NEGIMA! 15

Ken Akamatsu

TRANSLATED BY
Toshifumi Yoshida

ADAPTED BY
Ikoi Hiroe

LETTERING AND RETOUCH BY
Steve Palmer

BALLANTINE BOOKS · NEW YORK

Negima! volume 15 is a work of fiction. Names, characters, places, and incidents are the products of the author's imagination or are used fictitiously. Any resemblance to actual events, locales, or persons, living or dead, is entirely coincidental.

A Del Rey Trade Paperback Original

Published in the United States by Del Rey Books, an imprint of The Random House Publishing Group, a division of Random House, Inc., New York.

Del Rey is a registered trademark and the Del Rey colophon is a trademark of Random House, Inc.

Publication rights arranged through Kodansha Ltd.

First published in Japan in 2006 by Kodansha Ltd., Tokyo.

ISBN 978-0-345-49615-7

Printed in the United States of America

www.delreymanga.com

9 8 7 6 5 4 3 2

Translator: Toshifumi Yoshida
Adapter: Ikoi Hiroe
Lettering and retouch: Steve Palmer

Honorifics Explained

Throughout the Del Rey Manga books, you will find Japanese honorifics left intact in the translations. For those not familiar with how the Japanese use honorifics and, more important, how they differ from American honorifics, we present this brief overview.

Politeness has always been a critical facet of Japanese culture. Ever since the feudal era, when Japan was a highly stratified society, use of honorifics—which can be defined as polite speech that indicates relationship or status—has played an essential role in the Japanese language. When addressing someone in Japanese, an honorific usually takes the form of a suffix attached to one's name (example: "Asuna-san"), is used as a title at the end of one's name, or appears in place of the name itself (example: "Negi-sensei," or simply "Sensei!").

Honorifics can be expressions of respect or endearment. In the context of manga and anime, honorifics give insight into the nature of the relationship between characters. Many translations into English leave out these important honorifics and therefore distort the feel of the original Japanese. Because Japanese honorifics contain nuances that English honorifics lack, it is our policy at Del Rey not to translate them. Here, instead, is a guide to some of the honorifics you may encounter in Del Rey Manga.

-*san:* This is the most common honorific and is equivalent to Mr., Miss, Ms., or Mrs. It is the all-purpose honorific and can be used in any situation where politeness is required.

-*sama:* This is one level higher than "-san" and is used to confer great respect.

-*dono:* This comes from the word "tono," which means "lord." It is an even higher level than "-sama" and confers utmost respect.

-kun: This suffix is used at the end of boys' names to express familiarity or endearment. It is also sometimes used by men among friends, or when addressing someone younger or of a lower station.

-chan: This is used to express endearment, mostly toward girls. It is also used for little boys, pets, and even among lovers. It gives a sense of childish cuteness.

Bozu: This is an informal way to refer to a boy, similar to the English terms "kid" and "squirt."

Sempai/Senpai: This title suggests that the addressee is one's senior in a group or organization. It is most often used in a school setting, where underclassmen refer to their upperclassmen as "sempai." It can also be used in the workplace, such as when a newer employee addresses an employee who has seniority in the company.

Kohai: This is the opposite of "sempai," and is used toward underclassmen in school or newcomers in the workplace. It connotes that the addressee is of a lower station.

Sensei: Literally meaning "one who has come before," this title is used for teachers, doctors, or masters of any profession or art.

Anesan (or *nesan*): A generic term for a girl, usually older, that means sister.

Ojôsama: A way of referring to the daughter or sister of someone with high political or social status.

-[blank]: This is usually forgotten in these lists, but it is perhaps the most significant difference between Japanese and English. The lack of honorific means that the speaker has permission to address the person in a very intimate way. Usually, only family, spouses, or very close friends have this kind of permission. Known as *yobisute,* it can be gratifying when someone who has earned the intimacy starts to call one by one's name without an honorific. But when that intimacy hasn't been earned, it can be very insulting.

A Word from the Author

The Summer and Spring editions of the *Negima!* OVA releases have been revealed, and a new *Negima!* TV series has been announced! (^^) It's going to have a lot of original touches. I may be the creator, but I'm still looking forward to it. Please check the official site for broadcast times and stations.

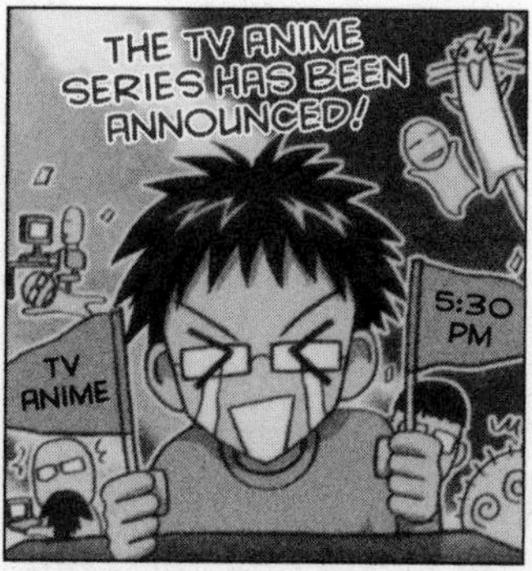
THE TV ANIME SERIES HAS BEEN ANNOUNCED!
5:30 PM
TV ANIME

Now I present *Negima!* volume 15 to my readers.

Once Asuna's story at the beginning of the volume is complete, we'll launch into the "vs. Chao" episode. Negi's new enemy is incredibly intelligent and powerful! What fate awaits Negi and his new party!?

There's a lot of info at the end of the book to prepare readers for upcoming volumes, so be sure to check it out!

Ken Akamatsu
www.ailove.net

魔法先生ネギま!

MAGISTER NEGI MAGI

15

赤松 健

Ken Akamatsu

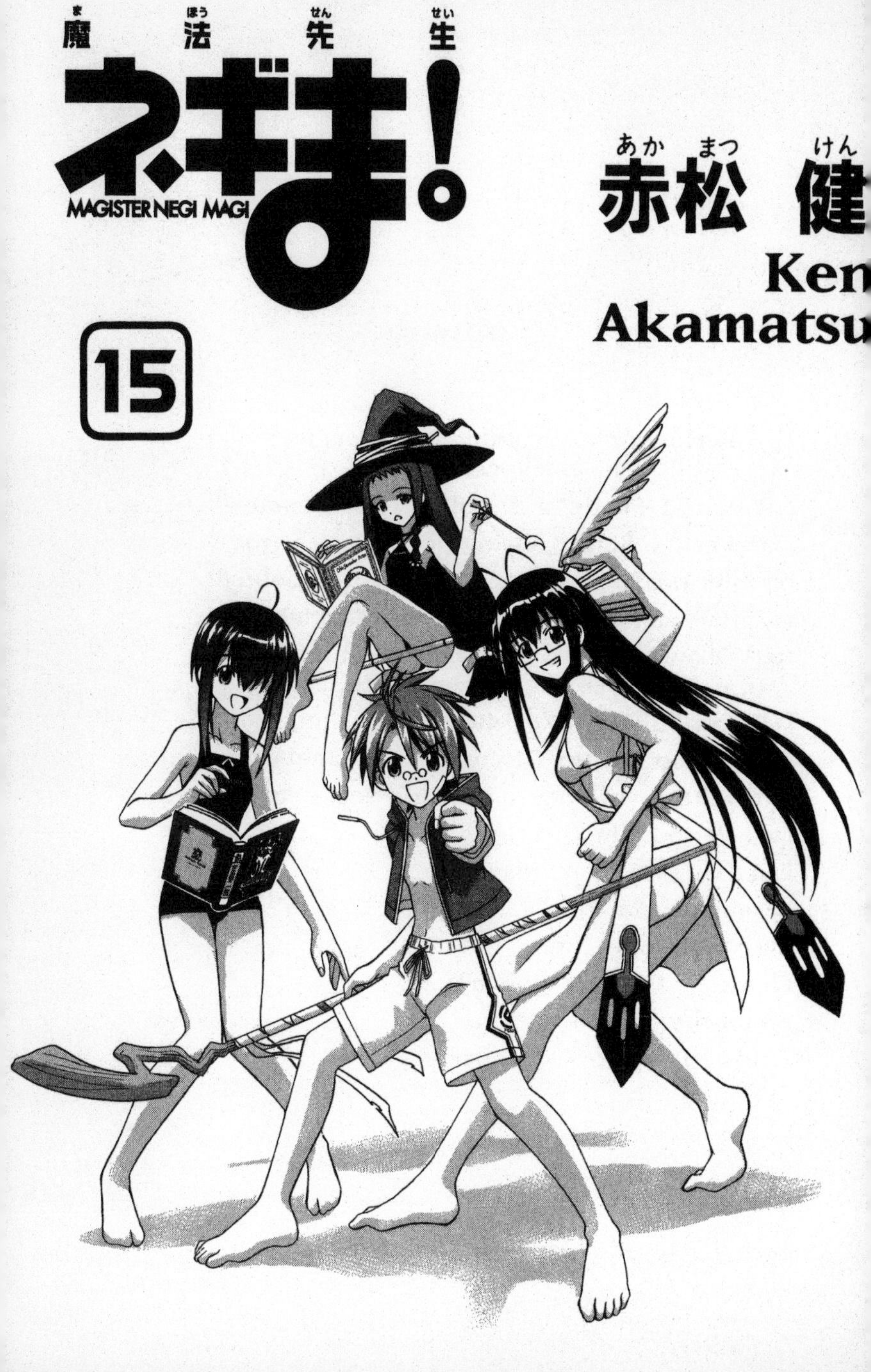

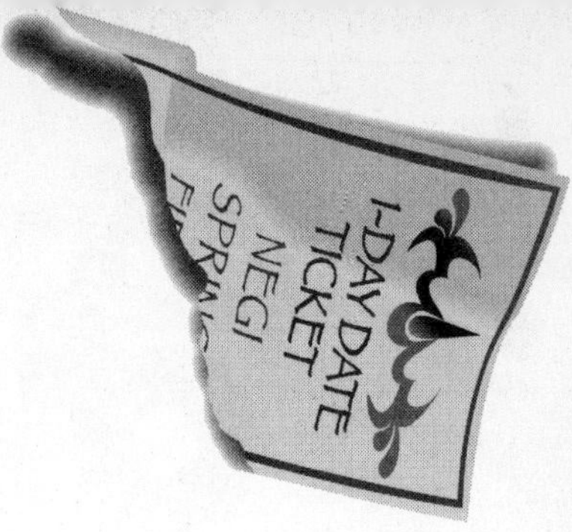
1-DAY DATE
TICKET
NEGI

Contents

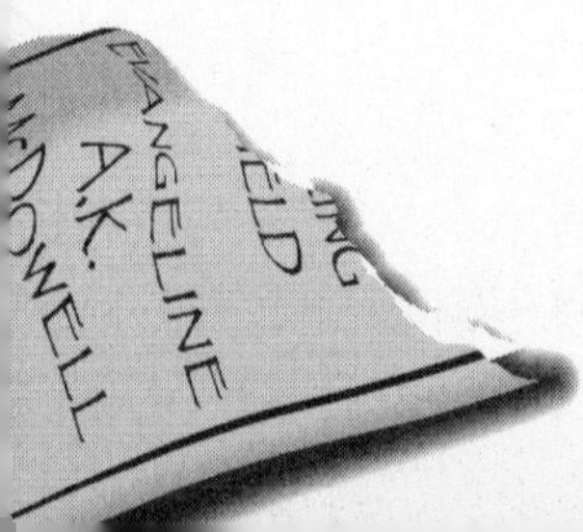
EVANGELINE
A.K.

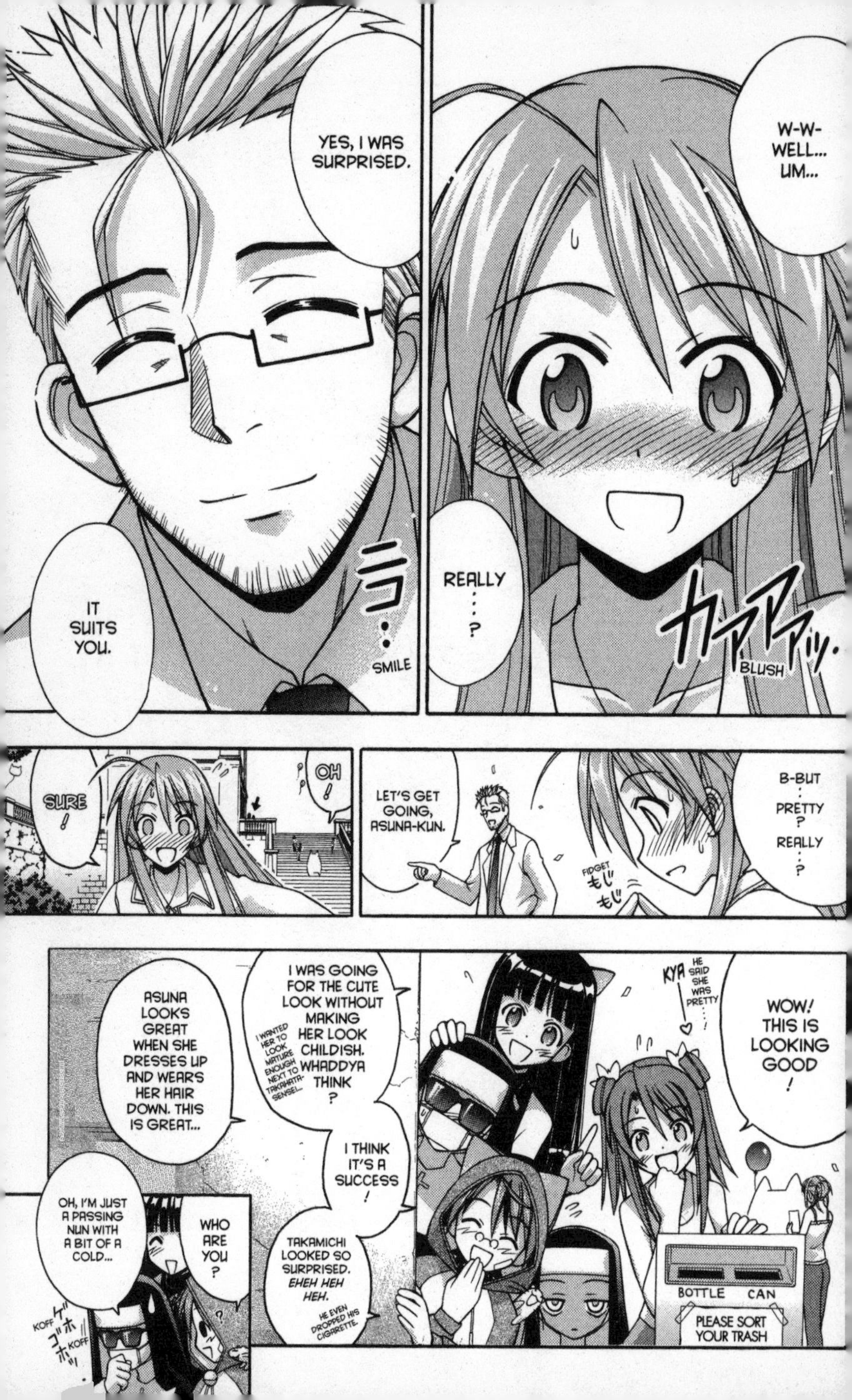

W-W-WELL... UM...
REALLY...?
BLUSH
YES, I WAS SURPRISED.
IT SUITS YOU.
SMILE
B-BUT... PRETTY? REALLY...?
FIDGET
LET'S GET GOING, ASUNA-KUN.
OH!
SURE!
WOW! THIS IS LOOKING GOOD!
KYA
HE SAID SHE WAS PRETTY...!
BOTTLE
CAN
PLEASE SORT YOUR TRASH
I WAS GOING FOR THE CUTE LOOK WITHOUT MAKING HER LOOK CHILDISH. WHADDYA THINK?
I WANTED HER TO LOOK MATURE ENOUGH NEXT TO TAKAHATA-SENSEI...
ASUNA LOOKS GREAT WHEN SHE DRESSES UP AND WEARS HER HAIR DOWN. THIS IS GREAT...
I THINK IT'S A SUCCESS!
TAKAMICHI LOOKED SO SURPRISED. EHEH HEH HEH.
HE EVEN DROPPED HIS CIGARETTE.
WHO ARE YOU?
OH, I'M JUST A PASSING NUN WITH A BIT OF A COLD...
KOFF
KOFF

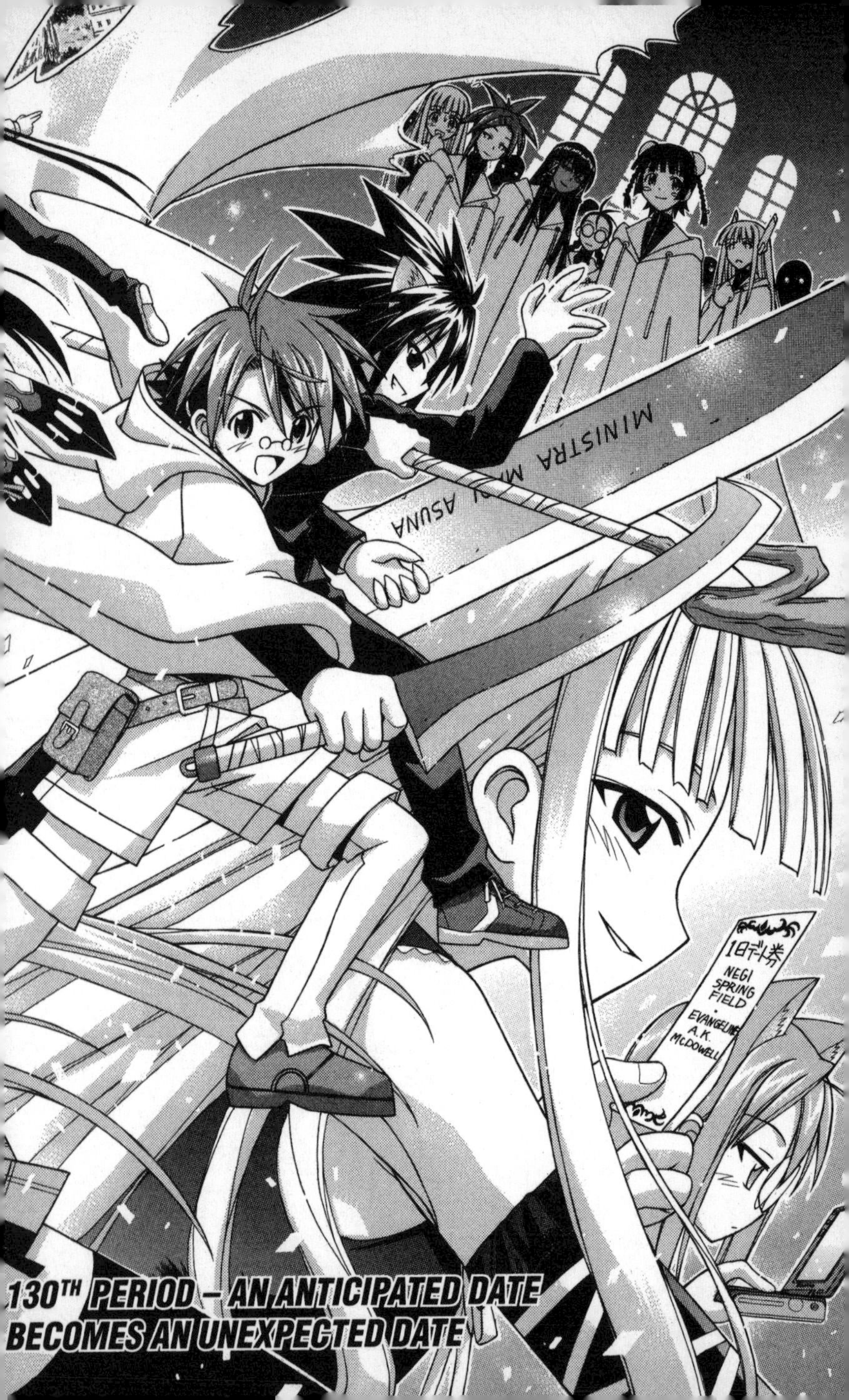
MINISTRA
ASUNA
1日デート券
NEGI SPRING FIELD
EVANGELINE A.K. McDOWELL

130TH PERIOD – AN ANTICIPATED DATE BECOMES AN UNEXPECTED DATE

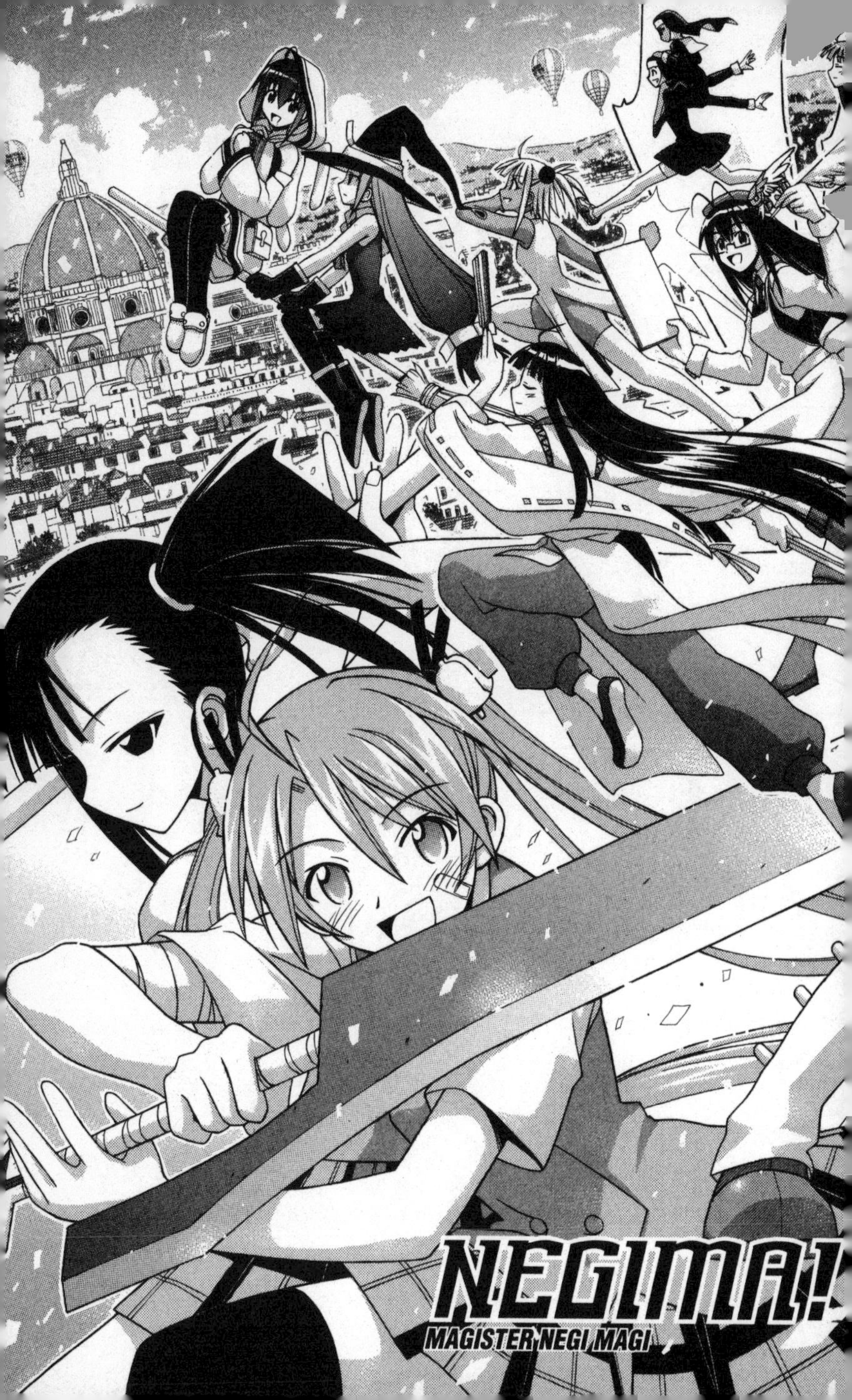
NEGIMA!
MAGISTER NEGI MAGI

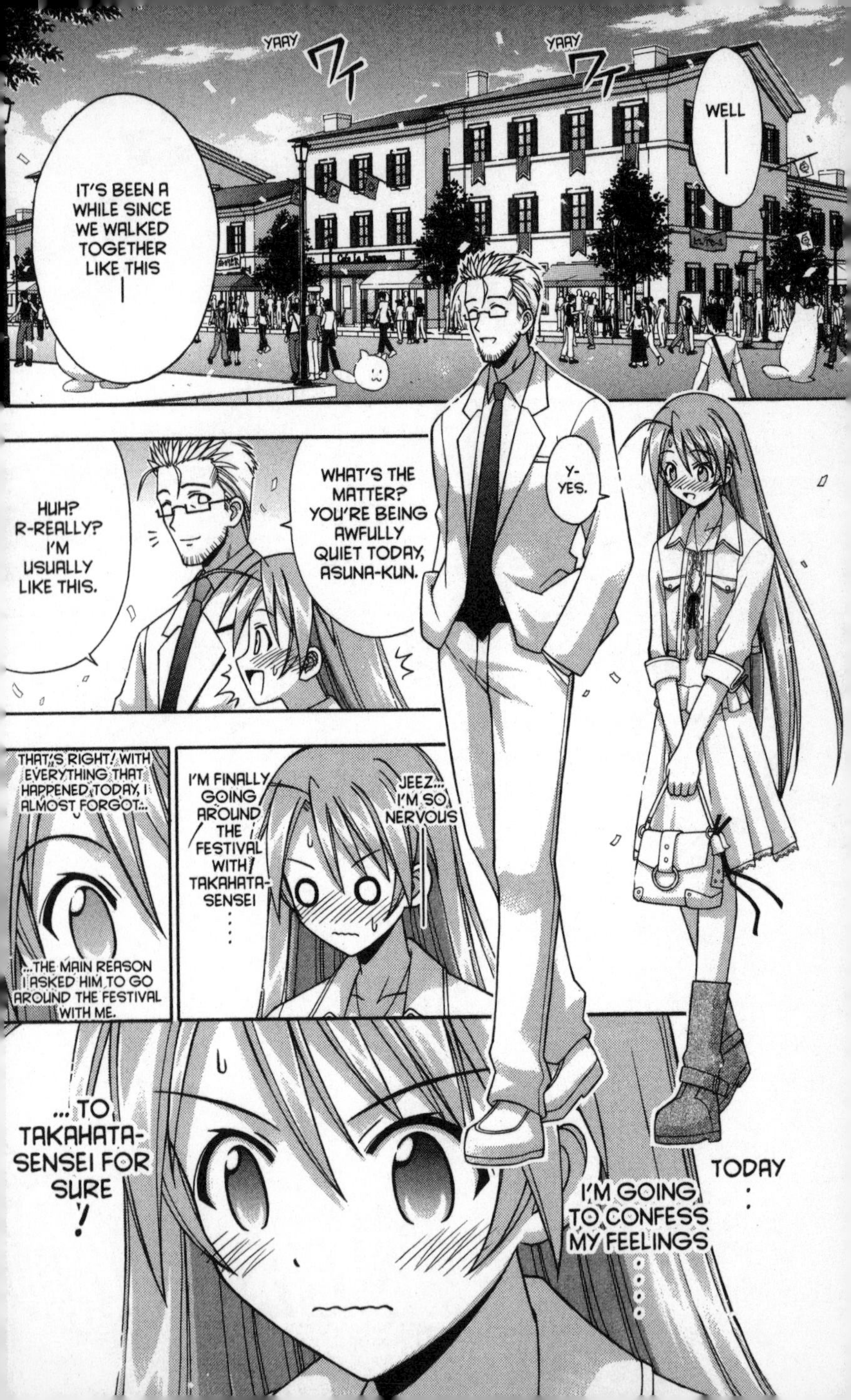

YAAY
ワイ
WELL—
YAAY
ワイ
IT'S BEEN A WHILE SINCE WE WALKED TOGETHER LIKE THIS—
Y-YES.
WHAT'S THE MATTER? YOU'RE BEING AWFULLY QUIET TODAY, ASUNA-KUN.
HUH? R-REALLY? I'M USUALLY LIKE THIS.
JEEZ... I'M SO NERVOUS
I'M FINALLY GOING AROUND THE FESTIVAL WITH TAKAHATA-SENSEI....
THAT'S RIGHT! WITH EVERYTHING THAT HAPPENED TODAY, I ALMOST FORGOT...
...THE MAIN REASON I ASKED HIM TO GO AROUND THE FESTIVAL WITH ME.
TODAY:
I'M GOING TO CONFESS MY FEELINGS....
...TO TAKAHATA-SENSEI FOR SURE!

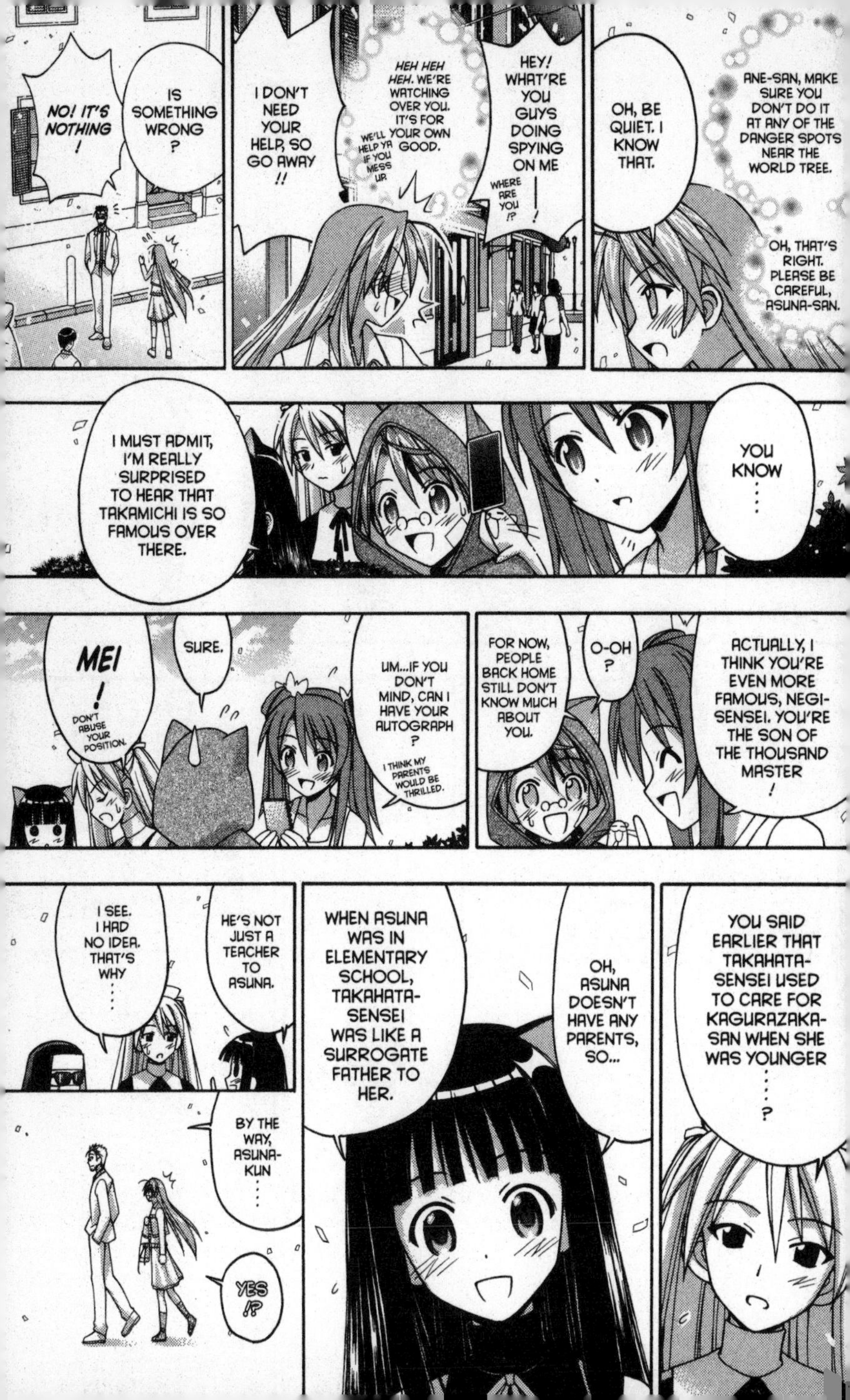
ANE-SAN, MAKE SURE YOU DON'T DO IT AT ANY OF THE DANGER SPOTS NEAR THE WORLD TREE.
OH, THAT'S RIGHT. PLEASE BE CAREFUL, ASUNA-SAN.
OH, BE QUIET. I KNOW THAT.
HEY! WHAT'RE YOU GUYS DOING SPYING ON ME!
WHERE ARE YOU!?
HEH HEH HEH. WE'RE WATCHING OVER YOU. IT'S FOR YOUR OWN GOOD.
WE'LL HELP YA IF YOU MESS UP.
I DON'T NEED YOUR HELP, SO GO AWAY!!
IS SOMETHING WRONG?
NO! IT'S NOTHING!
YOU KNOW.....
I MUST ADMIT, I'M REALLY SURPRISED TO HEAR THAT TAKAMICHI IS SO FAMOUS OVER THERE.
ACTUALLY, I THINK YOU'RE EVEN MORE FAMOUS, NEGI-SENSEI. YOU'RE THE SON OF THE THOUSAND MASTER!
O-OH?
FOR NOW, PEOPLE BACK HOME STILL DON'T KNOW MUCH ABOUT YOU.
UM...IF YOU DON'T MIND, CAN I HAVE YOUR AUTOGRAPH?
I THINK MY PARENTS WOULD BE THRILLED.
SURE.
MEI!
DON'T ABUSE YOUR POSITION.
YOU SAID EARLIER THAT TAKAHATA-SENSEI USED TO CARE FOR KAGURAZAKA-SAN WHEN SHE WAS YOUNGER.....?
OH, ASUNA DOESN'T HAVE ANY PARENTS, SO...
WHEN ASUNA WAS IN ELEMENTARY SCHOOL, TAKAHATA-SENSEI WAS LIKE A SURROGATE FATHER TO HER.
HE'S NOT JUST A TEACHER TO ASUNA.
I SEE. I HAD NO IDEA. THAT'S WHY.....
BY THE WAY, ASUNA-KUN.....
YES!?

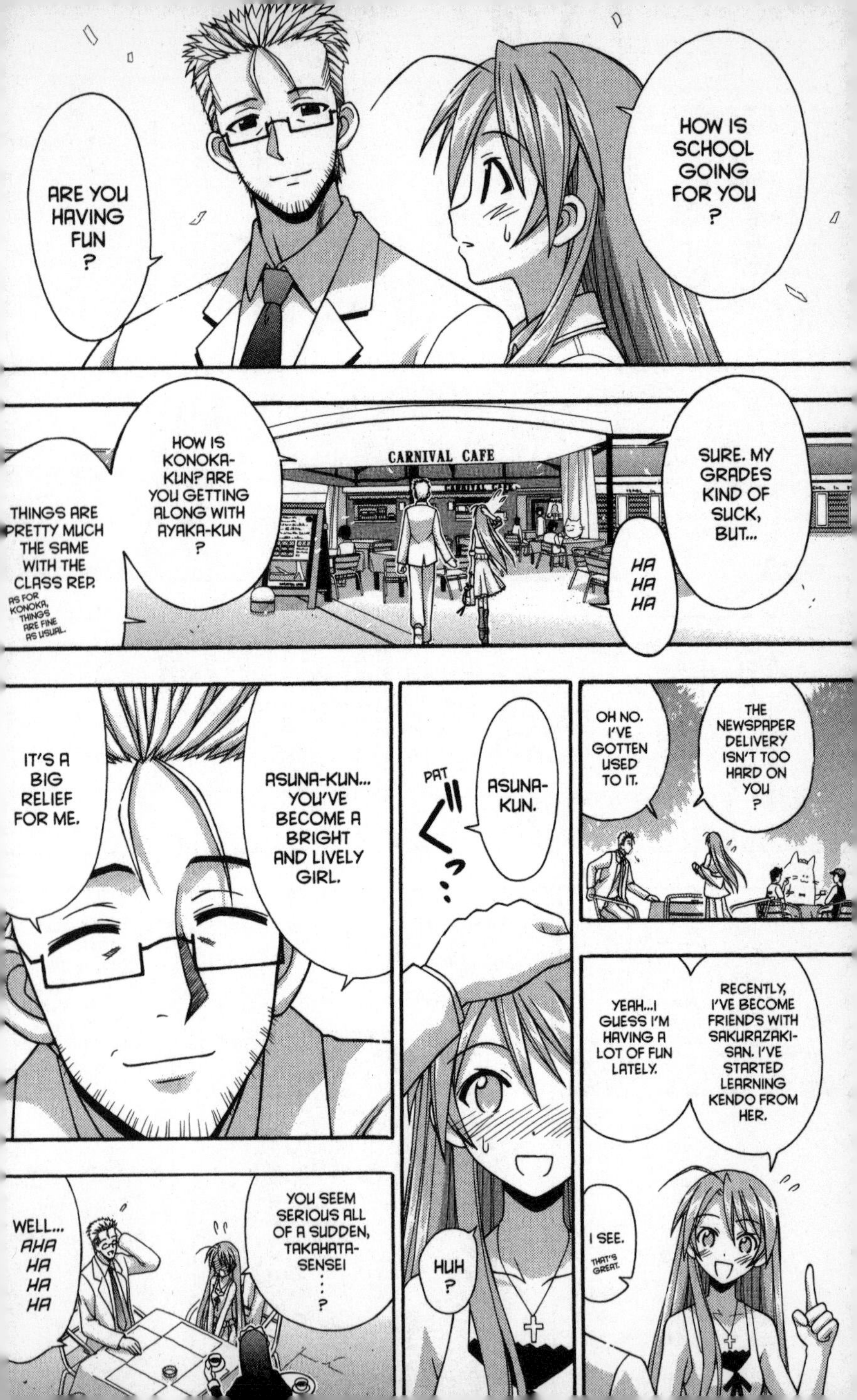
HOW IS SCHOOL GOING FOR YOU ?
ARE YOU HAVING FUN ?
SURE. MY GRADES KIND OF SUCK, BUT...
HA HA HA
HOW IS KONOKA-KUN? ARE YOU GETTING ALONG WITH AYAKA-KUN ?
THINGS ARE PRETTY MUCH THE SAME WITH THE CLASS REP.
AS FOR KONOKA, THINGS ARE FINE AS USUAL.
CARNIVAL CAFE
THE NEWSPAPER DELIVERY ISN'T TOO HARD ON YOU ?
OH NO. I'VE GOTTEN USED TO IT.
RECENTLY, I'VE BECOME FRIENDS WITH SAKURAZAKI-SAN. I'VE STARTED LEARNING KENDO FROM HER.
YEAH...I GUESS I'M HAVING A LOT OF FUN LATELY.
I SEE.
THAT'S GREAT.
ASUNA-KUN.
PAT
HUH ?
ASUNA-KUN... YOU'VE BECOME A BRIGHT AND LIVELY GIRL.
IT'S A BIG RELIEF FOR ME.
YOU SEEM SERIOUS ALL OF A SUDDEN, TAKAHATA-SENSEI ...?
WELL... AHA HA HA HA

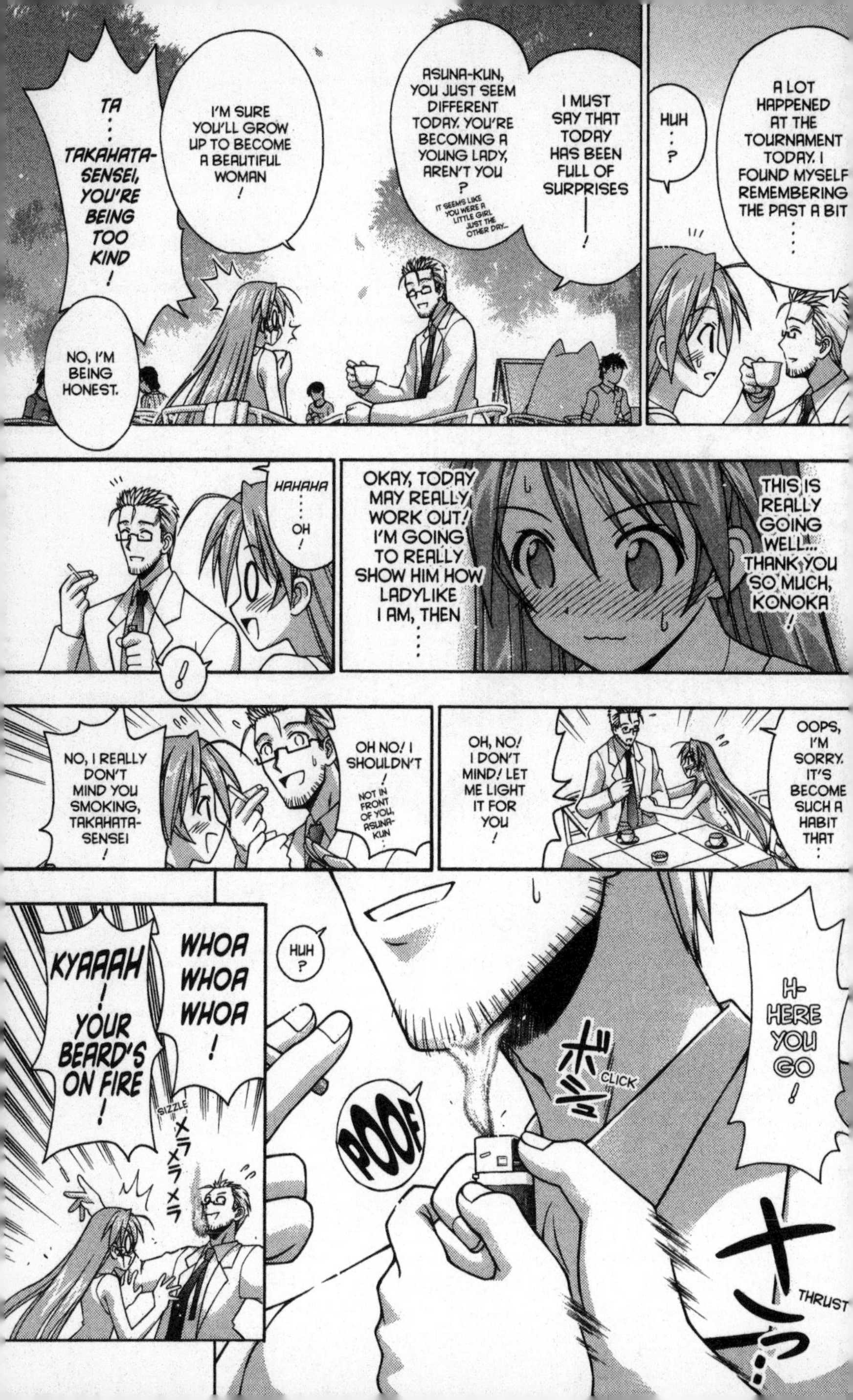
A LOT HAPPENED AT THE TOURNAMENT TODAY. I FOUND MYSELF REMEMBERING THE PAST A BIT...
HUH...?
I MUST SAY THAT TODAY HAS BEEN FULL OF SURPRISES—!
ASUNA-KUN, YOU JUST SEEM DIFFERENT TODAY. YOU'RE BECOMING A YOUNG LADY, AREN'T YOU?
IT SEEMS LIKE YOU WERE A LITTLE GIRL JUST THE OTHER DAY...
I'M SURE YOU'LL GROW UP TO BECOME A BEAUTIFUL WOMAN!
TA... TAKAHATA-SENSEI, YOU'RE BEING TOO KIND!
NO, I'M BEING HONEST.
THIS IS REALLY GOING WELL... THANK YOU SO MUCH, KONOKA!
OKAY, TODAY MAY REALLY WORK OUT! I'M GOING TO REALLY SHOW HIM HOW LADYLIKE I AM, THEN...
HAHAHA... OH!
!
OOPS, I'M SORRY. IT'S BECOME SUCH A HABIT THAT...
OH, NO! I DON'T MIND! LET ME LIGHT IT FOR YOU!
OH NO! I SHOULDN'T!
NOT IN FRONT OF YOU, ASUNA-KUN...
NO, I REALLY DON'T MIND YOU SMOKING, TAKAHATA-SENSEI!
H-HERE YOU GO!
THRUST
CLICK
POOF
HUH?
WHOA WHOA WHOA!
KYAAAH! YOUR BEARD'S ON FIRE!
SIZZLE

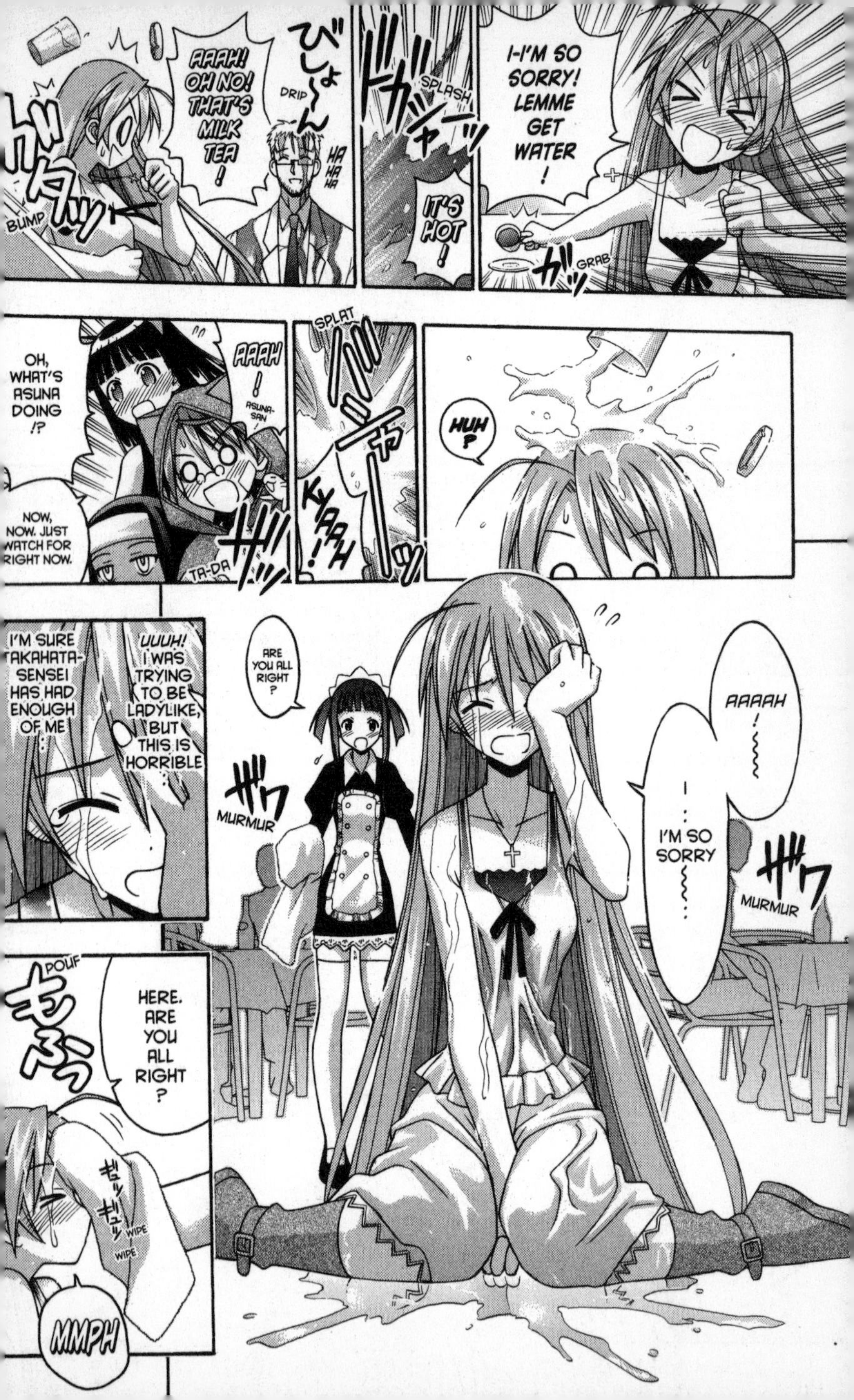
I-I'M SO SORRY! LEMME GET WATER!
GRAB
SPLASH
IT'S HOT!
AAAH! OH NO! THAT'S MILK TEA!
DRIP
HA HA HA
BUMP
HUH?
SPLAT
KYAAAH!
AAAH!
ASUNA-SAN!
OH, WHAT'S ASUNA DOING!?
NOW, NOW. JUST WATCH FOR RIGHT NOW.
TA-DA
AAAAH!
I... I'M SO SORRY...
MURMUR
ARE YOU ALL RIGHT?
MURMUR
UUUH! I WAS TRYING TO BE LADYLIKE, BUT THIS IS HORRIBLE...
I'M SURE TAKAHATA-SENSEI HAS HAD ENOUGH OF ME...
HERE. ARE YOU ALL RIGHT?
POUF
WIPE WIPE
MMPH

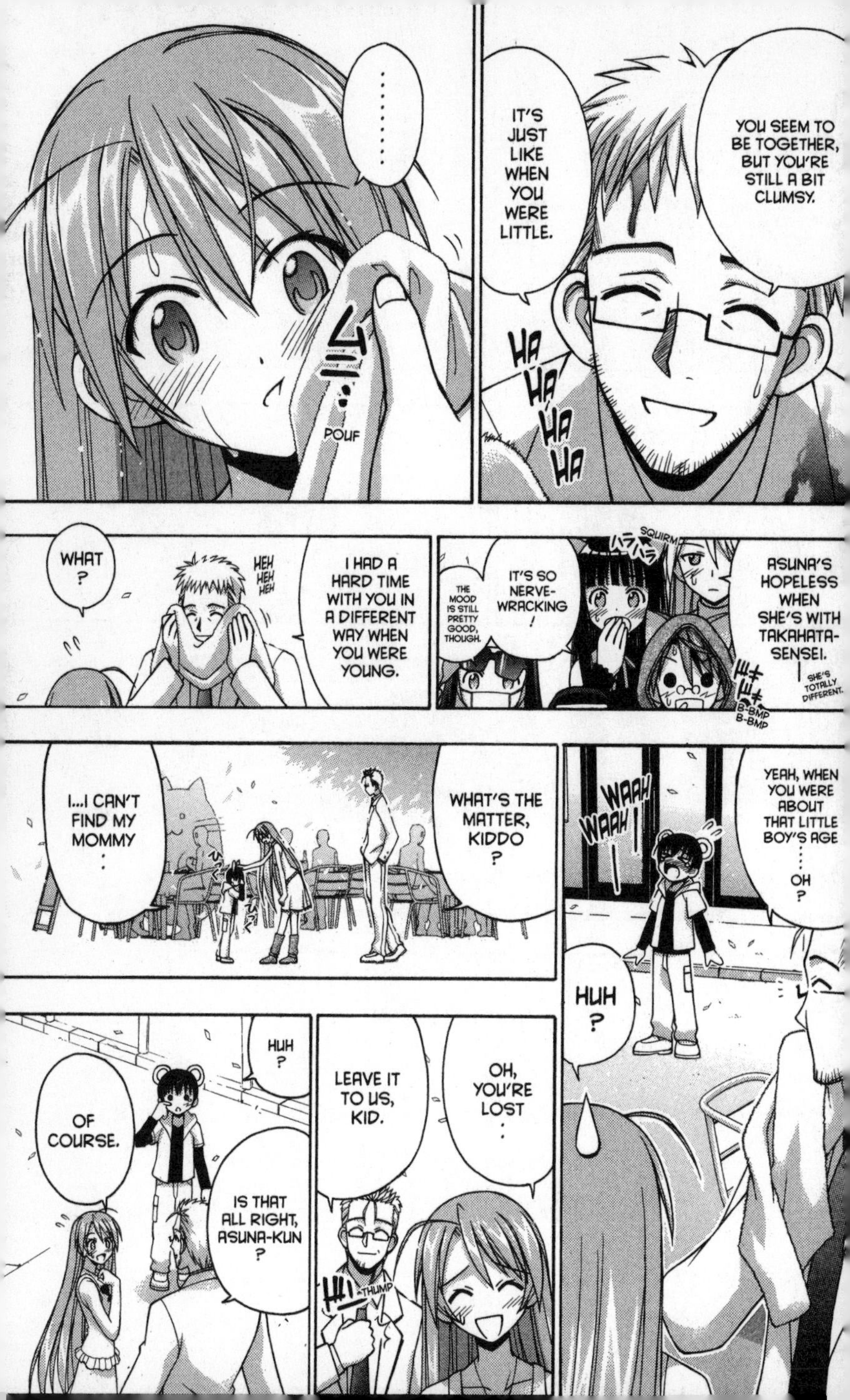
YOU SEEM TO BE TOGETHER, BUT YOU'RE STILL A BIT CLUMSY.
IT'S JUST LIKE WHEN YOU WERE LITTLE.
HA HA HA HA HA
......
POUF
ASUNA'S HOPELESS WHEN SHE'S WITH TAKAHATA-SENSEI.
SHE'S TOTALLY DIFFERENT.
SQUIRM
B-BMP B-BMP
IT'S SO NERVE-WRACKING!
THE MOOD IS STILL PRETTY GOOD, THOUGH.
I HAD A HARD TIME WITH YOU IN A DIFFERENT WAY WHEN YOU WERE YOUNG.
HEH HEH HEH
WHAT?
YEAH, WHEN YOU WERE ABOUT THAT LITTLE BOY'S AGE.....
OH?
WAAH WAAH!
HUH?
WHAT'S THE MATTER, KIDDO?
I...I CAN'T FIND MY MOMMY...
OH, YOU'RE LOST...
LEAVE IT TO US, KID.
THUMP
HUH?
IS THAT ALL RIGHT, ASUNA-KUN?
OF COURSE.

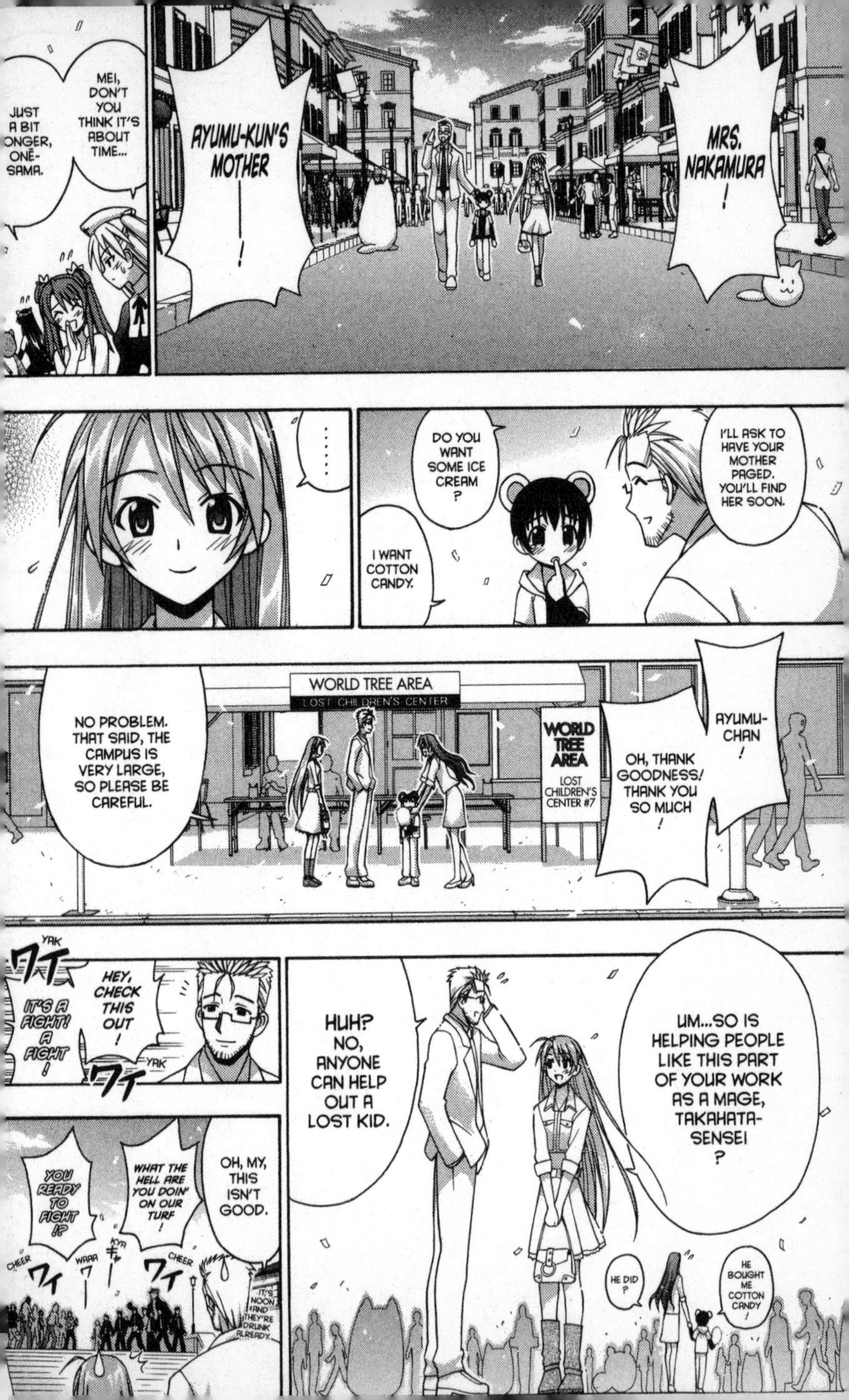
MRS. NAKAMURA!
AYUMU-KUN'S MOTHER!
MEI, DON'T YOU THINK IT'S ABOUT TIME...
JUST A BIT LONGER, ONĒ-SAMA.
I'LL ASK TO HAVE YOUR MOTHER PAGED. YOU'LL FIND HER SOON.
DO YOU WANT SOME ICE CREAM?
I WANT COTTON CANDY.
......
AYUMU-CHAN!
OH, THANK GOODNESS! THANK YOU SO MUCH!
WORLD TREE AREA LOST CHILDREN'S CENTER #7
WORLD TREE AREA
LOST CHILDREN'S CENTER
NO PROBLEM. THAT SAID, THE CAMPUS IS VERY LARGE, SO PLEASE BE CAREFUL.
UM...SO IS HELPING PEOPLE LIKE THIS PART OF YOUR WORK AS A MAGE, TAKAHATA-SENSEI?
HUH? NO, ANYONE CAN HELP OUT A LOST KID.
HE BOUGHT ME COTTON CANDY!
HE DID?
YAK
HEY, CHECK THIS OUT!
IT'S A FIGHT! A FIGHT!
YAK
OH, MY, THIS ISN'T GOOD.
WHAT THE HELL ARE YOU DOIN' ON OUR TURF!
YOU READY TO FIGHT!?
CHEER
KYA
WAAA
CHEER
IT'S NOON AND THEY'RE DRUNK ALREADY.

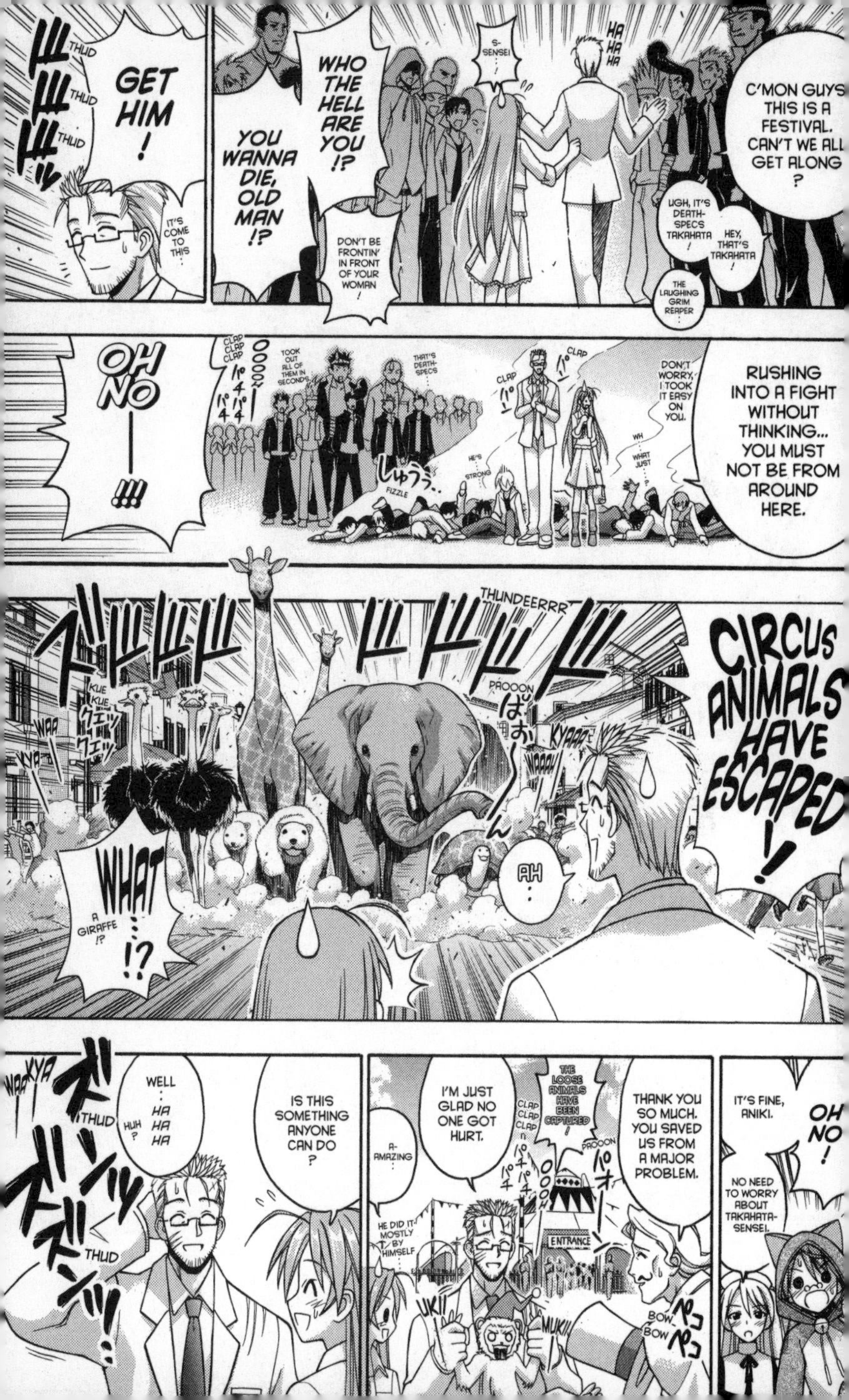
C'MON GUYS THIS IS A FESTIVAL. CAN'T WE ALL GET ALONG?
HA HA HA HA
S-SENSEI...!
HEY, THAT'S TAKAHATA!
UGH, IT'S DEATH-SPECS TAKAHATA!
THE LAUGHING GRIM REAPER...
WHO THE HELL ARE YOU!?
YOU WANNA DIE, OLD MAN!?
DON'T BE FRONTIN' IN FRONT OF YOUR WOMAN!
GET HIM!
THUD
THUD
THUD
IT'S COME TO THIS...
RUSHING INTO A FIGHT WITHOUT THINKING... YOU MUST NOT BE FROM AROUND HERE.
DON'T WORRY, I TOOK IT EASY ON YOU.
CLAP
CLAP
WH- WHAT JUST...?
HE'S STRONG...
FIZZLE
THAT'S DEATH-SPECS...
TOOK OUT ALL OF THEM IN SECONDS
OOOOH
CLAP CLAP CLAP
OH NO——!!!
CIRCUS ANIMALS HAVE ESCAPED!
THUNDEERRR
PAOOON
KYAAA
WAAAH
AH...
KUE KUE
WAA
KYA
WHAT!?
A GIRAFFE!?
OH NO!
IT'S FINE, ANIKI.
NO NEED TO WORRY ABOUT TAKAHATA-SENSEI.
THANK YOU SO MUCH. YOU SAVED US FROM A MAJOR PROBLEM.
PAOOON
BOW BOW
THE LOOSE ANIMALS HAVE BEEN CAPTURED!
ENTRANCE
OOOH
CLAP CLAP CLAP
I'M JUST GLAD NO ONE GOT HURT.
MUKI!
UKI!
A-AMAZING...
HE DID IT MOSTLY BY HIMSELF...
IS THIS SOMETHING ANYONE CAN DO?
WELL... HA HA HA
HUH?
KYA
WAA
THUD
THUD

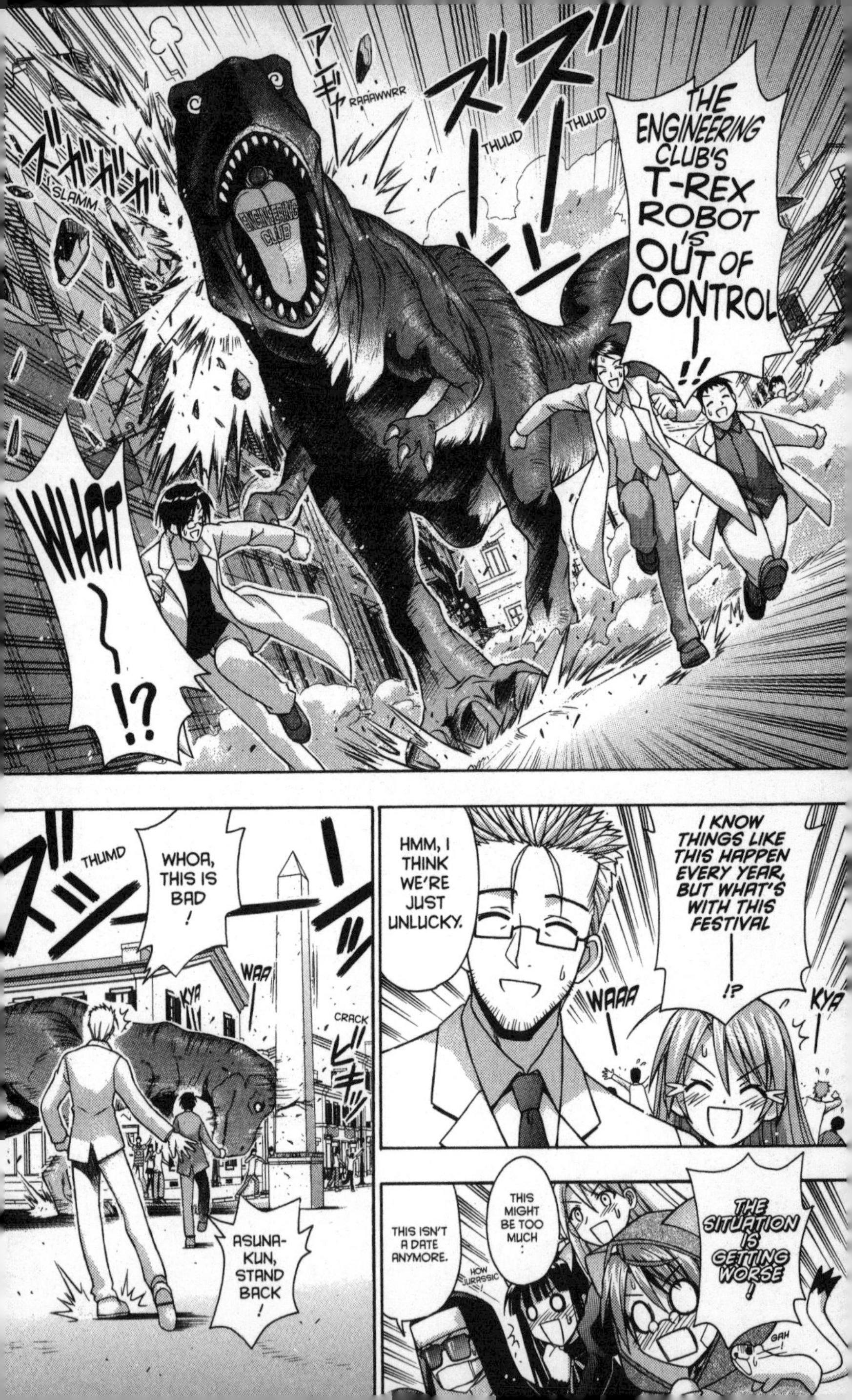
THE ENGINEERING CLUB'S T-REX ROBOT IS OUT OF CONTROL!!
THUUD
THUUD
RAAAWWRR
ENGINEERING CLUB
SLAMM
WHAT~~!?
I KNOW THINGS LIKE THIS HAPPEN EVERY YEAR, BUT WHAT'S WITH THIS FESTIVAL—!?
KYA!
WAAA!
HMM, I THINK WE'RE JUST UNLUCKY.
THE SITUATION IS GETTING WORSE!
GAH!
THIS MIGHT BE TOO MUCH
THIS ISN'T A DATE ANYMORE.
HOW JURASSIC!
WHOA, THIS IS BAD!
THUMD
WAA!
KYA!
CRACK
ASUNA-KUN, STAND BACK!

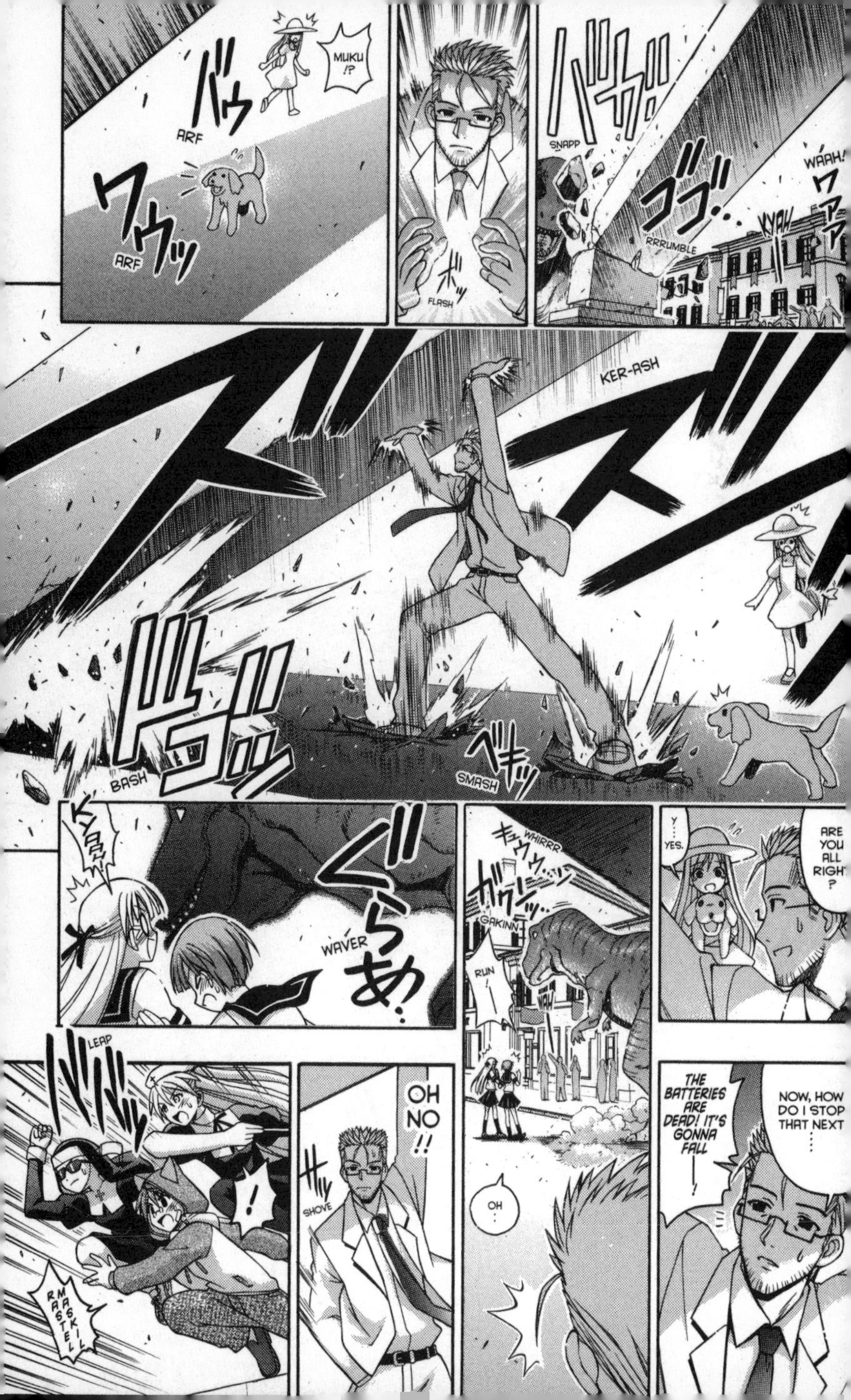
SNAPP
RRRUMBLE
WAAH!
KYAH
FLASH
MUKU !?
ARF
ARF
KER-ASH
BASH
SMASH
ARE YOU ALL RIGHT?
Y... YES.
WHIRRR
GAKINN
RUN!
WAH
KYAAH!
WAVER
NOW, HOW DO I STOP THAT NEXT.....
THE BATTERIES ARE DEAD! IT'S GONNA FALL—!
OH...
OH NO!!
SHOVE
LEAP
!
MASKIL
RASTEL

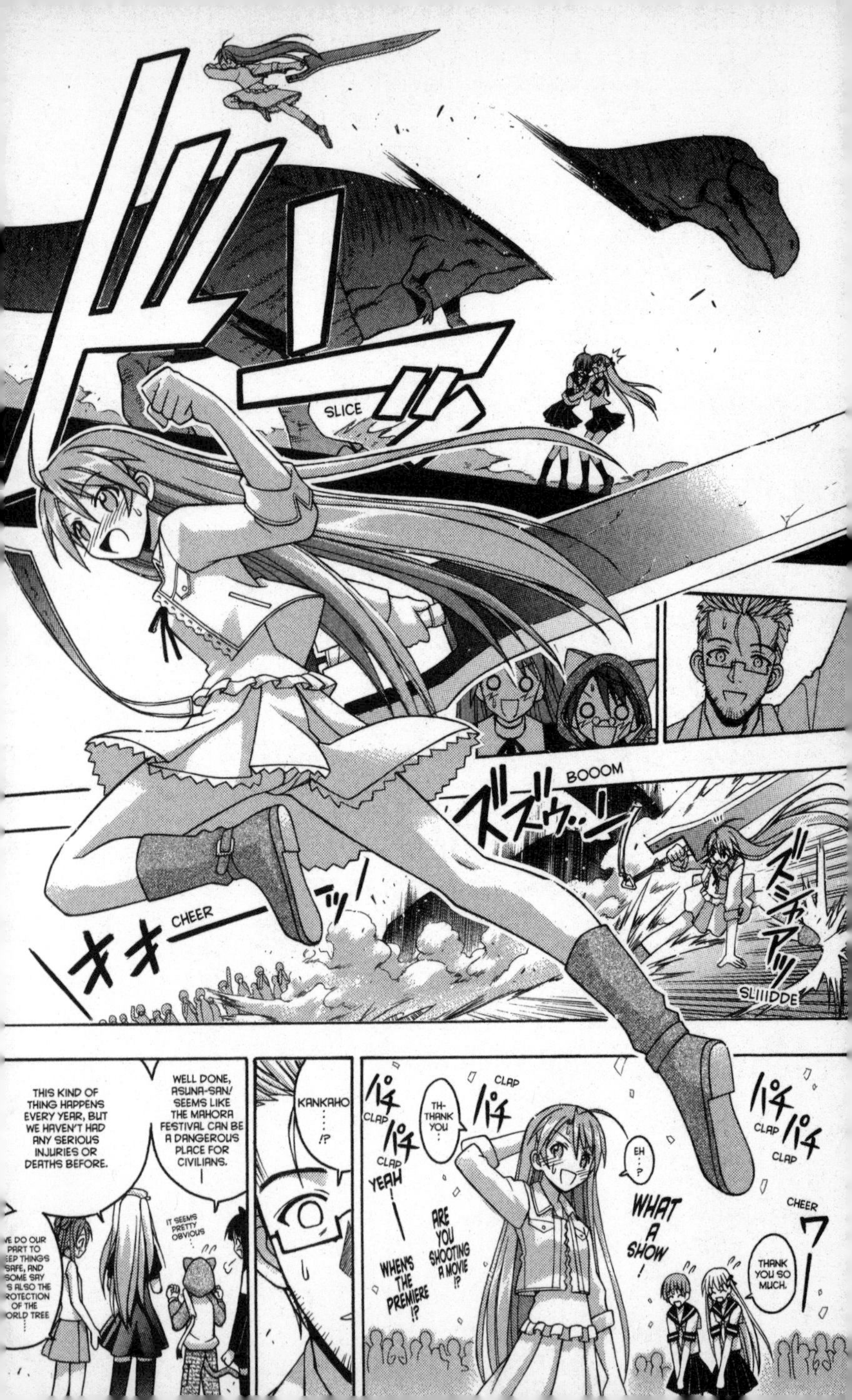
SLICE
BOOOM
SLIIIDDE
CHEER
CLAP
CLAP
CLAP
EH...?
TH-THANK YOU...
CLAP
CLAP
THANK YOU SO MUCH.
CHEER
WHAT A SHOW!
ARE YOU SHOOTING A MOVIE!?
YEAH!
WHEN'S THE PREMIERE!?
KANKAHO.....!?
WELL DONE, ASUNA-SAN! SEEMS LIKE THE MAHORA FESTIVAL CAN BE A DANGEROUS PLACE FOR CIVILIANS.
THIS KIND OF THING HAPPENS EVERY YEAR, BUT WE HAVEN'T HAD ANY SERIOUS INJURIES OR DEATHS BEFORE.
IT SEEMS PRETTY OBVIOUS...
E DO OUR PART TO EEP THINGS SAFE, AND SOME SAY 'S ALSO THE ROTECTION OF THE ORLD TREE.....

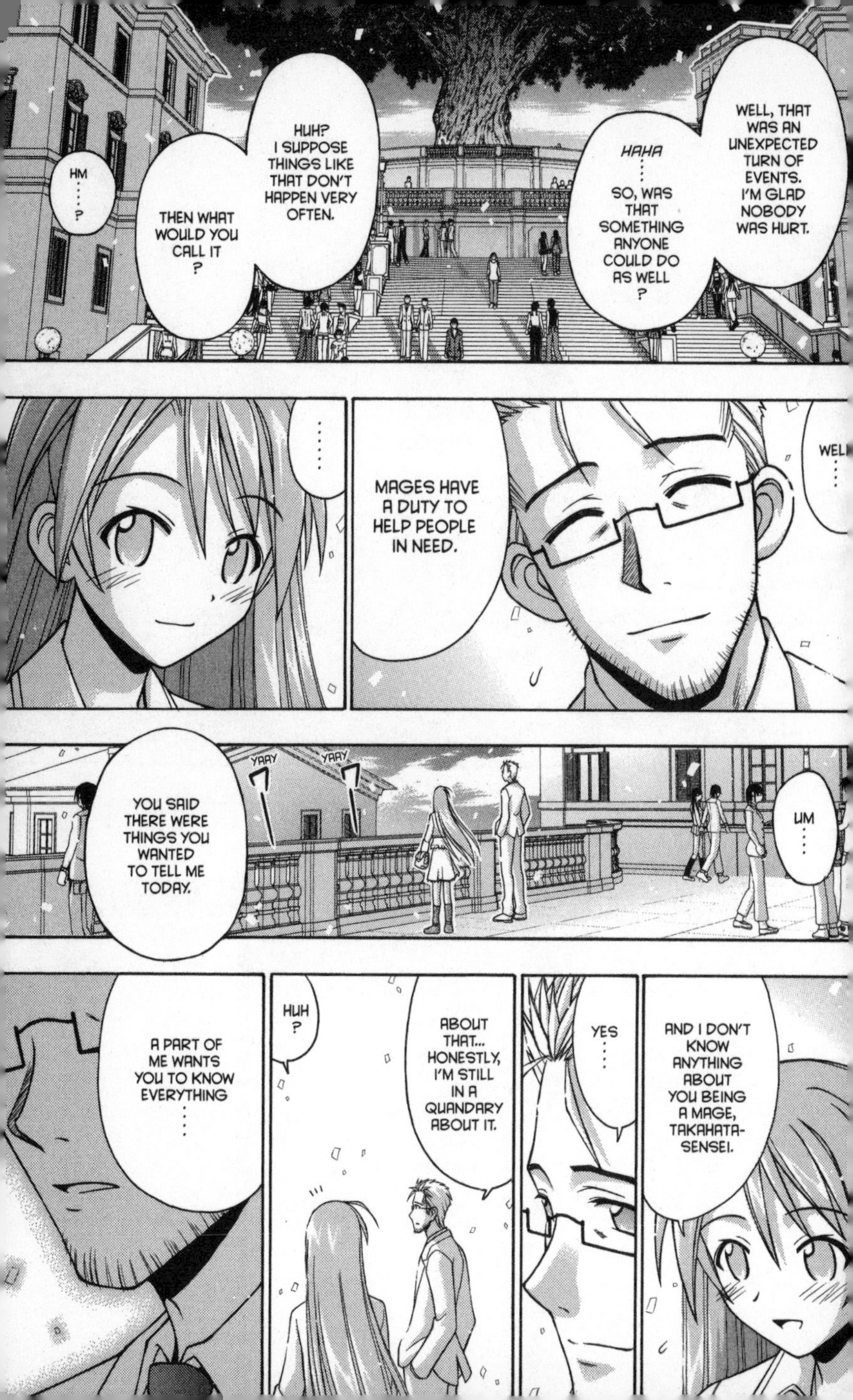
WELL, THAT WAS AN UNEXPECTED TURN OF EVENTS. I'M GLAD NOBODY WAS HURT.
HAHA ... SO, WAS THAT SOMETHING ANYONE COULD DO AS WELL?
HUH? I SUPPOSE THINGS LIKE THAT DON'T HAPPEN VERY OFTEN.
THEN WHAT WOULD YOU CALL IT?
HM.....?
WELL....
MAGES HAVE A DUTY TO HELP PEOPLE IN NEED.
......
UM....
YAAY
YAAY
YOU SAID THERE WERE THINGS YOU WANTED TO TELL ME TODAY.
AND I DON'T KNOW ANYTHING ABOUT YOU BEING A MAGE, TAKAHATA-SENSEI.
YES....
ABOUT THAT... HONESTLY, I'M STILL IN A QUANDARY ABOUT IT.
HUH?
A PART OF ME WANTS YOU TO KNOW EVERYTHING....

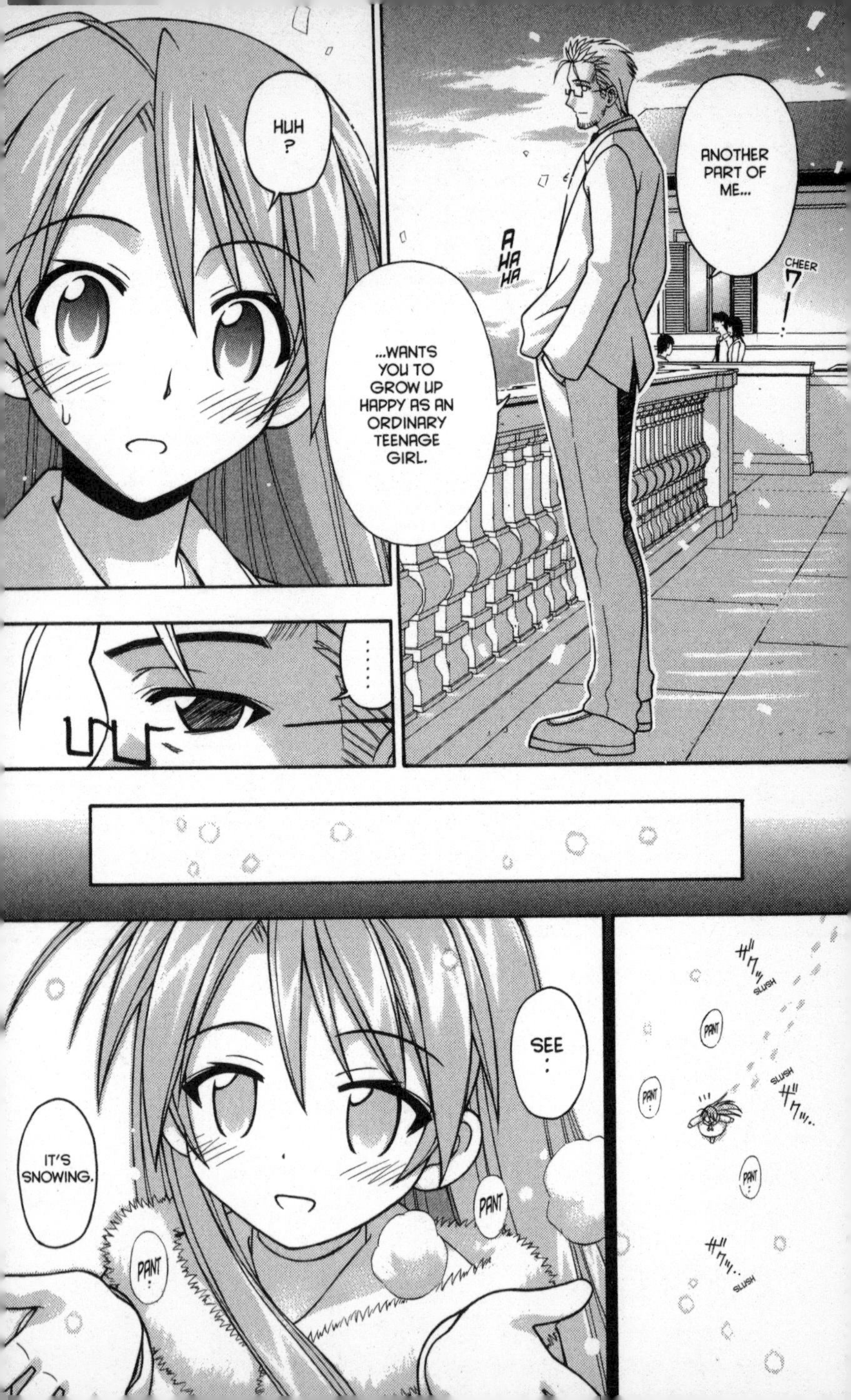
ANOTHER PART OF ME...
CHEER
AHAHA
...WANTS YOU TO GROW UP HAPPY AS AN ORDINARY TEENAGE GIRL.
HUH?
......
SLUSH
PANT
SLUSH
PANT
PANT
SLUSH
SEE...
PANT
PANT
IT'S SNOWING.

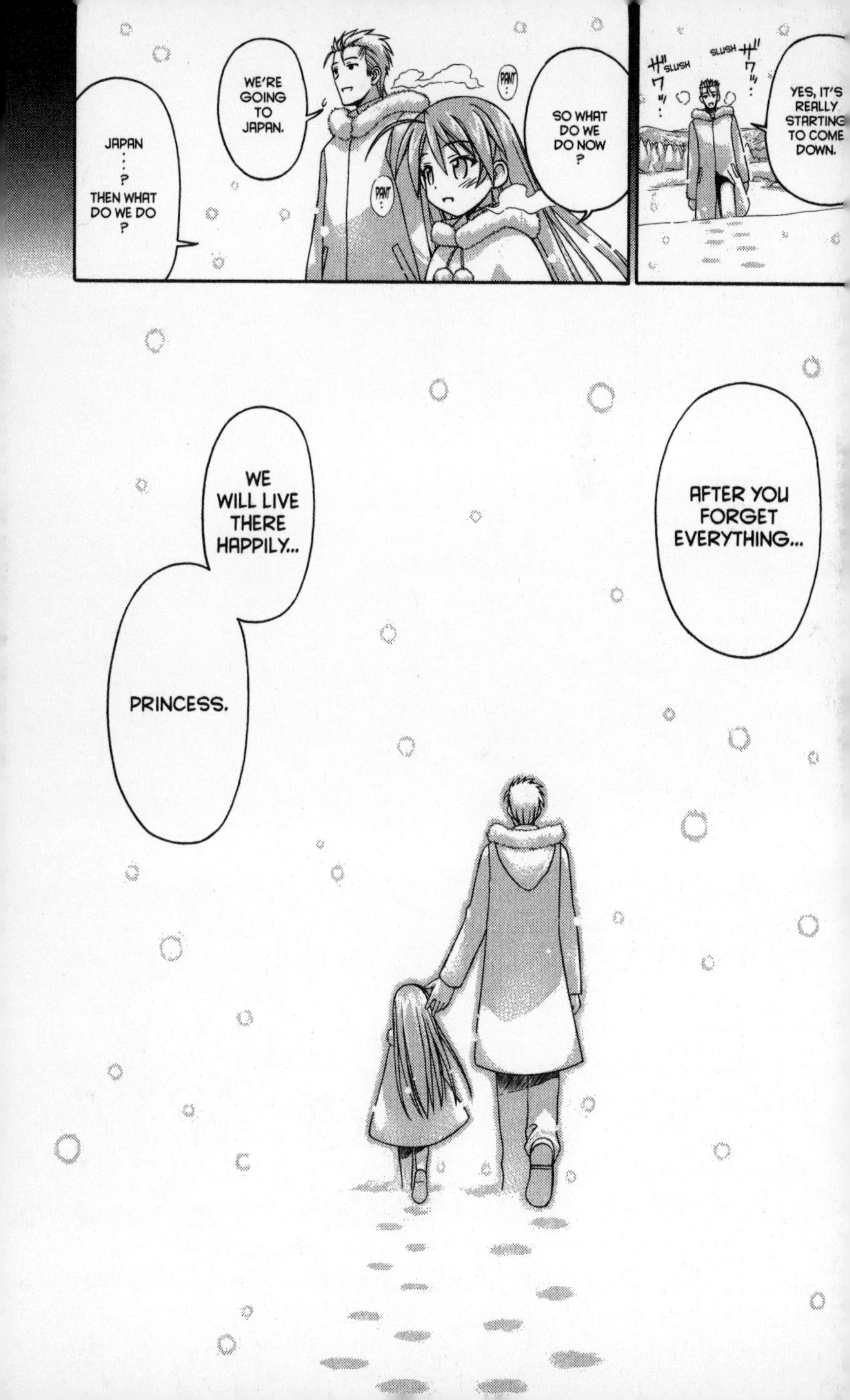
SLUSH
SLUSH
YES, IT'S REALLY STARTING TO COME DOWN.
PANT
PANT
SO WHAT DO WE DO NOW?
WE'RE GOING TO JAPAN.
JAPAN...? THEN WHAT DO WE DO?
AFTER YOU FORGET EVERYTHING...
WE WILL LIVE THERE HAPPILY...
PRINCESS.

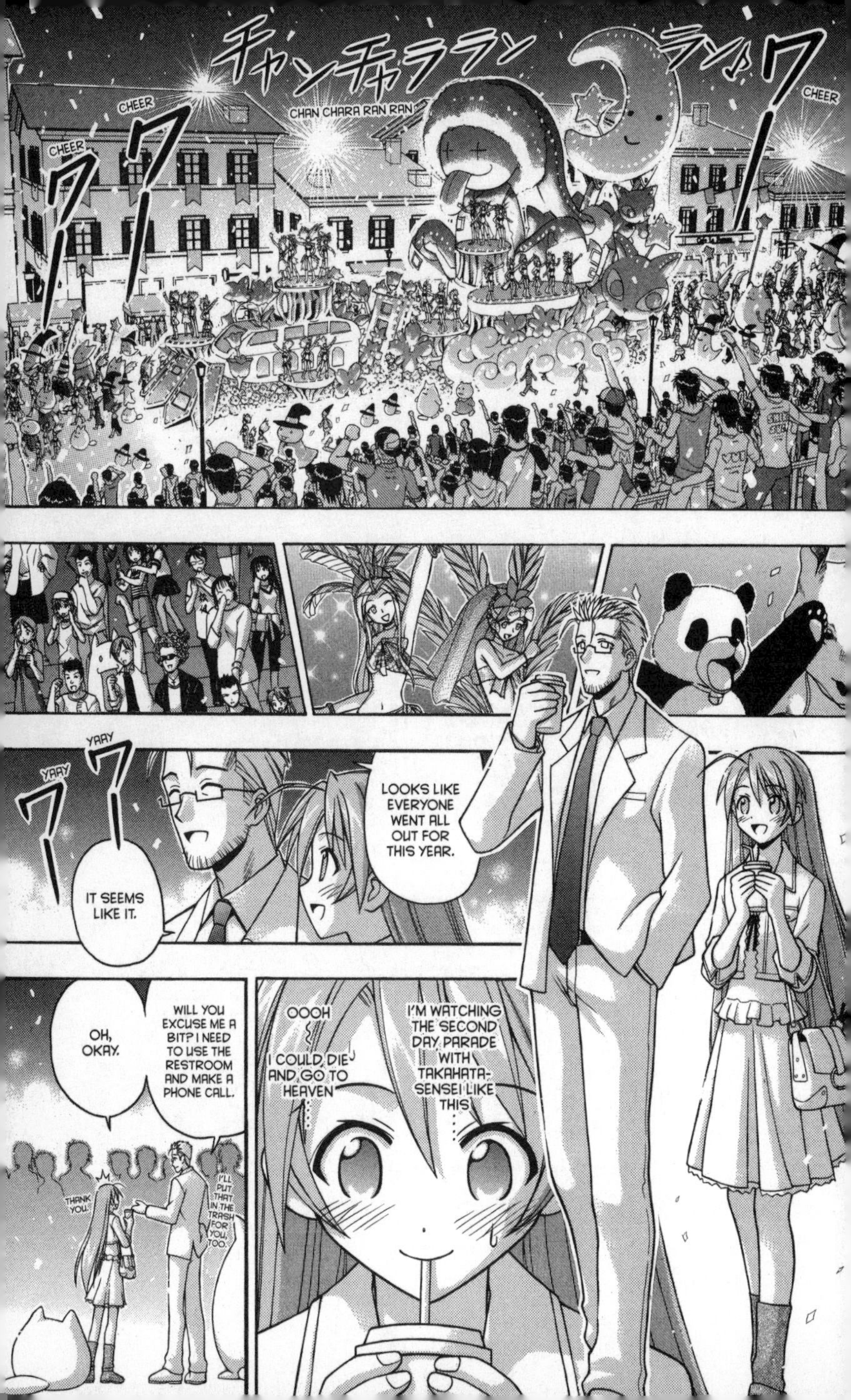

ランラン♪ワ
CHEER
チャンチャララン
CHAN CHARA RAN RAN
CHEER
ワ
CHEER
ワ
LOOKS LIKE EVERYONE WENT ALL OUT FOR THIS YEAR.
ワ
YAAY
ワ
YAAY
IT SEEMS LIKE IT.
I'M WATCHING THE SECOND DAY PARADE WITH TAKAHATA-SENSEI LIKE THIS
OOOH~
I COULD DIE AND GO TO HEAVEN
WILL YOU EXCUSE ME A BIT? I NEED TO USE THE RESTROOM AND MAKE A PHONE CALL.
OH, OKAY.
I'LL PUT THAT IN THE TRASH FOR YOU, TOO.
THANK YOU.

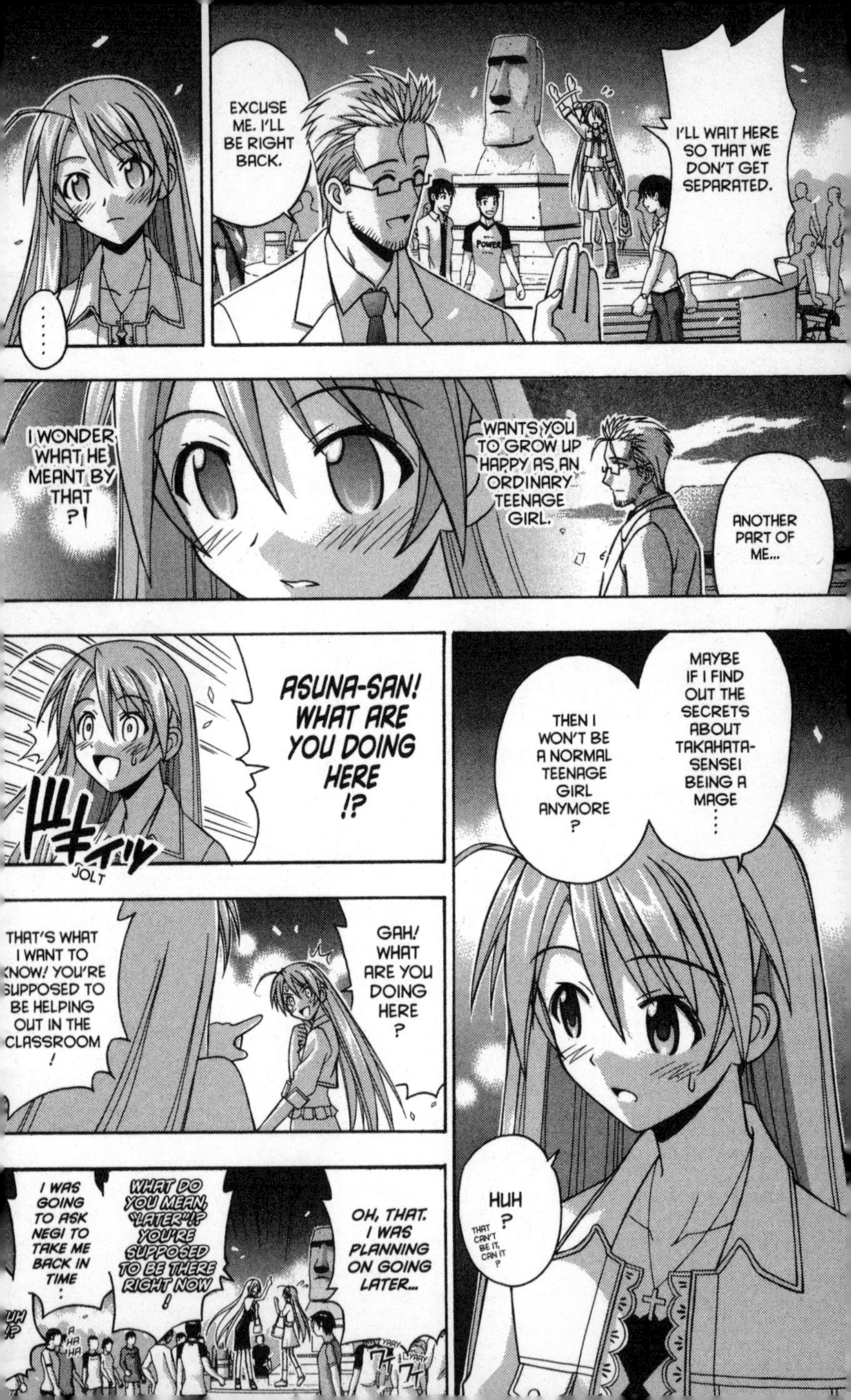
I'LL WAIT HERE SO THAT WE DON'T GET SEPARATED.
EXCUSE ME. I'LL BE RIGHT BACK.
......
ANOTHER PART OF ME...
WANTS YOU TO GROW UP HAPPY AS AN ORDINARY TEENAGE GIRL.
I WONDER WHAT HE MEANT BY THAT?!
MAYBE IF I FIND OUT THE SECRETS ABOUT TAKAHATA-SENSEI BEING A MAGE....
THEN I WON'T BE A NORMAL TEENAGE GIRL ANYMORE?
HUH?
THAT CAN'T BE IT, CAN IT?
ASUNA-SAN! WHAT ARE YOU DOING HERE!?
JOLT
GAH! WHAT ARE YOU DOING HERE?
THAT'S WHAT I WANT TO KNOW! YOU'RE SUPPOSED TO BE HELPING OUT IN THE CLASSROOM!
OH, THAT. I WAS PLANNING ON GOING LATER...
WHAT DO YOU MEAN, "LATER"!? YOU'RE SUPPOSED TO BE THERE RIGHT NOW!
I WAS GOING TO ASK NEGI TO TAKE ME BACK IN TIME...
HUH?
A HA HA
YAAY
YAAY

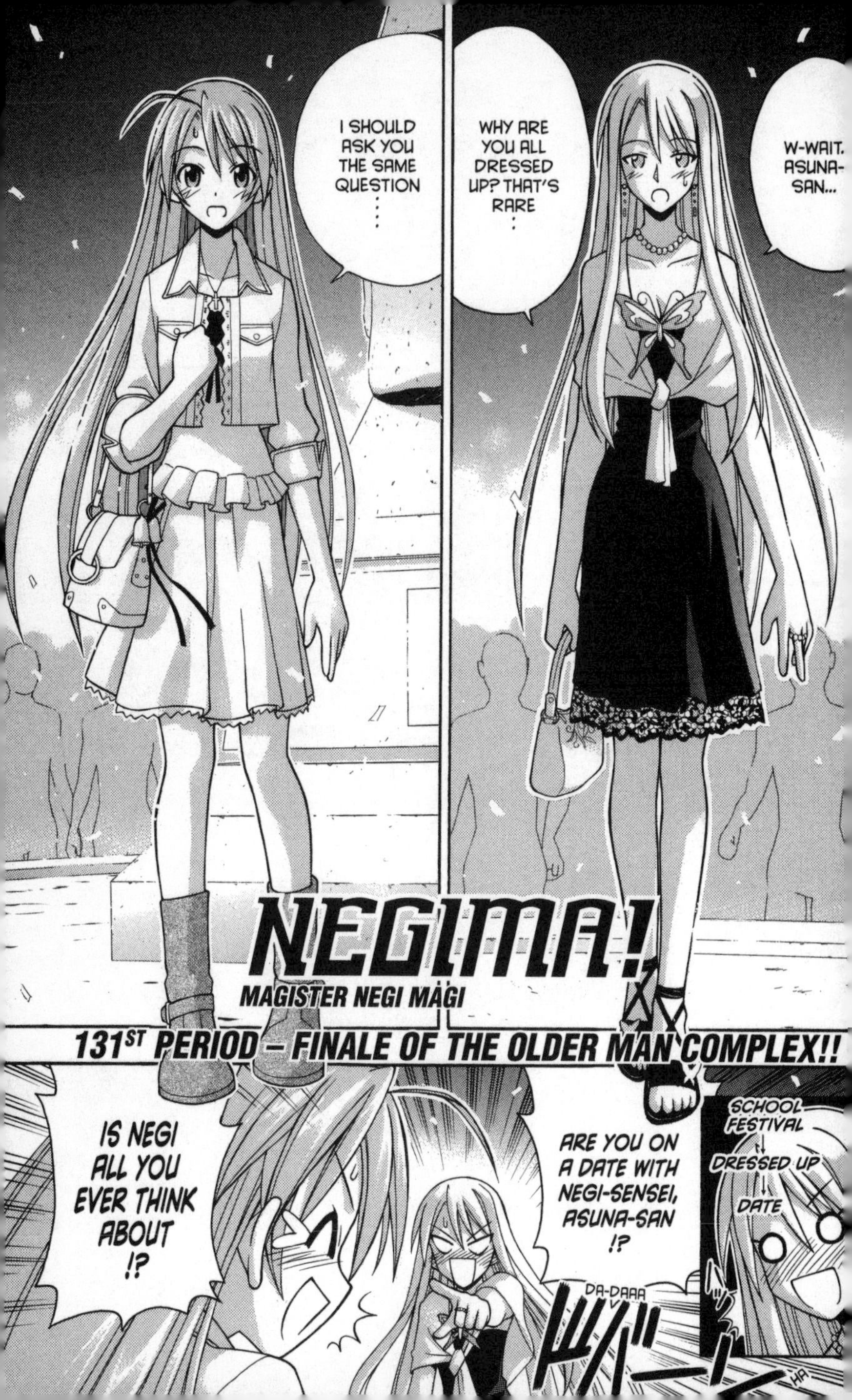
W-WAIT. ASUNA-SAN...
WHY ARE YOU ALL DRESSED UP? THAT'S RARE...
I SHOULD ASK YOU THE SAME QUESTION...
NEGIMA!
MAGISTER NEGI MAGI
131ST PERIOD – FINALE OF THE OLDER MAN COMPLEX!!
SCHOOL FESTIVAL ↓ DRESSED UP ↓ DATE
ARE YOU ON A DATE WITH NEGI-SENSEI, ASUNA-SAN!?
DA-DAAA
HA
IS NEGI ALL YOU EVER THINK ABOUT!?

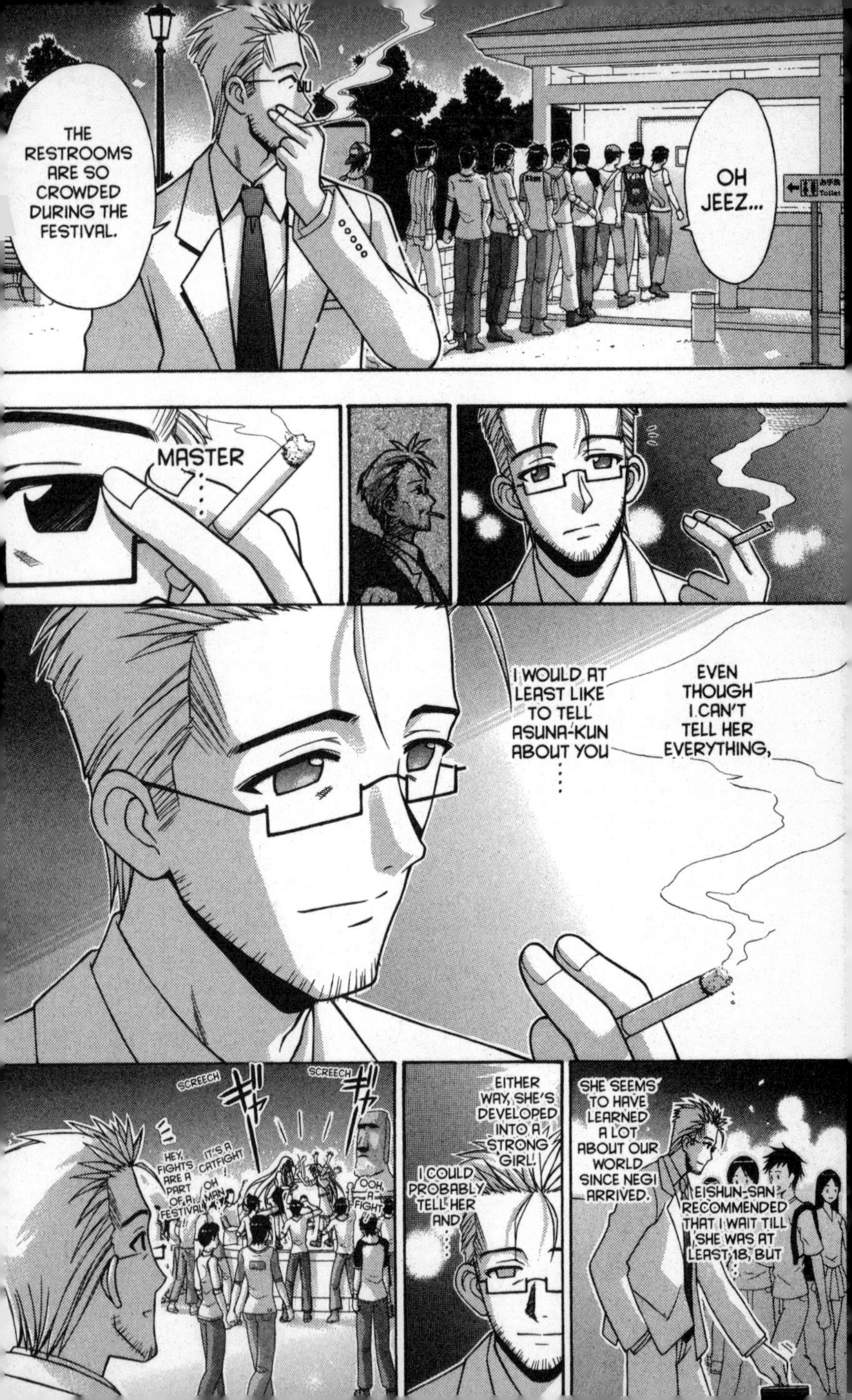
OH JEEZ...
THE RESTROOMS ARE SO CROWDED DURING THE FESTIVAL.
MASTER...
EVEN THOUGH I CAN'T TELL HER EVERYTHING,
I WOULD AT LEAST LIKE TO TELL ASUNA-KUN ABOUT YOU...
SHE SEEMS TO HAVE LEARNED A LOT ABOUT OUR WORLD SINCE NEGI ARRIVED.
EISHUN-SAN RECOMMENDED THAT I WAIT TILL SHE WAS AT LEAST 18, BUT
EITHER WAY, SHE'S DEVELOPED INTO A STRONG GIRL.
I COULD PROBABLY TELL HER AND...
SCREECH
SCREECH
OOH, A FIGHT
IT'S A CATFIGHT
OH MAN
HEY, FIGHTS ARE A PART OF A FESTIVAL

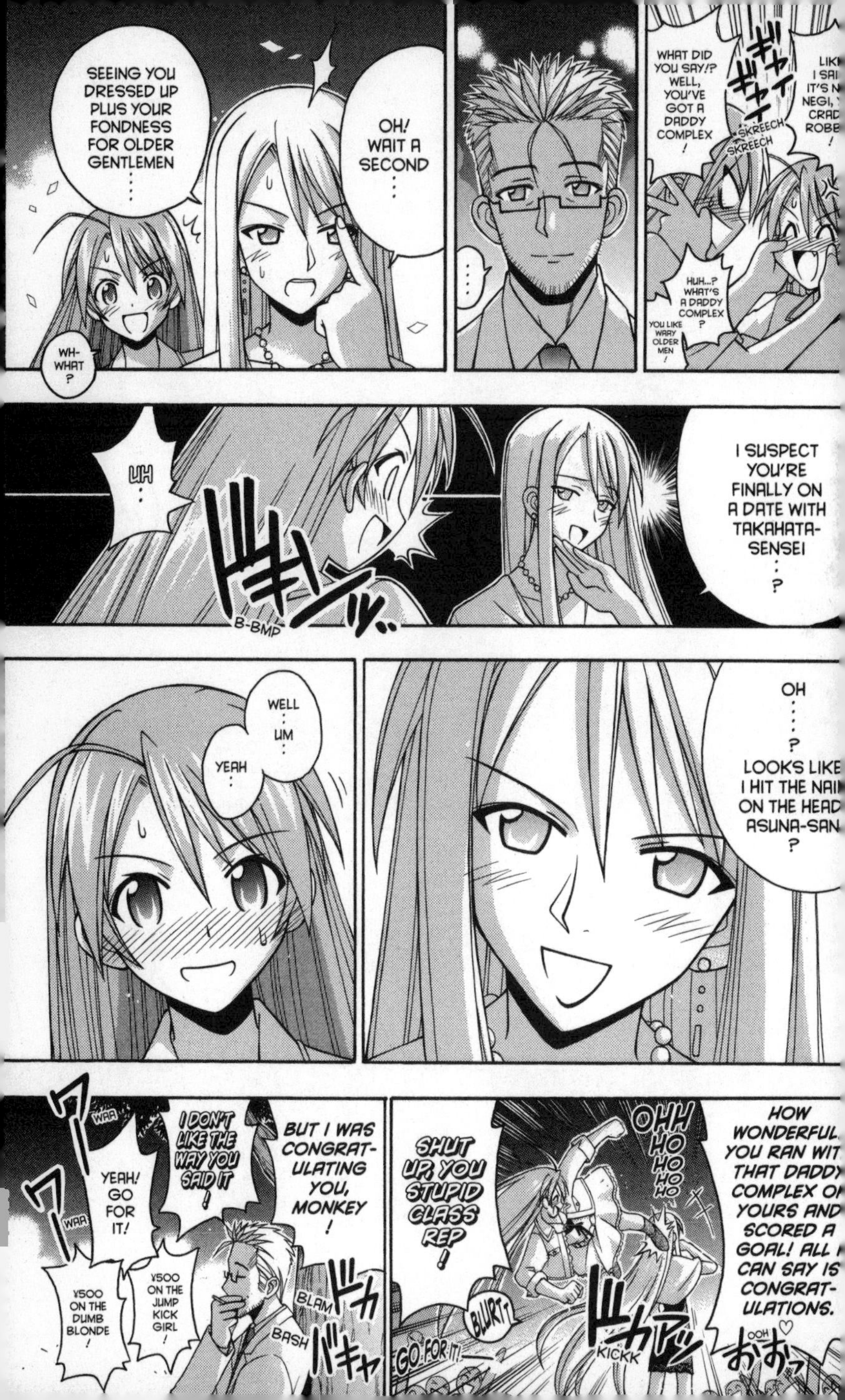
LIKE I SAI IT'S N NEGI, Y CRAD ROBB !
WHAT DID YOU SAY!? WELL, YOU'VE GOT A DADDY COMPLEX!
SKREECH SKREECH
HUH...? WHAT'S A DADDY COMPLEX?
YOU LIKE WAAY OLDER MEN!
....
OH! WAIT A SECOND...
SEEING YOU DRESSED UP PLUS YOUR FONDNESS FOR OLDER GENTLEMEN...
WH-WHAT?
I SUSPECT YOU'RE FINALLY ON A DATE WITH TAKAHATA-SENSEI...?
B-BMP
UH...
OH...? LOOKS LIKE I HIT THE NAI ON THE HEAD ASUNA-SAN?
WELL... UM... YEAH...
HOW WONDERFUL YOU RAN WIT THAT DADDY COMPLEX O YOURS AND SCORED A GOAL! ALL CAN SAY IS CONGRAT-ULATIONS.
OOH
OHH HO HO HO HO
KICKK
SHUT UP, YOU STUPID CLASS REP!
BLURT
GO FOR IT!
BUT I WAS CONGRAT-ULATING YOU, MONKEY!
I DON'T LIKE THE WAY YOU SAID IT!
BLAM
BASH
YEAH! GO FOR IT!
WAA
WAA
¥500 ON THE JUMP KICK GIRL!
¥500 ON THE DUMB BLONDE!

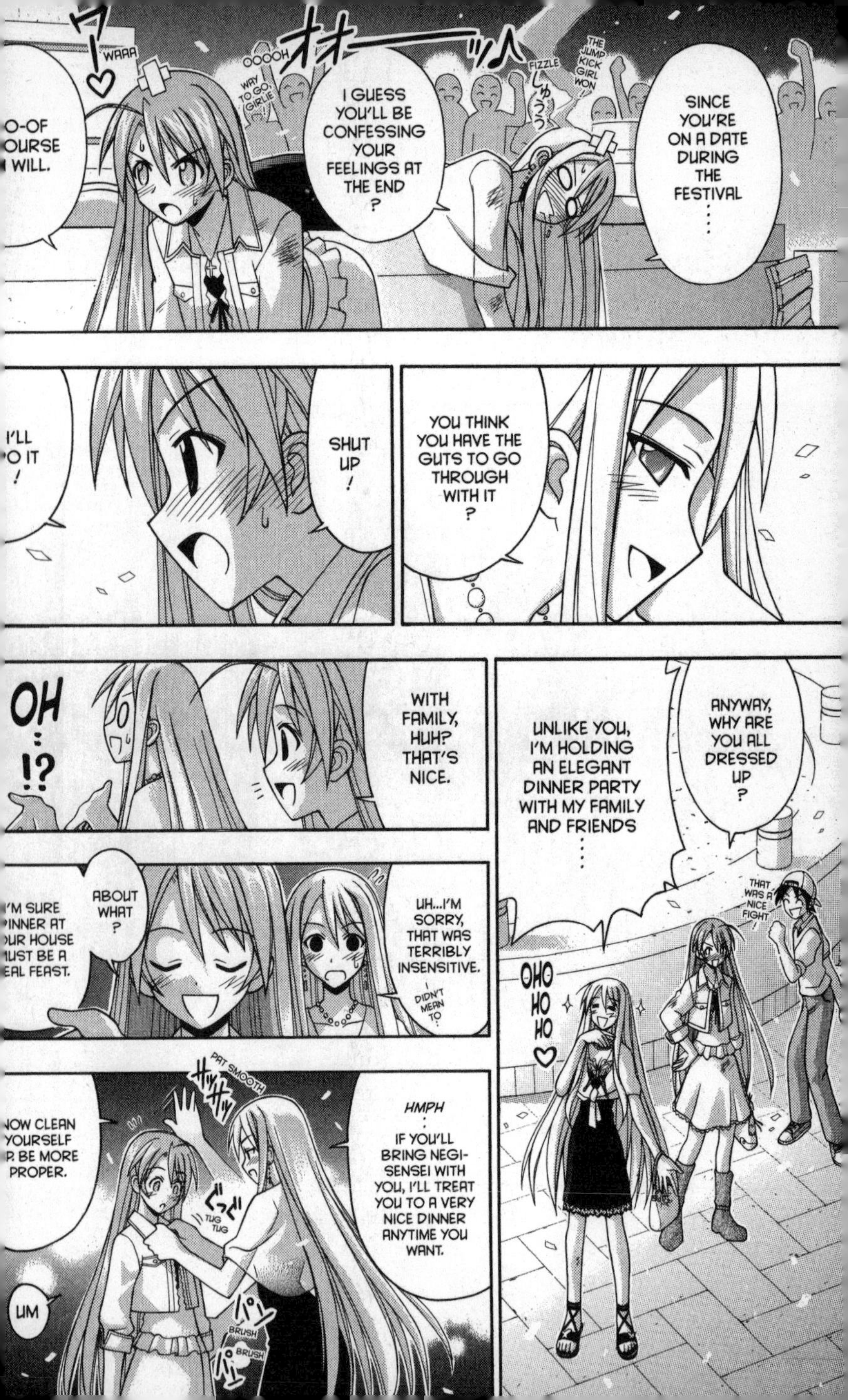
SINCE YOU'RE ON A DATE DURING THE FESTIVAL...
THE JUMP KICK GIRL WON!
FIZZLE
I GUESS YOU'LL BE CONFESSING YOUR FEELINGS AT THE END?
WAY TO GO, GIRLIE
OOOOH
WAAA
O-OF OURSE WILL.
YOU THINK YOU HAVE THE GUTS TO GO THROUGH WITH IT?
SHUT UP!
I'LL O IT!
ANYWAY, WHY ARE YOU ALL DRESSED UP?
UNLIKE YOU, I'M HOLDING AN ELEGANT DINNER PARTY WITH MY FAMILY AND FRIENDS...
THAT WAS A NICE FIGHT!
OHO HO HO♡
WITH FAMILY, HUH? THAT'S NICE.
OH...!?
UH...I'M SORRY, THAT WAS TERRIBLY INSENSITIVE.
I DIDN'T MEAN TO...
ABOUT WHAT?
I'M SURE INNER AT OUR HOUSE UST BE A EAL FEAST.
HMPH... IF YOU'LL BRING NEGI-SENSEI WITH YOU, I'LL TREAT YOU TO A VERY NICE DINNER ANYTIME YOU WANT.
PAT SMOOTH
TUG TUG
NOW CLEAN YOURSELF P. BE MORE PROPER.
BRUSH
BRUSH
UM

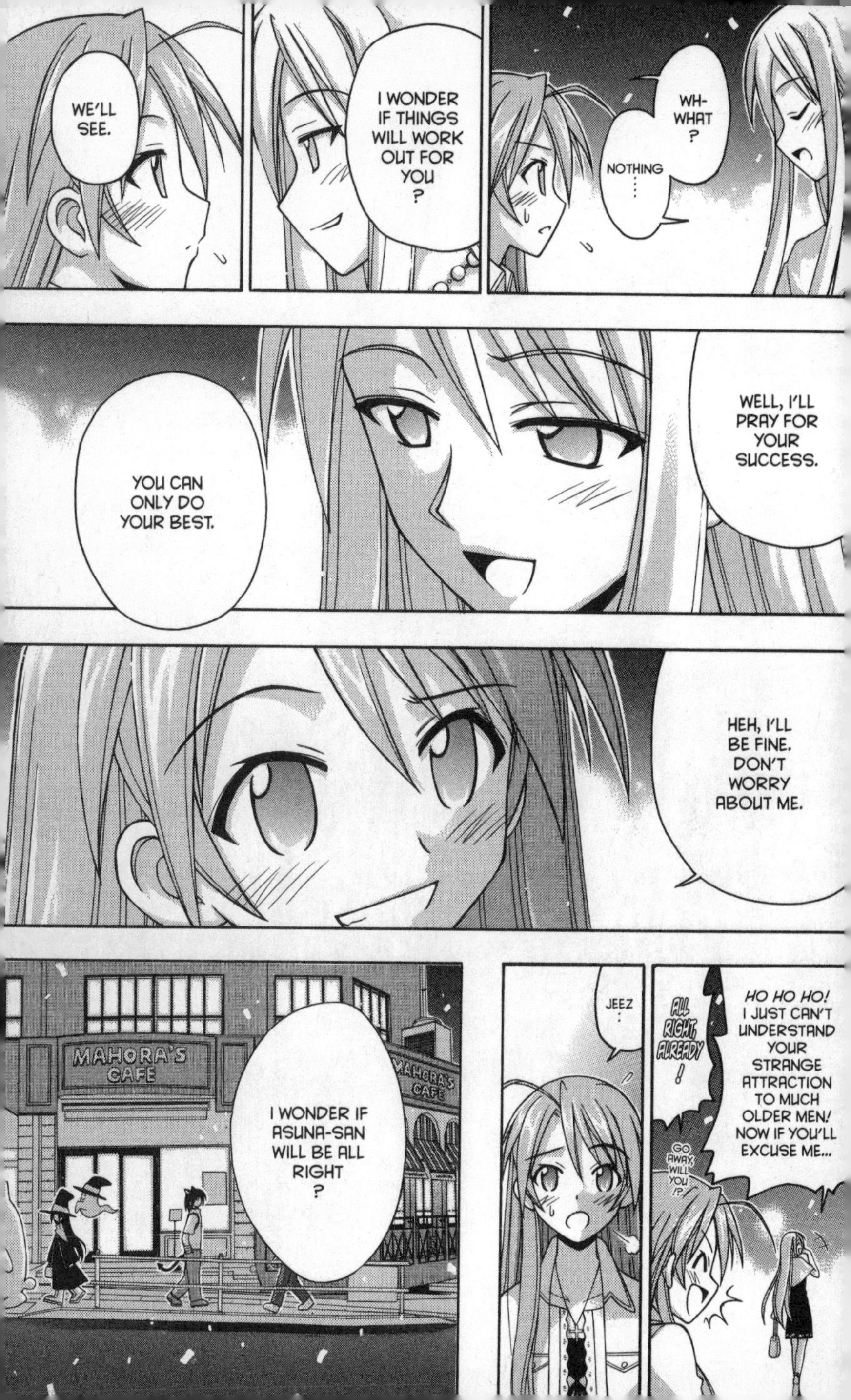
WH- WHAT ?
NOTHING ...
I WONDER IF THINGS WILL WORK OUT FOR YOU ?
WE'LL SEE.
WELL, I'LL PRAY FOR YOUR SUCCESS.
YOU CAN ONLY DO YOUR BEST.
HEH, I'LL BE FINE. DON'T WORRY ABOUT ME.
HO HO HO! I JUST CAN'T UNDERSTAND YOUR STRANGE ATTRACTION TO MUCH OLDER MEN! NOW IF YOU'LL EXCUSE ME...
ALL RIGHT, ALREADY!
GO AWAY, WILL YOU !?
JEEZ ...
MAHORA'S CAFE
MAHORA'S CAFE
I WONDER IF ASUNA-SAN WILL BE ALL RIGHT ?

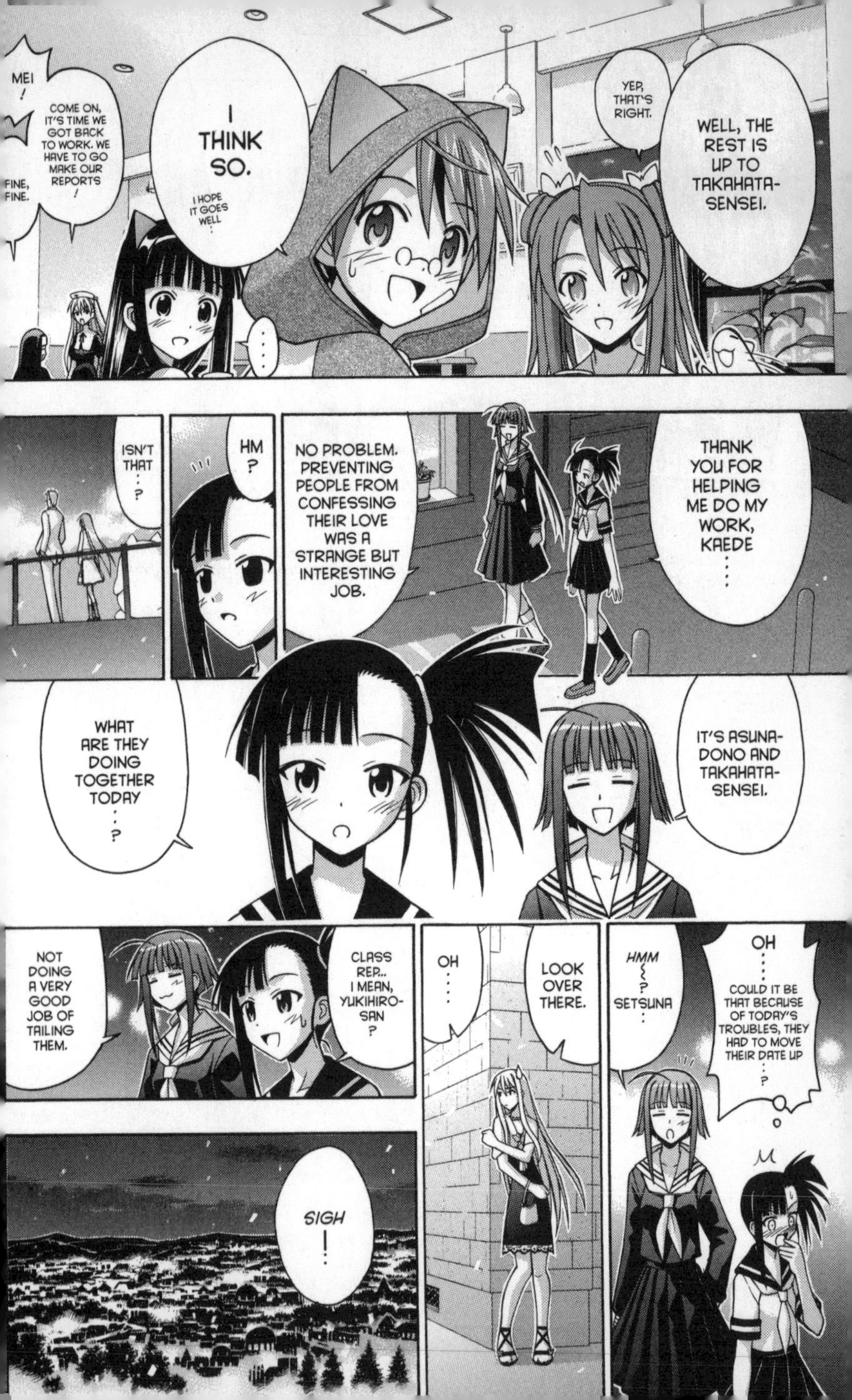
WELL, THE REST IS UP TO TAKAHATA-SENSEI.
YEP, THAT'S RIGHT.
I THINK SO.
I HOPE IT GOES WELL...
...
COME ON, IT'S TIME WE GOT BACK TO WORK. WE HAVE TO GO MAKE OUR REPORTS!
MEI!
FINE, FINE.
THANK YOU FOR HELPING ME DO MY WORK, KAEDE...
NO PROBLEM. PREVENTING PEOPLE FROM CONFESSING THEIR LOVE WAS A STRANGE BUT INTERESTING JOB.
HM?
ISN'T THAT...?
IT'S ASUNA-DONO AND TAKAHATA-SENSEI.
WHAT ARE THEY DOING TOGETHER TODAY...?
OH...
COULD IT BE THAT BECAUSE OF TODAY'S TROUBLES, THEY HAD TO MOVE THEIR DATE UP...?
HMM~? SETSUNA...
LOOK OVER THERE.
OH....
CLASS REP... I MEAN, YUKIHIRO-SAN?
NOT DOING A VERY GOOD JOB OF TAILING THEM.
SIGH!

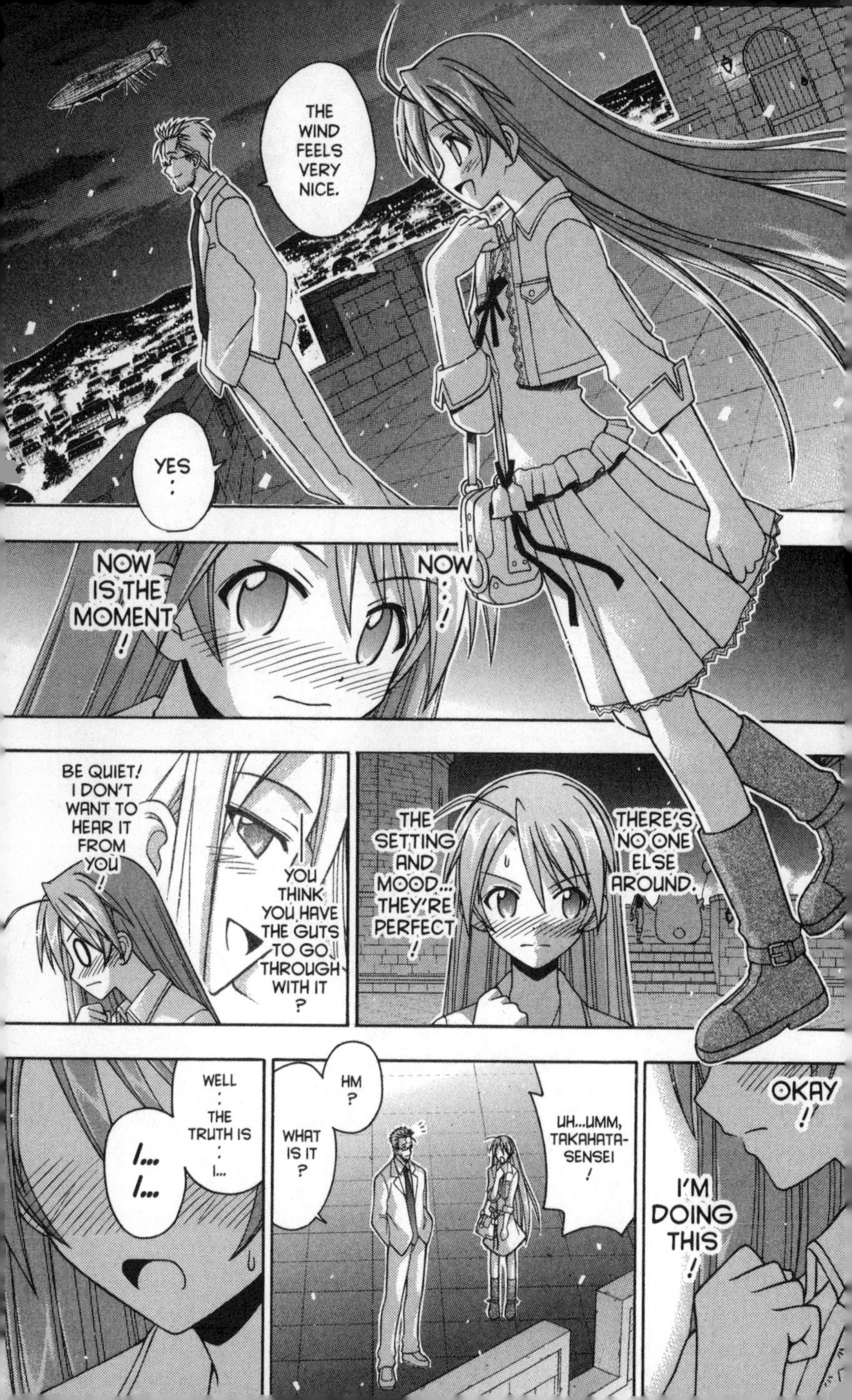
THE WIND FEELS VERY NICE.
YES...
NOW..!
NOW IS THE MOMENT!
THERE'S NO ONE ELSE AROUND.
THE SETTING AND MOOD... THEY'RE PERFECT!
YOU THINK YOU HAVE THE GUTS TO GO THROUGH WITH IT?
BE QUIET! I DON'T WANT TO HEAR IT FROM YOU!
OKAY!
I'M DOING THIS!
UH...UMM, TAKAHATA-SENSEI!
HM?
WHAT IS IT?
WELL... THE TRUTH IS... I...
I... I...

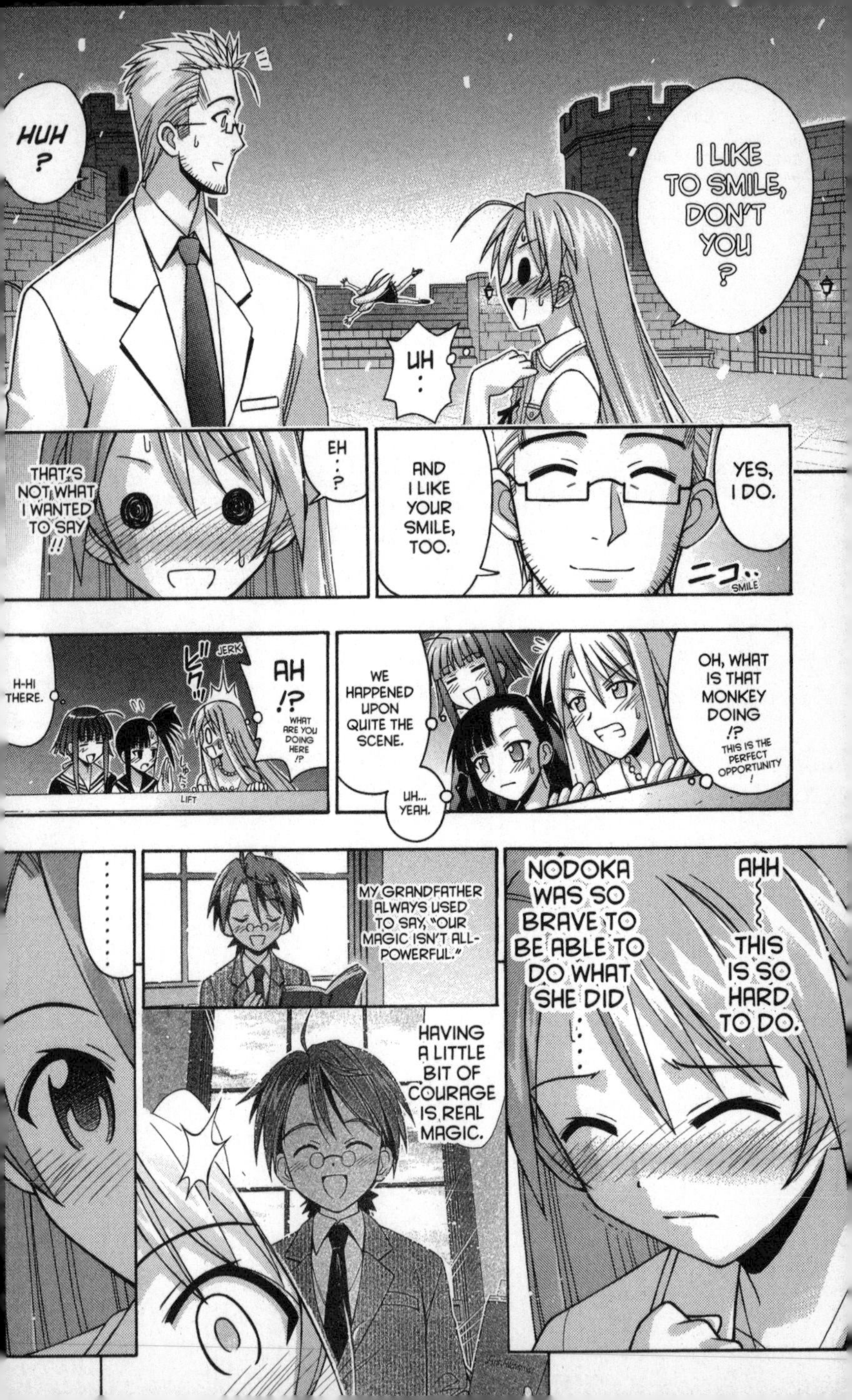
I LIKE TO SMILE, DON'T YOU?
UH...
HUH?
YES, I DO.
ニコ.. SMILE
AND I LIKE YOUR SMILE, TOO.
EH...?
THAT'S NOT WHAT I WANTED TO SAY!!
OH, WHAT IS THAT MONKEY DOING!?
THIS IS THE PERFECT OPPORTUNITY!
WE HAPPENED UPON QUITE THE SCENE.
UH... YEAH.
AH!?
WHAT ARE YOU DOING HERE!?
JERK
H-HI THERE.
LIFT
AHH~ THIS IS SO HARD TO DO.
NODOKA WAS SO BRAVE TO BE ABLE TO DO WHAT SHE DID...
MY GRANDFATHER ALWAYS USED TO SAY, "OUR MAGIC ISN'T ALL-POWERFUL."
HAVING A LITTLE BIT OF COURAGE IS REAL MAGIC.
......

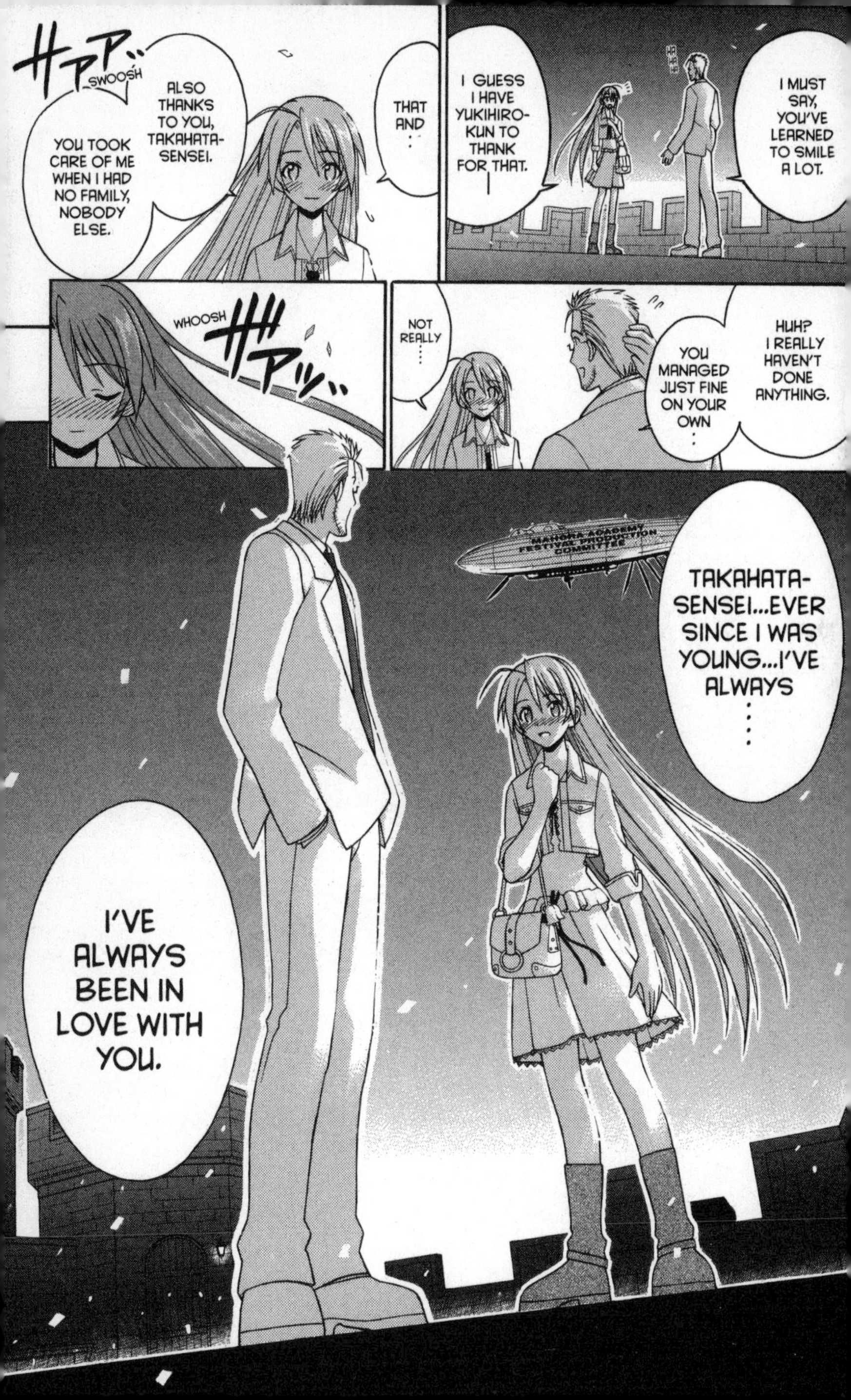
I MUST SAY, YOU'VE LEARNED TO SMILE A LOT.
I GUESS I HAVE YUKIHIRO-KUN TO THANK FOR THAT.
THAT AND...
ALSO THANKS TO YOU, TAKAHATA-SENSEI.
SWOOSH
YOU TOOK CARE OF ME WHEN I HAD NO FAMILY, NOBODY ELSE.
HUH? I REALLY HAVEN'T DONE ANYTHING.
YOU MANAGED JUST FINE ON YOUR OWN...
NOT REALLY...
WHOOSH
TAKAHATA-SENSEI...EVER SINCE I WAS YOUNG...I'VE ALWAYS...
MAHORA ACADEMY FESTIVAL PRODUCTION COMMITTEE
I'VE ALWAYS BEEN IN LOVE WITH YOU.

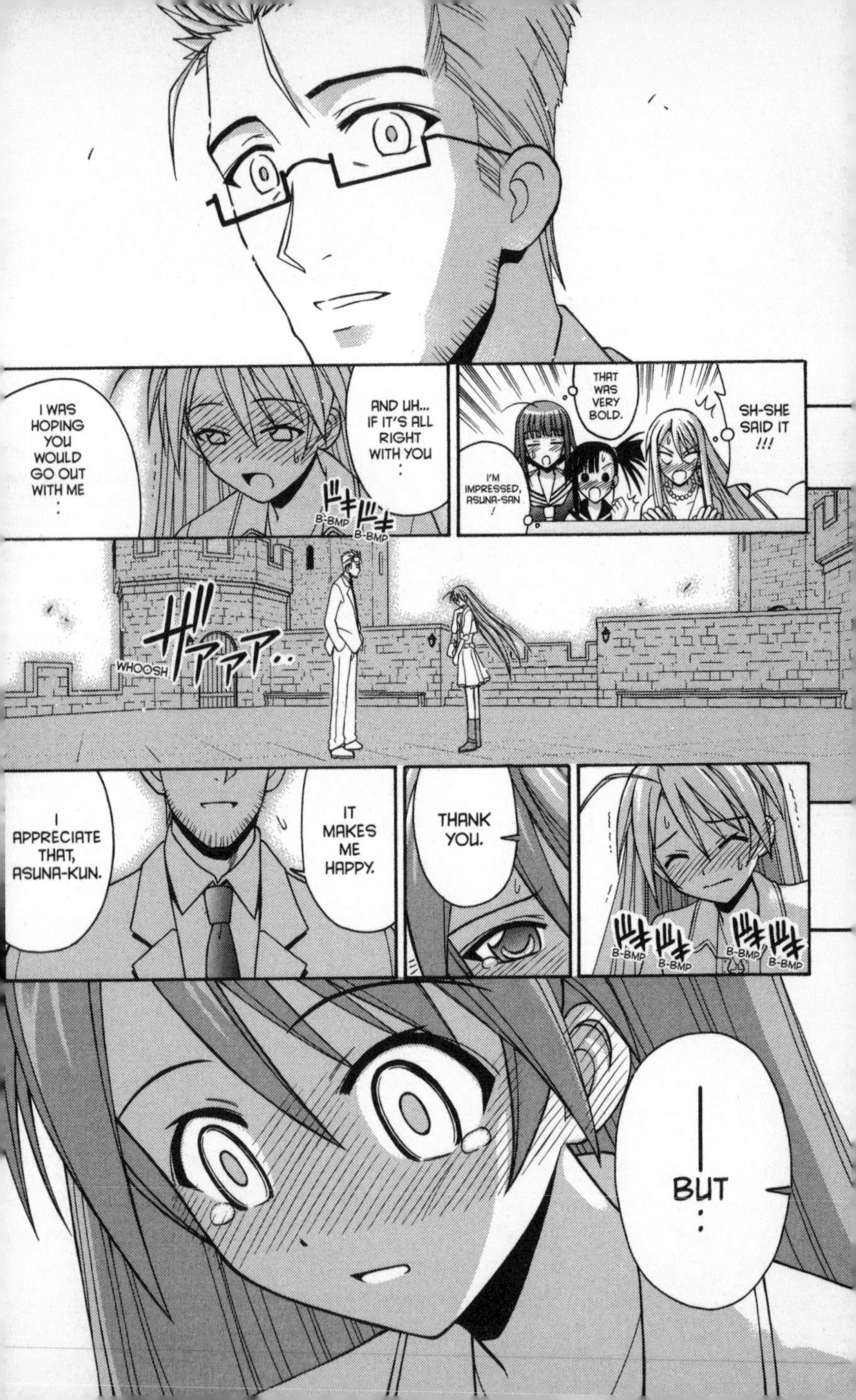

SH-SHE SAID IT !!!
THAT WAS VERY BOLD.
I'M IMPRESSED, ASUNA-SAN!
AND UH... IF IT'S ALL RIGHT WITH YOU :
ドキドキ
B-BMP B-BMP
I WAS HOPING YOU WOULD GO OUT WITH ME :
ザァァア..
WHOOSH
ドキドキ ドキドキ
B-BMP B-BMP B-BMP B-BMP
THANK YOU.
IT MAKES ME HAPPY.
I APPRECIATE THAT, ASUNA-KUN.
— BUT :

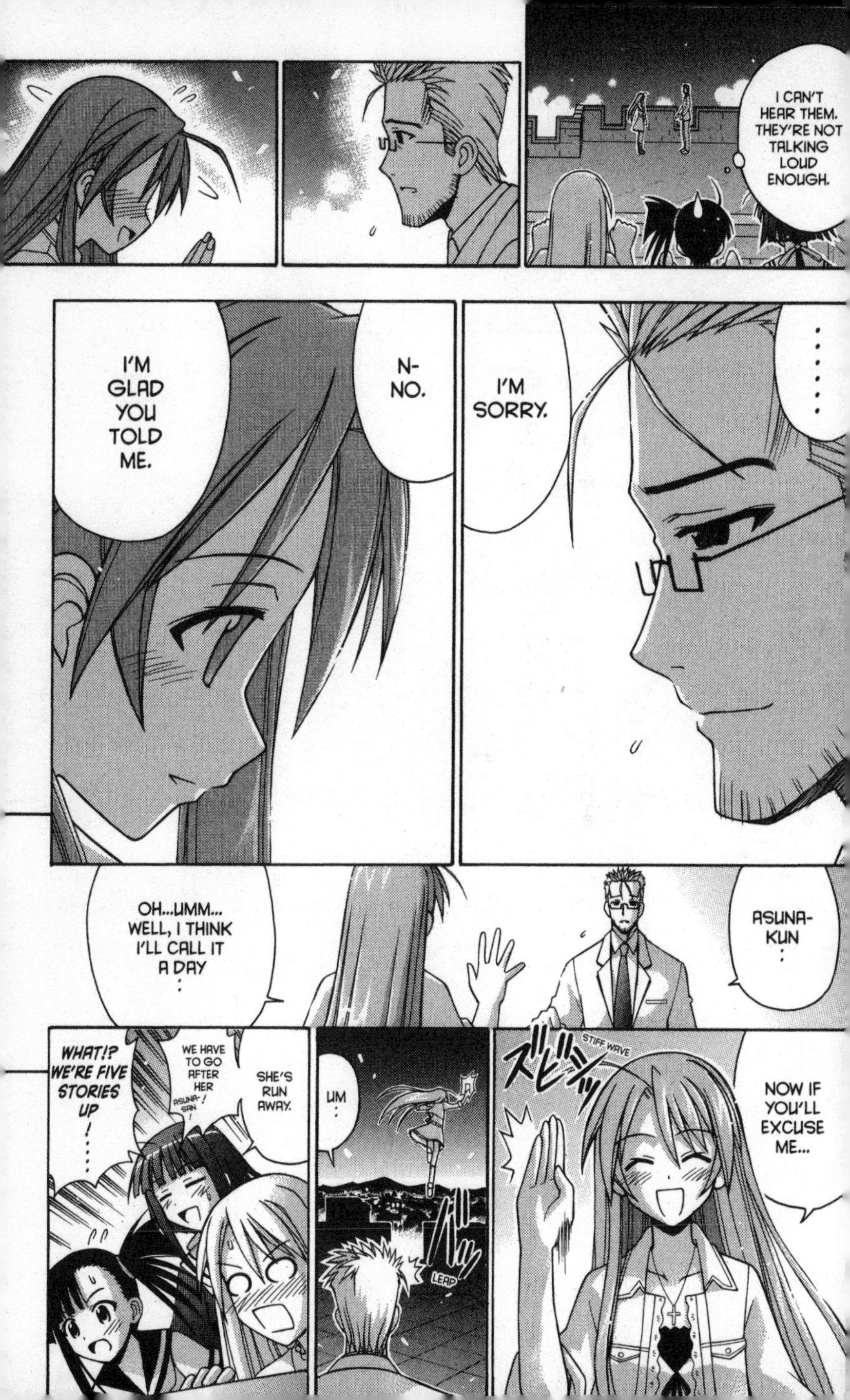
I CAN'T HEAR THEM. THEY'RE NOT TALKING LOUD ENOUGH.
......
I'M SORRY.
N-NO.
I'M GLAD YOU TOLD ME.
ASUNA-KUN:
OH...UMM... WELL, I THINK I'LL CALL IT A DAY:
STIFF WAVE
NOW IF YOU'LL EXCUSE ME...
UM:
LEAP
SHE'S RUN AWAY.
WE HAVE TO GO AFTER HER
ASUNA-SAN!
WHAT!? WE'RE FIVE STORIES UP!.....

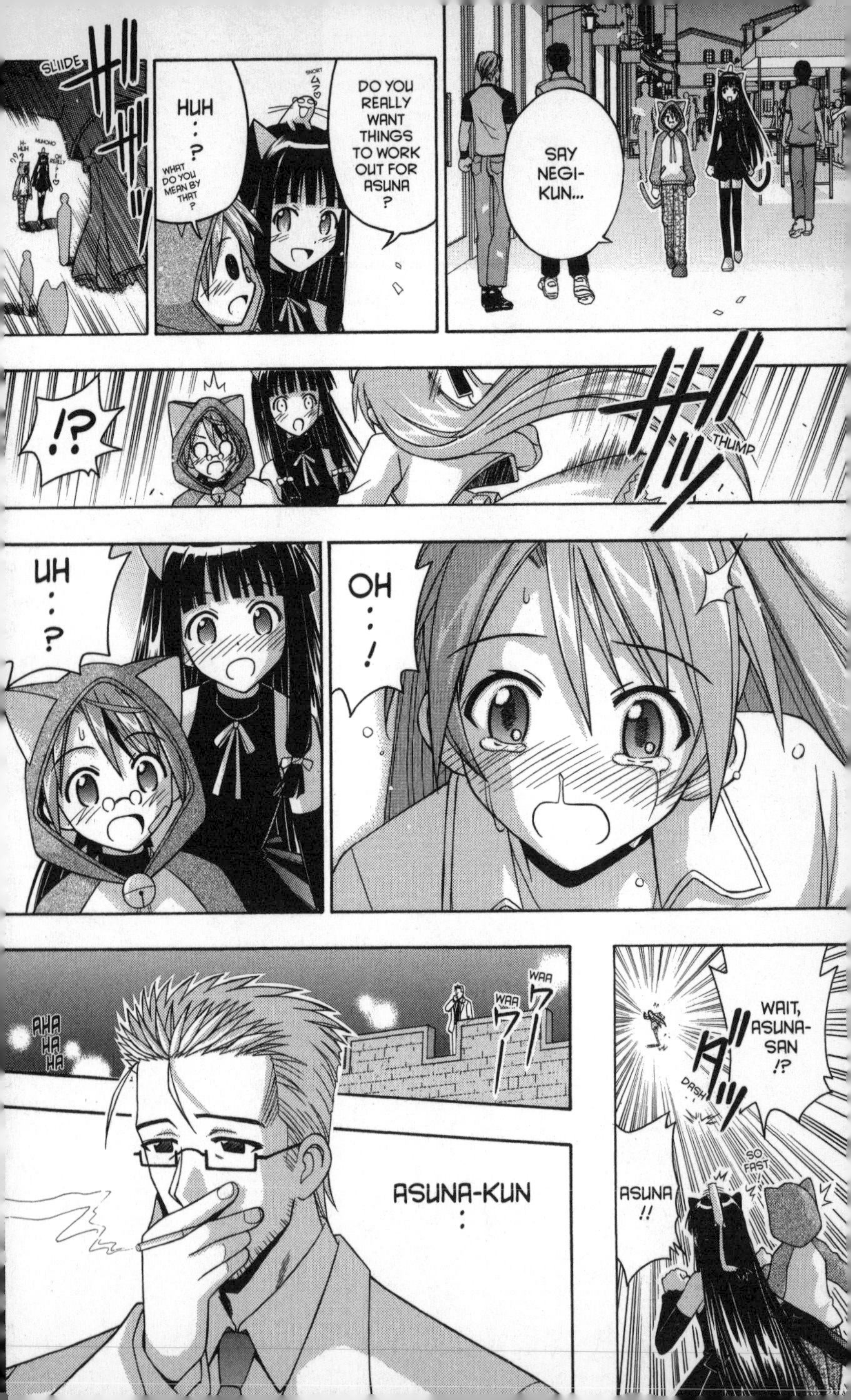
SAY NEGI-KUN...
DO YOU REALLY WANT THINGS TO WORK OUT FOR ASUNA?
SNORT
HUH...?
WHAT DO YOU MEAN BY THAT?
SLIIDE
MUHOHO
OH REALLY
H-HUH
THUMP
!?
OH...!
UH...?
WAIT, ASUNA-SAN!?
DASH
SO FAST
ASUNA!!
WAA
WAA
AHA HA HA
ASUNA-KUN...

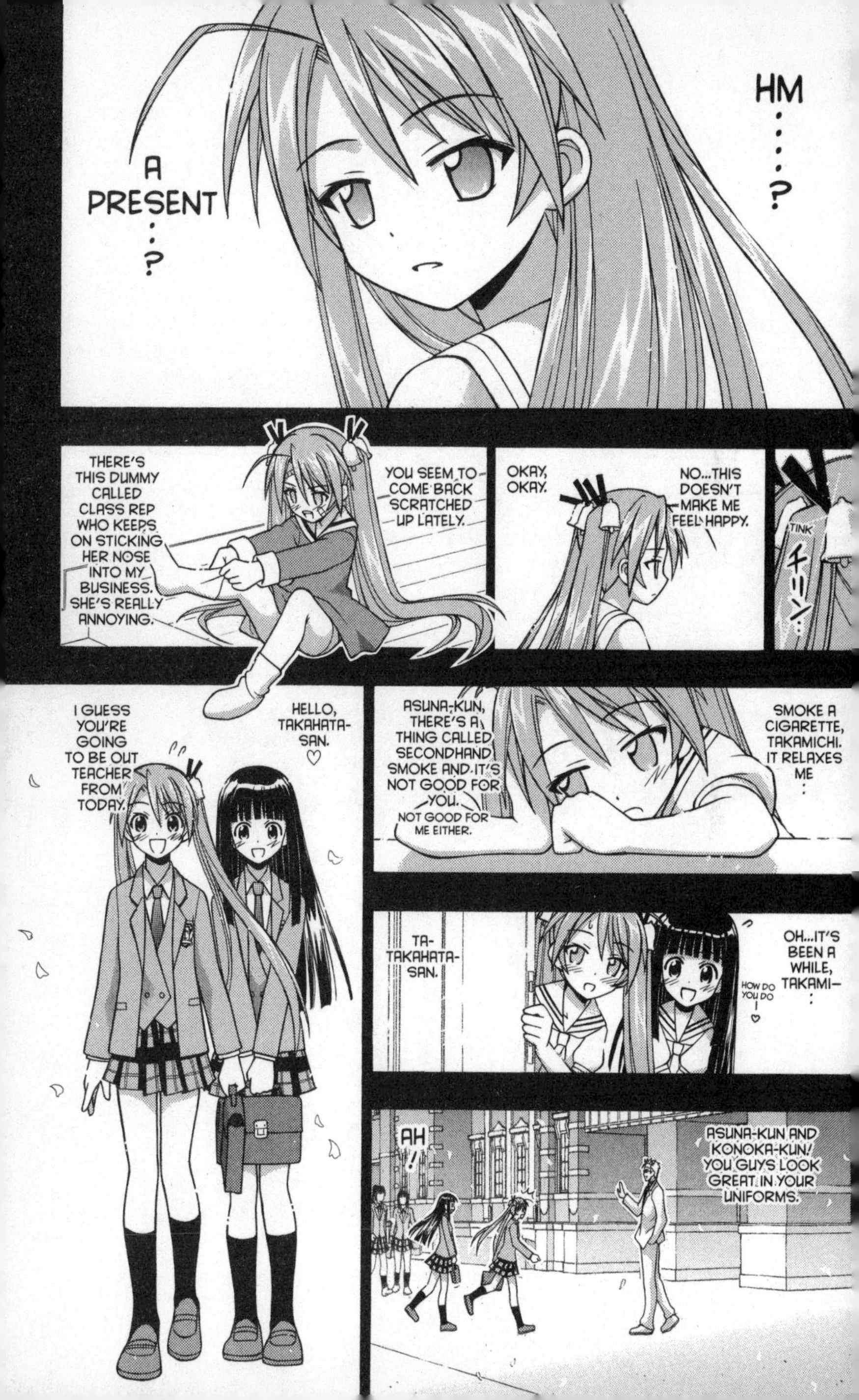
HM...?
A PRESENT...?
TINK
チリーン...
NO...THIS DOESN'T MAKE ME FEEL HAPPY.
OKAY, OKAY.
YOU SEEM TO COME BACK SCRATCHED UP LATELY.
THERE'S THIS DUMMY CALLED CLASS REP WHO KEEPS ON STICKING HER NOSE INTO MY BUSINESS. SHE'S REALLY ANNOYING.
SMOKE A CIGARETTE, TAKAMICHI. IT RELAXES ME...
ASUNA-KUN, THERE'S A THING CALLED SECONDHAND SMOKE AND IT'S NOT GOOD FOR YOU.
NOT GOOD FOR ME EITHER.
OH...IT'S BEEN A WHILE, TAKAMI-...
HOW DO YOU DO! ♡
TA-TAKAHATA-SAN.
ASUNA-KUN AND KONOKA-KUN! YOU GUYS LOOK GREAT IN YOUR UNIFORMS.
AH!
HELLO, TAKAHATA-SAN. ♡
I GUESS YOU'RE GOING TO BE OUT TEACHER FROM TODAY.

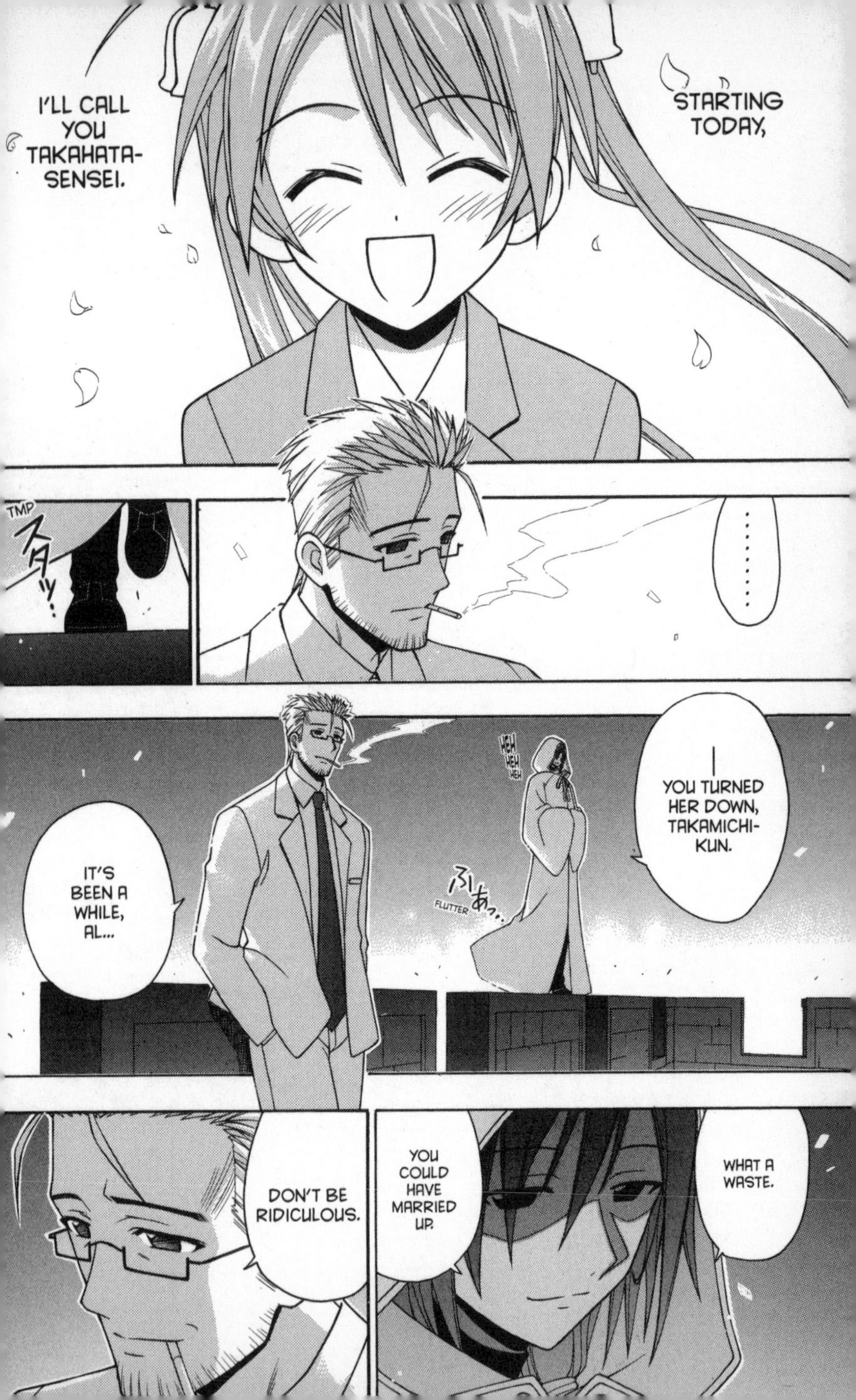
STARTING TODAY,
I'LL CALL YOU TAKAHATA-SENSEI.
......
TMP
スタッ
YOU TURNED HER DOWN, TAKAMICHI-KUN.
HEH HEH HEH
ふぁっ
FLUTTER
IT'S BEEN A WHILE, AL...
WHAT A WASTE.
YOU COULD HAVE MARRIED UP.
DON'T BE RIDICULOUS.

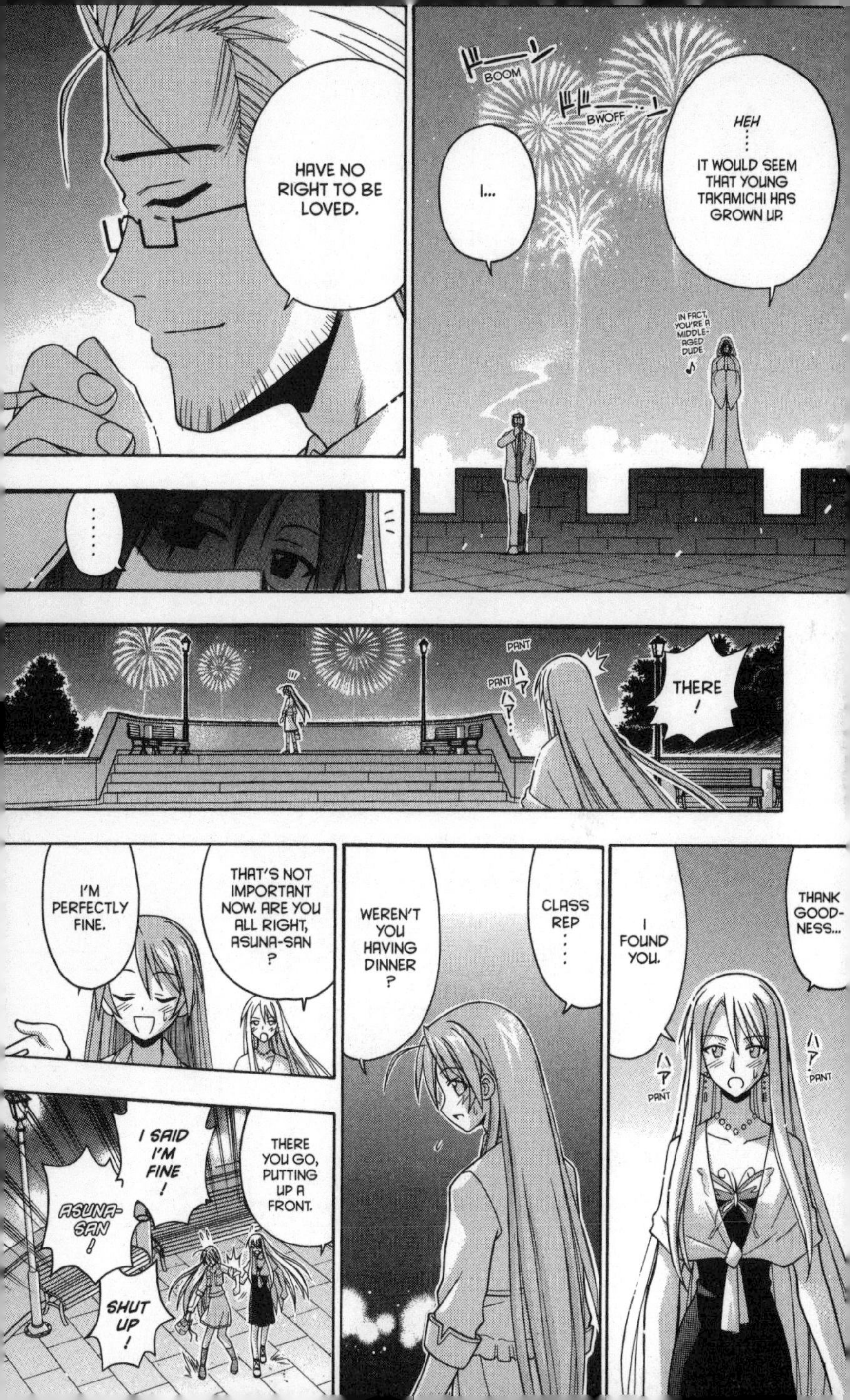
BOOM
BWOFF
HEH... IT WOULD SEEM THAT YOUNG TAKAMICHI HAS GROWN UP.
IN FACT, YOU'RE A MIDDLE-AGED DUDE ♪
I...
HAVE NO RIGHT TO BE LOVED.
......
THERE!
PANT
PANT
THANK GOODNESS...
I FOUND YOU.
PANT
PANT
CLASS REP...
WEREN'T YOU HAVING DINNER?
THAT'S NOT IMPORTANT NOW. ARE YOU ALL RIGHT, ASUNA-SAN?
I'M PERFECTLY FINE.
THERE YOU GO, PUTTING UP A FRONT.
I SAID I'M FINE!
ASUNA-SAN!
SHUT UP!

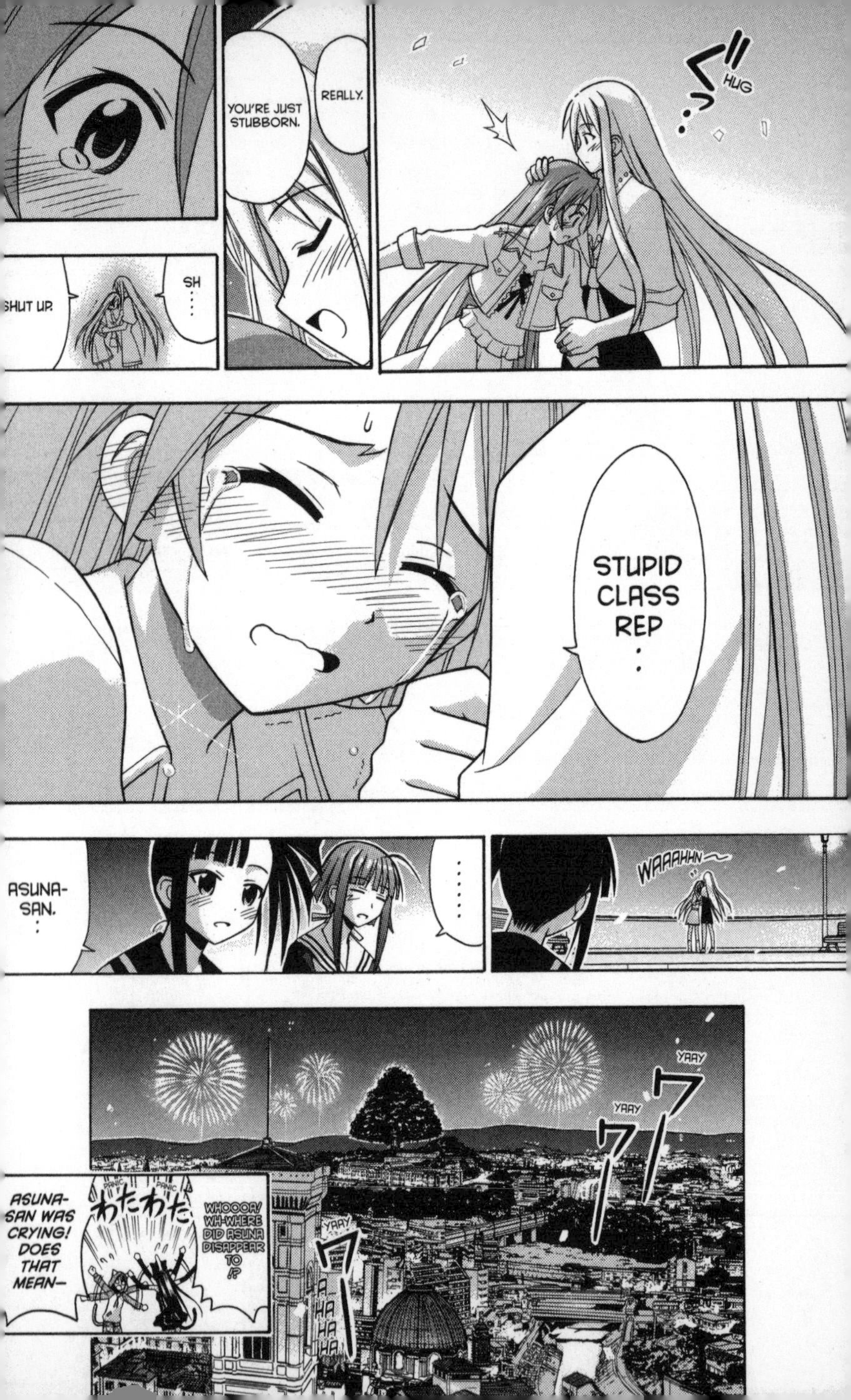
HUG
REALLY.
YOU'RE JUST STUBBORN.
SH....
SHUT UP.
STUPID CLASS REP...
WAAAHHN~
......
ASUNA-SAN...
YAAY
YAAY
YAAY
A HA HA HA
WHOOOA! WH-WHERE DID ASUNA DISAPPEAR TO!?
わたわた
PANIC PANIC
ASUNA-SAN WAS CRYING! DOES THAT MEAN—

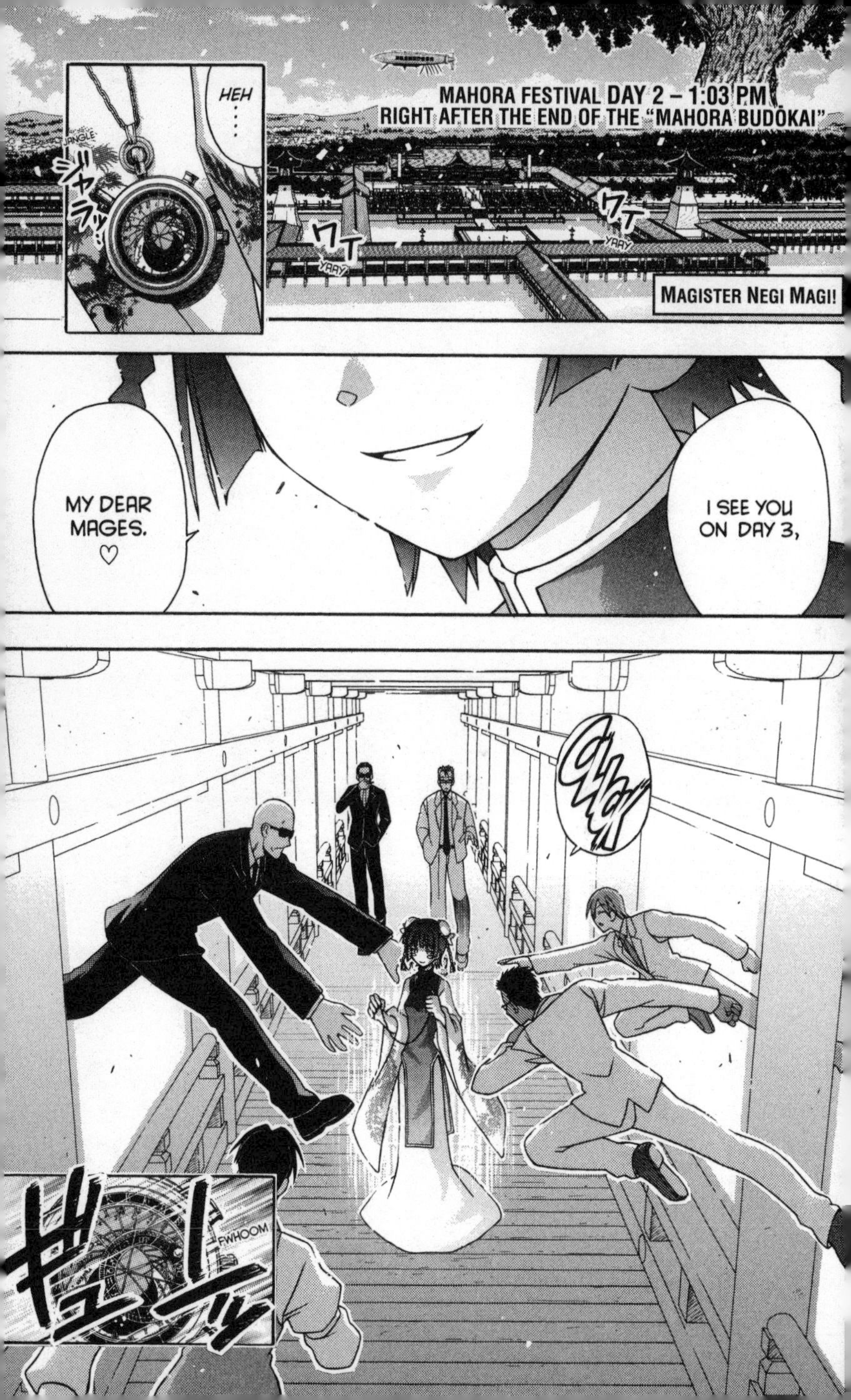
MAHORA FESTIVAL DAY 2 – 1:03 PM
RIGHT AFTER THE END OF THE "MAHORA BUDŌKAI"
YAAY
YAAY
MAGISTER NEGI MAGI!
HEH
. . . .
JANGLE
I SEE YOU ON DAY 3,
MY DEAR MAGES. ♡
FWHOOM

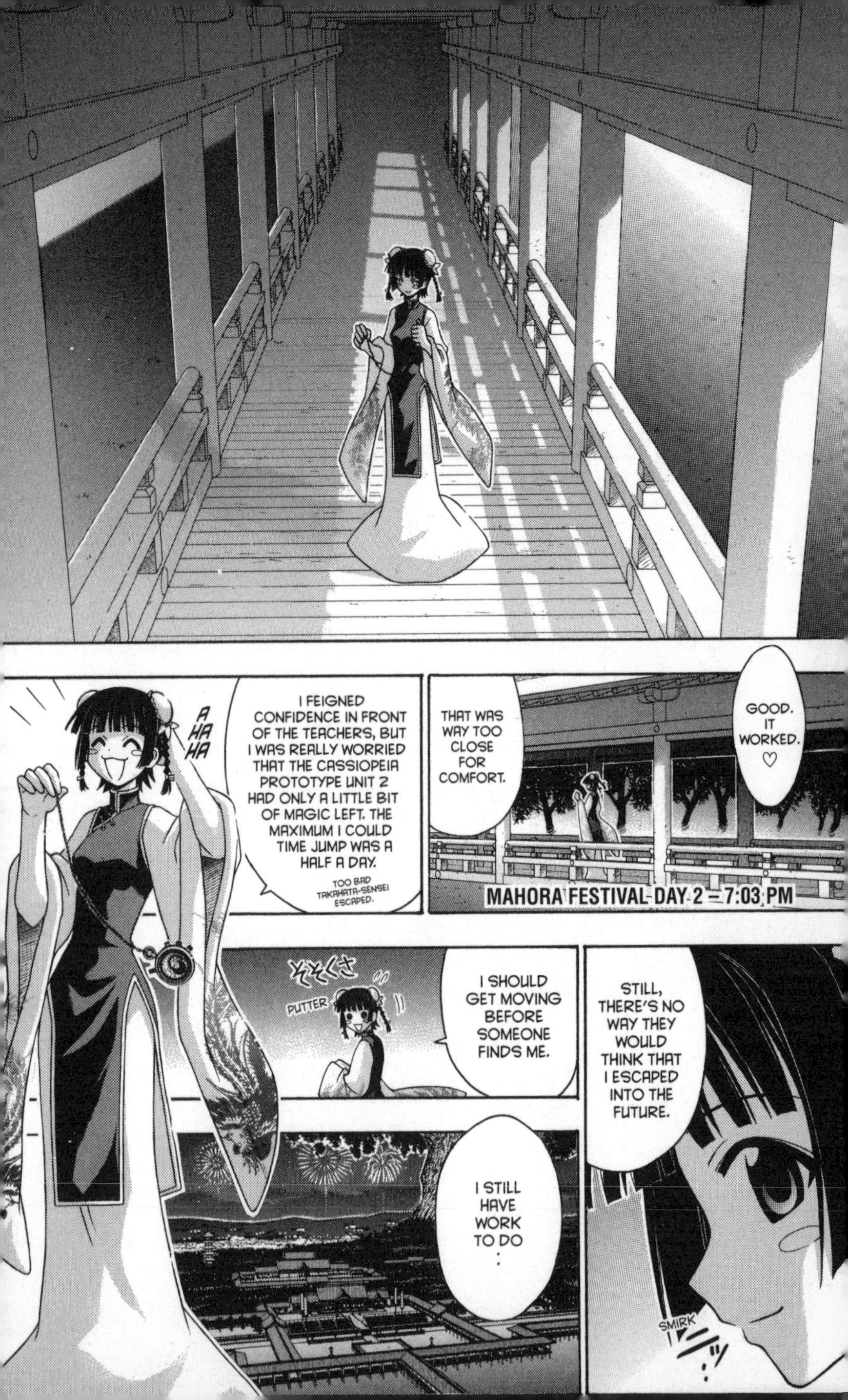
GOOD. IT WORKED. ♡
THAT WAS WAY TOO CLOSE FOR COMFORT.
MAHORA FESTIVAL DAY 2 — 7:03 PM
I FEIGNED CONFIDENCE IN FRONT OF THE TEACHERS, BUT I WAS REALLY WORRIED THAT THE CASSIOPEIA PROTOTYPE UNIT 2 HAD ONLY A LITTLE BIT OF MAGIC LEFT. THE MAXIMUM I COULD TIME JUMP WAS A HALF A DAY.
TOO BAD TAKAHATA-SENSEI ESCAPED.
A HA HA
STILL, THERE'S NO WAY THEY WOULD THINK THAT I ESCAPED INTO THE FUTURE.
I SHOULD GET MOVING BEFORE SOMEONE FINDS ME.
PUTTER
I STILL HAVE WORK TO DO
SMIRK

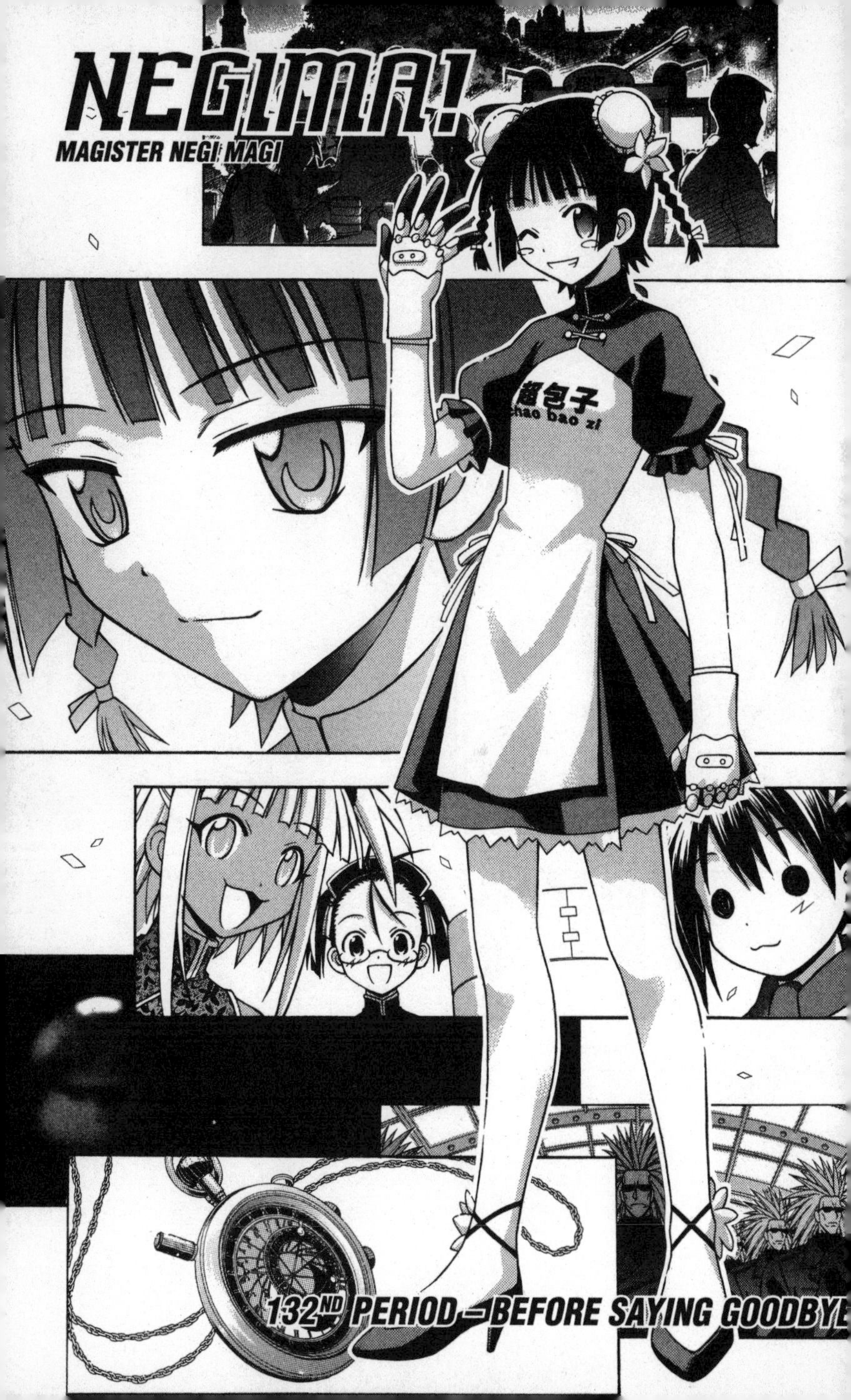
NEGIMA!
MAGISTER NEGI MAGI
超包子
chao bao zi
132ND PERIOD – BEFORE SAYING GOODBYE

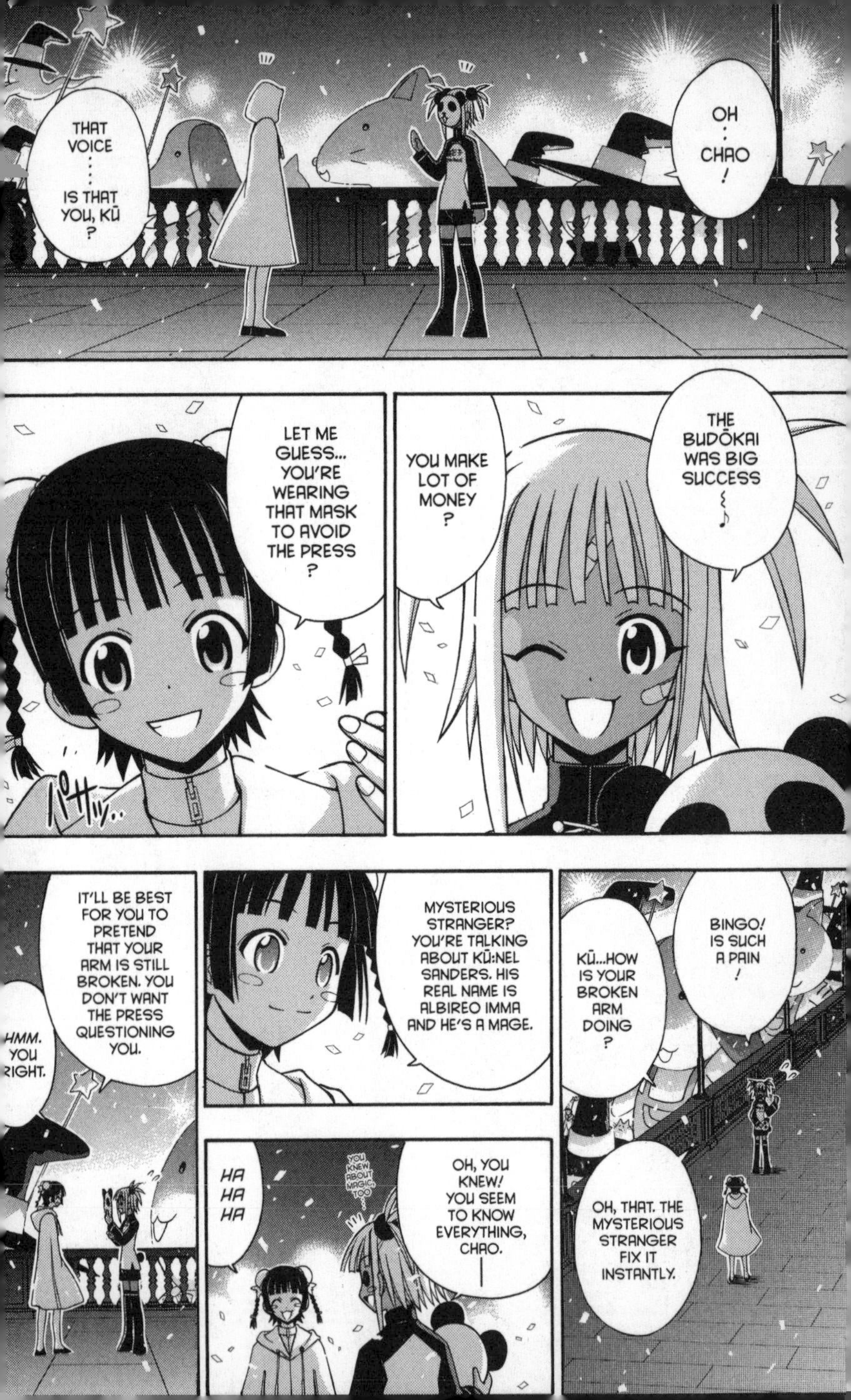
OH... CHAO!
THAT VOICE...... IS THAT YOU, KŪ?
THE BUDŌKAI WAS BIG SUCCESS~♪
YOU MAKE LOT OF MONEY?
LET ME GUESS... YOU'RE WEARING THAT MASK TO AVOID THE PRESS?
パサッ..
BINGO! IS SUCH A PAIN!
KŪ...HOW IS YOUR BROKEN ARM DOING?
OH, THAT. THE MYSTERIOUS STRANGER FIX IT INSTANTLY.
MYSTERIOUS STRANGER? YOU'RE TALKING ABOUT KŪ:NEL SANDERS. HIS REAL NAME IS ALBIREO IMMA AND HE'S A MAGE.
OH, YOU KNEW! YOU SEEM TO KNOW EVERYTHING, CHAO.
YOU KNEW ABOUT MAGIC, TOO...
HA HA HA
IT'LL BE BEST FOR YOU TO PRETEND THAT YOUR ARM IS STILL BROKEN. YOU DON'T WANT THE PRESS QUESTIONING YOU.
HMM. YOU RIGHT.

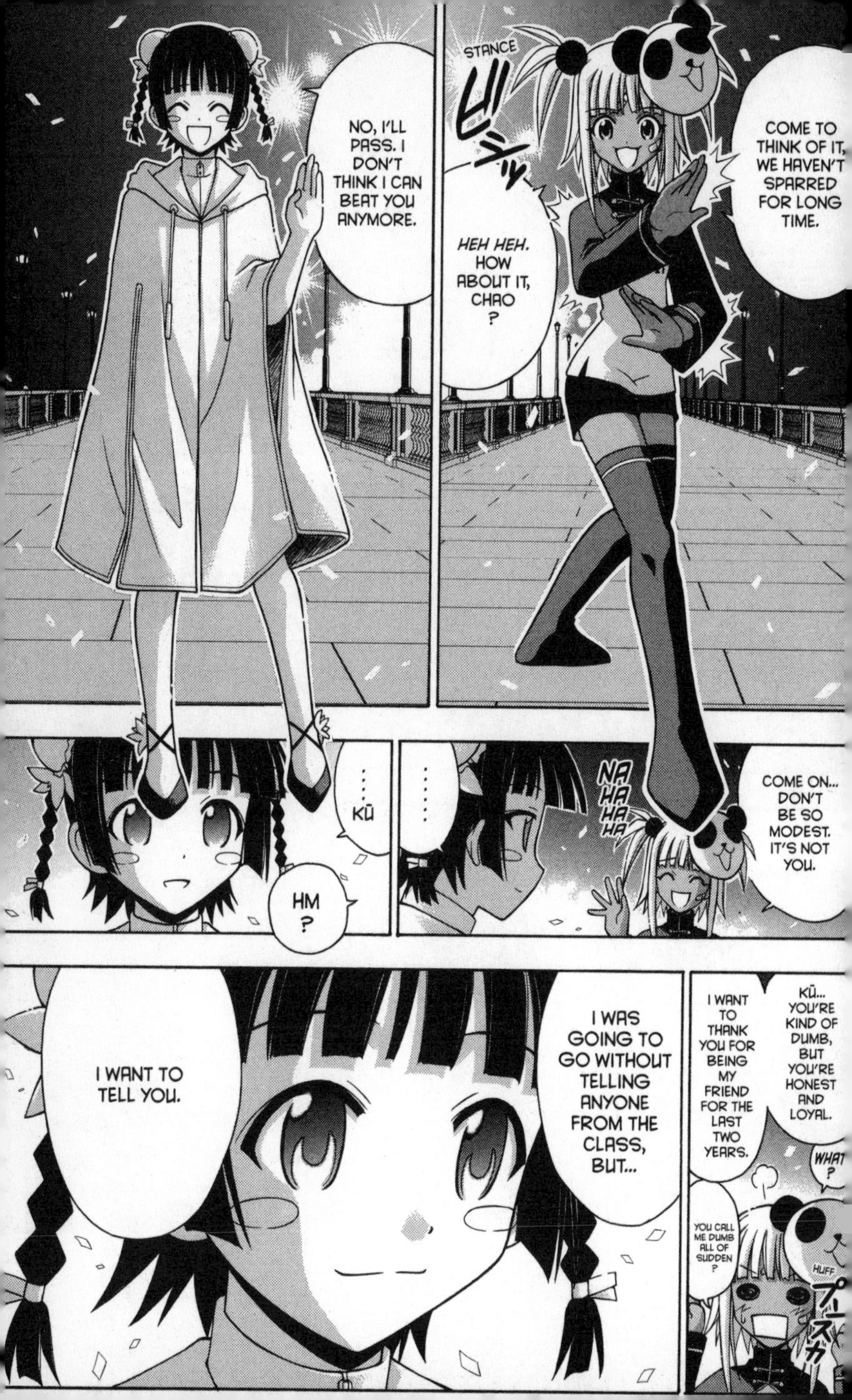

STANCE
COME TO THINK OF IT, WE HAVEN'T SPARRED FOR LONG TIME.
HEH HEH. HOW ABOUT IT, CHAO?
NO, I'LL PASS. I DON'T THINK I CAN BEAT YOU ANYMORE.
NA HA HA HA
COME ON... DON'T BE SO MODEST. IT'S NOT YOU.
......
......KŪ
HM?
KŪ... YOU'RE KIND OF DUMB, BUT YOU'RE HONEST AND LOYAL.
I WANT TO THANK YOU FOR BEING MY FRIEND FOR THE LAST TWO YEARS.
WHAT?
YOU CALL ME DUMB ALL OF SUDDEN?
HUFF
I WAS GOING TO GO WITHOUT TELLING ANYONE FROM THE CLASS, BUT...
I WANT TO TELL YOU.

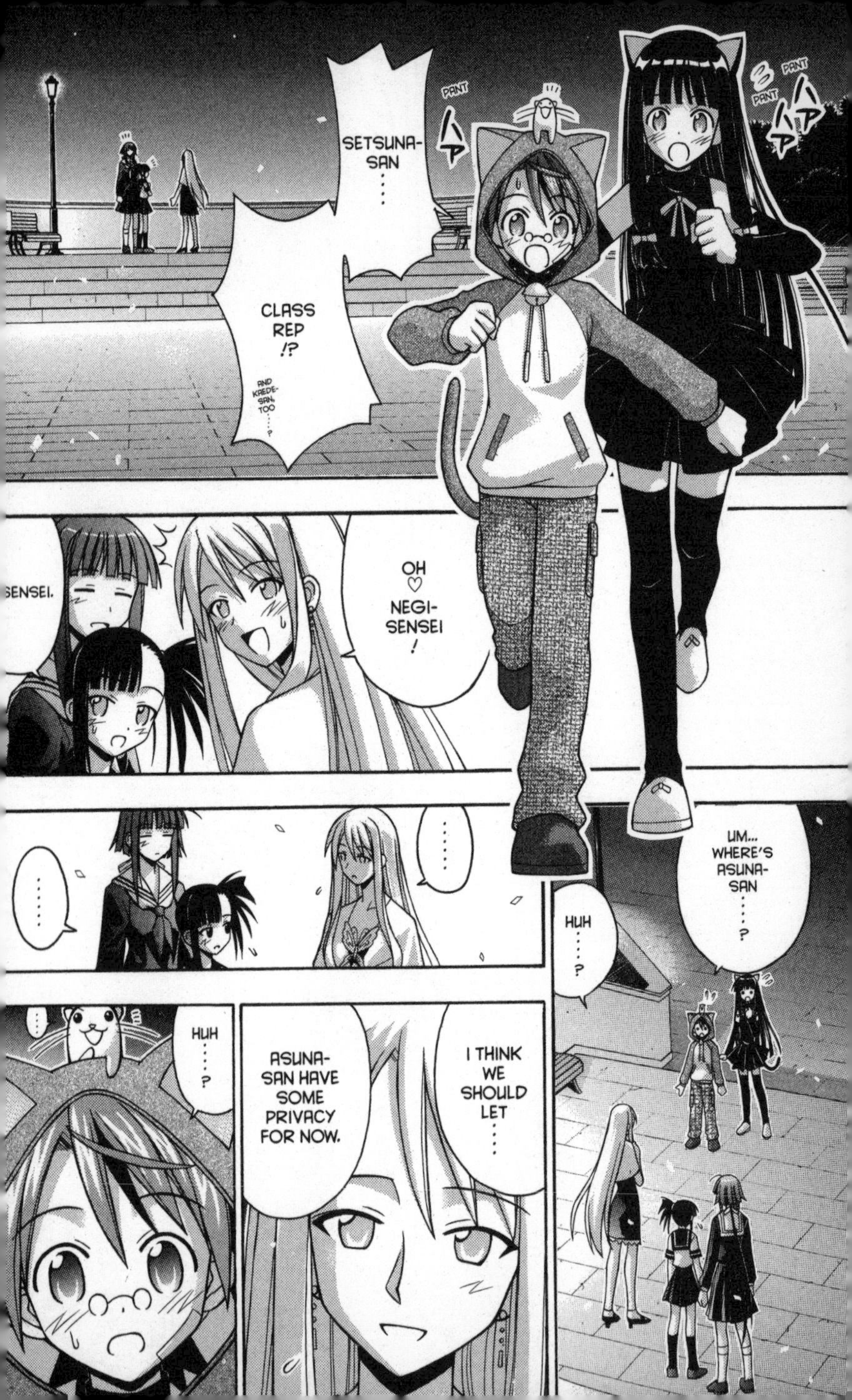

PANT
PANT
PANT
SETSUNA-SAN....
CLASS REP!?
AND KAEDE-SAN, TOO....?
OH ♡ NEGI-SENSEI!
SENSEI.
UM... WHERE'S ASUNA-SAN....?
HUH....?
......
......
I THINK WE SHOULD LET....
ASUNA-SAN HAVE SOME PRIVACY FOR NOW.
HUH....?
...

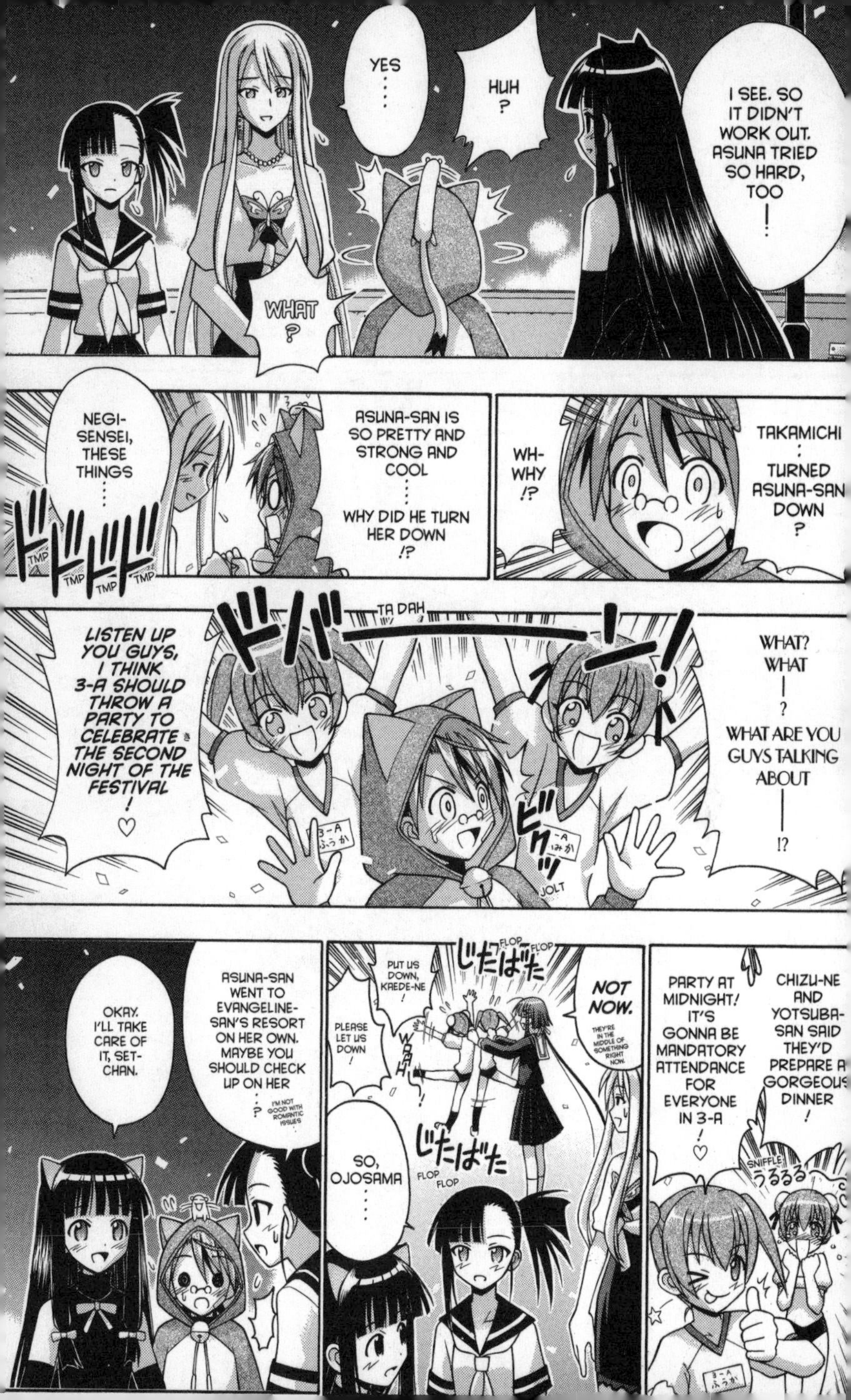
I SEE. SO IT DIDN'T WORK OUT. ASUNA TRIED SO HARD, TOO!
HUH?
YES...
WHAT?
TAKAMICHI: TURNED ASUNA-SAN DOWN?
WH-WHY!?
ASUNA-SAN IS SO PRETTY AND STRONG AND COOL... WHY DID HE TURN HER DOWN!?
NEGI-SENSEI, THESE THINGS...
TMP TMP TMP TMP
WHAT? WHAT—? WHAT ARE YOU GUYS TALKING ABOUT—!?
TA DAH
LISTEN UP YOU GUYS, I THINK 3-A SHOULD THROW A PARTY TO CELEBRATE THE SECOND NIGHT OF THE FESTIVAL! ♡
3-A ふうか
JOLT
CHIZU-NE AND YOTSUBA-SAN SAID THEY'D PREPARE A GORGEOUS DINNER!
PARTY AT MIDNIGHT! IT'S GONNA BE MANDATORY ATTENDANCE FOR EVERYONE IN 3-A! ♡
SNIFFLE
うるるる
FLOP FLOP
NOT NOW.
THEY'RE IN THE MIDDLE OF SOMETHING RIGHT NOW.
PUT US DOWN, KAEDE-NE!
PLEASE LET US DOWN!
SO, OJOSAMA...
FLOP FLOP
ASUNA-SAN WENT TO EVANGELINE-SAN'S RESORT ON HER OWN. MAYBE YOU SHOULD CHECK UP ON HER..?
I'M NOT GOOD WITH ROMANTIC ISSUES
OKAY. I'LL TAKE CARE OF IT, SET-CHAN.

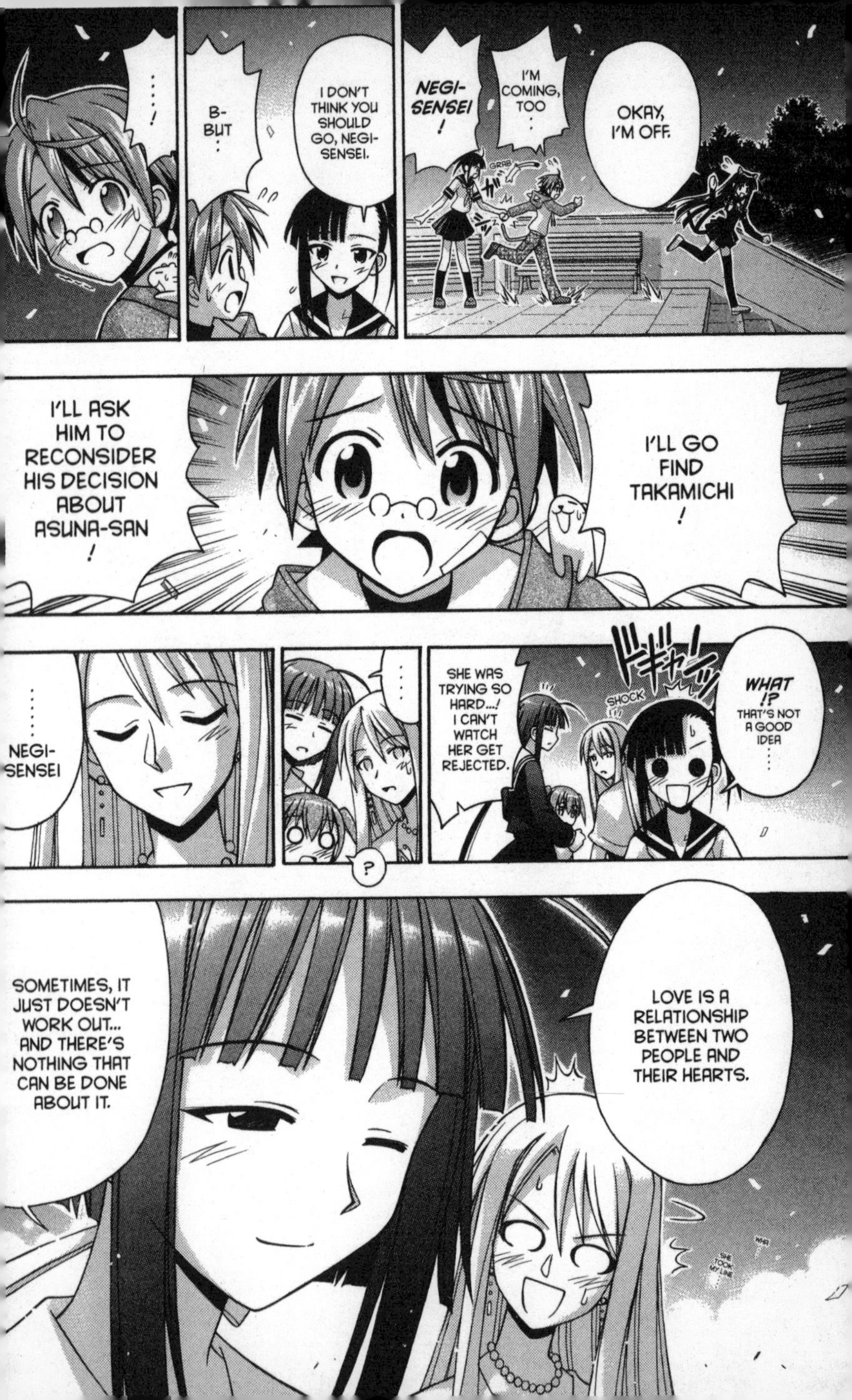
OKAY, I'M OFF.
I'M COMING, TOO...
GRAB
NEGI-SENSEI!
I DON'T THINK YOU SHOULD GO, NEGI-SENSEI.
B-BUT...
...!
I'LL GO FIND TAKAMICHI!
I'LL ASK HIM TO RECONSIDER HIS DECISION ABOUT ASUNA-SAN!
WHAT!? THAT'S NOT A GOOD IDEA...
SHOCK
SHE WAS TRYING SO HARD...! I CAN'T WATCH HER GET REJECTED.
...
?
......NEGI-SENSEI
LOVE IS A RELATIONSHIP BETWEEN TWO PEOPLE AND THEIR HEARTS.
SOMETIMES, IT JUST DOESN'T WORK OUT... AND THERE'S NOTHING THAT CAN BE DONE ABOUT IT.
WHA
SHE TOOK MY LINE

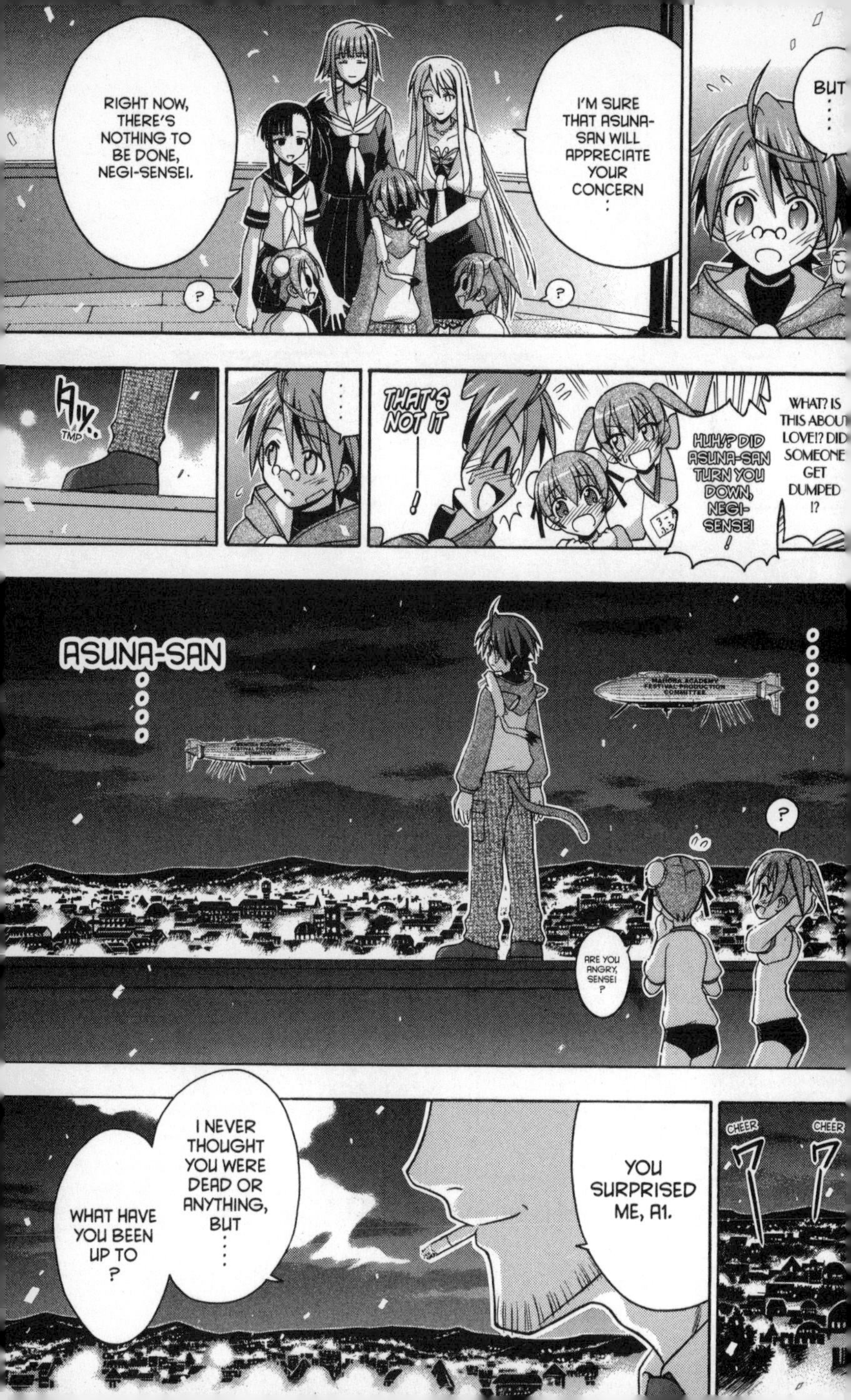
BUT . . .
I'M SURE THAT ASUNA-SAN WILL APPRECIATE YOUR CONCERN . . .
?
RIGHT NOW, THERE'S NOTHING TO BE DONE, NEGI-SENSEI.
?
WHAT? IS THIS ABOUT LOVE!? DID SOMEONE GET DUMPED!?
HUH!? DID ASUNA-SAN TURN YOU DOWN, NEGI-SENSEI!
THAT'S NOT IT—!
. . .
TMP
MAHORA ACADEMY FESTIVAL PRODUCTION COMMITTEE
ASUNA-SAN ooooo
?
ARE YOU ANGRY, SENSEI?
CHEER
CHEER
YOU SURPRISED ME, A1.
I NEVER THOUGHT YOU WERE DEAD OR ANYTHING, BUT . . . .
WHAT HAVE YOU BEEN UP TO?

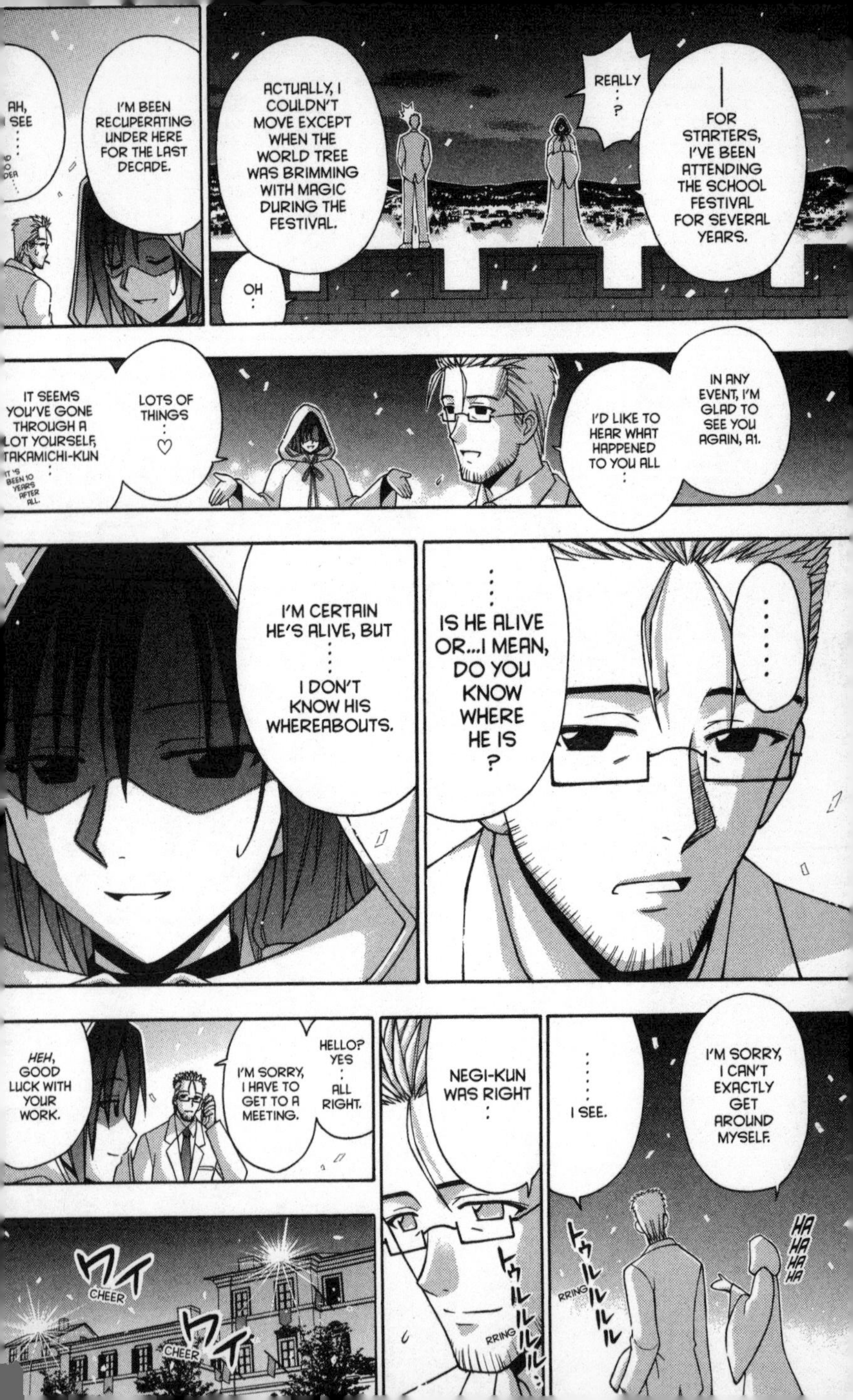

FOR STARTERS, I'VE BEEN ATTENDING THE SCHOOL FESTIVAL FOR SEVERAL YEARS.
REALLY...?
ACTUALLY, I COULDN'T MOVE EXCEPT WHEN THE WORLD TREE WAS BRIMMING WITH MAGIC DURING THE FESTIVAL.
OH...
I'M BEEN RECUPERATING UNDER HERE FOR THE LAST DECADE.
AH, I SEE...
IN ANY EVENT, I'M GLAD TO SEE YOU AGAIN, A1.
I'D LIKE TO HEAR WHAT HAPPENED TO YOU ALL...
LOTS OF THINGS...♡
IT SEEMS YOU'VE GONE THROUGH A LOT YOURSELF, TAKAMICHI-KUN...
IT'S BEEN 10 YEARS AFTER ALL.
......
...IS HE ALIVE OR...I MEAN, DO YOU KNOW WHERE HE IS?
I'M CERTAIN HE'S ALIVE, BUT... I DON'T KNOW HIS WHEREABOUTS.
I'M SORRY, I CAN'T EXACTLY GET AROUND MYSELF.
HAHAHAHA
...I SEE.
RRING
NEGI-KUN WAS RIGHT...
RRING
HELLO? YES... ALL RIGHT.
I'M SORRY, I HAVE TO GET TO A MEETING.
HEH, GOOD LUCK WITH YOUR WORK.
CHEER
CHEER

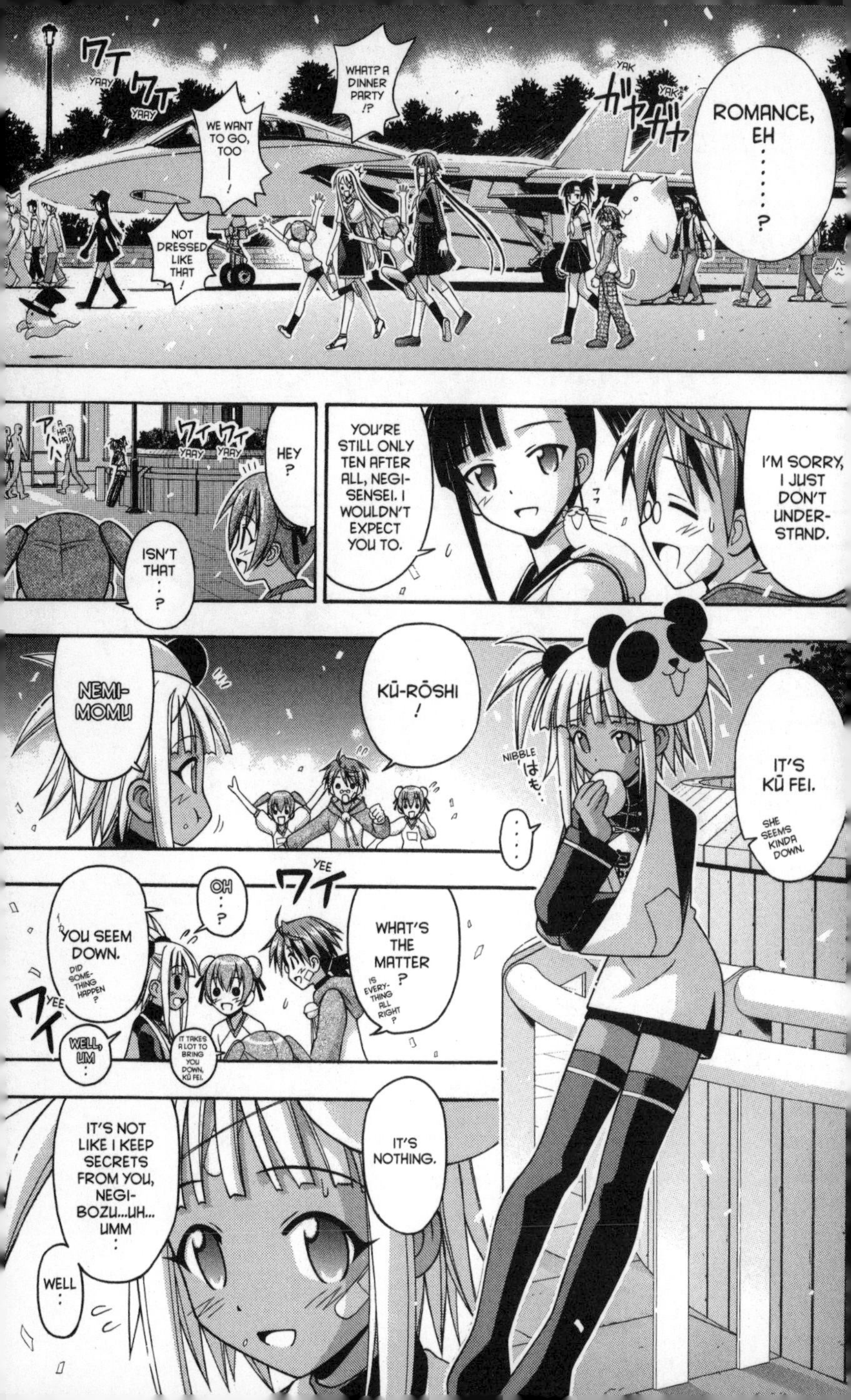
ROMANCE, EH......?
ガヤガヤ
YAK YAK
WHAT? A DINNER PARTY!?
WE WANT TO GO, TOO—!
NOT DRESSED LIKE THAT!
ワイワイ
YAAY YAAY
I'M SORRY, I JUST DON'T UNDERSTAND.
YOU'RE STILL ONLY TEN AFTER ALL, NEGI-SENSEI. I WOULDN'T EXPECT YOU TO.
HEY?
ISN'T THAT...?
ワイワイ
YAAY YAAY
アハハ
A HA HA
IT'S KŪ FEI.
SHE SEEMS KINDA DOWN.
はも
NIBBLE
...
KŪ-RŌSHI!
NEMI-MOMU
ワイ
YEE
WHAT'S THE MATTER?
IS EVERYTHING ALL RIGHT?
OH...?
YOU SEEM DOWN.
DID SOMETHING HAPPEN?
IT TAKES A LOT TO BRING YOU DOWN, KŪ FEI.
WELL, UM...
ワイ
YEE
IT'S NOTHING.
IT'S NOT LIKE I KEEP SECRETS FROM YOU, NEGI-BOZU...UH... UMM...
WELL...

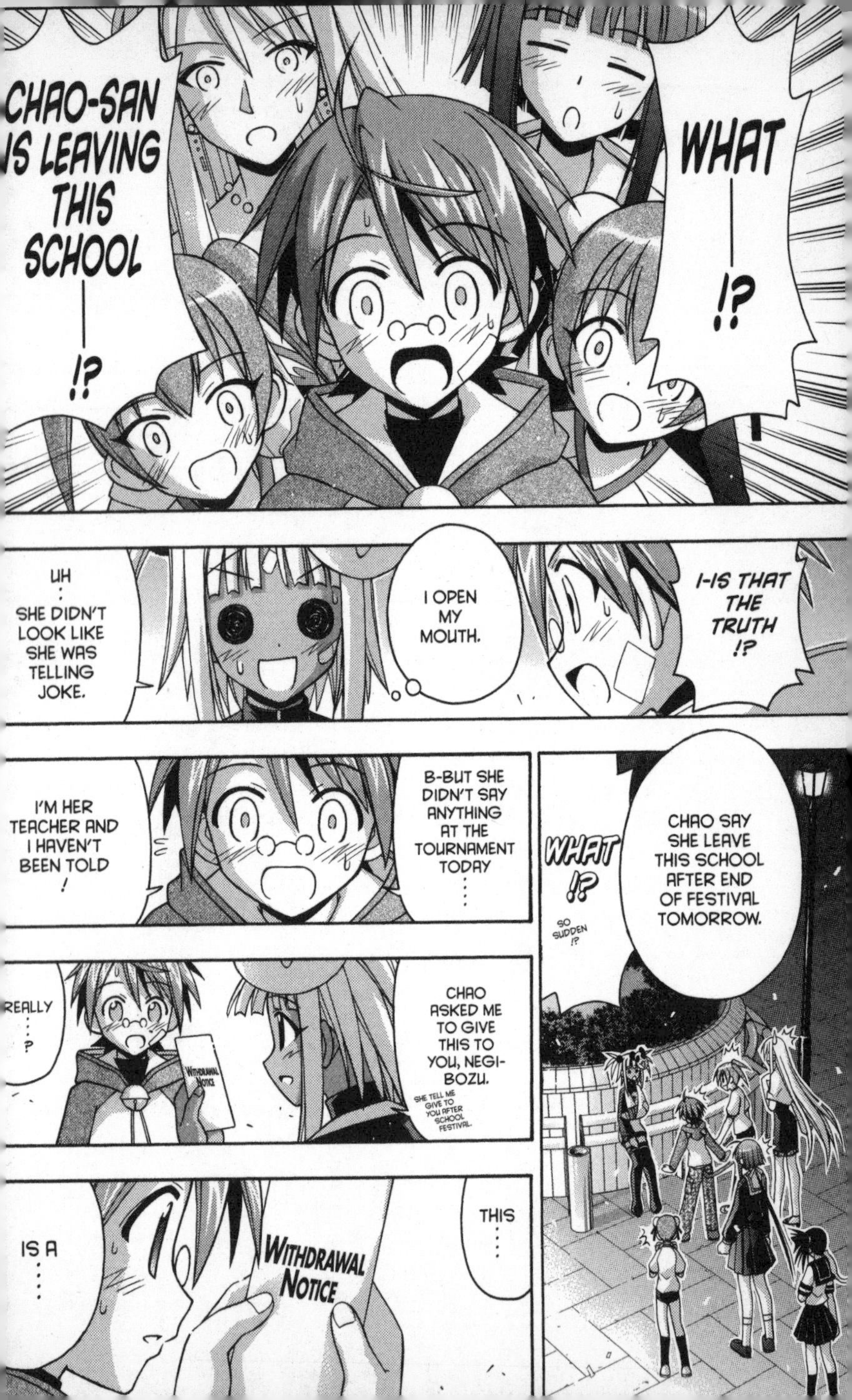
WHAT—!?
CHAO-SAN IS LEAVING THIS SCHOOL—!?
I-IS THAT THE TRUTH!?
I OPEN MY MOUTH.
UH... SHE DIDN'T LOOK LIKE SHE WAS TELLING JOKE.
CHAO SAY SHE LEAVE THIS SCHOOL AFTER END OF FESTIVAL TOMORROW.
WHAT!?
SO SUDDEN!?
B-BUT SHE DIDN'T SAY ANYTHING AT THE TOURNAMENT TODAY...
I'M HER TEACHER AND I HAVEN'T BEEN TOLD!
CHAO ASKED ME TO GIVE THIS TO YOU, NEGI-BOZU.
SHE TELL ME GIVE TO YOU AFTER SCHOOL FESTIVAL.
WITHDRAWAL NOTICE
REALLY...?
THIS...
WITHDRAWAL NOTICE
IS A...

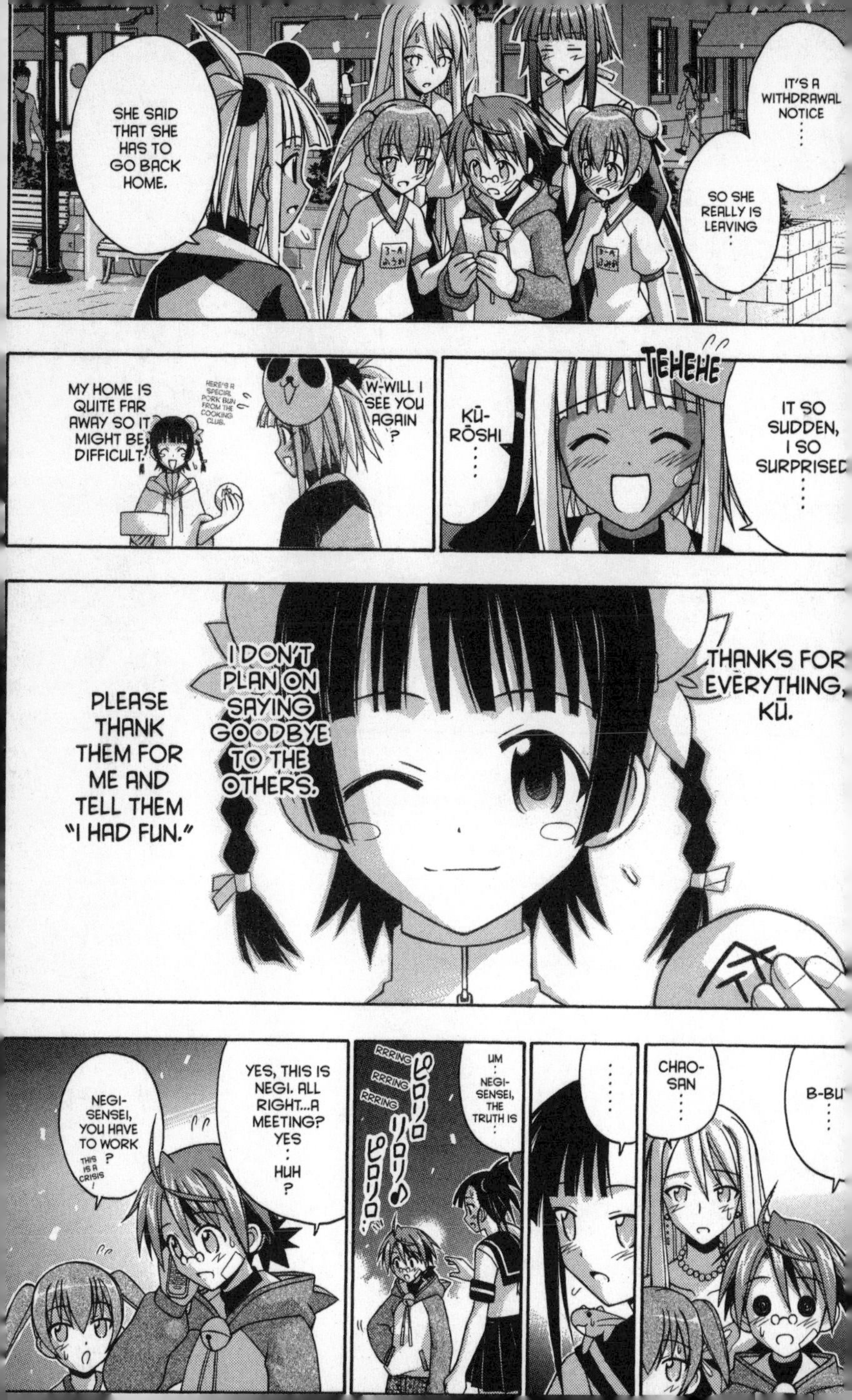
IT'S A WITHDRAWAL NOTICE...
SO SHE REALLY IS LEAVING...
SHE SAID THAT SHE HAS TO GO BACK HOME.
TEHEHE
IT SO SUDDEN, I SO SURPRISED...
KŪ-RŌSHI...
W-WILL I SEE YOU AGAIN?
HERE'S A SPECIAL PORK BUN FROM THE COOKING CLUB.
MY HOME IS QUITE FAR AWAY SO IT MIGHT BE DIFFICULT.
THANKS FOR EVERYTHING, KŪ.
I DON'T PLAN ON SAYING GOODBYE TO THE OTHERS.
PLEASE THANK THEM FOR ME AND TELL THEM "I HAD FUN."
B-BU...
CHAO-SAN...
......
UM... NEGI-SENSEI, THE TRUTH IS...
RRRING RRRING RRRING
ピロリロ リロリ♪ ピロリロ...
YES, THIS IS NEGI. ALL RIGHT...A MEETING? YES... HUH?
NEGI-SENSEI, YOU HAVE TO WORK?
THIS IS A CRISIS!

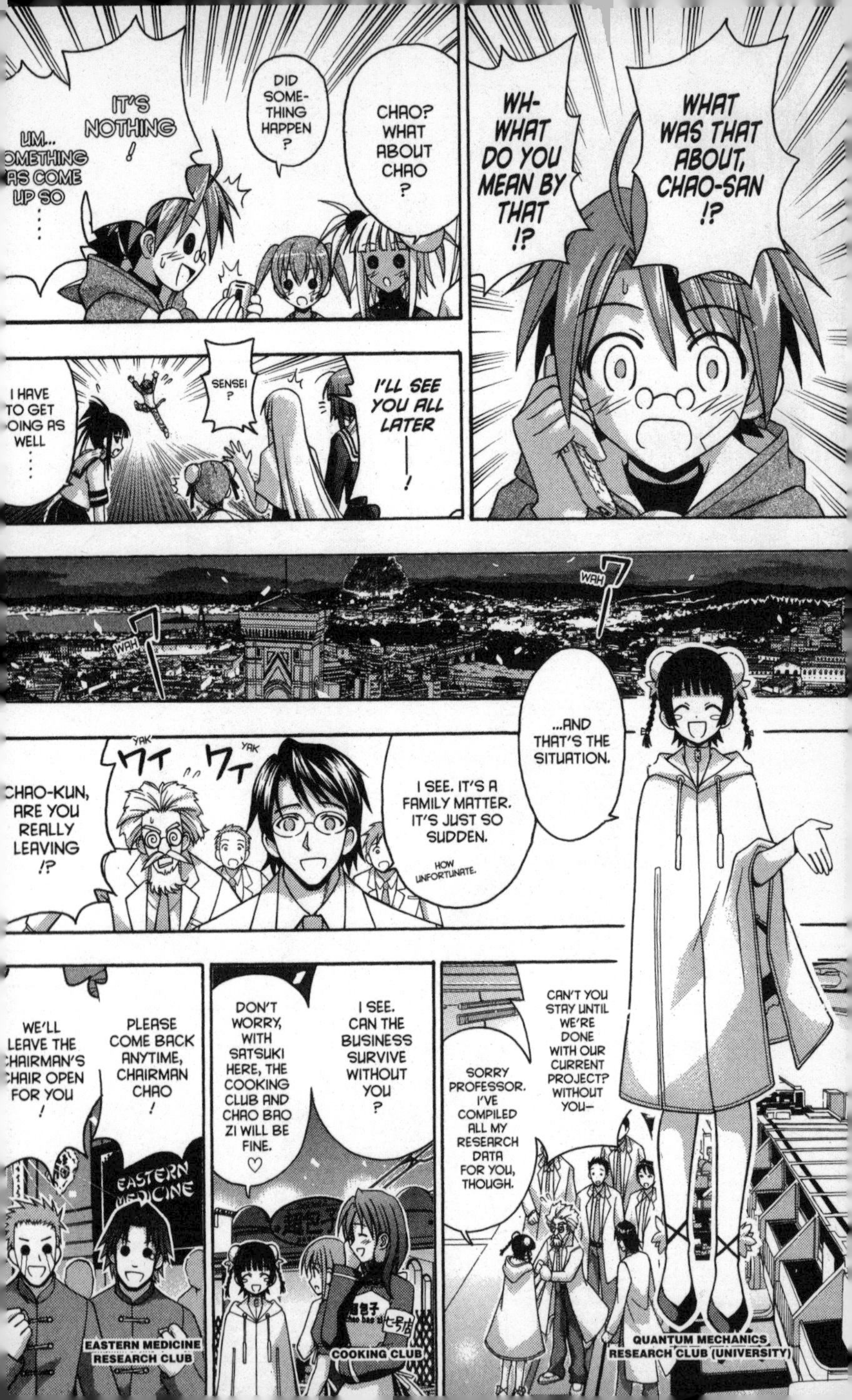
WHAT WAS THAT ABOUT, CHAO-SAN !?
WH-WHAT DO YOU MEAN BY THAT !?
CHAO? WHAT ABOUT CHAO ?
DID SOME-THING HAPPEN ?
IT'S NOTHING !
UM... OMETHING AS COME UP SO ...
I'LL SEE YOU ALL LATER—!
SENSEI ?
I HAVE TO GET OING AS WELL ...
WAH
WAH
...AND THAT'S THE SITUATION.
I SEE. IT'S A FAMILY MATTER. IT'S JUST SO SUDDEN.
HOW UNFORTUNATE.
ワイ YAK
ワイ YAK
CHAO-KUN, ARE YOU REALLY LEAVING !?
CAN'T YOU STAY UNTIL WE'RE DONE WITH OUR CURRENT PROJECT? WITHOUT YOU—
SORRY PROFESSOR. I'VE COMPILED ALL MY RESEARCH DATA FOR YOU, THOUGH.
QUANTUM MECHANICS RESEARCH CLUB (UNIVERSITY)
I SEE. CAN THE BUSINESS SURVIVE WITHOUT YOU ?
DON'T WORRY, WITH SATSUKI HERE, THE COOKING CLUB AND CHAO BAO ZI WILL BE FINE. ♡
COOKING CLUB
PLEASE COME BACK ANYTIME, CHAIRMAN CHAO !
WE'LL LEAVE THE HAIRMAN'S HAIR OPEN FOR YOU !
EASTERN MEDICINE
EASTERN MEDICINE RESEARCH CLUB

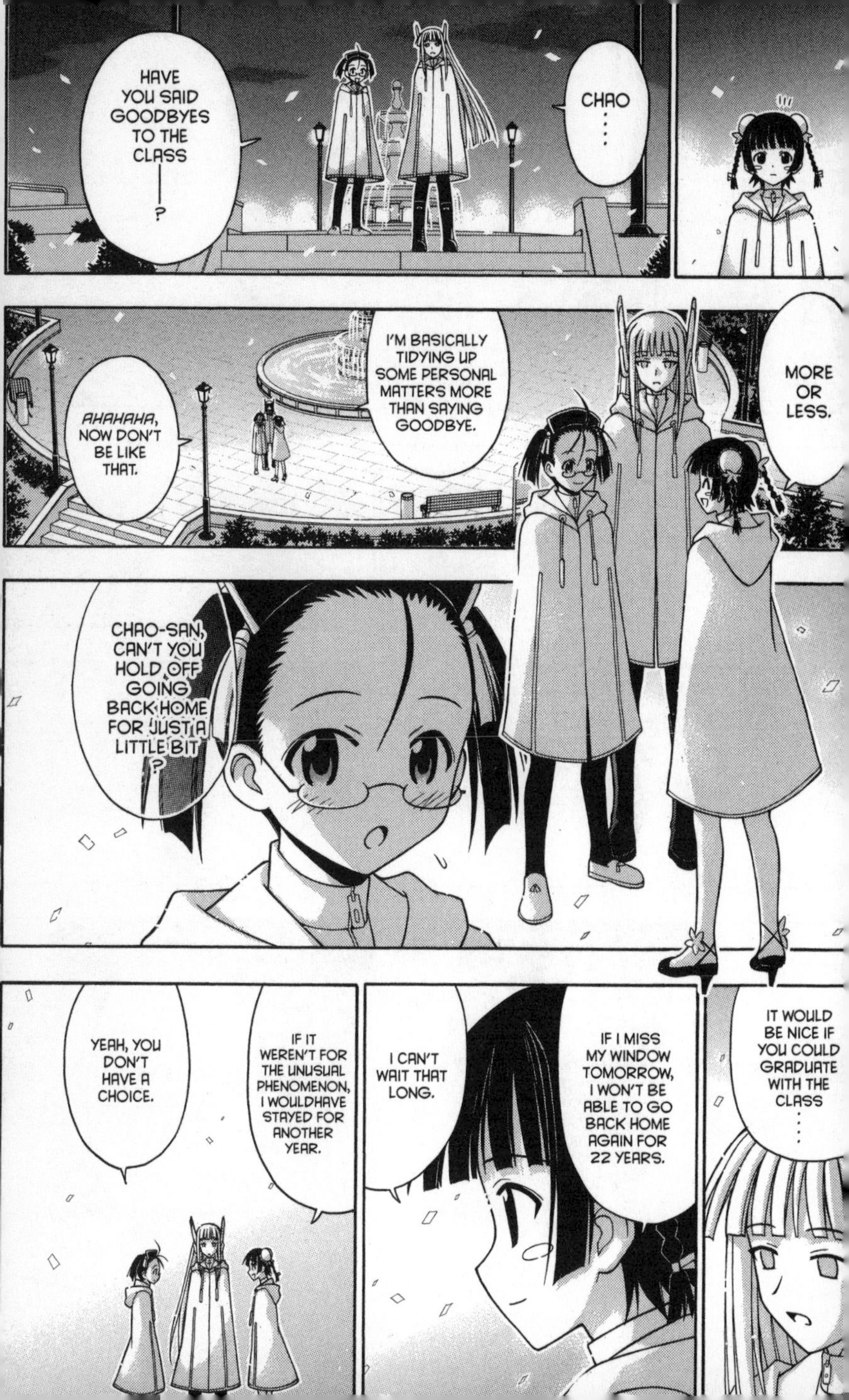
CHAO ...
HAVE YOU SAID GOODBYES TO THE CLASS—?
MORE OR LESS.
I'M BASICALLY TIDYING UP SOME PERSONAL MATTERS MORE THAN SAYING GOODBYE.
AHAHAHA, NOW DON'T BE LIKE THAT.
CHAO-SAN, CAN'T YOU HOLD OFF GOING BACK HOME FOR JUST A LITTLE BIT?
IT WOULD BE NICE IF YOU COULD GRADUATE WITH THE CLASS ...
IF I MISS MY WINDOW TOMORROW, I WON'T BE ABLE TO GO BACK HOME AGAIN FOR 22 YEARS.
I CAN'T WAIT THAT LONG.
IF IT WEREN'T FOR THE UNUSUAL PHENOMENON, I WOULDHAVE STAYED FOR ANOTHER YEAR.
YEAH, YOU DON'T HAVE A CHOICE.

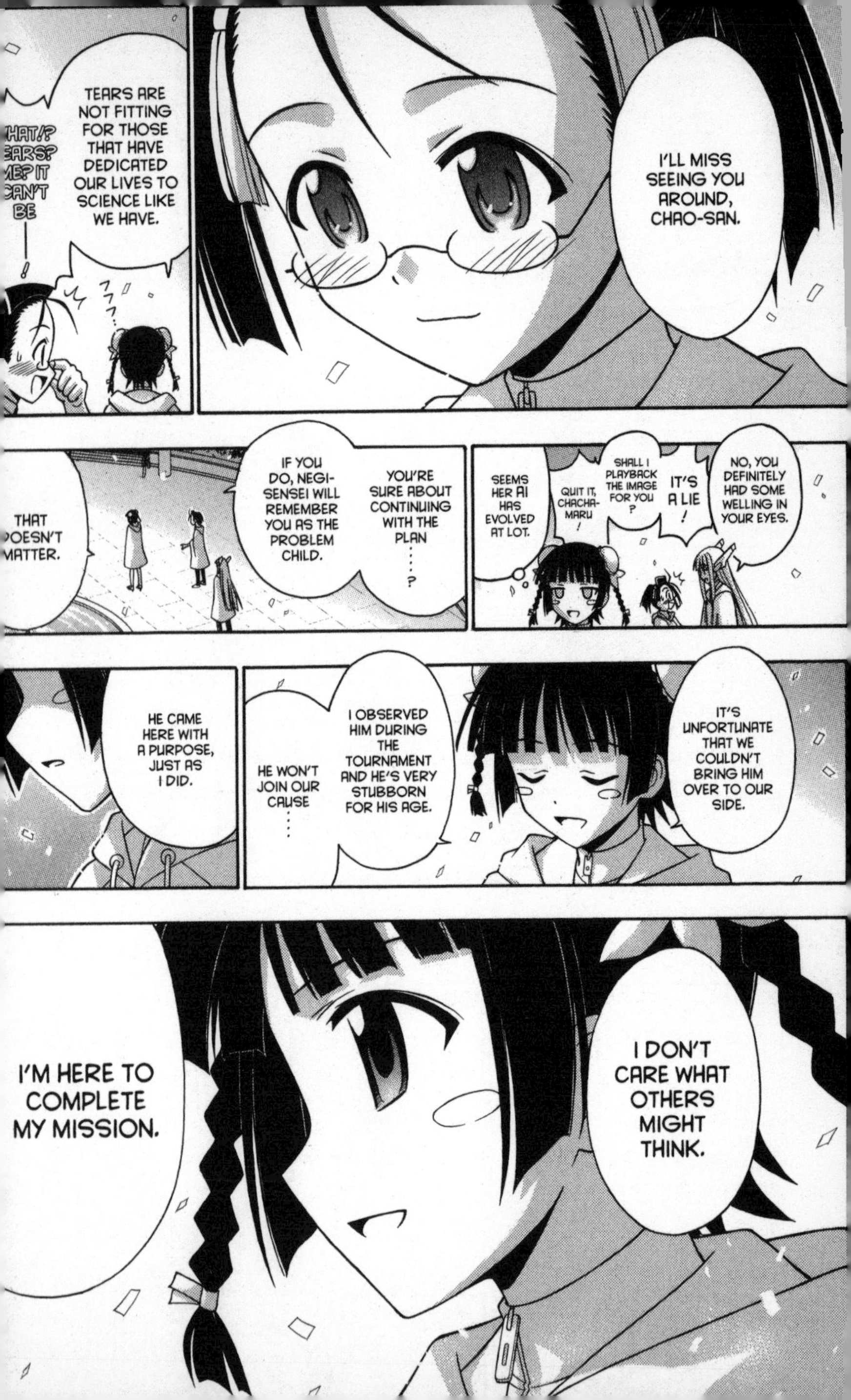
I'LL MISS SEEING YOU AROUND, CHAO-SAN.
TEARS ARE NOT FITTING FOR THOSE THAT HAVE DEDICATED OUR LIVES TO SCIENCE LIKE WE HAVE.
HAT!? EARS? ME? IT CAN'T BE —!
NO, YOU DEFINITELY HAD SOME WELLING IN YOUR EYES.
IT'S A LIE!
SHALL I PLAYBACK THE IMAGE FOR YOU?
QUIT IT, CHACHAMARU!
SEEMS HER AI HAS EVOLVED AT LOT.
YOU'RE SURE ABOUT CONTINUING WITH THE PLAN...?
IF YOU DO, NEGI-SENSEI WILL REMEMBER YOU AS THE PROBLEM CHILD.
THAT OESN'T MATTER.
IT'S UNFORTUNATE THAT WE COULDN'T BRING HIM OVER TO OUR SIDE.
I OBSERVED HIM DURING THE TOURNAMENT AND HE'S VERY STUBBORN FOR HIS AGE.
HE WON'T JOIN OUR CAUSE...
HE CAME HERE WITH A PURPOSE, JUST AS I DID.
I DON'T CARE WHAT OTHERS MIGHT THINK.
I'M HERE TO COMPLETE MY MISSION.

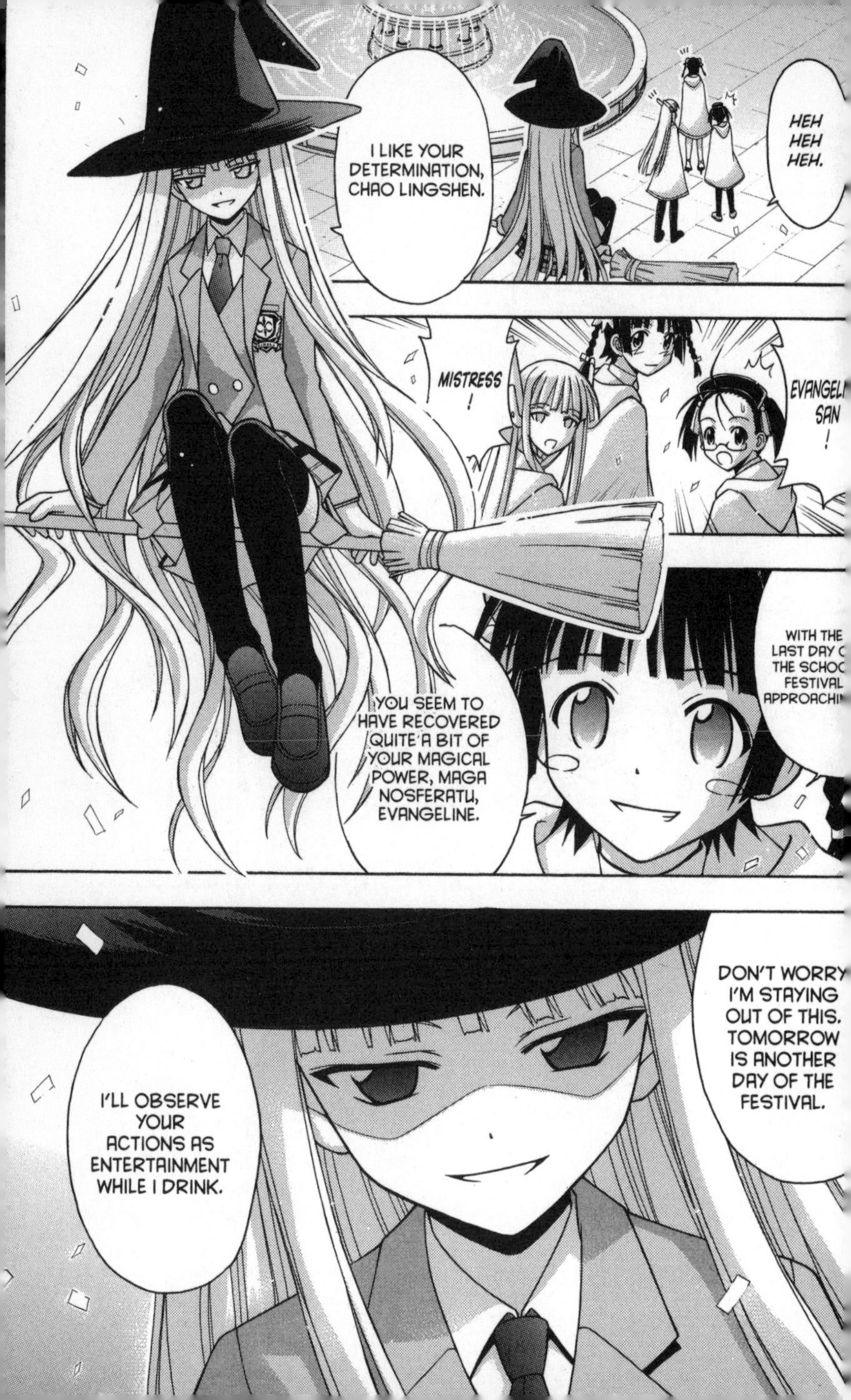
HEH HEH HEH.
I LIKE YOUR DETERMINATION, CHAO LINGSHEN.
EVANGELI SAN!
MISTRESS!
WITH THE LAST DAY O THE SCHOO FESTIVAL APPROACHIN
YOU SEEM TO HAVE RECOVERED QUITE A BIT OF YOUR MAGICAL POWER, MAGA NOSFERATU, EVANGELINE.
DON'T WORRY I'M STAYING OUT OF THIS. TOMORROW IS ANOTHER DAY OF THE FESTIVAL.
I'LL OBSERVE YOUR ACTIONS AS ENTERTAINMENT WHILE I DRINK.

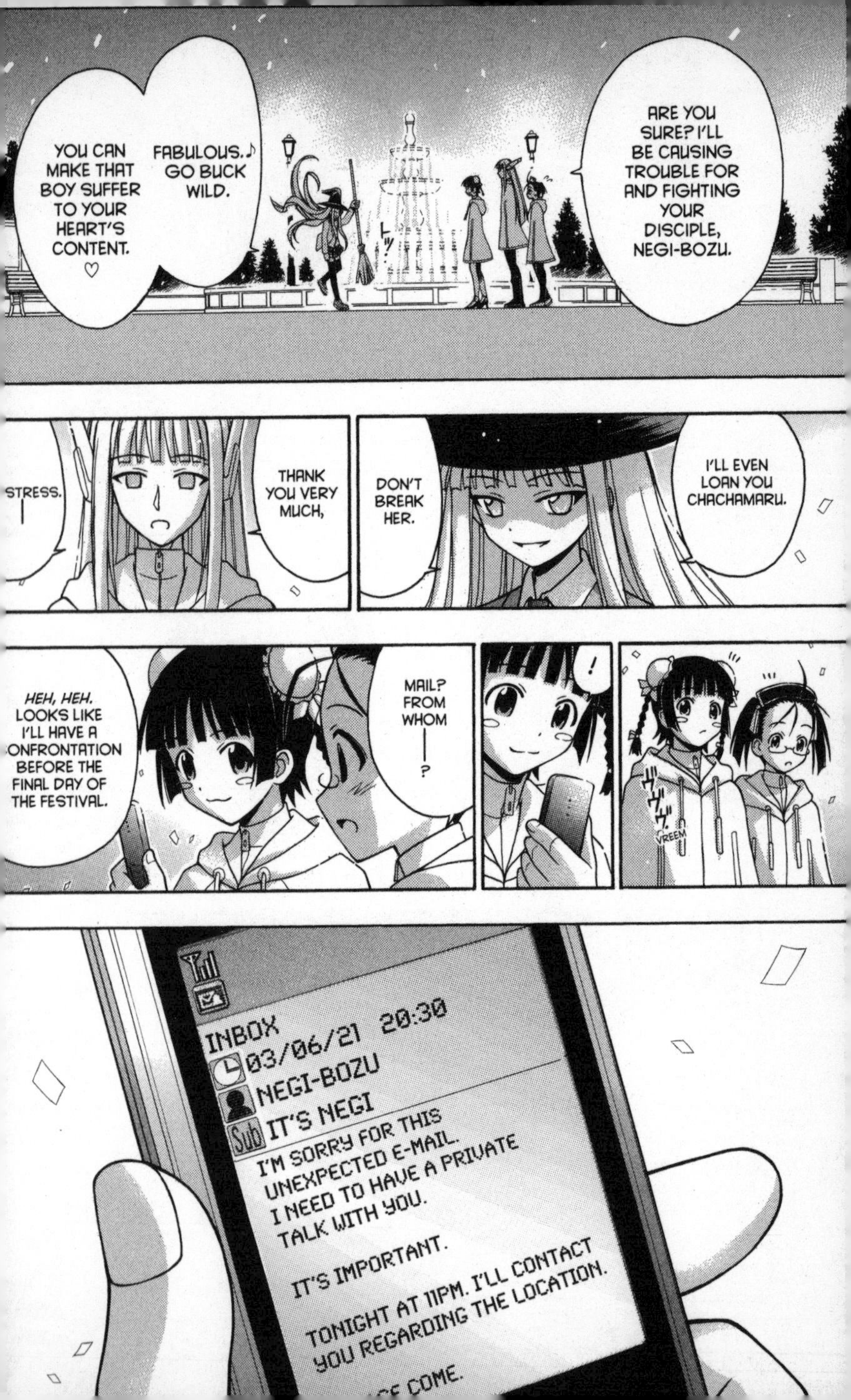

ARE YOU SURE? I'LL BE CAUSING TROUBLE FOR AND FIGHTING YOUR DISCIPLE, NEGI-BOZU.
FABULOUS.♪ GO BUCK WILD.
YOU CAN MAKE THAT BOY SUFFER TO YOUR HEART'S CONTENT. ♡
I'LL EVEN LOAN YOU CHACHAMARU.
DON'T BREAK HER.
THANK YOU VERY MUCH,
STRESS.
VREEM
!
MAIL? FROM WHOM ?
HEH, HEH. LOOKS LIKE I'LL HAVE A ONFRONTATION BEFORE THE FINAL DAY OF THE FESTIVAL.
INBOX 03/06/21 20:30
NEGI-BOZU
IT'S NEGI
I'M SORRY FOR THIS UNEXPECTED E-MAIL. I NEED TO HAVE A PRIVATE TALK WITH YOU.
IT'S IMPORTANT.
TONIGHT AT 11PM. I'LL CONTACT YOU REGARDING THE LOCATION.
E COME.

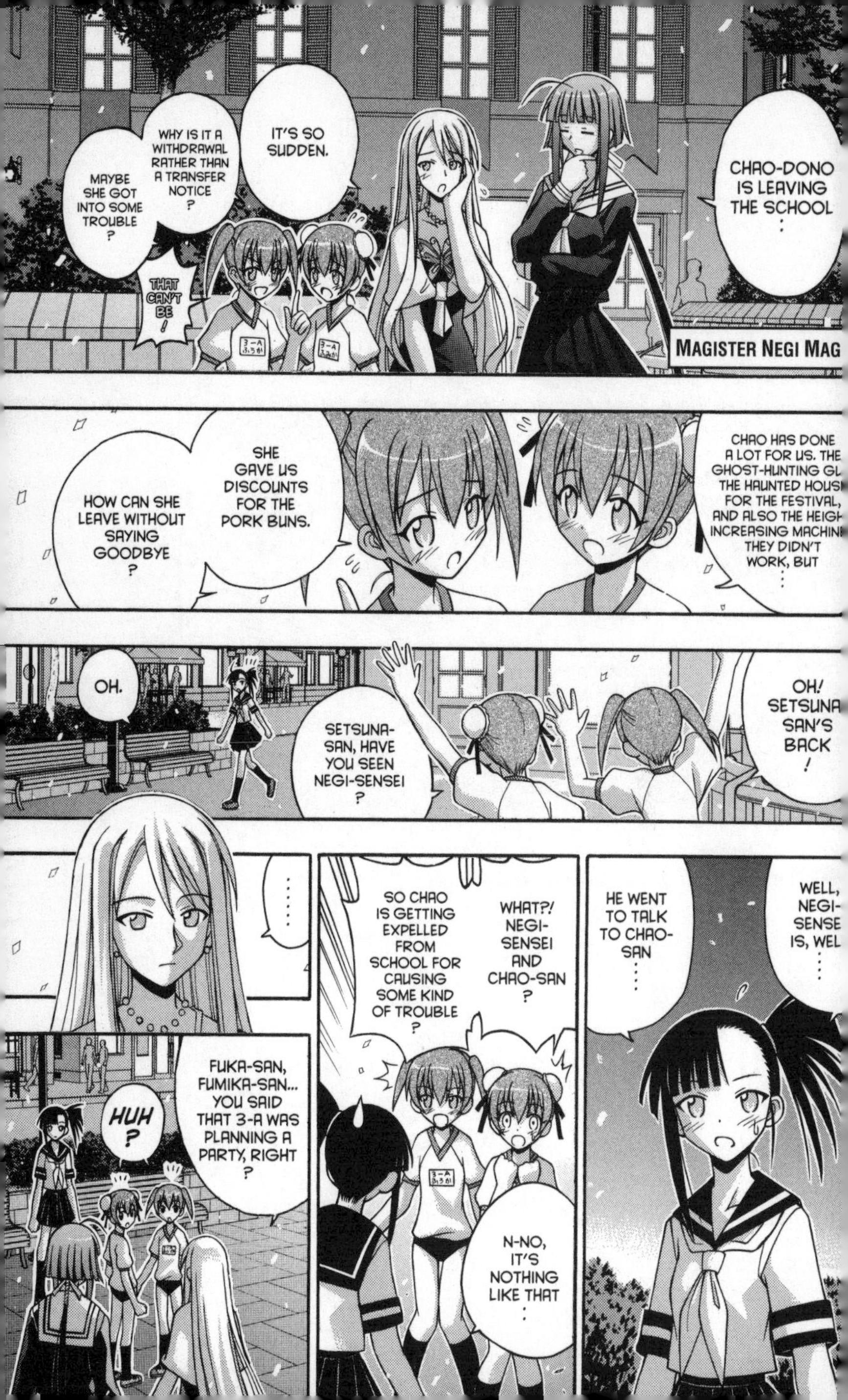

MAGISTER NEGI MAG
CHAO-DONO IS LEAVING THE SCHOOL...
IT'S SO SUDDEN.
WHY IS IT A WITHDRAWAL RATHER THAN A TRANSFER NOTICE?
MAYBE SHE GOT INTO SOME TROUBLE?
THAT CAN'T BE!
CHAO HAS DONE A LOT FOR US. THE GHOST-HUNTING GL THE HAUNTED HOUS FOR THE FESTIVAL, AND ALSO THE HEIGH INCREASING MACHIN THEY DIDN'T WORK, BUT...
SHE GAVE US DISCOUNTS FOR THE PORK BUNS.
HOW CAN SHE LEAVE WITHOUT SAYING GOODBYE?
OH! SETSUNA SAN'S BACK!
SETSUNA-SAN, HAVE YOU SEEN NEGI-SENSEI?
OH.
WELL, NEGI-SENSE IS, WEL...
HE WENT TO TALK TO CHAO-SAN...
WHAT?! NEGI-SENSEI AND CHAO-SAN?
SO CHAO IS GETTING EXPELLED FROM SCHOOL FOR CAUSING SOME KIND OF TROUBLE?
......
N-NO, IT'S NOTHING LIKE THAT...
FUKA-SAN, FUMIKA-SAN... YOU SAID THAT 3-A WAS PLANNING A PARTY, RIGHT?
HUH?

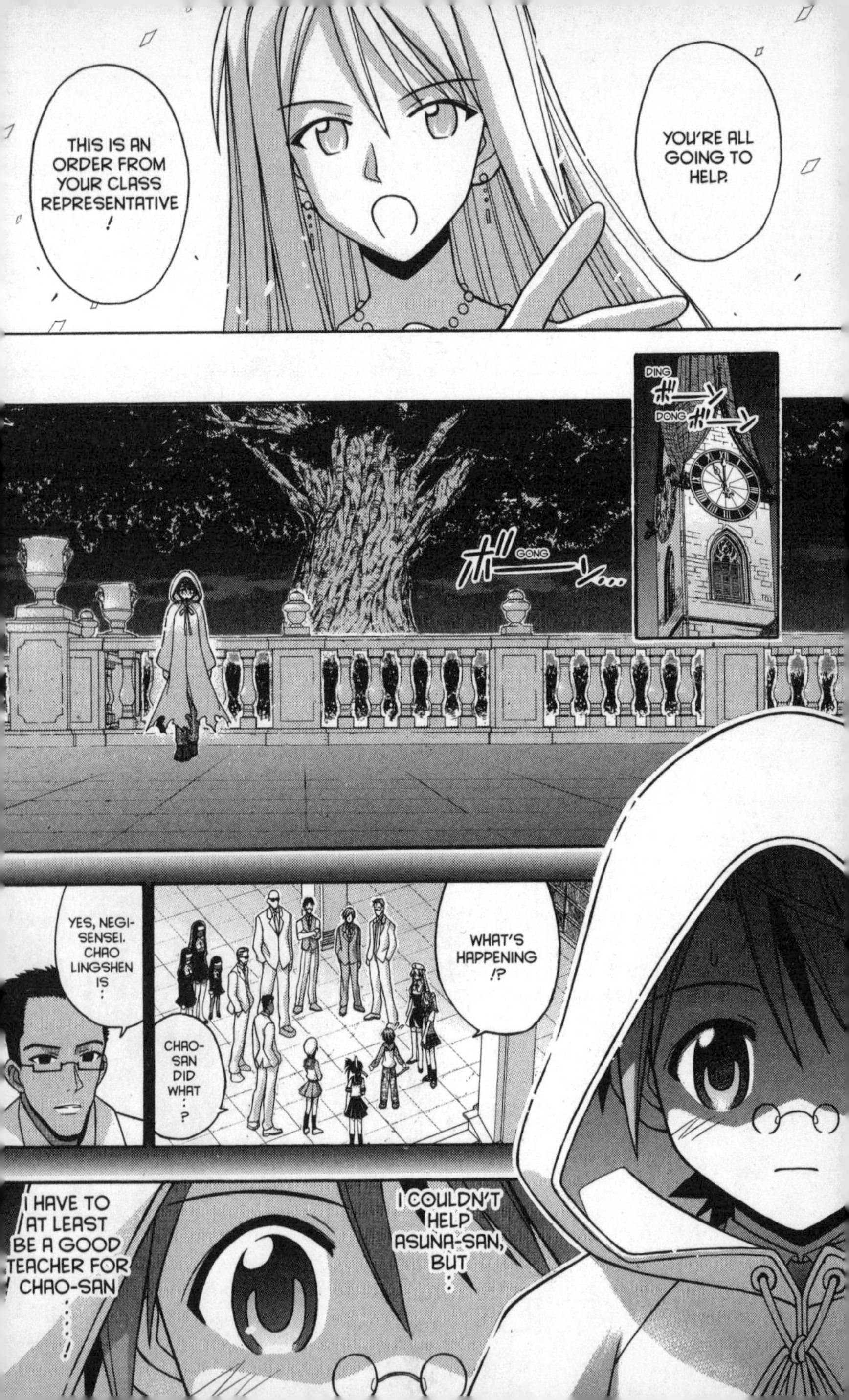
YOU'RE ALL GOING TO HELP.
THIS IS AN ORDER FROM YOUR CLASS REPRESENTATIVE!
DING
DONG
GONG
WHAT'S HAPPENING!?
CHAO-SAN DID WHAT...?
YES, NEGI-SENSEI. CHAO LINGSHEN IS...
I COULDN'T HELP ASUNA-SAN, BUT...
I HAVE TO AT LEAST BE A GOOD TEACHER FOR CHAO-SAN...!

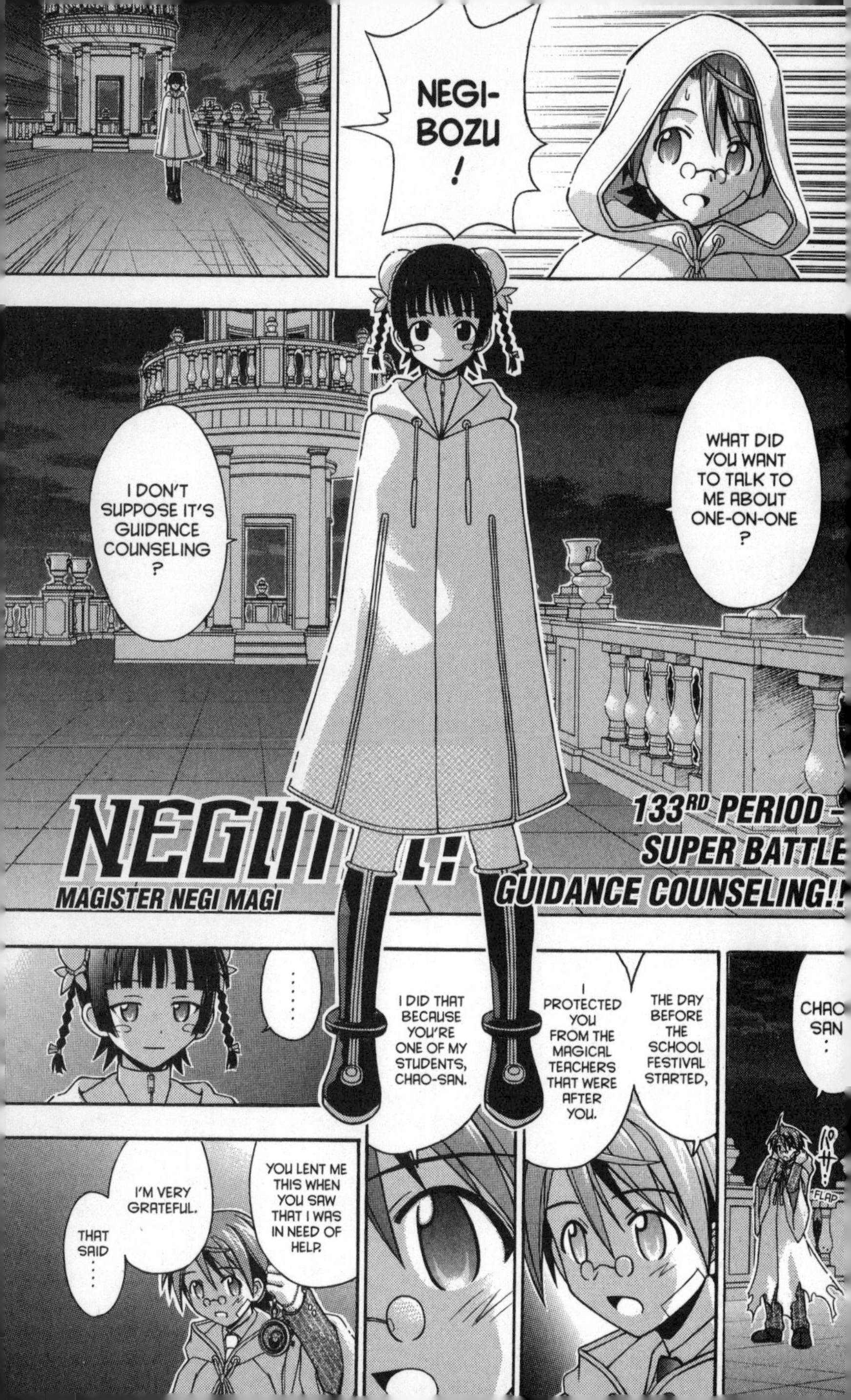

NEGI-BOZU!
WHAT DID YOU WANT TO TALK TO ME ABOUT ONE-ON-ONE?
I DON'T SUPPOSE IT'S GUIDANCE COUNSELING?
133RD PERIOD - SUPER BATTLE GUIDANCE COUNSELING!!
NEGIMA!
MAGISTER NEGI MAGI
CHAO SAN:
THE DAY BEFORE THE SCHOOL FESTIVAL STARTED,
I PROTECTED YOU FROM THE MAGICAL TEACHERS THAT WERE AFTER YOU.
I DID THAT BECAUSE YOU'RE ONE OF MY STUDENTS, CHAO-SAN.
......
FLAP
YOU LENT ME THIS WHEN YOU SAW THAT I WAS IN NEED OF HELP.
I'M VERY GRATEFUL.
THAT SAID....

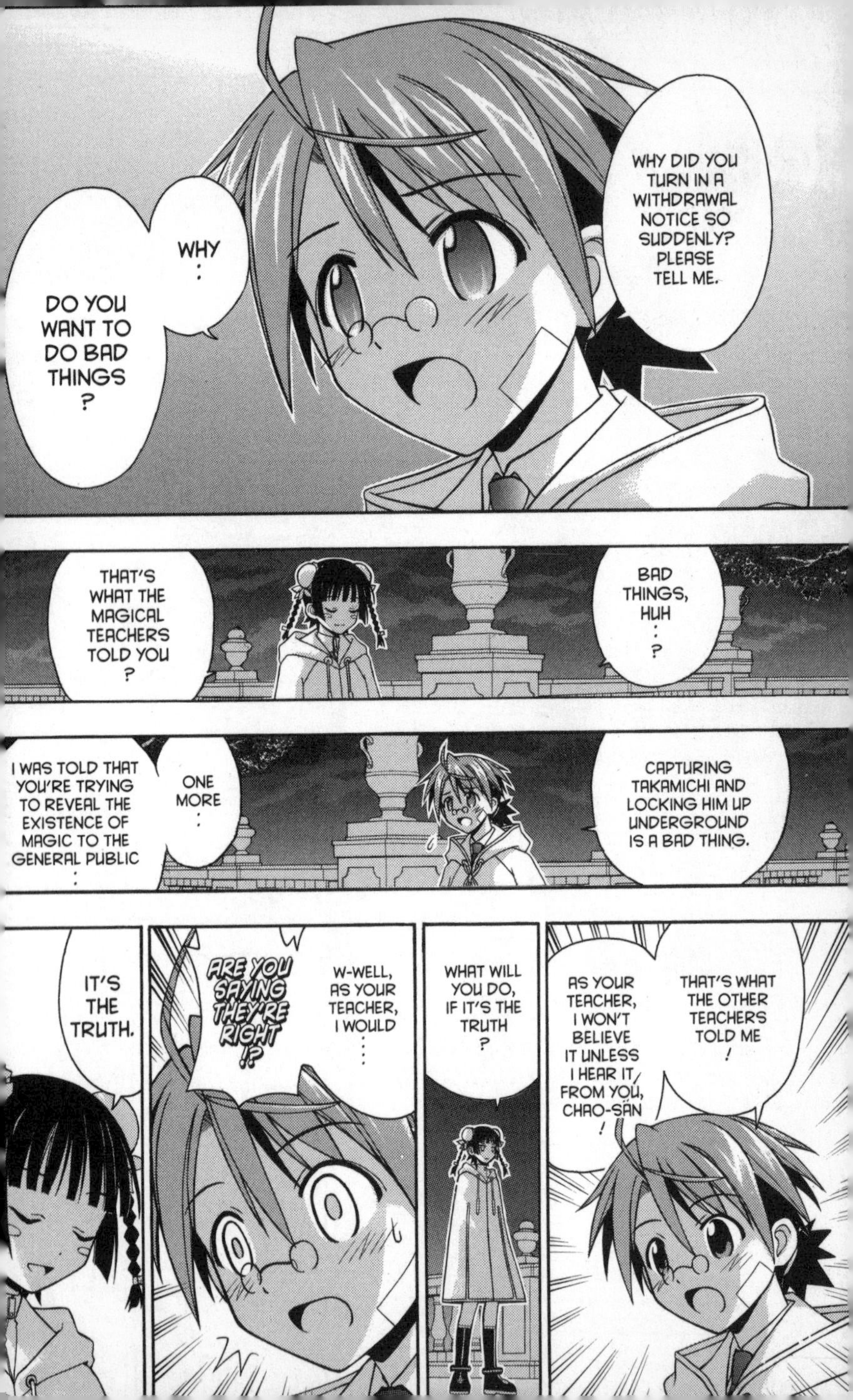
WHY DID YOU TURN IN A WITHDRAWAL NOTICE SO SUDDENLY? PLEASE TELL ME.
WHY :
DO YOU WANT TO DO BAD THINGS ?
BAD THINGS, HUH . . ?
THAT'S WHAT THE MAGICAL TEACHERS TOLD YOU ?
CAPTURING TAKAMICHI AND LOCKING HIM UP UNDERGROUND IS A BAD THING.
ONE MORE :
I WAS TOLD THAT YOU'RE TRYING TO REVEAL THE EXISTENCE OF MAGIC TO THE GENERAL PUBLIC :
THAT'S WHAT THE OTHER TEACHERS TOLD ME !
AS YOUR TEACHER, I WON'T BELIEVE IT UNLESS I HEAR IT FROM YOU, CHAO-SAN !
WHAT WILL YOU DO, IF IT'S THE TRUTH ?
W-WELL, AS YOUR TEACHER, I WOULD . . . .
ARE YOU SAYING THEY'RE RIGHT !?
IT'S THE TRUTH.

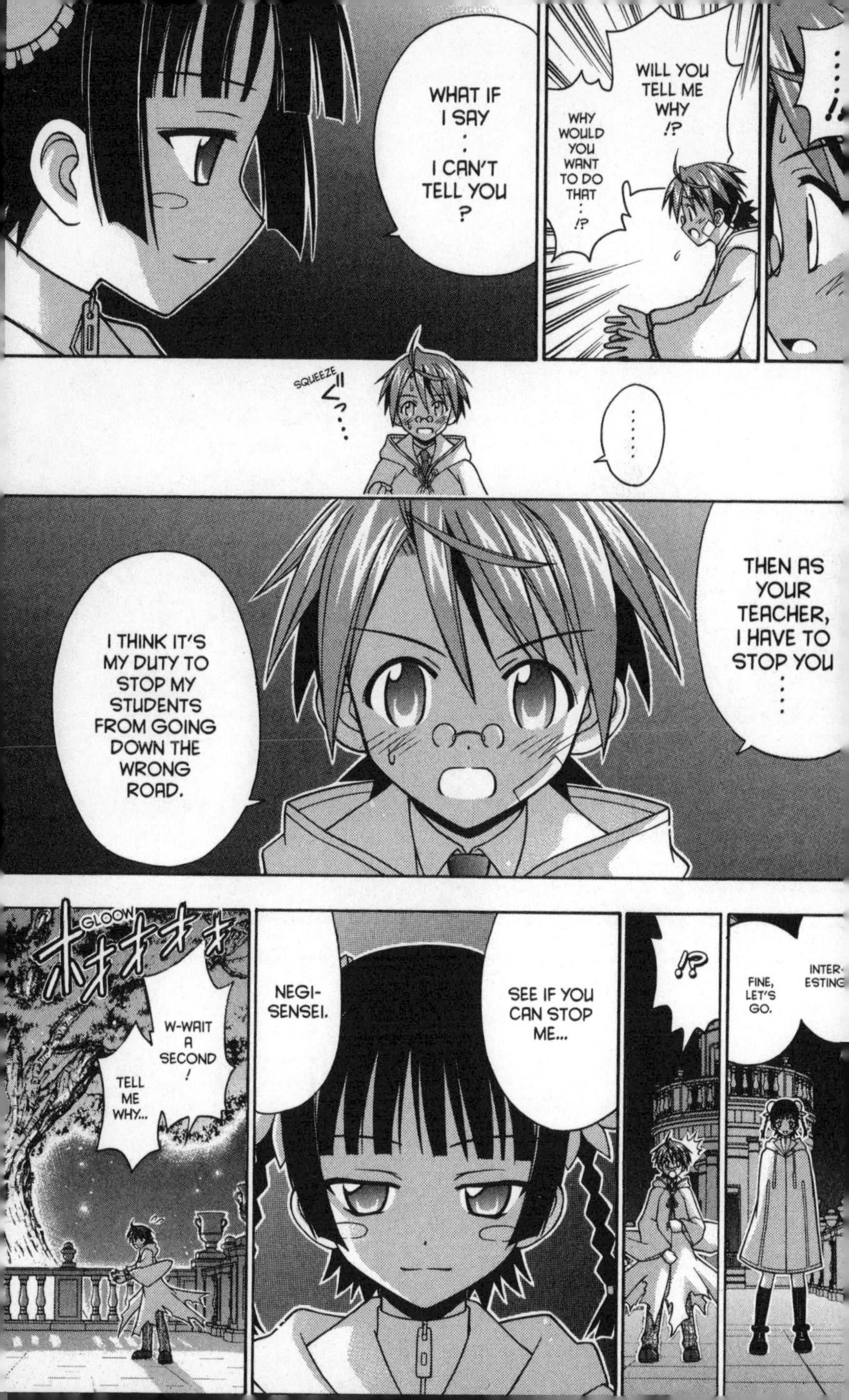
....!!
WILL YOU TELL ME WHY !?
WHY WOULD YOU WANT TO DO THAT ..!?
WHAT IF I SAY . . I CAN'T TELL YOU ?
......
SQUEEZE
THEN AS YOUR TEACHER, I HAVE TO STOP YOU ....
I THINK IT'S MY DUTY TO STOP MY STUDENTS FROM GOING DOWN THE WRONG ROAD.
INTER-ESTING
FINE, LET'S GO.
!?
SEE IF YOU CAN STOP ME...
NEGI-SENSEI.
GLOOW
W-WAIT A SECOND !
TELL ME WHY...

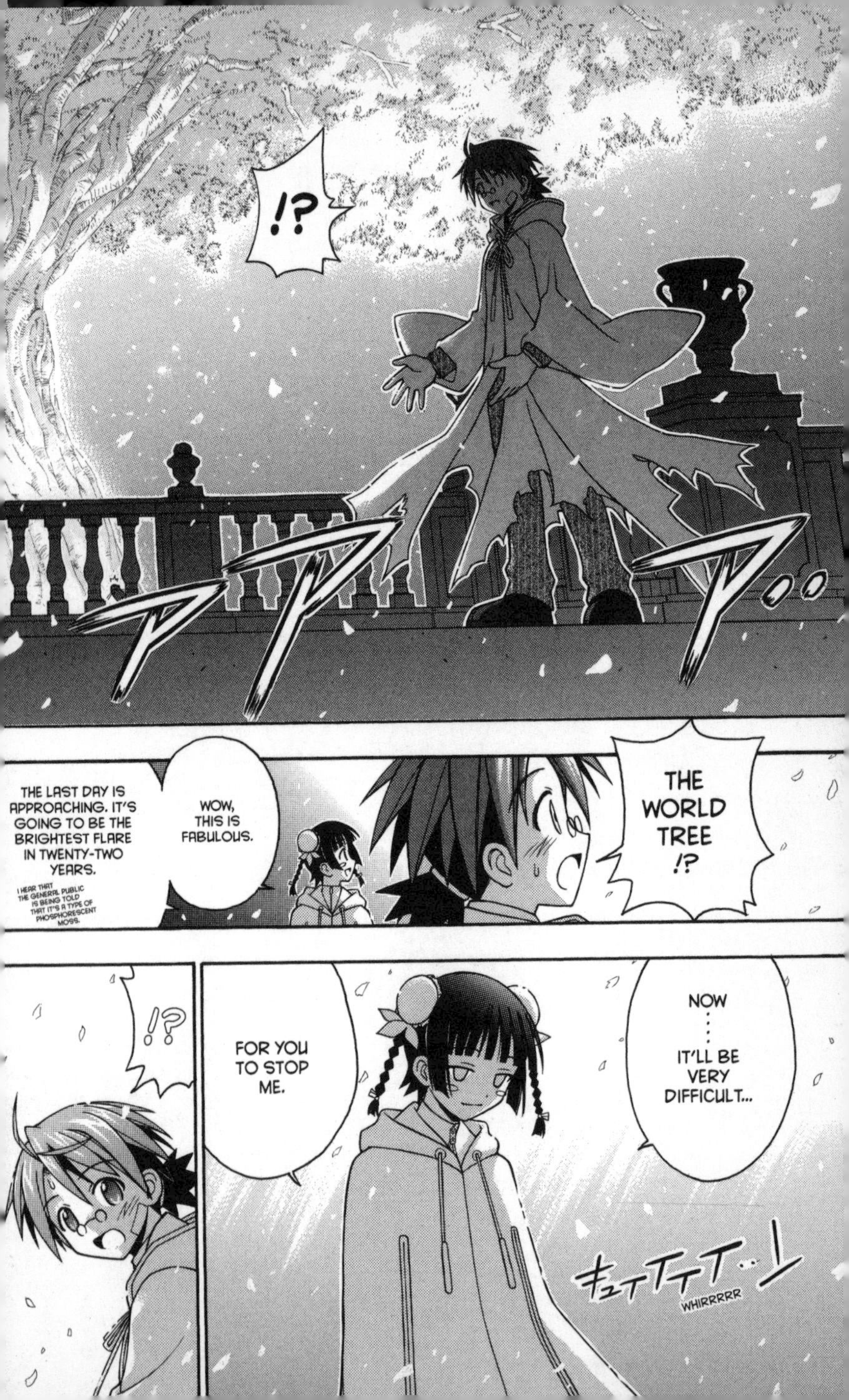
!?
THE WORLD TREE !?
WOW, THIS IS FABULOUS.
THE LAST DAY IS APPROACHING. IT'S GOING TO BE THE BRIGHTEST FLARE IN TWENTY-TWO YEARS.
I HEAR THAT THE GENERAL PUBLIC IS BEING TOLD THAT IT'S A TYPE OF PHOSPHORESCENT MOSS.
NOW... IT'LL BE VERY DIFFICULT...
FOR YOU TO STOP ME.
WHIRRRRR
!?

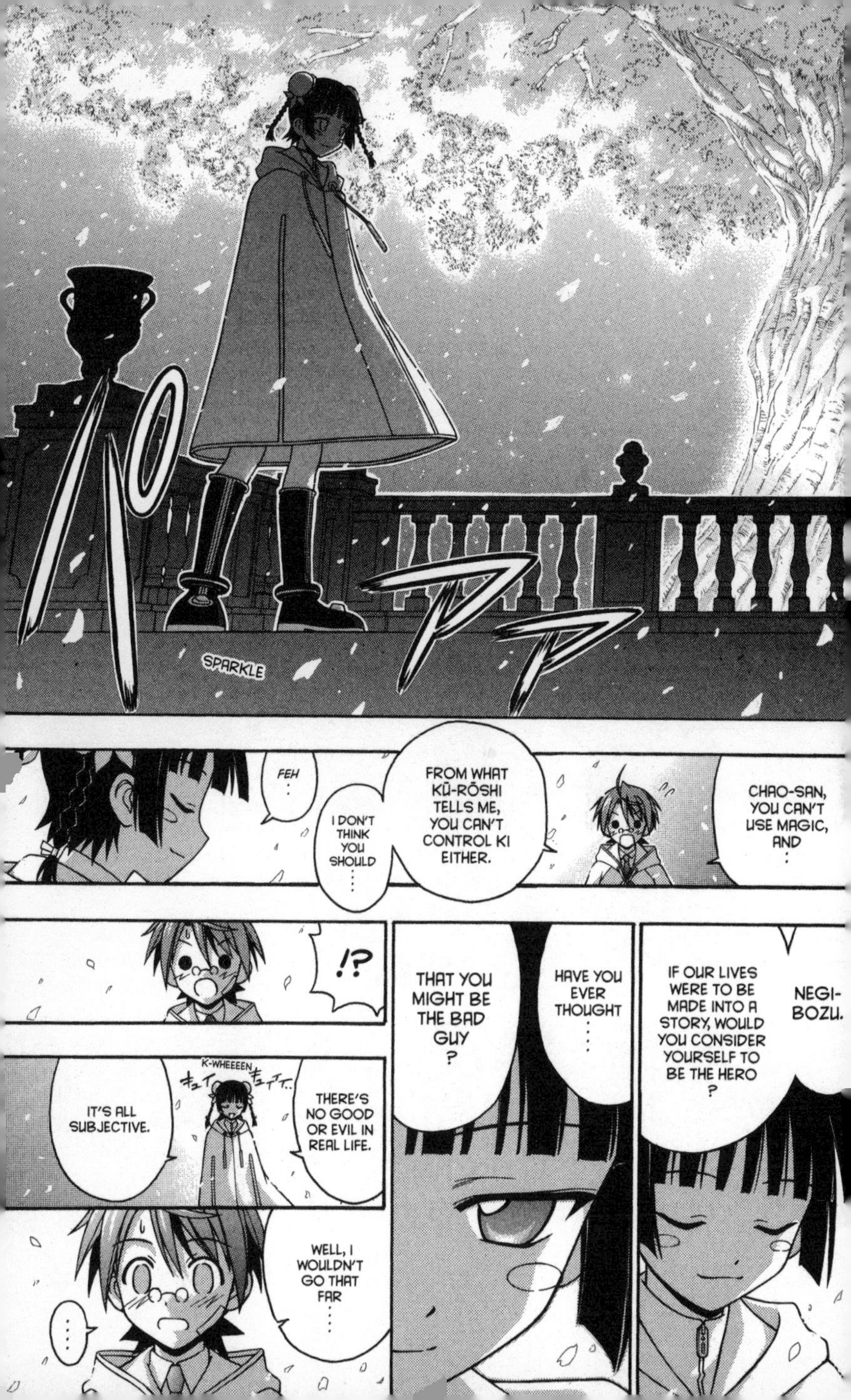
SPARKLE
CHAO-SAN, YOU CAN'T USE MAGIC, AND ...
FROM WHAT KŪ-RŌSHI TELLS ME, YOU CAN'T CONTROL KI EITHER.
I DON'T THINK YOU SHOULD ...
FEH ...
NEGI-BOZU.
IF OUR LIVES WERE TO BE MADE INTO A STORY, WOULD YOU CONSIDER YOURSELF TO BE THE HERO ?
HAVE YOU EVER THOUGHT ...
THAT YOU MIGHT BE THE BAD GUY ?
!?
THERE'S NO GOOD OR EVIL IN REAL LIFE.
K-WHEEEEN
IT'S ALL SUBJECTIVE.
WELL, I WOULDN'T GO THAT FAR ...
...

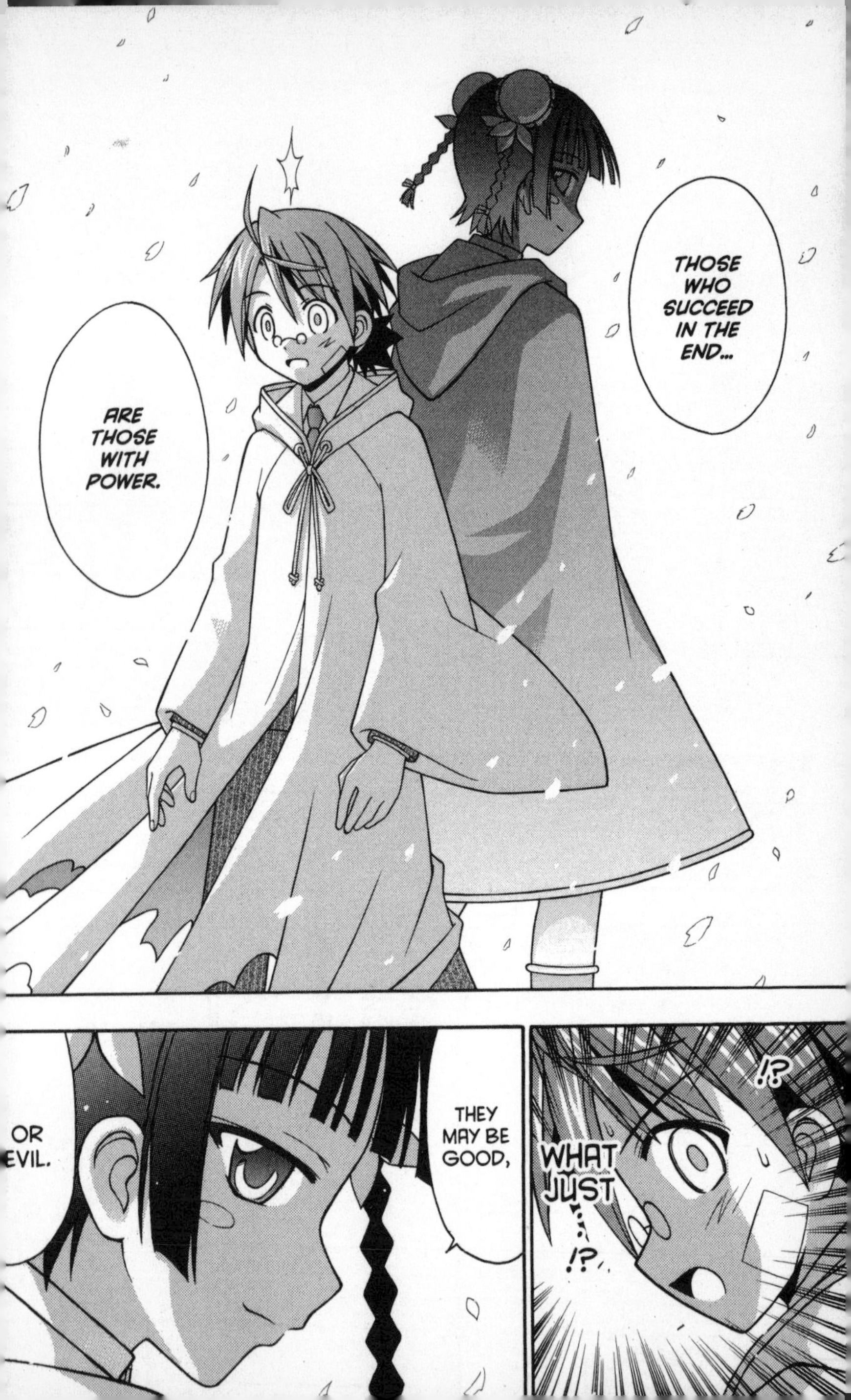
THOSE WHO SUCCEED IN THE END...
ARE THOSE WITH POWER.
!?
WHAT JUST...!?
THEY MAY BE GOOD,
OR EVIL.

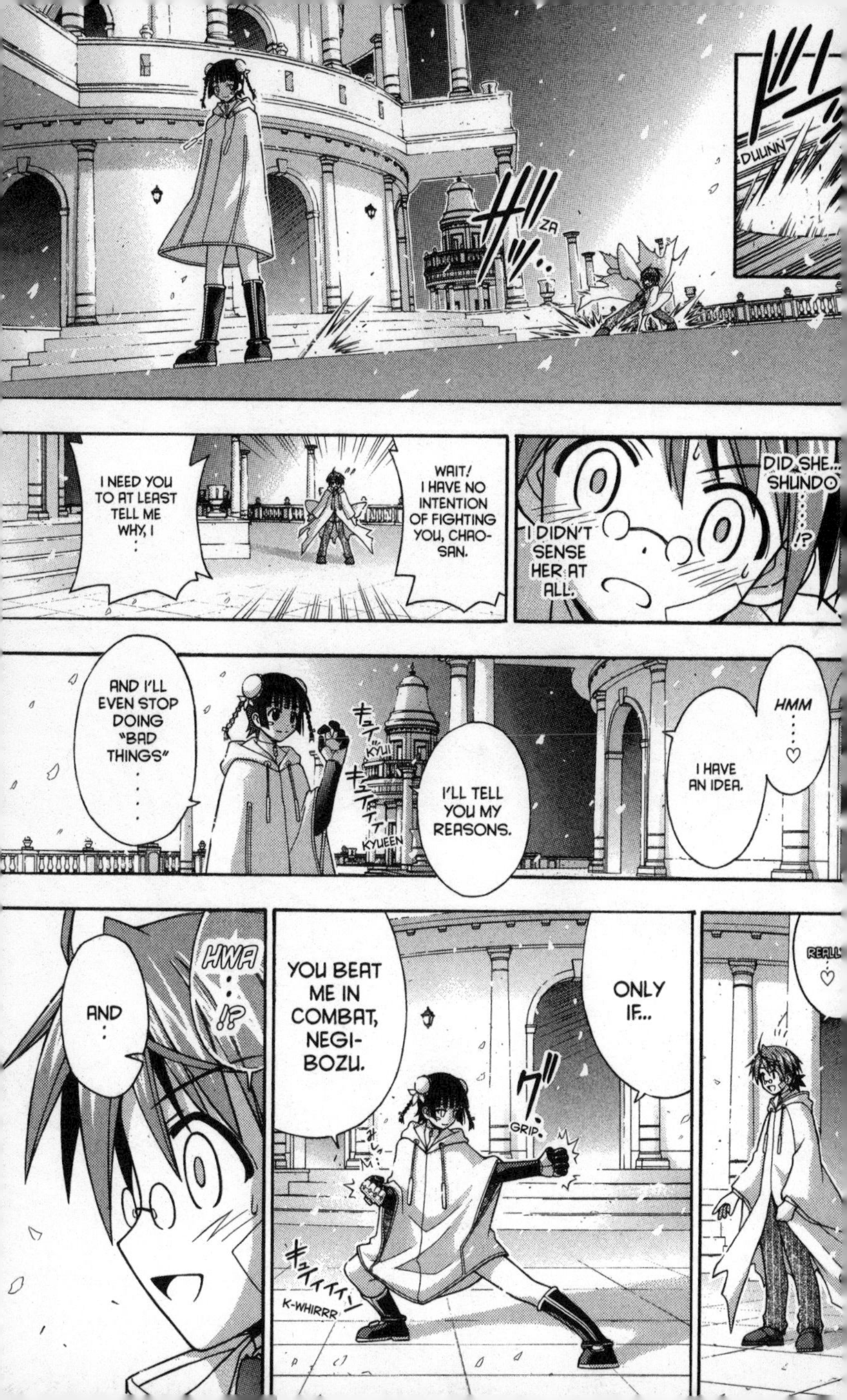
DUUNN
ZA
DID SHE... SHUNDO......!?
I DIDN'T SENSE HER AT ALL.
WAIT! I HAVE NO INTENTION OF FIGHTING YOU, CHAO-SAN.
I NEED YOU TO AT LEAST TELL ME WHY, I...
HMM...♡
I HAVE AN IDEA.
I'LL TELL YOU MY REASONS.
KYU
KYUEEN
AND I'LL EVEN STOP DOING "BAD THINGS"......
REALL...♡
ONLY IF...
YOU BEAT ME IN COMBAT, NEGI-BOZU.
GRIP
K-WHIRRR
HWA...!?
AND...

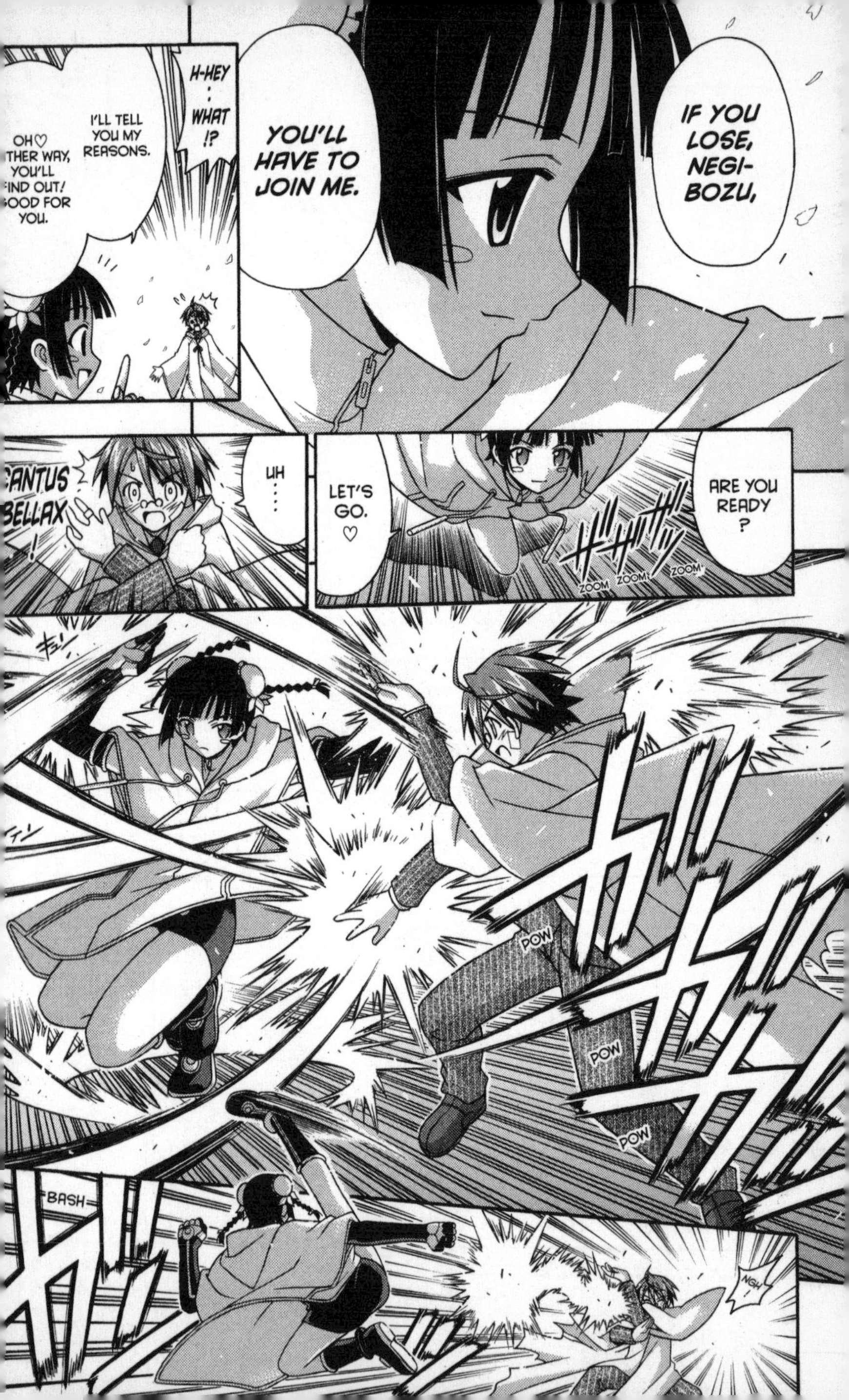
IF YOU LOSE, NEGI-BOZU,
YOU'LL HAVE TO JOIN ME.
H-HEY : WHAT !?
I'LL TELL YOU MY REASONS.
OH♡ THER WAY, YOU'LL FIND OUT! OOD FOR YOU.
ARE YOU READY ?
ZOOM ZOOM ZOOM
LET'S GO. ♡
UH .....
ANTUS BELLAX !
POW
POW
POW
BASH
NGH !

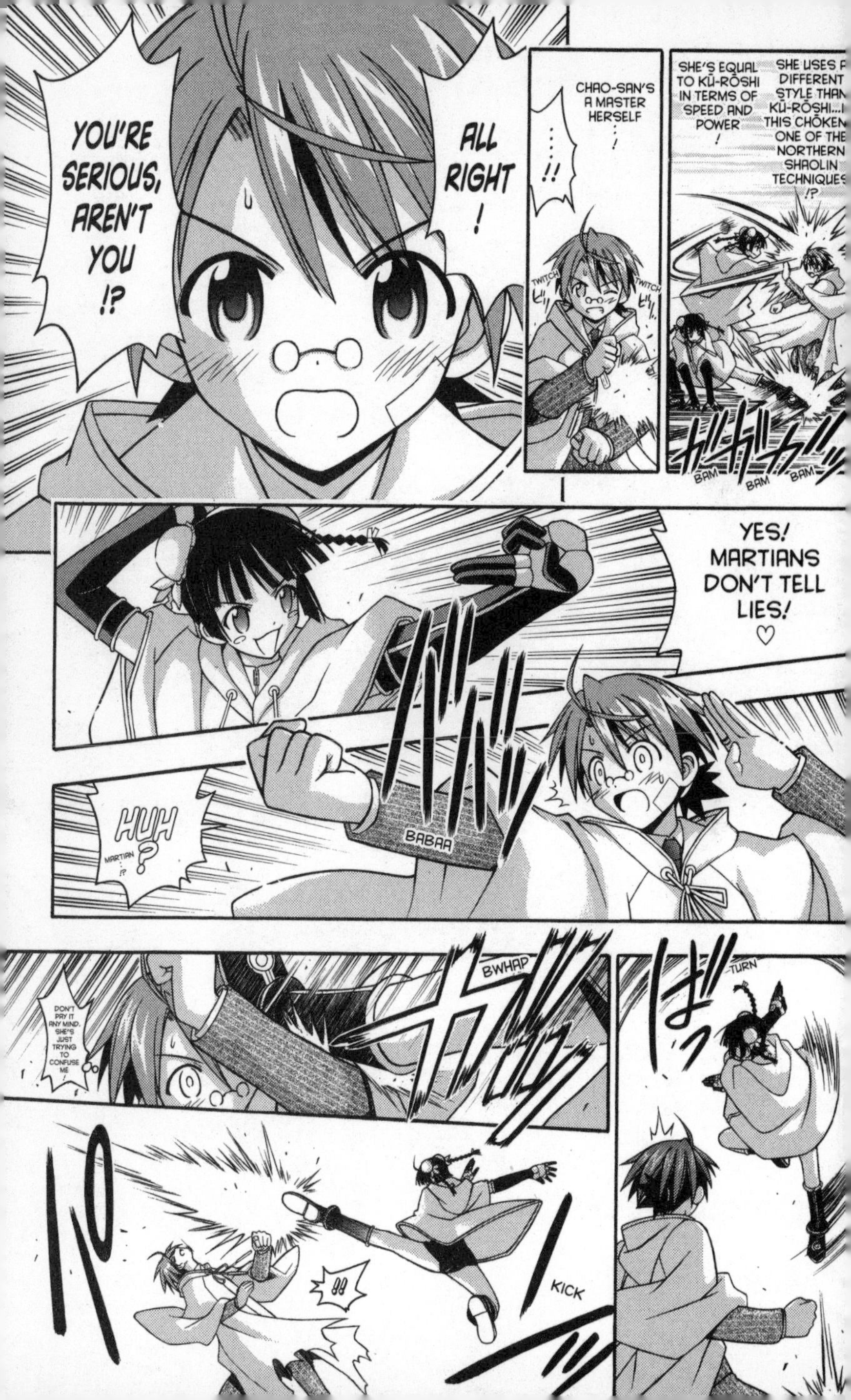
SHE USES A DIFFERENT STYLE THAN KŪ-RŌSHI...I THIS CHŌKEN ONE OF THE NORTHERN SHAOLIN TECHNIQUES !?
SHE'S EQUAL TO KŪ-RŌSHI IN TERMS OF SPEED AND POWER !
BAM BAM BAM
CHAO-SAN'S A MASTER HERSELF ...!
......!!
TWITCH TWITCH
ALL RIGHT !
YOU'RE SERIOUS, AREN'T YOU !?
YES! MARTIANS DON'T TELL LIES! ♡
BABAA
HUH ?
MARTIAN ...!?
TURN
BWHAP
DON'T PAY IT ANY MIND. SHE'S JUST TRYING TO CONFUSE ME !
KICK
!!

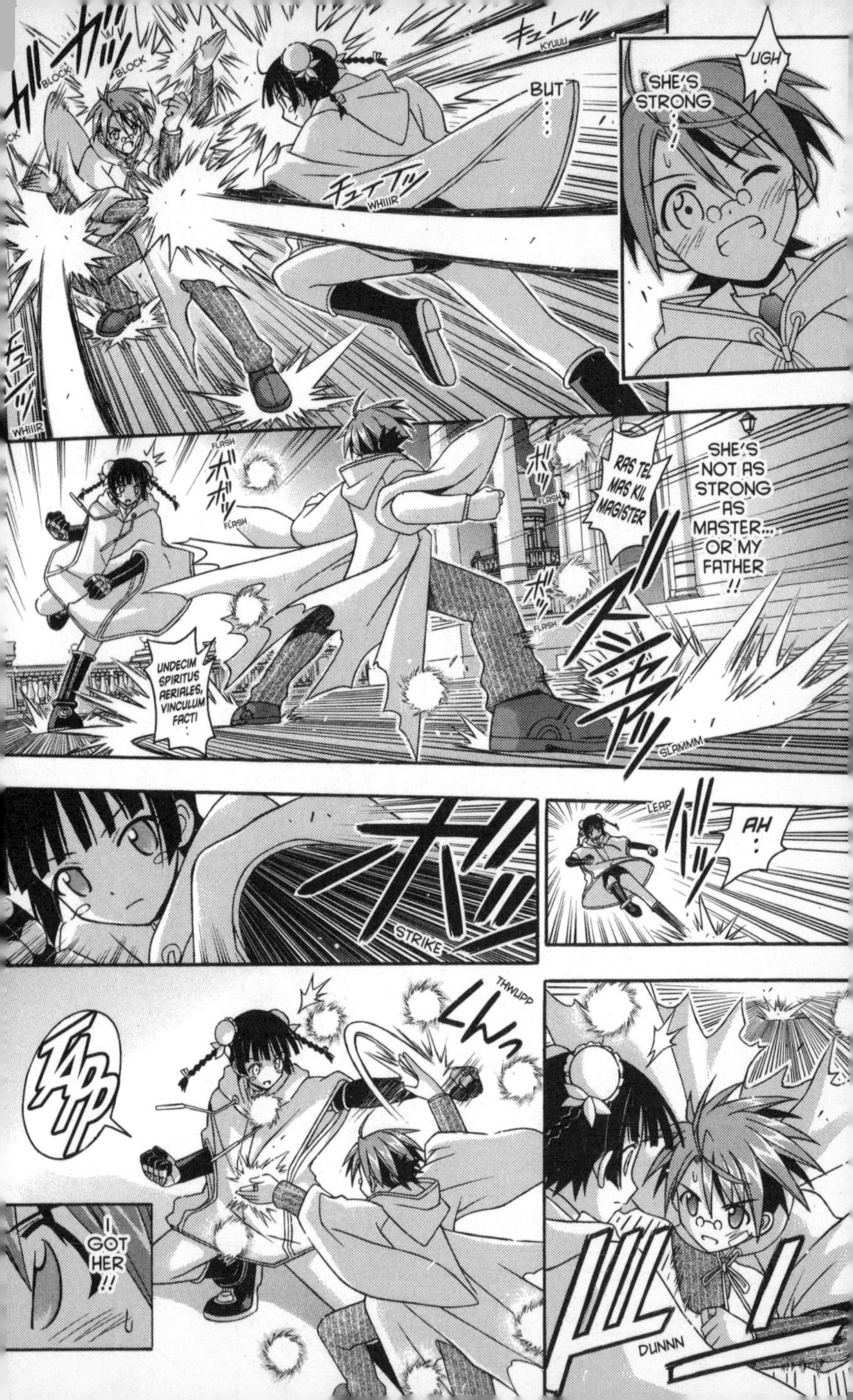
UGH
SHE'S STRONG...!
KYUUU
BUT...
BLOCK
BLOCK
WHIIIR
WHIIIR
SHE'S NOT AS STRONG AS MASTER... OR MY FATHER!!
RAS TEL MAS KIL MAGISTER
FLASH
FLASH
FLASH
FLASH
UNDECIM SPIRITUS AERIALES, VINCULUM FACTI!
SLAMMM
LEAP
AH...
STRIKE
DUNNN
THWUPP
TAP
I GOT HER!!

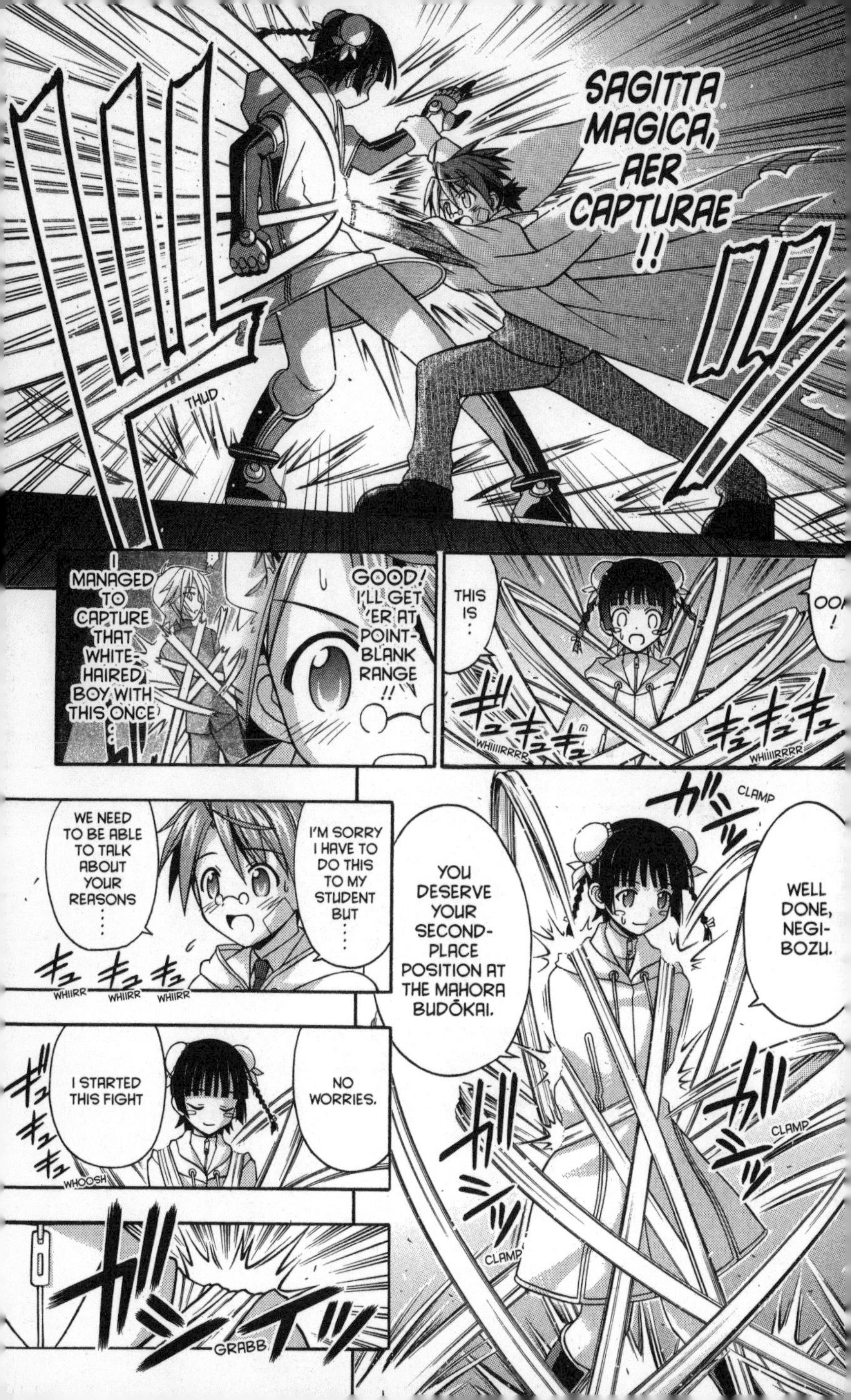

SAGITTA MAGICA, AER CAPTURAE !!
THUD
OO!
THIS IS . . .
WHIIIRRRR
WHIIIRRRR
GOOD! I'LL GET 'ER AT POINT-BLANK RANGE !!
I MANAGED TO CAPTURE THAT WHITE-HAIRED BOY WITH THIS ONCE . . .
CLAMP
WELL DONE, NEGI-BOZU.
YOU DESERVE YOUR SECOND-PLACE POSITION AT THE MAHORA BUDŌKAI.
CLAMP
CLAMP
I'M SORRY I HAVE TO DO THIS TO MY STUDENT BUT . . .
WE NEED TO BE ABLE TO TALK ABOUT YOUR REASONS . . . . .
WHIIRR
WHIIRR
WHIIRR
NO WORRIES.
I STARTED THIS FIGHT
WHOOSH
GRABB

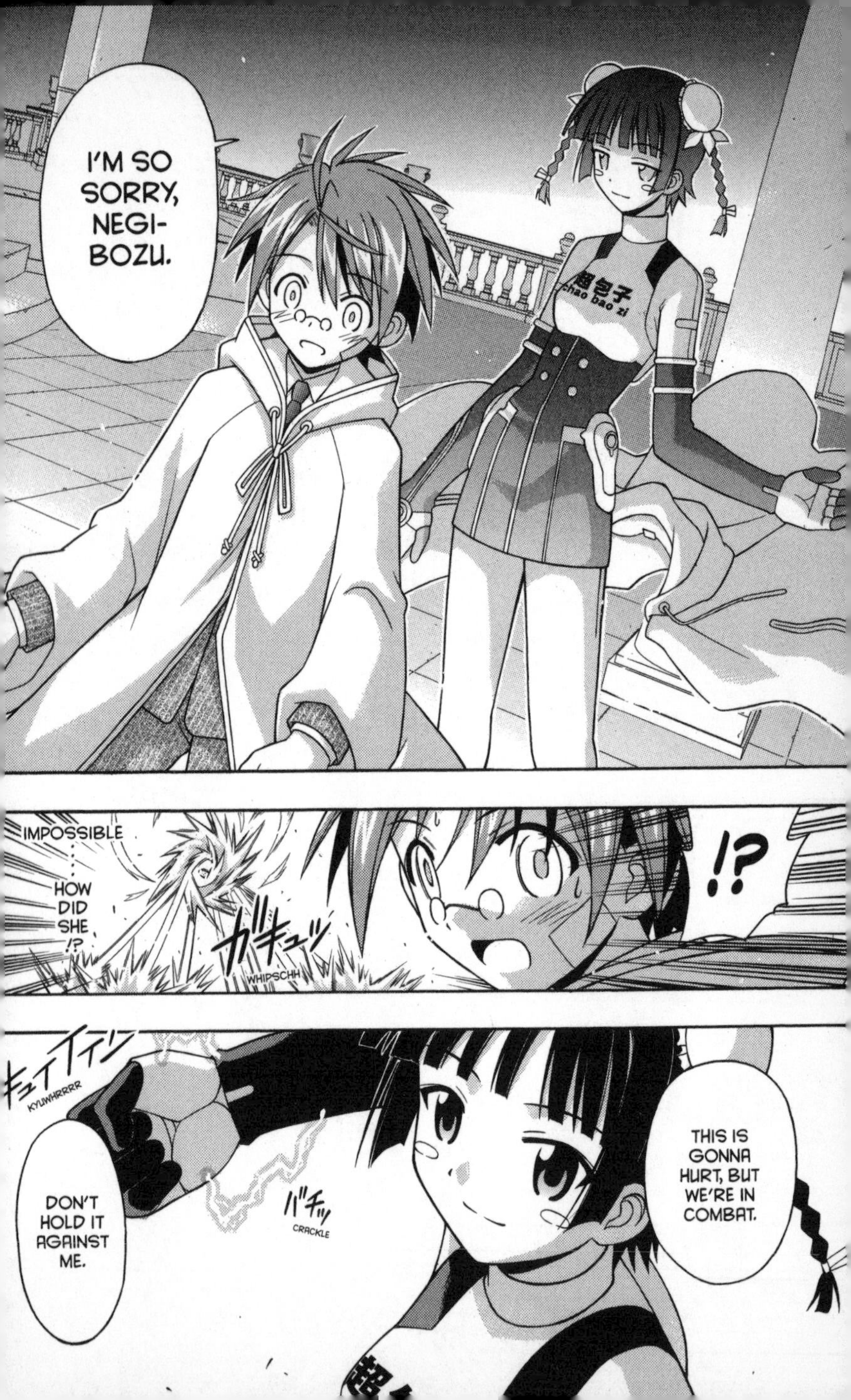
I'M SO SORRY, NEGI-BOZU.
超包子 chao bao zi
!?
ガキュッ
WHIPSCHH
IMPOSSIBLE …… HOW DID SHE !?
THIS IS GONNA HURT, BUT WE'RE IN COMBAT.
バチッ
CRACKLE
DON'T HOLD IT AGAINST ME.
キュイイイン
KYUWHRRRR

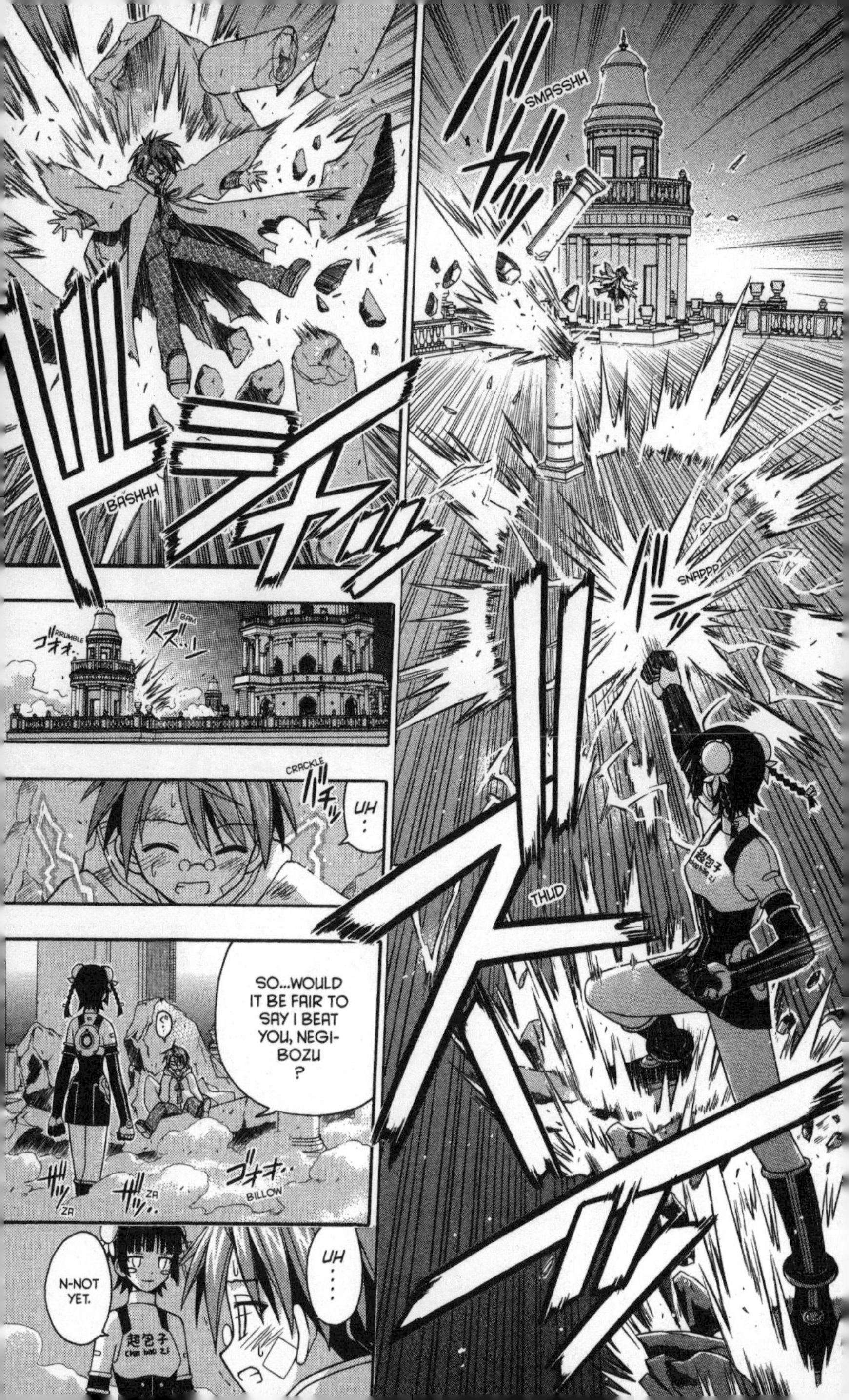
SMASSHH
SNAPPP
THUD
BASHHH
BAM
RRUMBLE
UH...
CRACKLE
SO...WOULD IT BE FAIR TO SAY I BEAT YOU, NEGI-BOZU?
BILLOW
ZA
ZA
UH...
N-NOT YET.

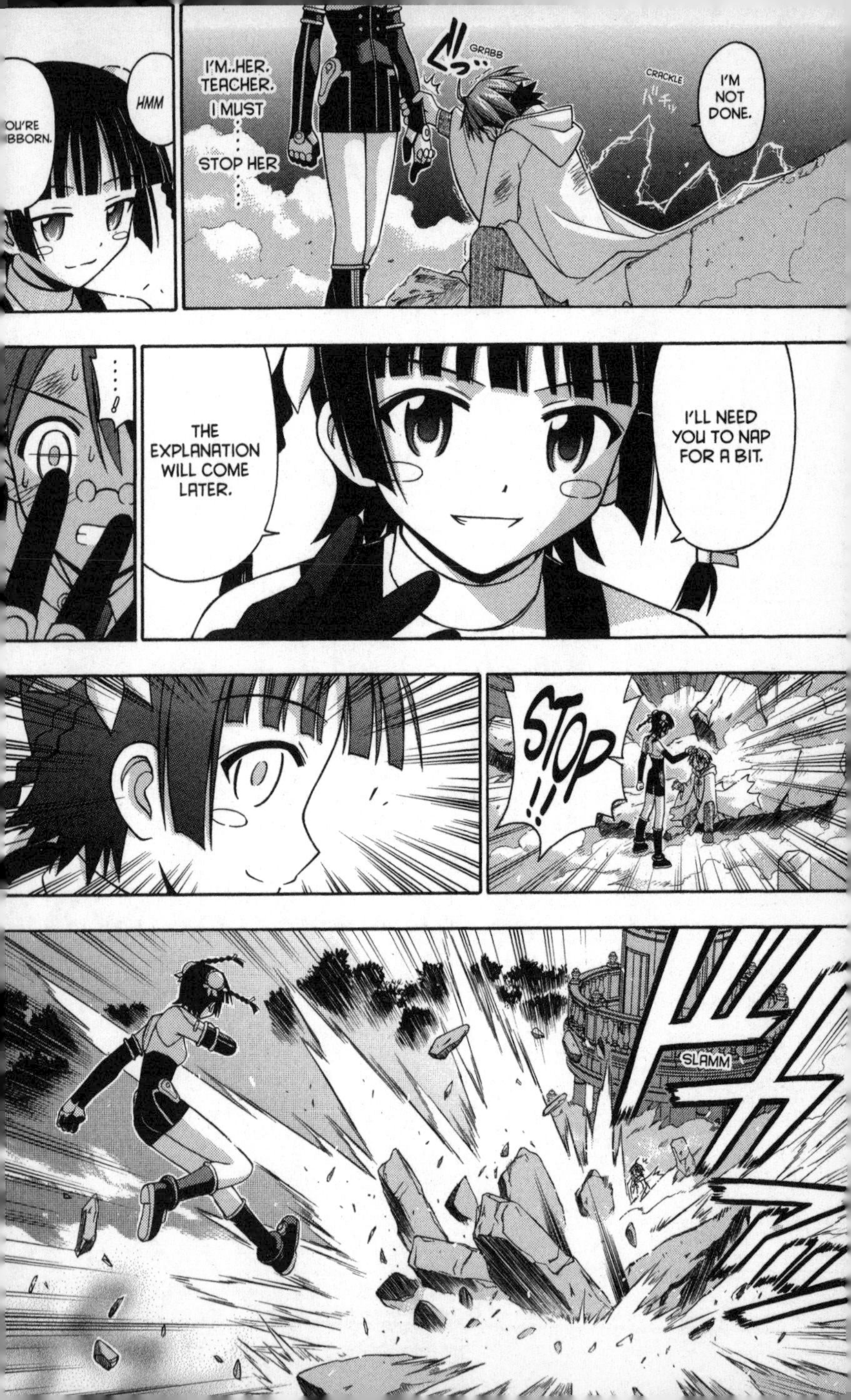
GRABB
CRACKLE
I'M NOT DONE.
I'M..HER. TEACHER. I MUST
...STOP HER...
HMM
OU'RE
IBBORN.
I'LL NEED YOU TO NAP FOR A BIT.
THE EXPLANATION WILL COME LATER.
...!
STOP!!
SLAMM

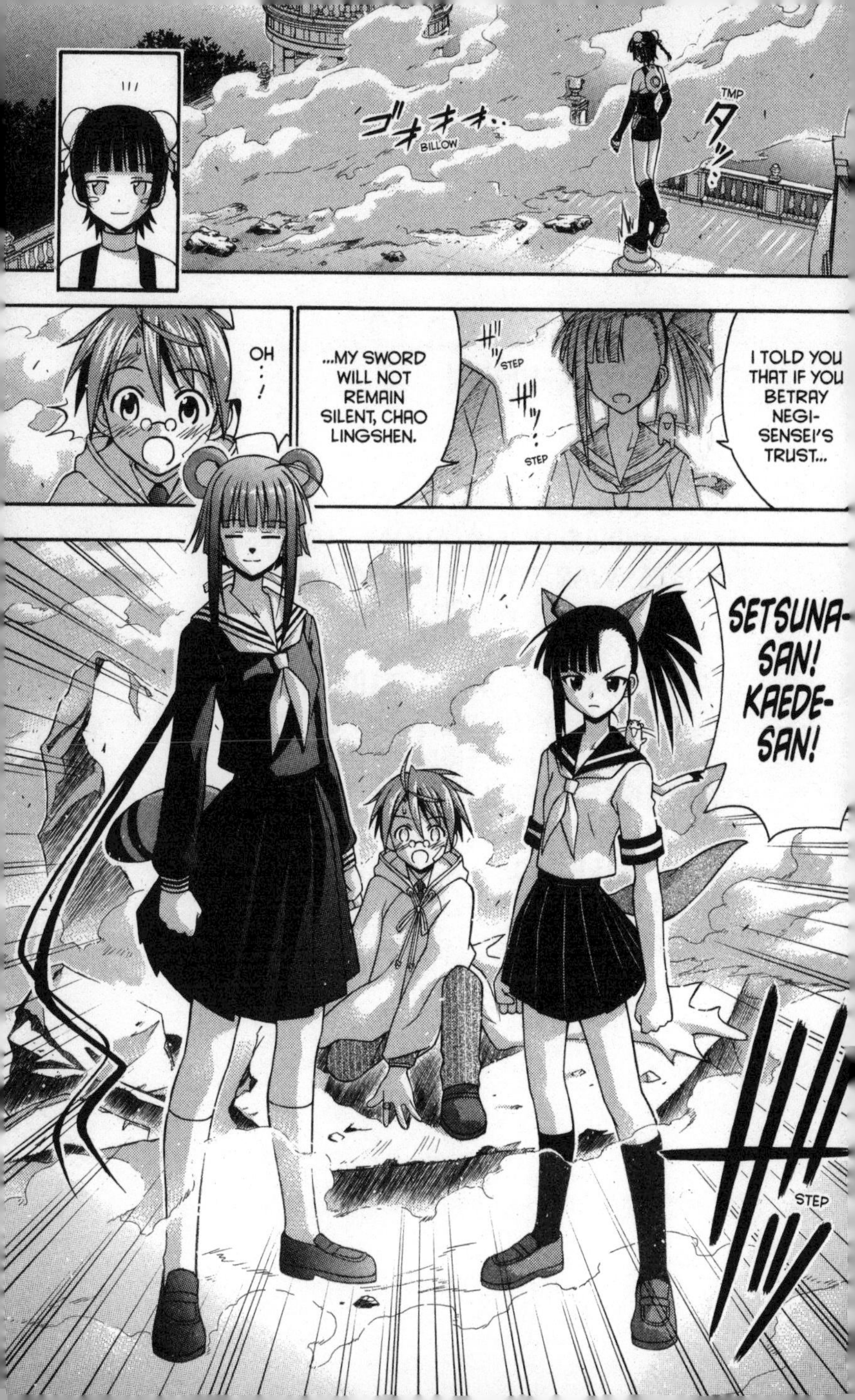

タッ
TMP
ゴオオオ…
BILLOW
I TOLD YOU THAT IF YOU BETRAY NEGI-SENSEI'S TRUST...
STEP
STEP
...MY SWORD WILL NOT REMAIN SILENT, CHAO LINGSHEN.
OH...!
SETSUNA-SAN! KAEDE-SAN!
STEP

STUDENT NUMBER 19
CHAO LINGSHEN

BORN: DECEMBER 1, 1988
BLOOD TYPE: O
LIKES: WORLD DOMINATION
DISLIKES: WAR, CYCLES OF HATRED,
    UNILATERAL WORLD DOMINATION
    BY A SINGLE NATION
AFFILIATIONS: COOKING CLUB, CHINESE
    MARTIAL ARTS RESEARCH CLUB,
    ROBOT ENGINEERING RESEARCH
    CLUB, EASTERN MEDICINE
    RESEARCH CLUB, BIOENGINEERING
    RESEARCH CLUB, QUANTUM
    MECHANICS RESEARCH CLUB
    (UNIVERSITY)

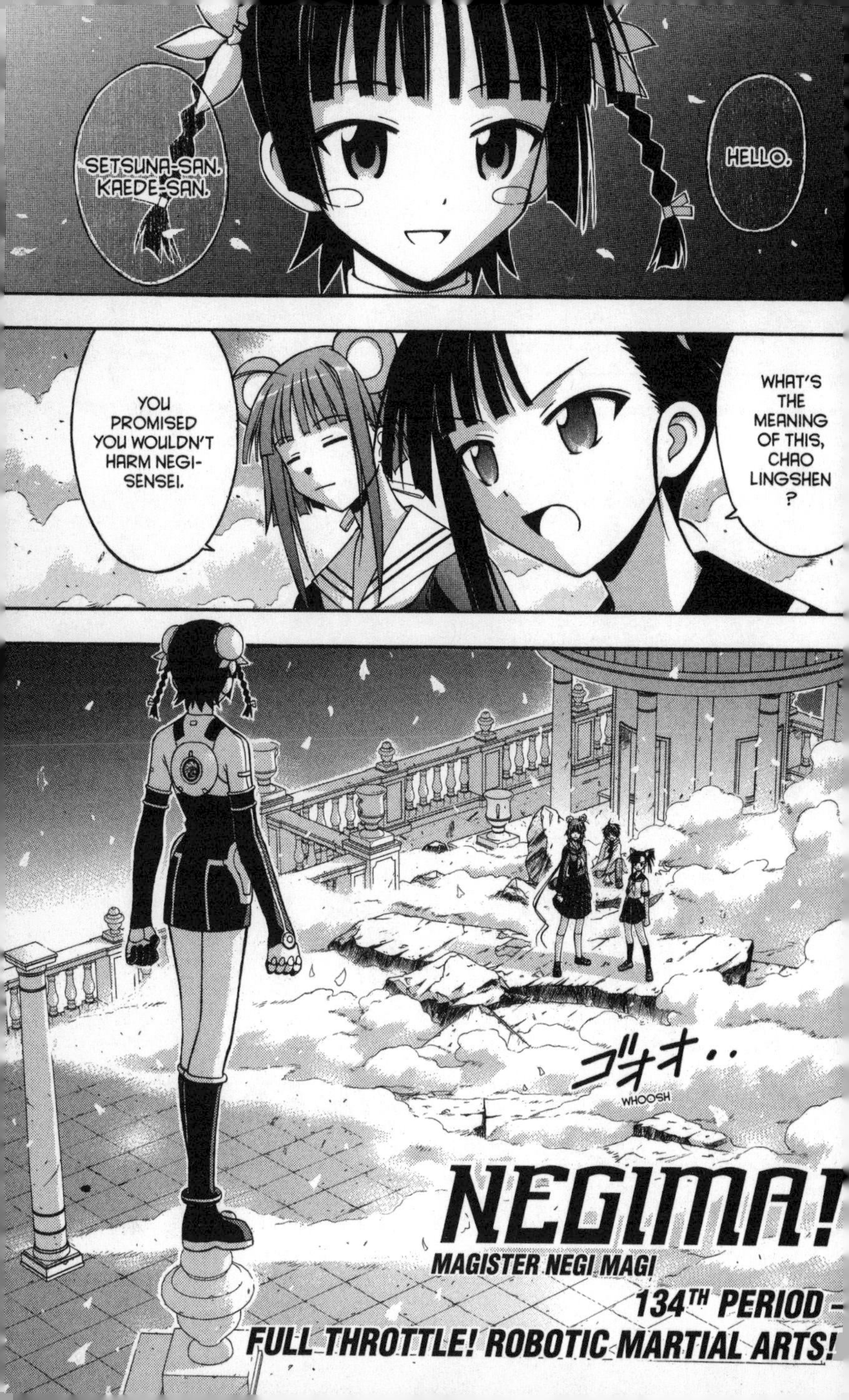
HELLO.
SETSUNA-SAN. KAEDE-SAN.
WHAT'S THE MEANING OF THIS, CHAO LINGSHEN?
YOU PROMISED YOU WOULDN'T HARM NEGI-SENSEI.
ゴォオ・・
WHOOSH
NEGIMA!
MAGISTER NEGI MAGI
134TH PERIOD –
FULL THROTTLE! ROBOTIC MARTIAL ARTS!

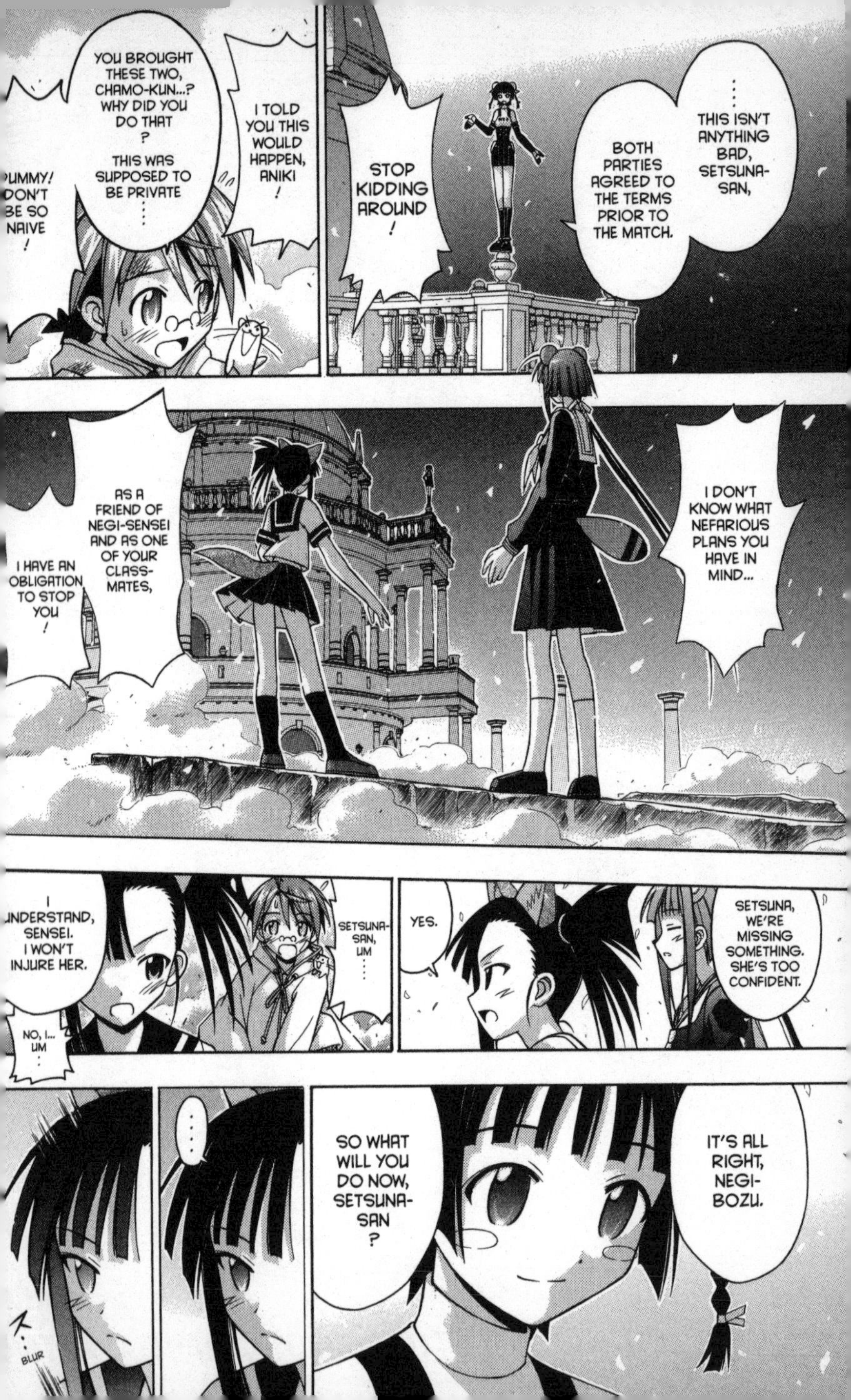
...THIS ISN'T ANYTHING BAD, SETSUNA-SAN,
BOTH PARTIES AGREED TO THE TERMS PRIOR TO THE MATCH.
STOP KIDDING AROUND!
I TOLD YOU THIS WOULD HAPPEN, ANIKI!
YOU BROUGHT THESE TWO, CHAMO-KUN...? WHY DID YOU DO THAT? THIS WAS SUPPOSED TO BE PRIVATE....
UMMY! DON'T BE SO NAIVE!
I DON'T KNOW WHAT NEFARIOUS PLANS YOU HAVE IN MIND...
AS A FRIEND OF NEGI-SENSEI AND AS ONE OF YOUR CLASSMATES,
I HAVE AN OBLIGATION TO STOP YOU!
SETSUNA, WE'RE MISSING SOMETHING. SHE'S TOO CONFIDENT.
YES.
SETSUNA-SAN, UM...
I NDERSTAND, SENSEI. I WON'T INJURE HER.
NO, I... UM...
IT'S ALL RIGHT, NEGI-BOZU.
SO WHAT WILL YOU DO NOW, SETSUNA-SAN?
....
BLUR

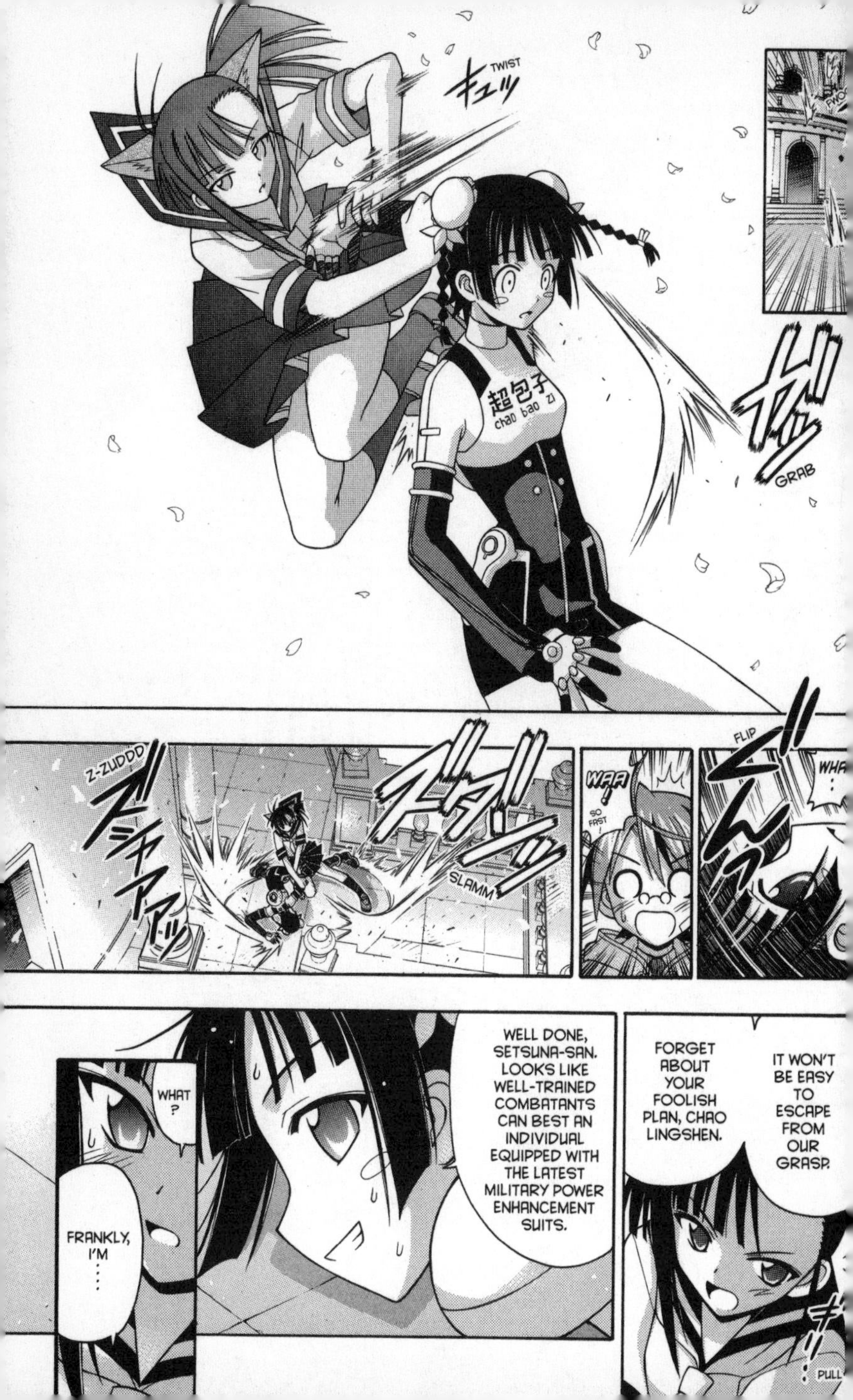

FWOO
TWIST
超包子 chao bao zi
GRAB
FLIP
WHA :
WAA!
SO FAST!
SLAMM
Z-ZUDDD
IT WON'T BE EASY TO ESCAPE FROM OUR GRASP.
FORGET ABOUT YOUR FOOLISH PLAN, CHAO LINGSHEN.
PULL
WELL DONE, SETSUNA-SAN. LOOKS LIKE WELL-TRAINED COMBATANTS CAN BEST AN INDIVIDUAL EQUIPPED WITH THE LATEST MILITARY POWER ENHANCEMENT SUITS.
WHAT?
FRANKLY, I'M ....

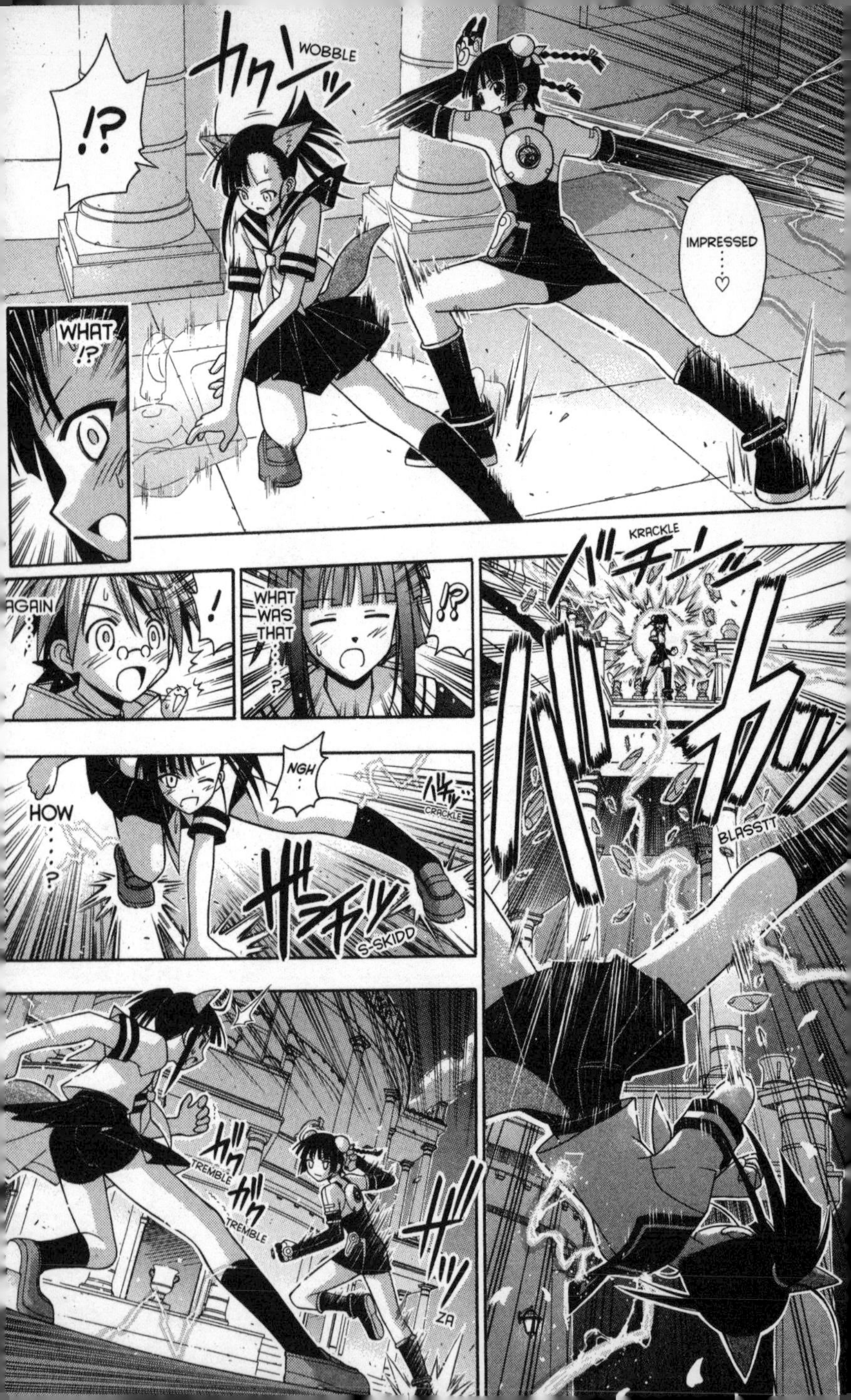

IMPRESSED ... ♡
WOBBLE
!?
WHAT !?
KRACKLE
BLASSTT
!?
WHAT WAS THAT ...?
!
AGAIN ...
NGH ...
CRACKLE
HOW ...?
S-SKIDD
TREMBLE
TREMBLE
ZA

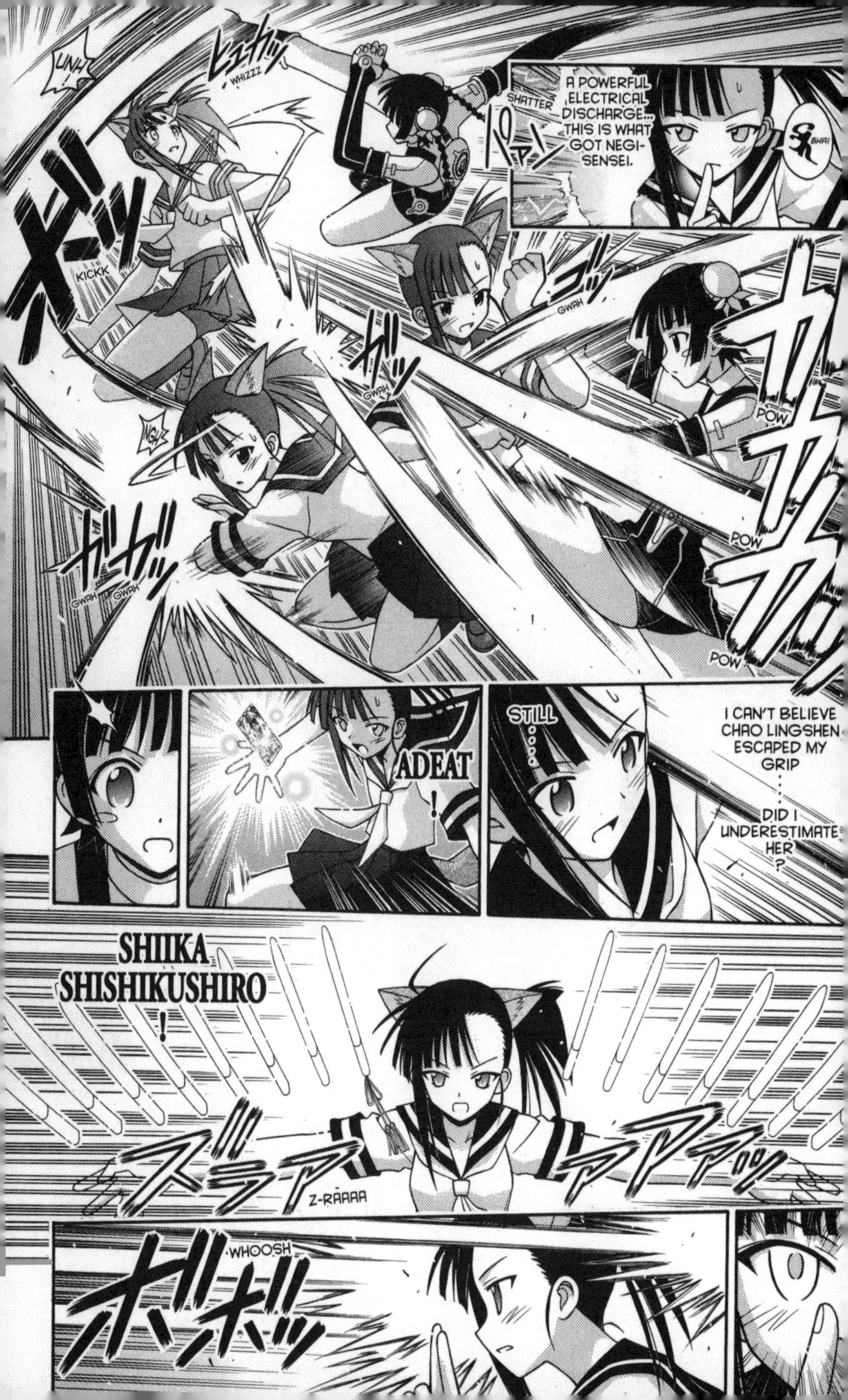
BHAI
A POWERFUL ELECTRICAL DISCHARGE... THIS IS WHAT GOT NEGI-SENSEI.
SHATTER
WHIZZZ
UNH!
KICKK
GWAH
POW
GWAH
NGH
POW
POW
GWAH GWAH
I CAN'T BELIEVE CHAO LINGSHEN ESCAPED MY GRIP...
DID I UNDERESTIMATE HER?
STILL....
ADEAT!
SHIIKA SHISHIKUSHIRO!
Z-RAAAA
WHOOSH

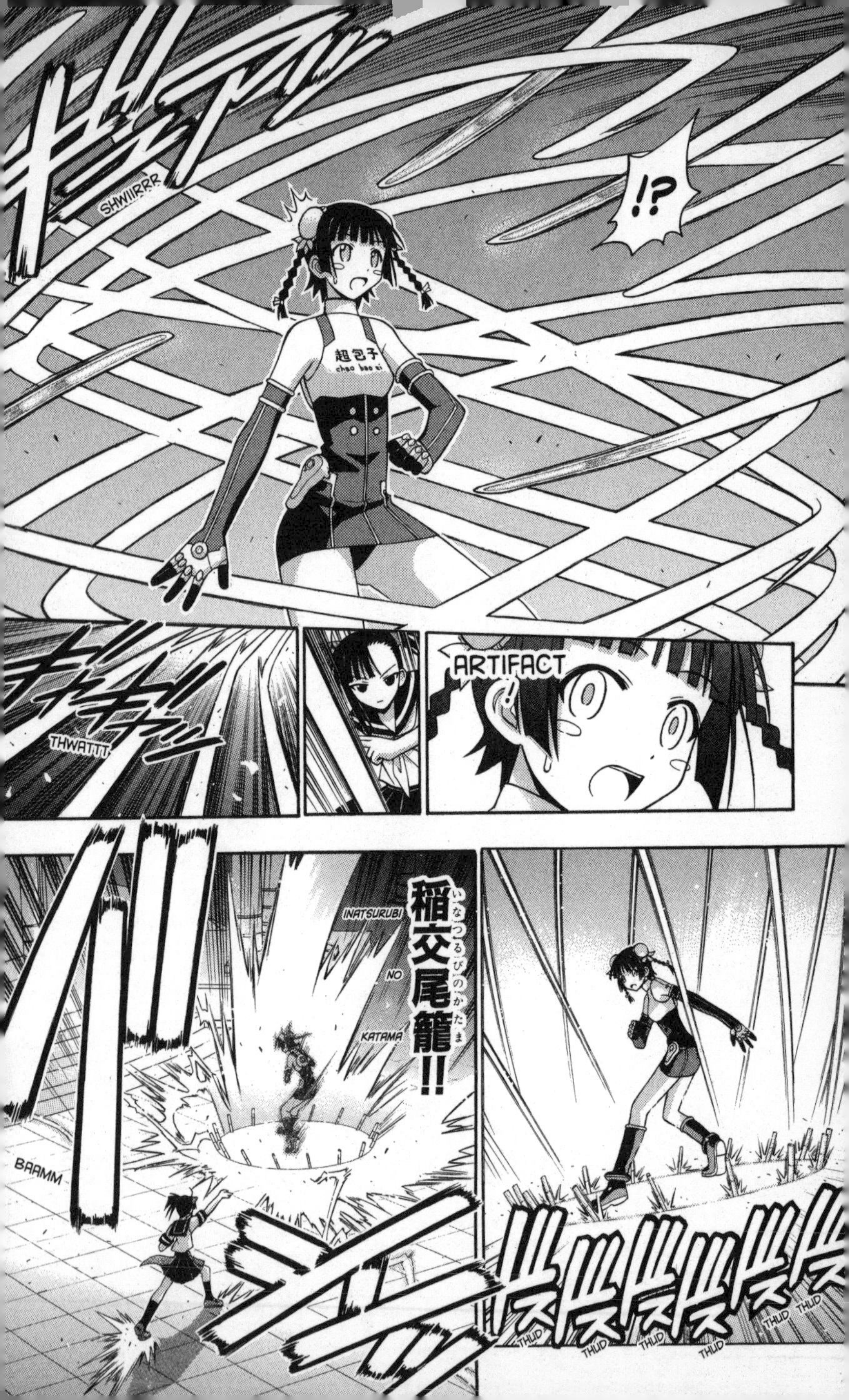
SHWIIRRR
!?
ARTIFACT!
THWATTT
THUD THUD THUD THUD THUD THUD
稲交尾籠!!
いなつるびのかたま
INATSURUBI NO KATAMA
BAAMM

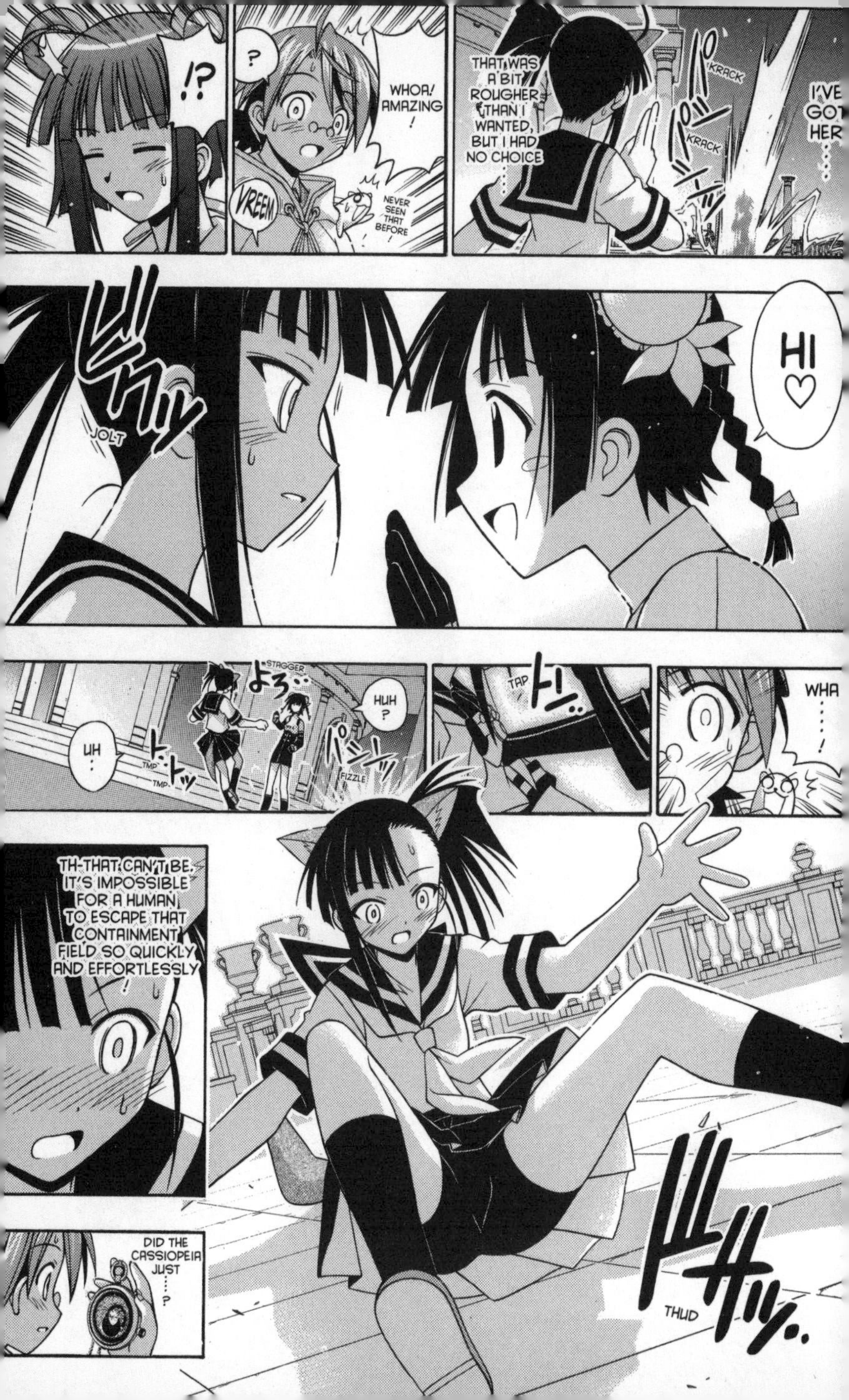
I'VE GOT HER......
KRACK
KRACK
THAT WAS A BIT ROUGHER THAN I WANTED, BUT I HAD NO CHOICE......
?
WHOA! AMAZING!
VREEM
NEVER SEEN THAT BEFORE!
!?
HI ♡
JOLT
WHA......!
TAP
HUH?
STAGGER
FIZZLE
UH...
TMP
TMP
THUD
TH-THAT CAN'T BE. IT'S IMPOSSIBLE FOR A HUMAN TO ESCAPE THAT CONTAINMENT FIELD SO QUICKLY AND EFFORTLESSLY!
DID THE CASSIOPEIA JUST......?

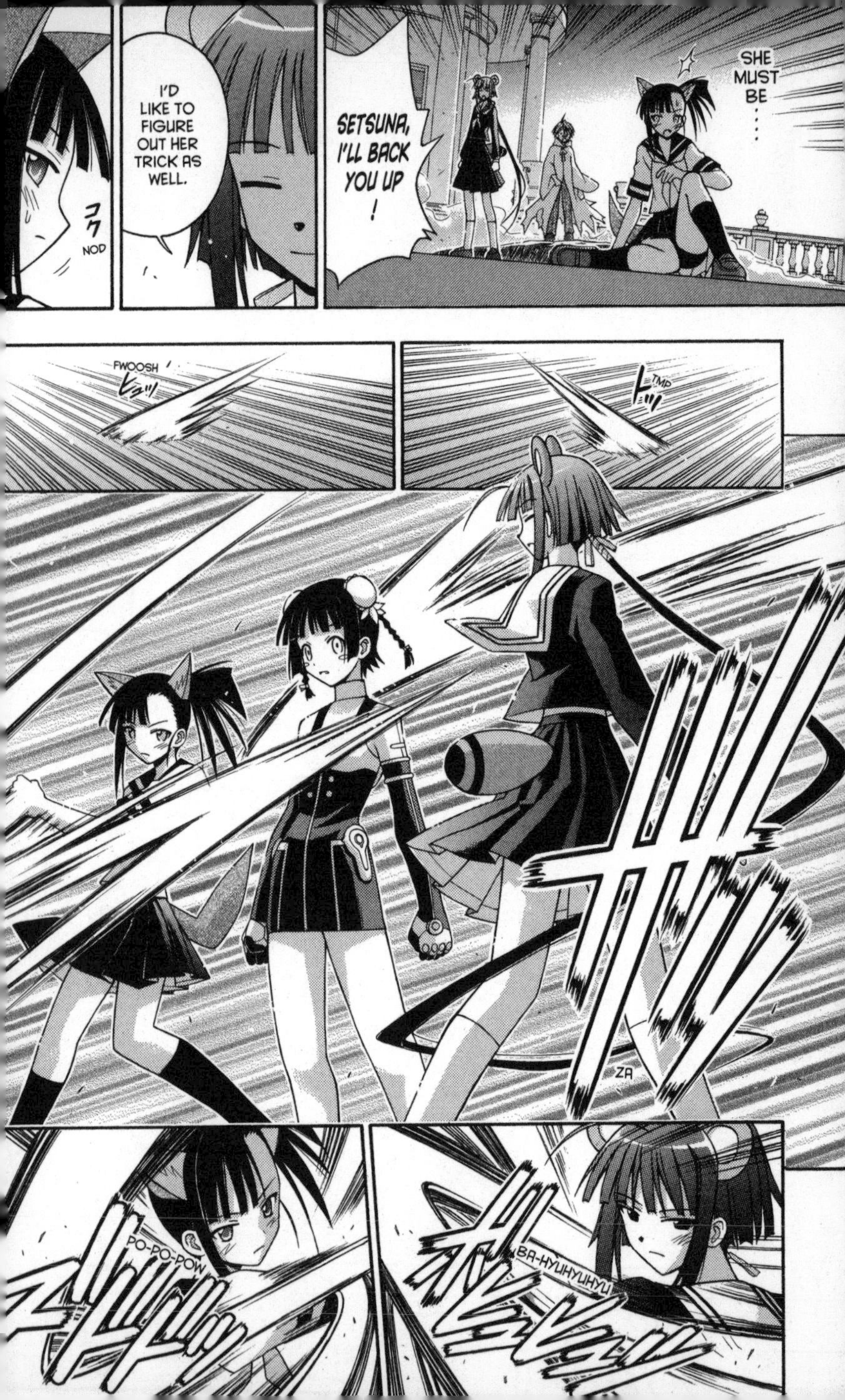
SHE MUST BE ....
SETSUNA, I'LL BACK YOU UP!
I'D LIKE TO FIGURE OUT HER TRICK AS WELL.
コク
NOD
TMP
FWOOSH
ZA
BA-HYUHYUHYU
PO-PO-POW

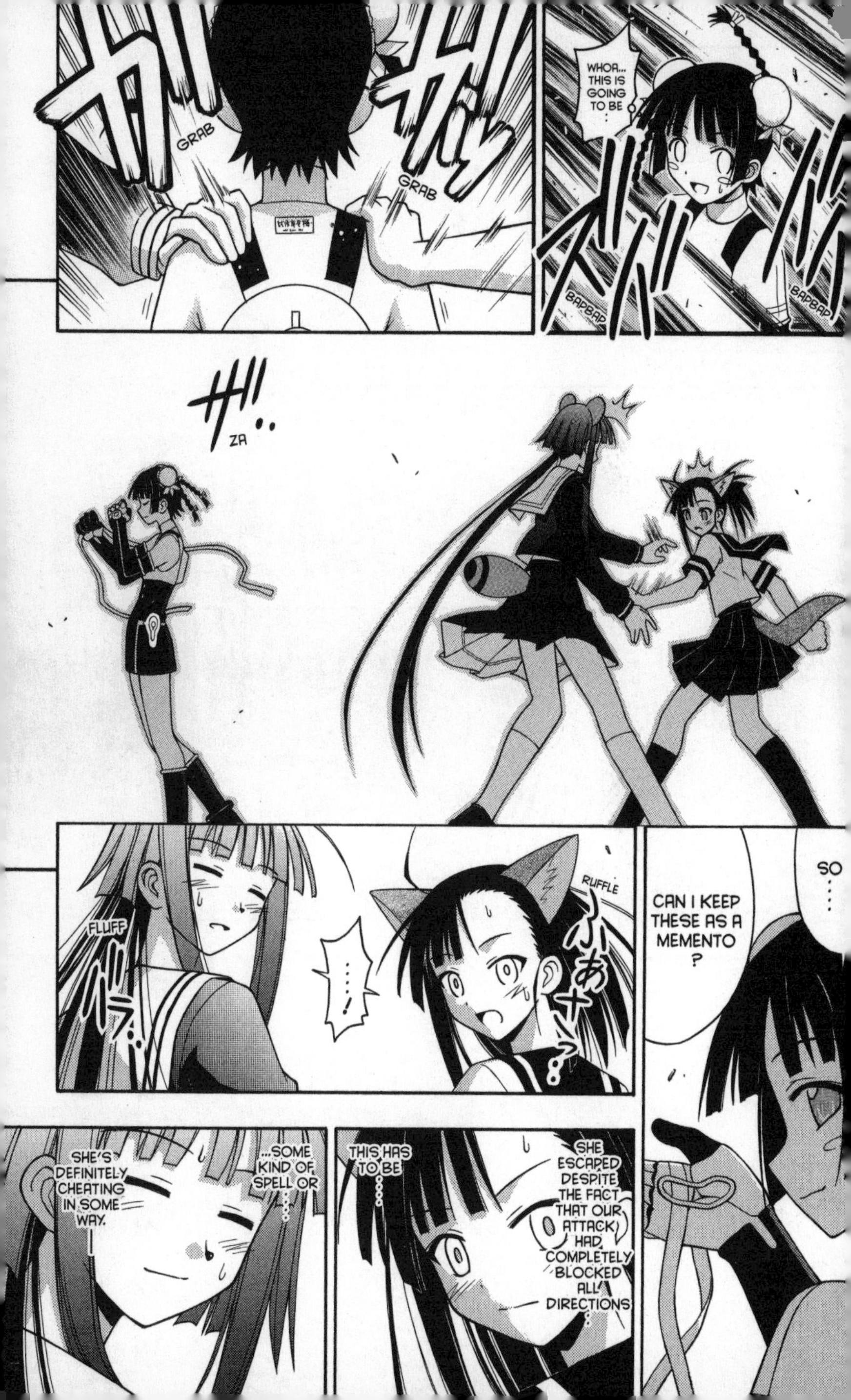
WHOA... THIS IS GOING TO BE ...
BAPBAP
BAPBAP
GRAB
GRAB
ZA
SO....
CAN I KEEP THESE AS A MEMENTO?
RUFFLE
...!
FLUFF
SHE ESCAPED DESPITE THE FACT THAT OUR ATTACK HAD COMPLETELY BLOCKED ALL DIRECTIONS...
THIS HAS TO BE....
...SOME KIND OF SPELL OR...
SHE'S DEFINITELY CHEATING IN SOME WAY.

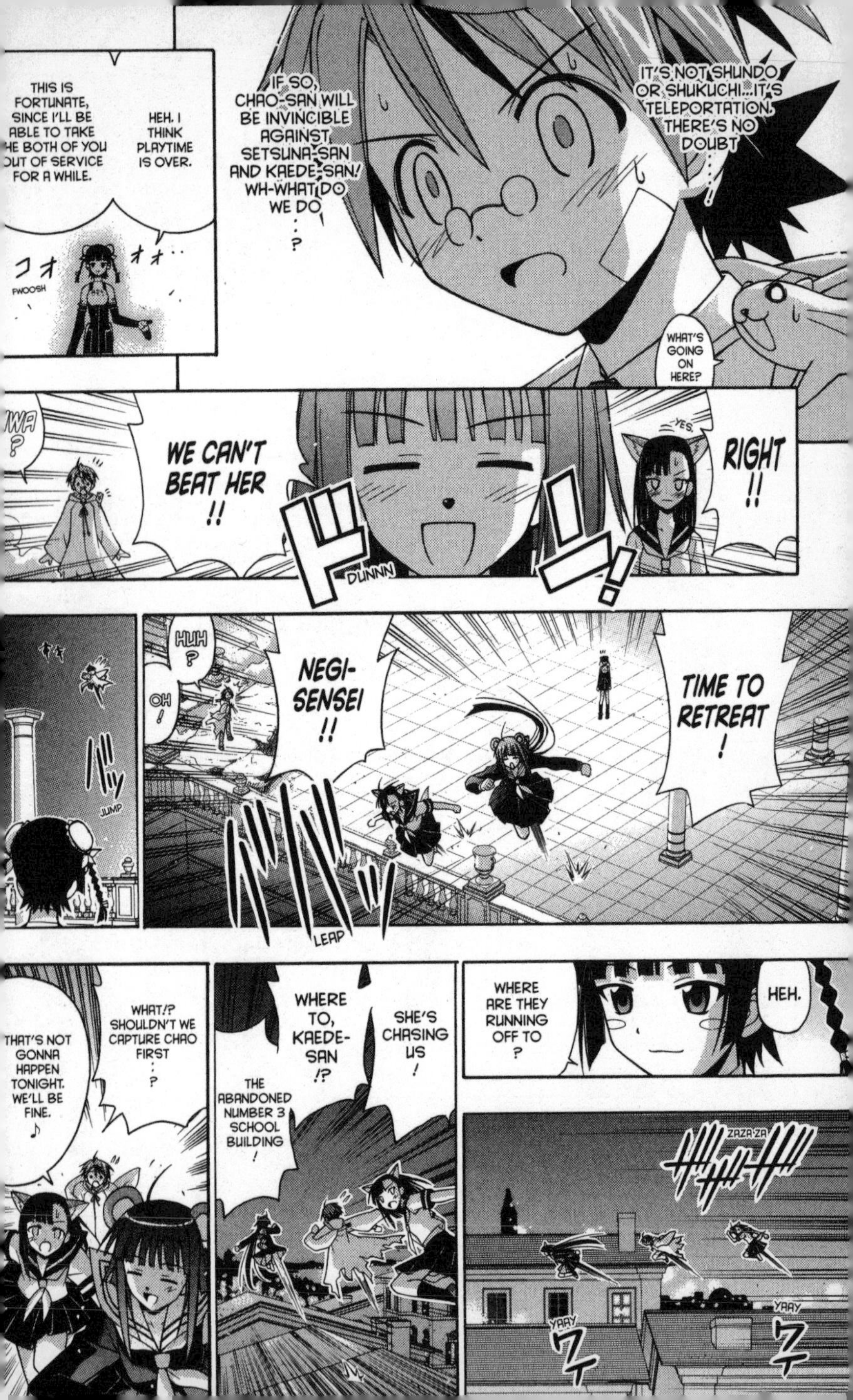
IT'S NOT SHUNDO OR SHUKUCHI...IT'S TELEPORTATION. THERE'S NO DOUBT
IF SO, CHAO-SAN WILL BE INVINCIBLE AGAINST SETSUNA-SAN AND KAEDE-SAN! WH-WHAT DO WE DO...?
WHAT'S GOING ON HERE?
HEH. I THINK PLAYTIME IS OVER.
THIS IS FORTUNATE, SINCE I'LL BE ABLE TO TAKE THE BOTH OF YOU OUT OF SERVICE FOR A WHILE.
コオオ‥
FWOOSH
—YES.
RIGHT!!
DUNNN
WE CAN'T BEAT HER!!
TIME TO RETREAT!
NEGI-SENSEI!!
HUH?
OH!
LEAP
JUMP
HEH.
WHERE ARE THEY RUNNING OFF TO?
ZAZAZA
YAAY
YAAY
SHE'S CHASING US!
WHERE TO, KAEDE-SAN!?
THE ABANDONED NUMBER 3 SCHOOL BUILDING!
WHAT!? SHOULDN'T WE CAPTURE CHAO FIRST...?
THAT'S NOT GONNA HAPPEN TONIGHT. WE'LL BE FINE. ♪

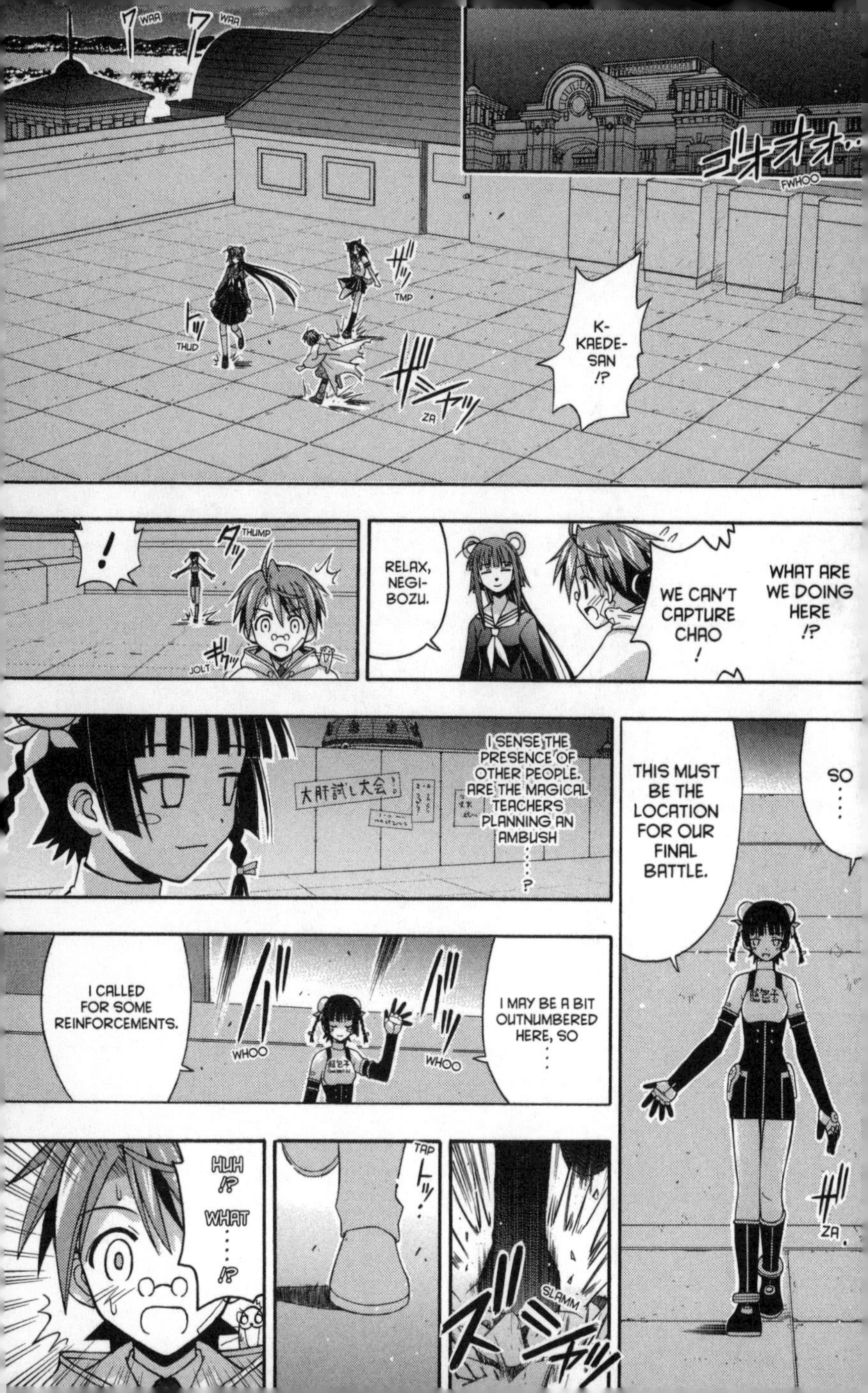
FWHOO
WAA
WAA
K-KAEDE-SAN!?
TMP
ZA
THUD
WHAT ARE WE DOING HERE!?
WE CAN'T CAPTURE CHAO!
RELAX, NEGI-BOZU.
!
THUMP
JOLT
SO......
THIS MUST BE THE LOCATION FOR OUR FINAL BATTLE.
ZA
I SENSE THE PRESENCE OF OTHER PEOPLE. ARE THE MAGICAL TEACHERS PLANNING AN AMBUSH.....?
大肝試し大会!
I MAY BE A BIT OUTNUMBERED HERE, SO...
WHOO
WHOO
I CALLED FOR SOME REINFORCEMENTS.
SLAMM
TAP
HUH!?
WHAT.....!?

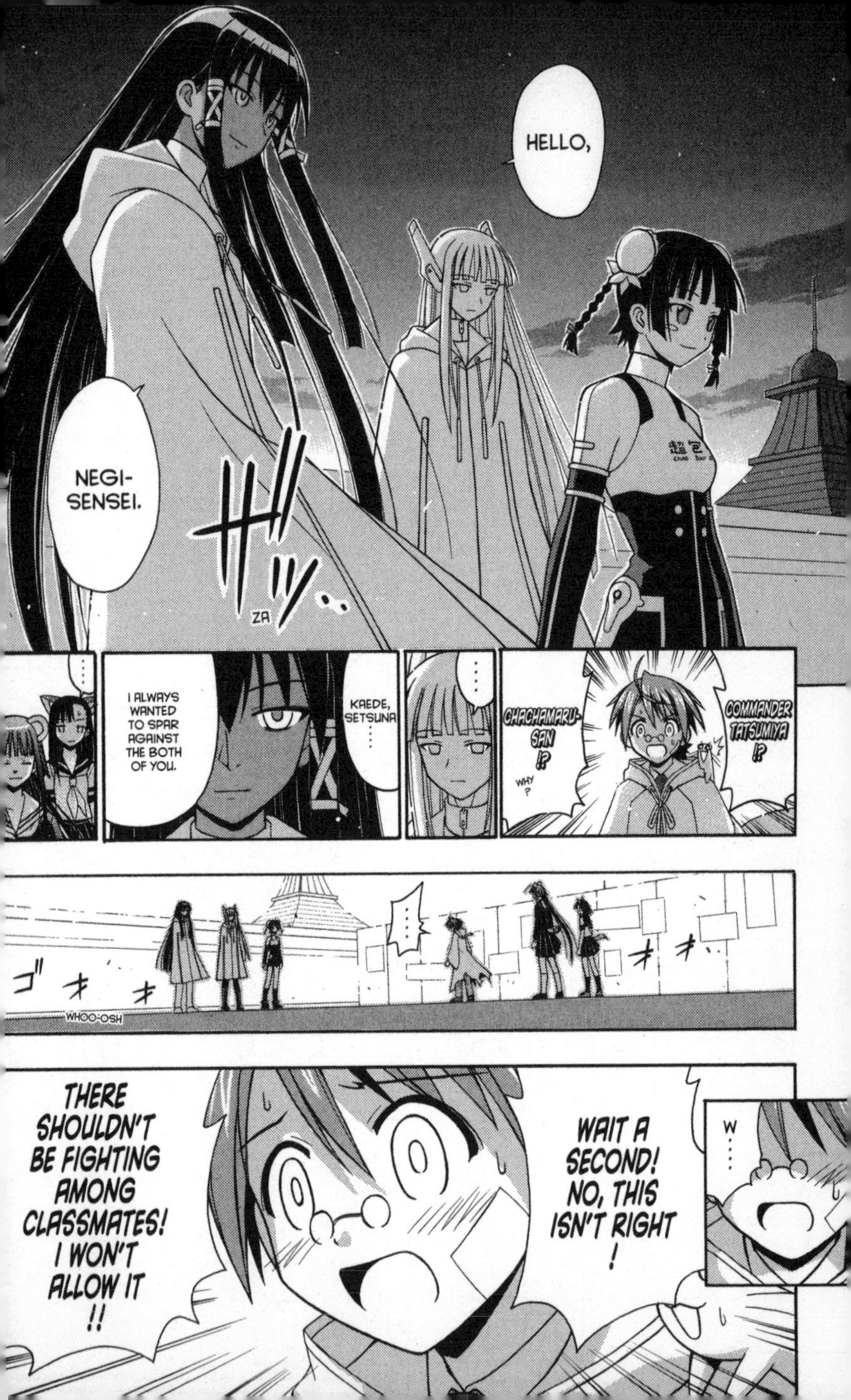
HELLO,
NEGI-SENSEI.
ZA
COMMANDER TATSUMIYA !?
CHACHAMARU-SAN !?
WHY ?
. . . .
KAEDE, SETSUNA . . . .
I ALWAYS WANTED TO SPAR AGAINST THE BOTH OF YOU.
. . . .
. . . .
WHOO-OSH
W . . . .
WAIT A SECOND! NO, THIS ISN'T RIGHT !
THERE SHOULDN'T BE FIGHTING AMONG CLASSMATES! I WON'T ALLOW IT !!

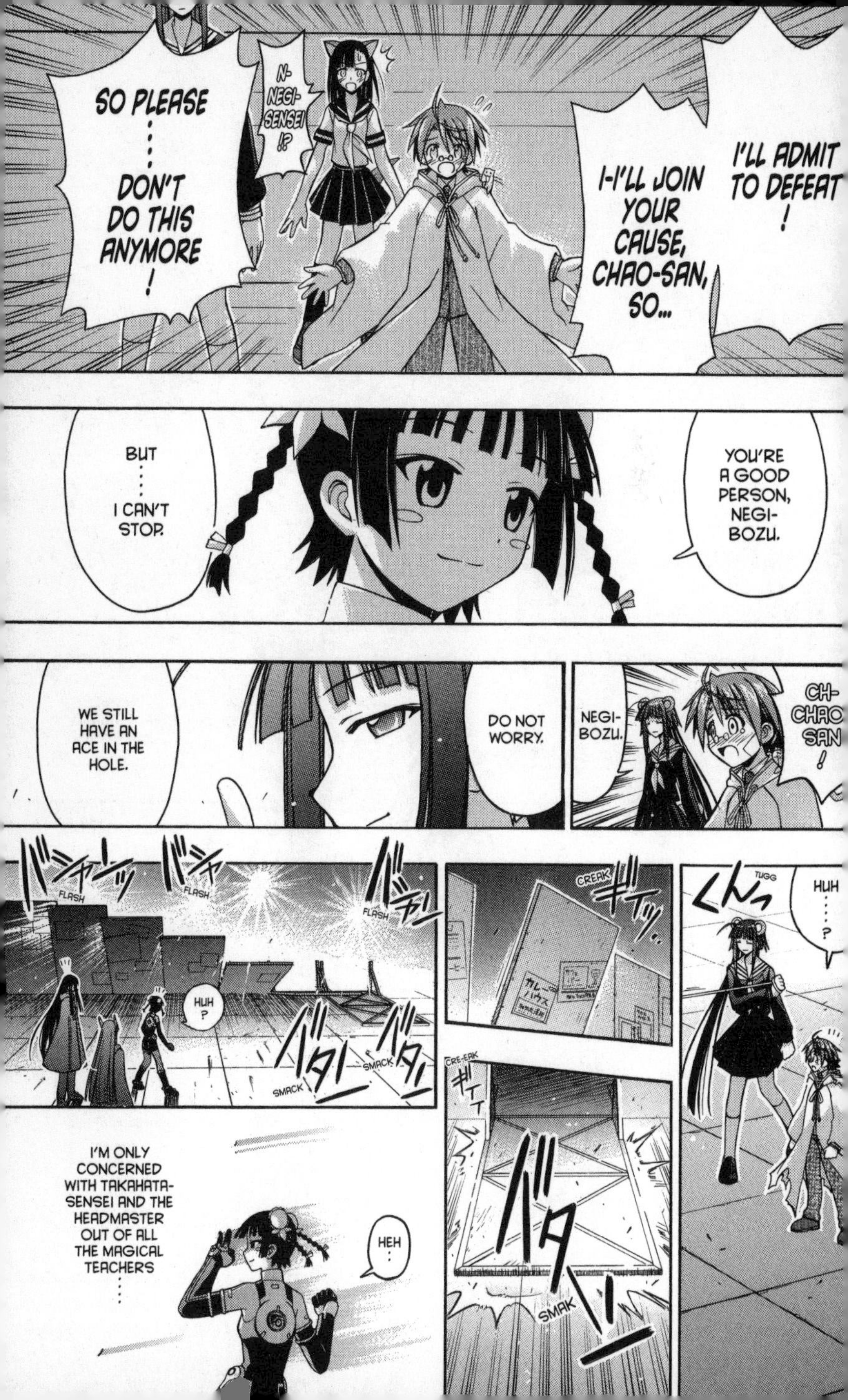
I'LL ADMIT TO DEFEAT!
I-I'LL JOIN YOUR CAUSE, CHAO-SAN, SO...
N-NEGI-SENSEI!?
SO PLEASE... DON'T DO THIS ANYMORE!
YOU'RE A GOOD PERSON, NEGI-BOZU.
BUT... I CAN'T STOP.
CH-CHAO SAN!
NEGI-BOZU.
DO NOT WORRY.
WE STILL HAVE AN ACE IN THE HOLE.
TUGG
HUH...?
CREAK
CRE-EAK
SMAK
FLASH
FLASH
FLASH
HUH?
SMACK
SMACK
HEH...
I'M ONLY CONCERNED WITH TAKAHATA-SENSEI AND THE HEADMASTER OUT OF ALL THE MAGICAL TEACHERS...

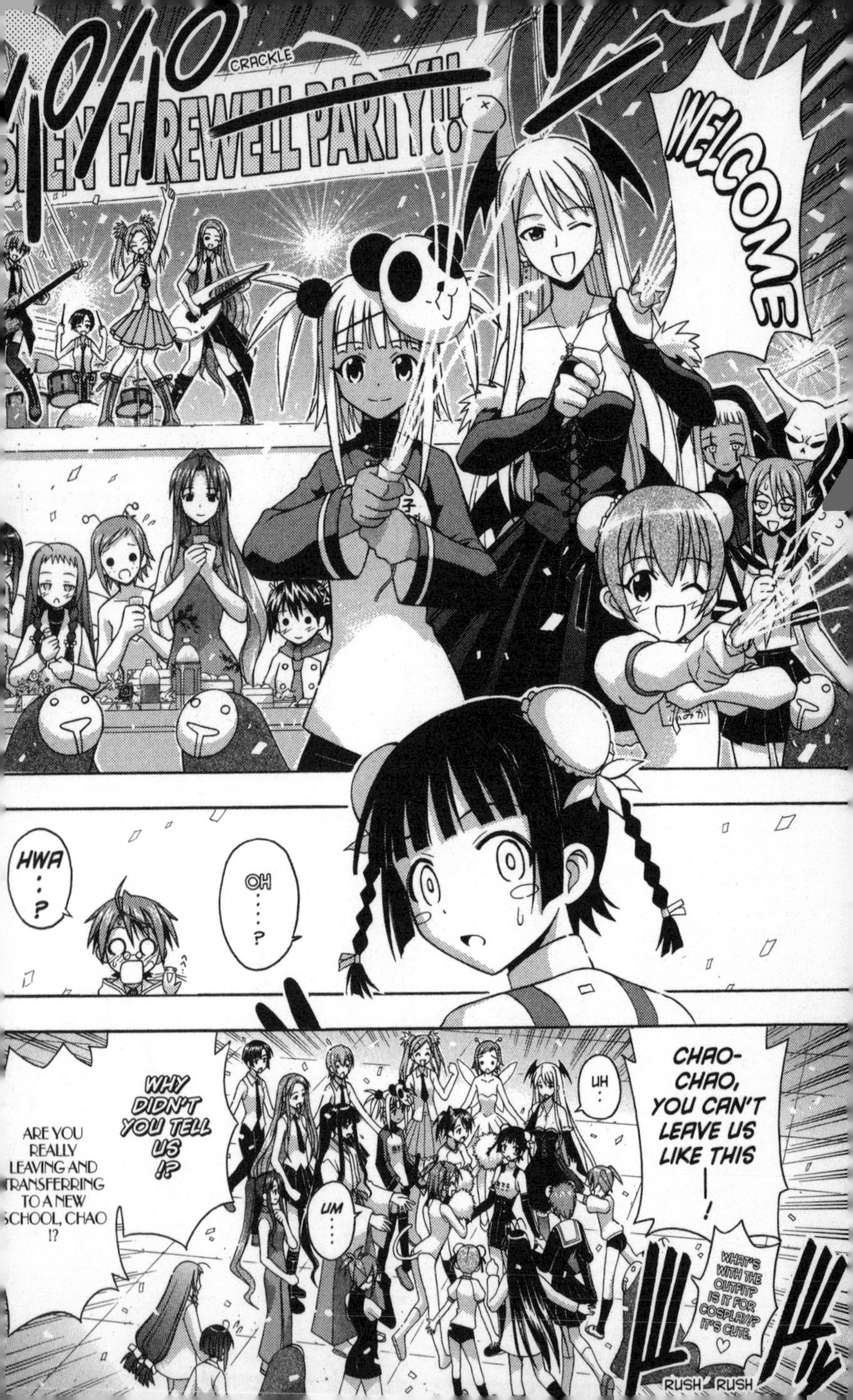
WELCOME
CRACKLE
SIEN FAREWELL PARTY!!
OH.....?
HWA...?
CHAO-CHAO, YOU CAN'T LEAVE US LIKE THIS—!
WHAT'S WITH THE OUTFIT? IS IT FOR COSPLAY? IT'S CUTE. ♡
RUSH RUSH
UH...
WHY DIDN'T YOU TELL US!?
UM.....
ARE YOU REALLY LEAVING AND TRANSFERRING TO A NEW SCHOOL, CHAO!?

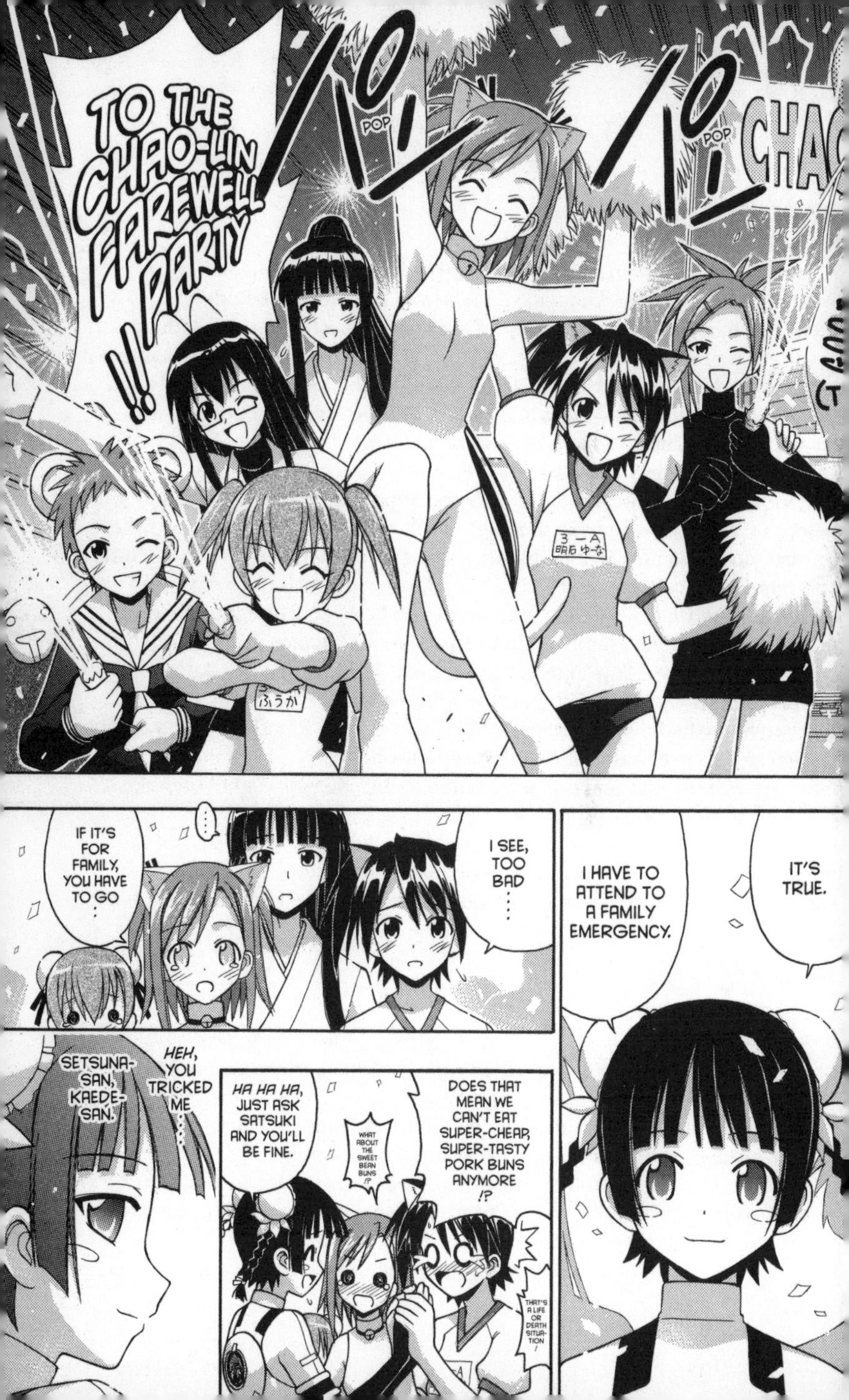
POP
POP
TO THE CHAO-LIN FAREWELL PARTY!!
3ーA 明石ゆーな
ふうか
IT'S TRUE.
I HAVE TO ATTEND TO A FAMILY EMERGENCY.
I SEE, TOO BAD...
...
IF IT'S FOR FAMILY, YOU HAVE TO GO...
DOES THAT MEAN WE CAN'T EAT SUPER-CHEAP, SUPER-TASTY PORK BUNS ANYMORE!?
WHAT ABOUT THE SWEET BEAN BUNS!?
HA HA HA, JUST ASK SATSUKI AND YOU'LL BE FINE.
THAT'S A LIFE OR DEATH SITUATION!
HEH, YOU TRICKED ME...
SETSUNA-SAN, KAEDE-SAN.

LEXICON MAGICUM NEGIMARUM

Negima! 134th Period

■「𑀪」

BHAI

In Genjyou's (Xuanzang, AD 602–664) translation of *Yakushi Rurikounyorai Hongan Kudokukyou* (Sutra of the Medicine Buddha), there is a passage that reads "East of the world—past countless Buddha-lands—more numerous than the grains of sand in ten Ganges Rivers, there exists a world called Pure Lapiz Lazuli. The Buddha of that world is called the Medicine Buddha...When the World-Honored Medicine Buddha was treading the Bodhisattva path, he solemnly made Twelve Great Vows to grant sentient beings whatever they desired...'Seventh Great Vow. I vow that in a future life, when I have attained Supreme Enlightenment, sentient beings afflicted with various illnesses—with no one to help them—nowhere to turn, no physicians, no medicine, no family, no home, who are destitute and miserable, will, as soon as my name passes through their ears, be relieved of all their illnesses. With mind and body peaceful and content, they will enjoy home, family, and property in abundance and eventually realize Unsurpassed Supreme Enlightenment.'" The text says Yakushi Nyorai (Bhaisajyaguru) is the Buddha who made the Great Vow saying that anyone who hears his name will be cured of all illnesses. 𑀪 is a *shuji*, or seed syllable, of Yakushi Nyorai and takes the place of the Buddha's name. Hence, by uttering this seed syllable, the speaker is able to make a connection to the Yakushi Nyorai.

In the story, Setsuna uttered the seed syllable 𑀪 to rid herself of the effects of Chao's electrical attack. As you can, her knees are shaking and she's unable to stand in one panel, but in the next panel, her agility is back.

■稲交尾籠

INATSURUBI NO KATAMA

This is one of Setsuna's anti-demon spells. By throwing a *shuriken* or *vajra* around the target, a spiritual zone is formed, trapping it inside. *Katama* refers to "an extremely tightly woven basket," and *inatsurubi* means "lightning." Hence, this is a high-level technique in which the target is surrounded, then stunned, with lightning strikes.

In the story, this technique was performed using the *tanto*, Setsuna's artifact. The artifact's ability to split into multiple blades midair and remain under control is ideal for casting this spell. Now whether or not the magical properties of the artifact conflicts with Setsuna's ki-based abilities remains unknown.

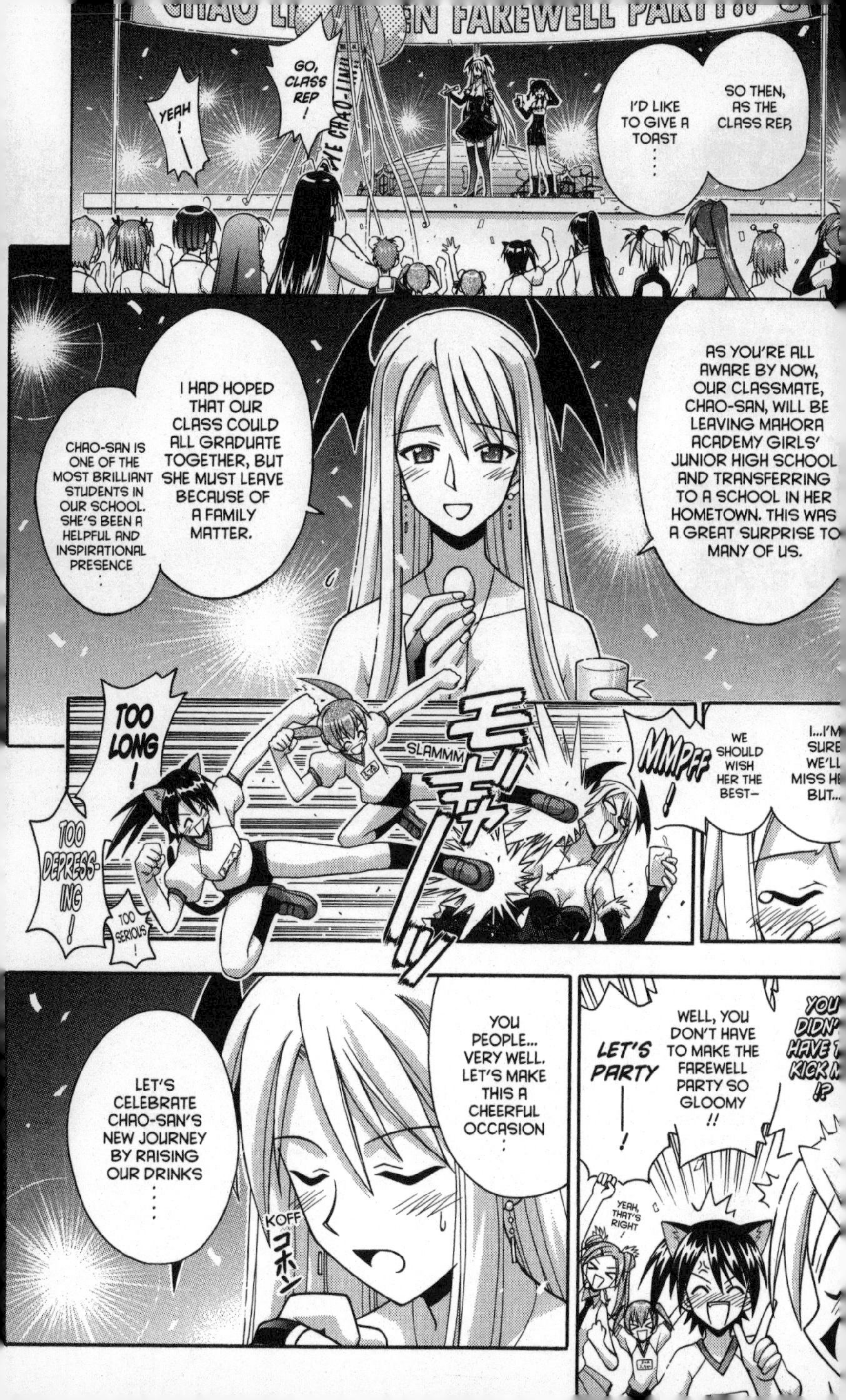
FAREWELL PARTY!!
SO THEN, AS THE CLASS REP,
I'D LIKE TO GIVE A TOAST ....
GO, CLASS REP!
YEAH!
AS YOU'RE ALL AWARE BY NOW, OUR CLASSMATE, CHAO-SAN, WILL BE LEAVING MAHORA ACADEMY GIRLS' JUNIOR HIGH SCHOOL AND TRANSFERRING TO A SCHOOL IN HER HOMETOWN. THIS WAS A GREAT SURPRISE TO MANY OF US.
I HAD HOPED THAT OUR CLASS COULD ALL GRADUATE TOGETHER, BUT SHE MUST LEAVE BECAUSE OF A FAMILY MATTER.
CHAO-SAN IS ONE OF THE MOST BRILLIANT STUDENTS IN OUR SCHOOL. SHE'S BEEN A HELPFUL AND INSPIRATIONAL PRESENCE :
I...I'M SURE WE'LL MISS HE BUT...
WE SHOULD WISH HER THE BEST—
MMPFF!
SLAMMM
TOO LONG!
TOO DEPRESSING!
TOO SERIOUS!
WELL, YOU DON'T HAVE TO MAKE THE FAREWELL PARTY SO GLOOMY !!
LET'S PARTY —!
YEAH, THAT'S RIGHT!
YOU PEOPLE... VERY WELL. LET'S MAKE THIS A CHEERFUL OCCASION :
LET'S CELEBRATE CHAO-SAN'S NEW JOURNEY BY RAISING OUR DRINKS ....
KOFF

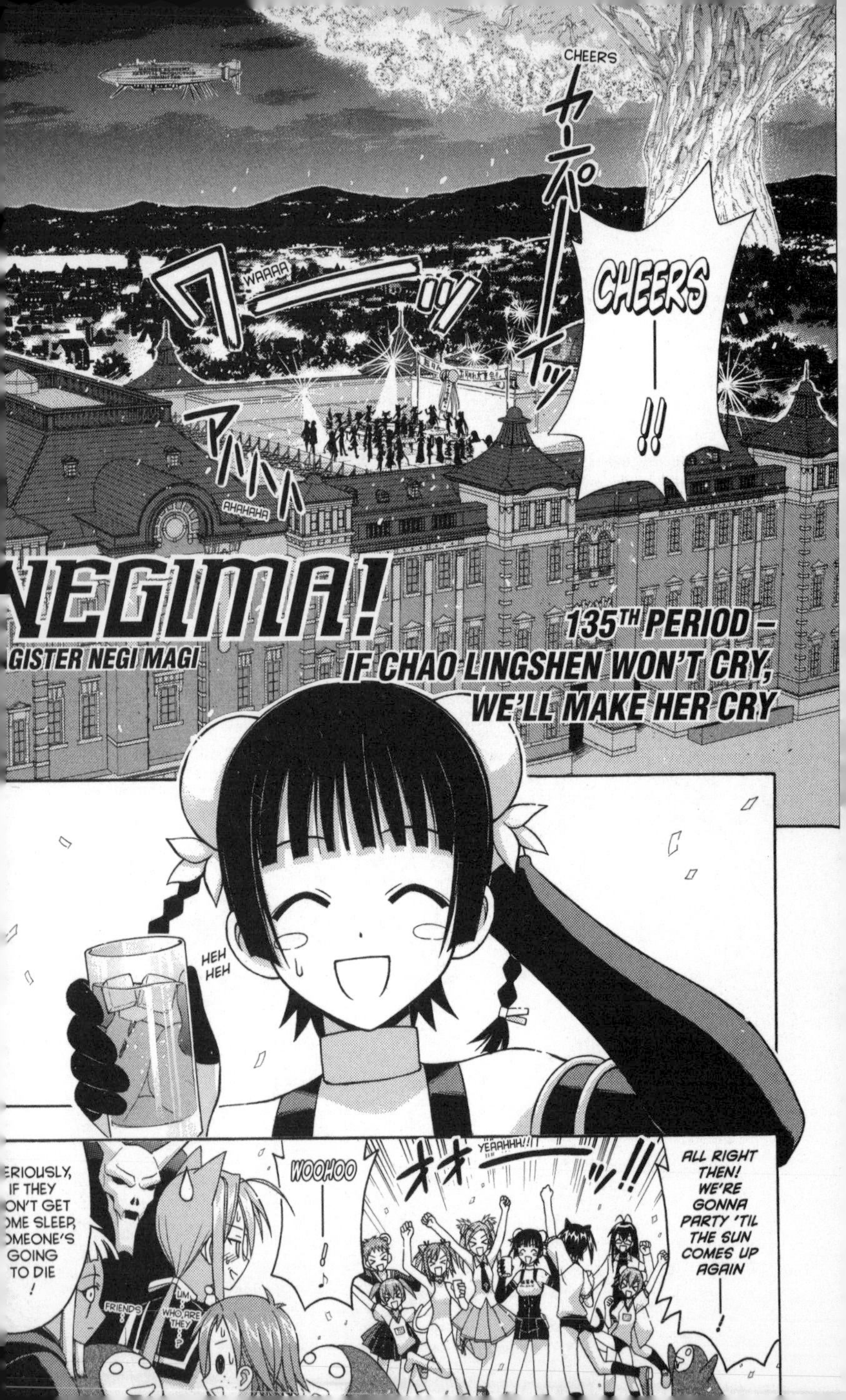
CHEERS
CHEERS —— !!
WAAAA
AHAHAHA
NEGIMA!
GISTER NEGI MAGI
135TH PERIOD – IF CHAO LINGSHEN WON'T CRY, WE'LL MAKE HER CRY
HEH HEH
ALL RIGHT THEN! WE'RE GONNA PARTY 'TIL THE SUN COMES UP AGAIN —— !
YEAAHHH!!
WOOHOO —— !
UM, WHO ARE THEY?
FRIENDS
ERIOUSLY, IF THEY ON'T GET OME SLEEP, OMEONE'S GOING TO DIE!

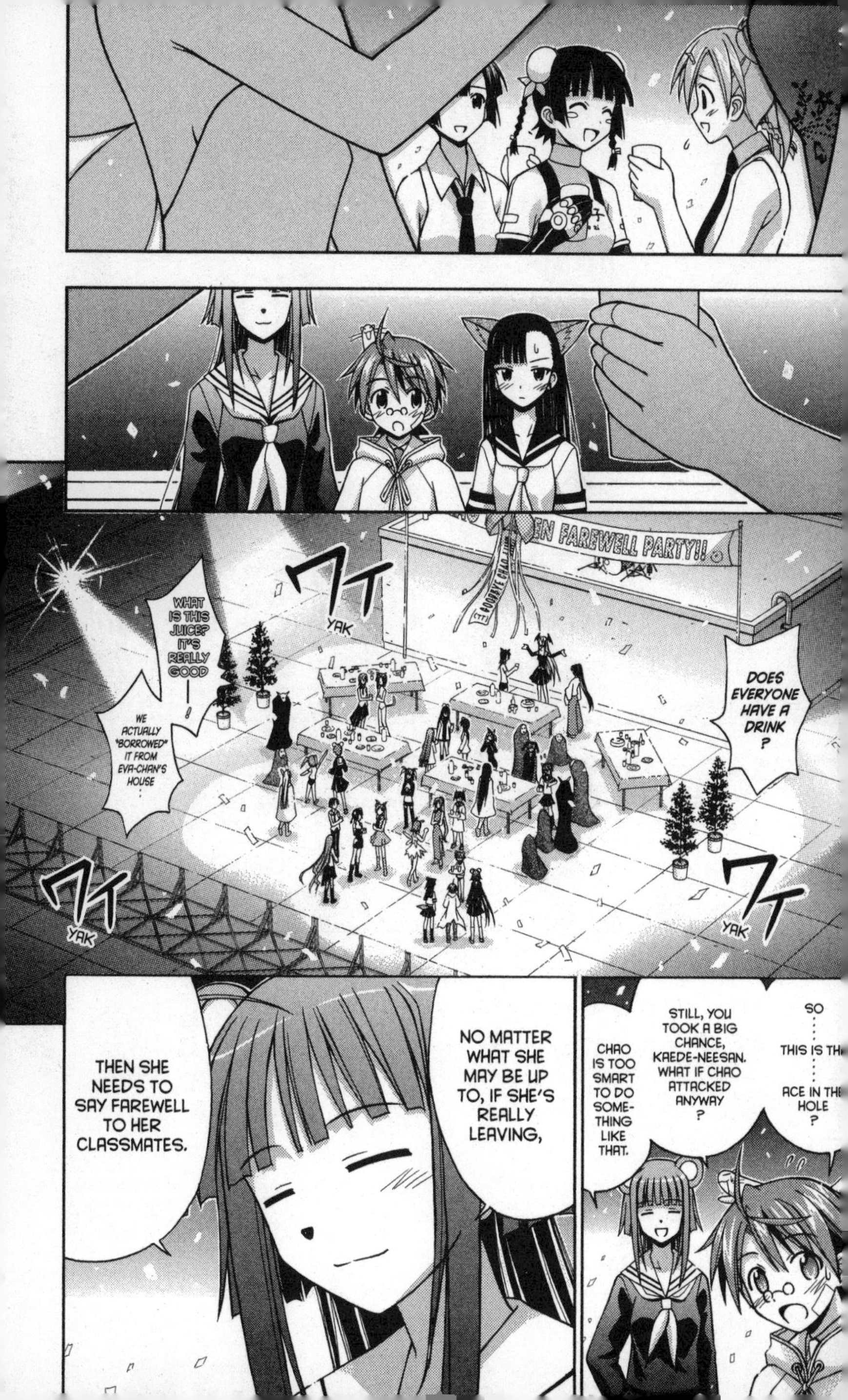
DOES EVERYONE HAVE A DRINK?
EN FAREWELL PARTY!!
YAK
YAK
WHAT IS THIS JUICE? IT'S REALLY GOOD—!
WE ACTUALLY "BORROWED" IT FROM EVA-CHAN'S HOUSE...
YAK
SO...... THIS IS TH...... ACE IN THE HOLE?
STILL, YOU TOOK A BIG CHANCE, KAEDE-NEESAN. WHAT IF CHAO ATTACKED ANYWAY?
CHAO IS TOO SMART TO DO SOME-THING LIKE THAT.
NO MATTER WHAT SHE MAY BE UP TO, IF SHE'S REALLY LEAVING,
THEN SHE NEEDS TO SAY FAREWELL TO HER CLASSMATES.

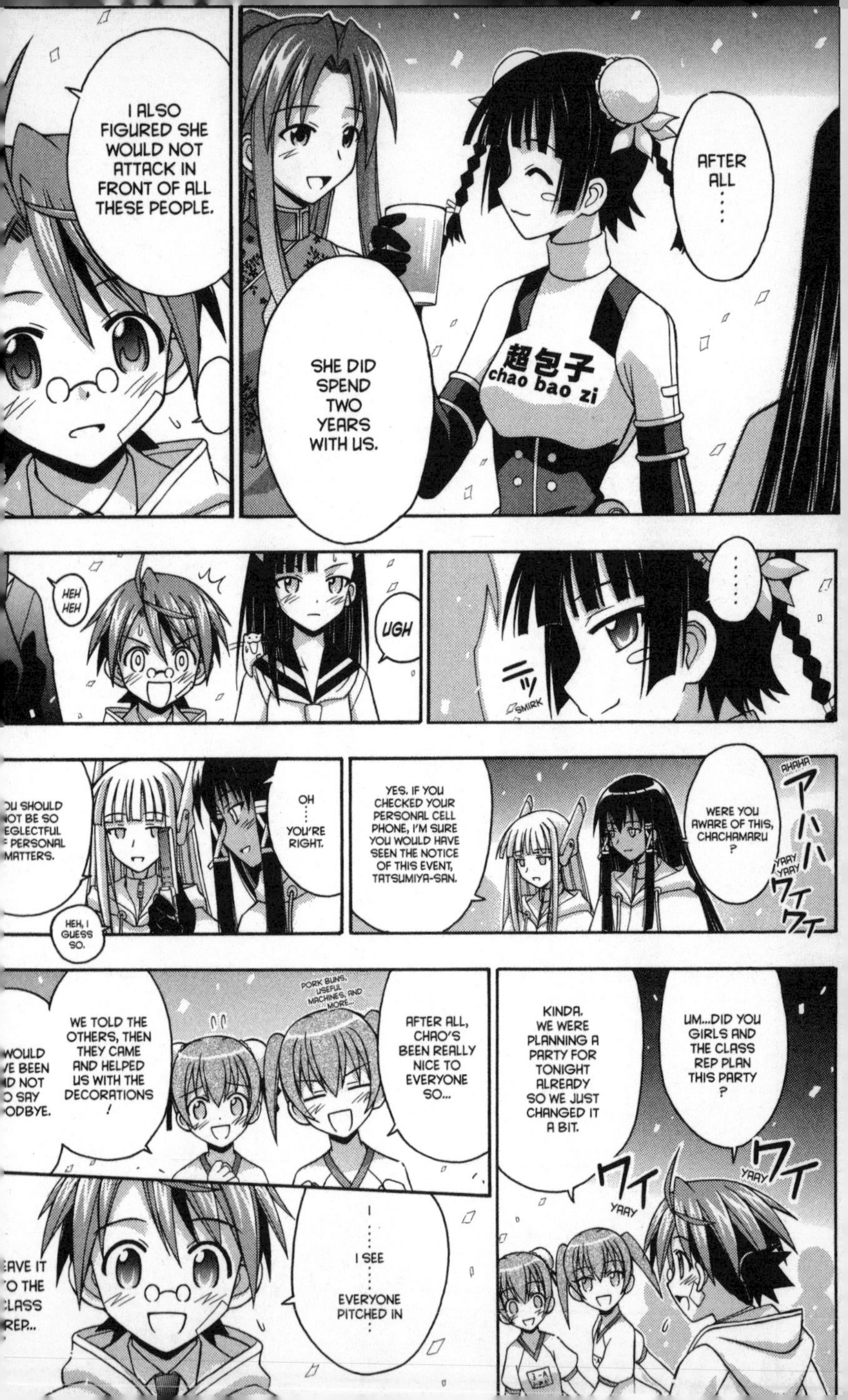
AFTER ALL......
SHE DID SPEND TWO YEARS WITH US.
超包子 chao bao zi
I ALSO FIGURED SHE WOULD NOT ATTACK IN FRONT OF ALL THESE PEOPLE.
......
ニッ SMIRK
UGH
HEH HEH
AHAHA アハハ
WERE YOU AWARE OF THIS, CHACHAMARU?
YAAY YAAY ワイワイ
YES. IF YOU CHECKED YOUR PERSONAL CELL PHONE, I'M SURE YOU WOULD HAVE SEEN THE NOTICE OF THIS EVENT, TATSUMIYA-SAN.
OH... YOU'RE RIGHT.
OU SHOULD OT BE SO EGLECTFUL F PERSONAL MATTERS.
HEH, I GUESS SO.
UM...DID YOU GIRLS AND THE CLASS REP PLAN THIS PARTY?
KINDA. WE WERE PLANNING A PARTY FOR TONIGHT ALREADY SO WE JUST CHANGED IT A BIT.
ワイ YAAY
ワイ YAAY
AFTER ALL, CHAO'S BEEN REALLY NICE TO EVERYONE SO...
PORK BUNS, USEFUL MACHINES, AND MORE...
WE TOLD THE OTHERS, THEN THEY CAME AND HELPED US WITH THE DECORATIONS!
WOULD VE BEEN D NOT O SAY ODBYE.
I...... I SEE...... EVERYONE PITCHED IN......
EAVE IT TO THE CLASS REP...

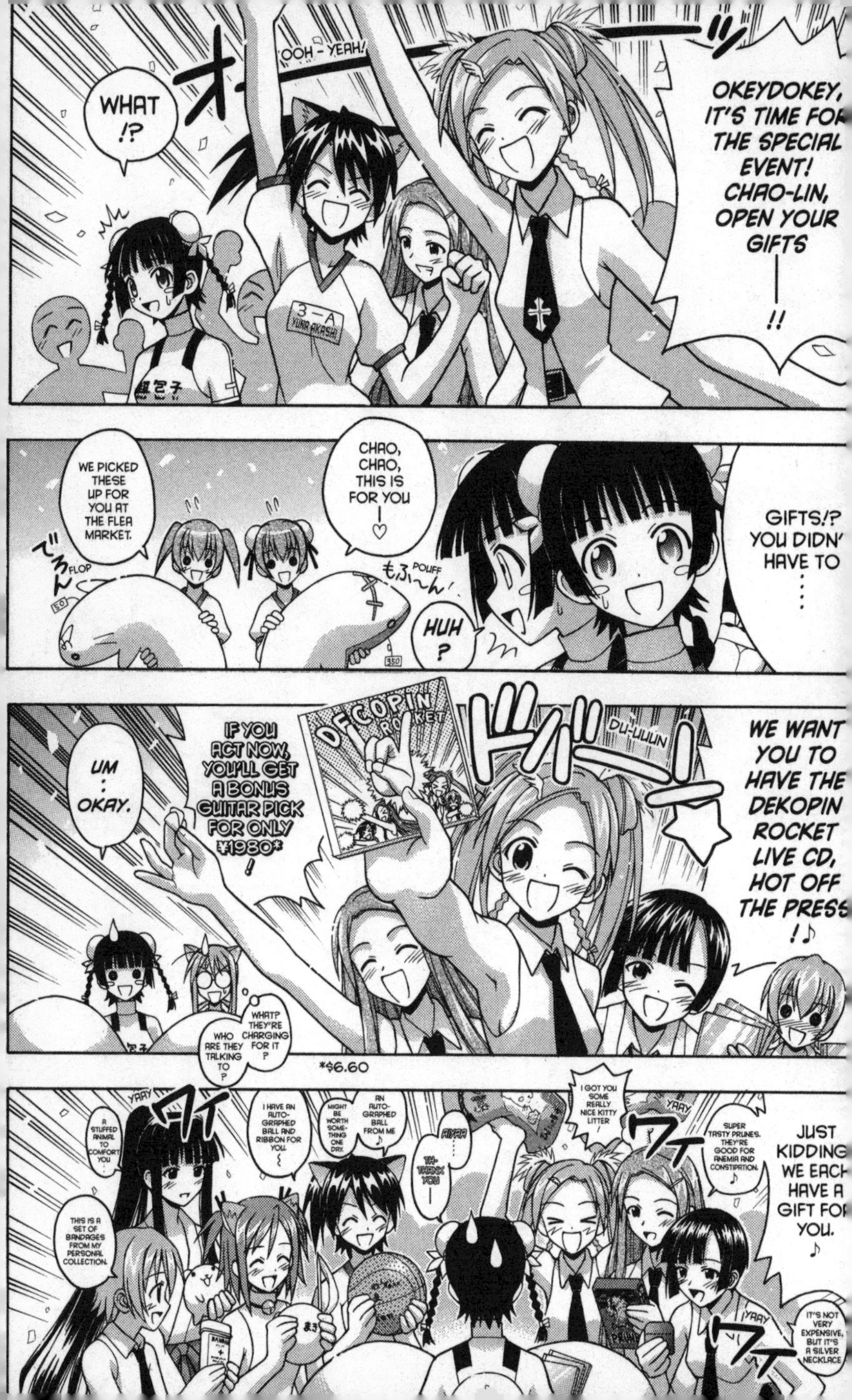
OKEYDOKEY, IT'S TIME FOR THE SPECIAL EVENT! CHAO-LIN, OPEN YOUR GIFTS—!!
OOH - YEAH!
WHAT !?
GIFTS!? YOU DIDN'T HAVE TO ....
HUH ?
CHAO, CHAO, THIS IS FOR YOU ♡
もふ~ん POUFF
WE PICKED THESE UP FOR YOU AT THE FLEA MARKET.
でろん FLOP
50
350
WE WANT YOU TO HAVE THE DEKOPIN ROCKET LIVE CD, HOT OFF THE PRESS !♪
DU-UUUN
DECOPIN ROCKET
IF YOU ACT NOW, YOU'LL GET A BONUS GUITAR PICK FOR ONLY ¥1980* !
UM : OKAY.
WHAT? THEY'RE CHARGING FOR IT ?
WHO ARE THEY TALKING TO ?
*$6.60
JUST KIDDING. WE EACH HAVE A GIFT FOR YOU. ♪
IT'S NOT VERY EXPENSIVE, BUT IT'S A SILVER NECKLACE
YAAY
SUPER TASTY PRUNES. THEY'RE GOOD FOR ANEMIA AND CONSTIPATION. ♪
YAAY
I GOT YOU SOME REALLY NICE KITTY LITTER !
AIYAA
TH-THANK YOU !
AN AUTO-GRAPHED BALL FROM ME
MIGHT BE WORTH SOME-THING ONE DAY.
I HAVE AN AUTO-GRAPHED BALL AND RIBBON FOR YOU. ~
A STUFFED ANIMAL TO COMFORT YOU.
YAAY
THIS IS A SET OF BANDAGES FROM MY PERSONAL COLLECTION.

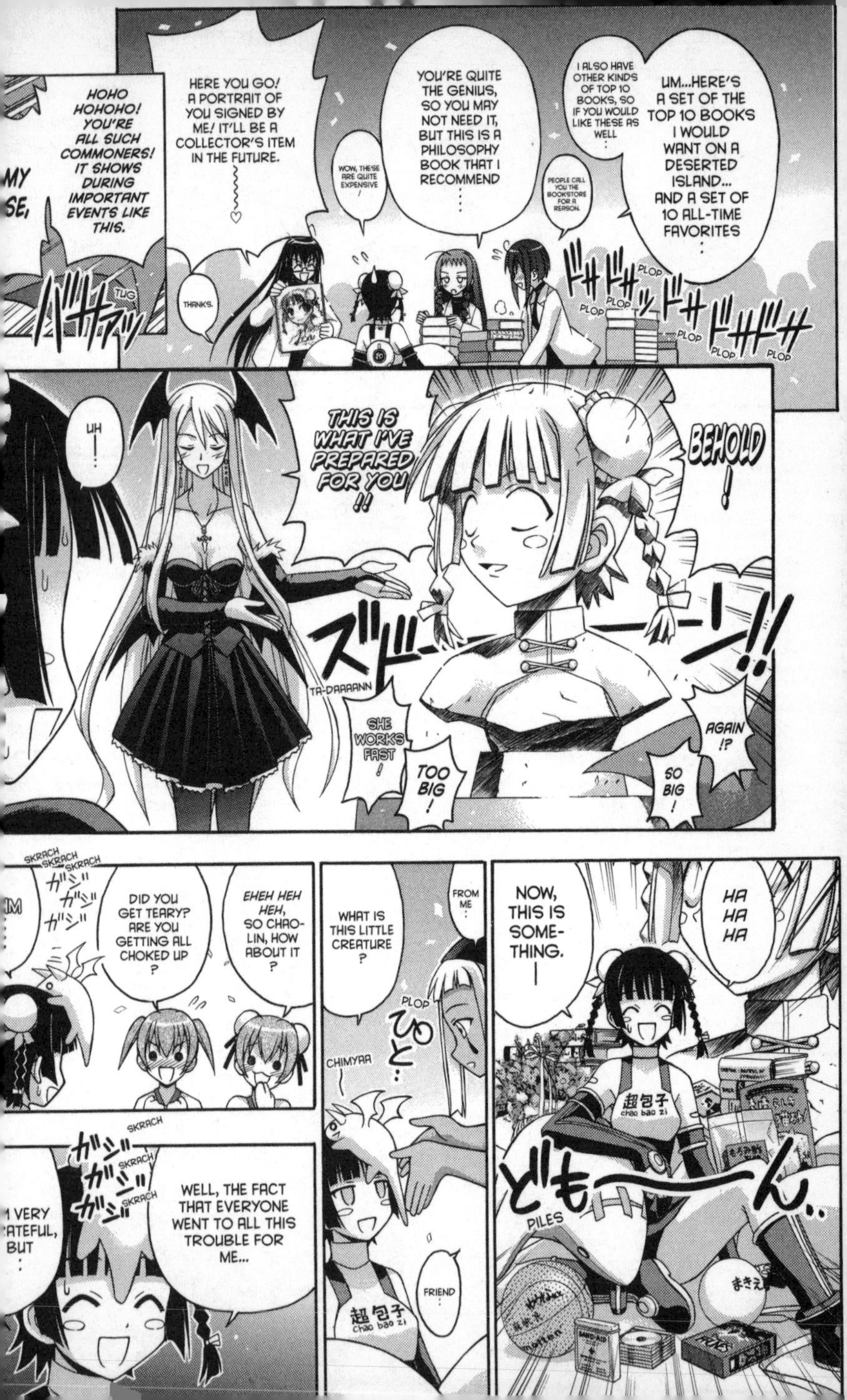
UM...HERE'S A SET OF THE TOP 10 BOOKS I WOULD WANT ON A DESERTED ISLAND... AND A SET OF 10 ALL-TIME FAVORITES :
I ALSO HAVE OTHER KINDS OF TOP 10 BOOKS, SO IF YOU WOULD LIKE THESE AS WELL :
PLOP
PLOP
PLOP
PLOP
PLOP
PLOP
PEOPLE CALL YOU THE BOOKSTORE FOR A REASON.
YOU'RE QUITE THE GENIUS, SO YOU MAY NOT NEED IT, BUT THIS IS A PHILOSOPHY BOOK THAT I RECOMMEND ......
WOW, THESE ARE QUITE EXPENSIVE !
HERE YOU GO! A PORTRAIT OF YOU SIGNED BY ME! IT'LL BE A COLLECTOR'S ITEM IN THE FUTURE. ♡
THANKS.
HOHO HOHOHO! YOU'RE ALL SUCH COMMONERS! IT SHOWS DURING IMPORTANT EVENTS LIKE THIS.
MY
SE,
TUG
BEHOLD !
THIS IS WHAT I'VE PREPARED FOR YOU !!
UH —!
ズドーーーン!!
TA-DAAAANN
AGAIN !?
SO BIG !
SHE WORKS FAST !
TOO BIG !
HA HA HA
NOW, THIS IS SOME-THING. —
超包子
chao bao zi
どもーーーん..
PILES
まきえ
FROM ME :
WHAT IS THIS LITTLE CREATURE ?
PLOP
ひょと..
CHIMYAA —
FRIEND :
超包子
Chao bao zi
EHEH HEH HEH, SO CHAO-LIN, HOW ABOUT IT ?
DID YOU GET TEARY? ARE YOU GETTING ALL CHOKED UP ?
SKRACH
SKRACH
SKRACH
ガジガジガジ
SKRACH
SKRACH
SKRACH
ガジガジガジ
WELL, THE FACT THAT EVERYONE WENT TO ALL THIS TROUBLE FOR ME...
VERY
ATEFUL, BUT :

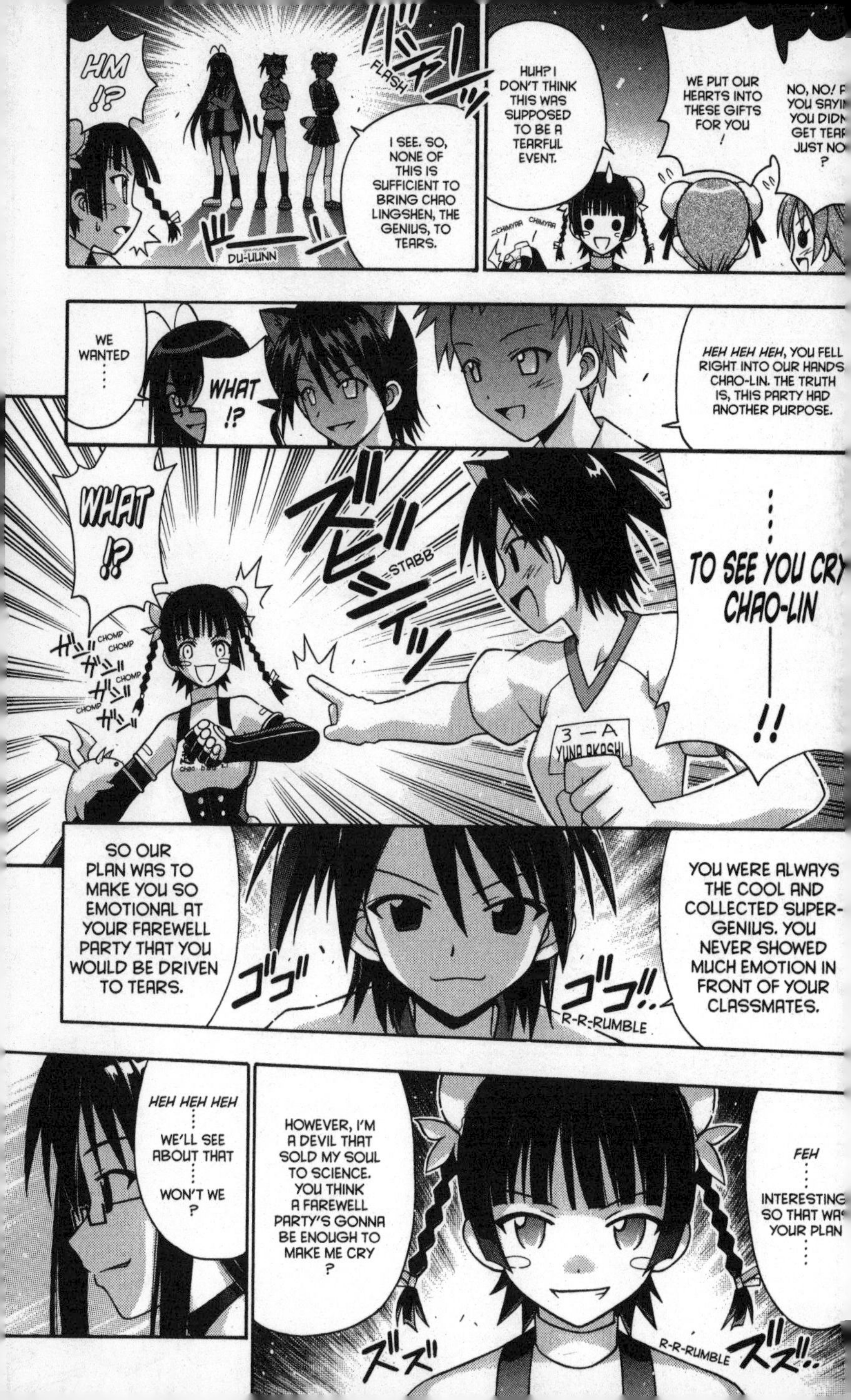
NO, NO! YOU SAYIN YOU DIDN GET TEAR JUST NO ?
WE PUT OUR HEARTS INTO THESE GIFTS FOR YOU !
CHIMYAA CHIMYAA
HUH? I DON'T THINK THIS WAS SUPPOSED TO BE A TEARFUL EVENT.
FLASH
I SEE. SO, NONE OF THIS IS SUFFICIENT TO BRING CHAO LINGSHEN, THE GENIUS, TO TEARS.
HM !?
DU-UUNN
HEH HEH HEH, YOU FELL RIGHT INTO OUR HANDS CHAO-LIN. THE TRUTH IS, THIS PARTY HAD ANOTHER PURPOSE.
WHAT !?
WE WANTED ....
.... TO SEE YOU CRY CHAO-LIN —— !!
STABB
3-A YUNA AKASHI
WHAT !?
CHOMP CHOMP CHOMP CHOMP
YOU WERE ALWAYS THE COOL AND COLLECTED SUPER-GENIUS. YOU NEVER SHOWED MUCH EMOTION IN FRONT OF YOUR CLASSMATES.
R-R-RUMBLE
SO OUR PLAN WAS TO MAKE YOU SO EMOTIONAL AT YOUR FAREWELL PARTY THAT YOU WOULD BE DRIVEN TO TEARS.
FEH .... INTERESTING SO THAT WA YOUR PLAN ....
R-R-RUMBLE
HOWEVER, I'M A DEVIL THAT SOLD MY SOUL TO SCIENCE. YOU THINK A FAREWELL PARTY'S GONNA BE ENOUGH TO MAKE ME CRY ?
HEH HEH HEH .... WE'LL SEE ABOUT THAT .... WON'T WE ?

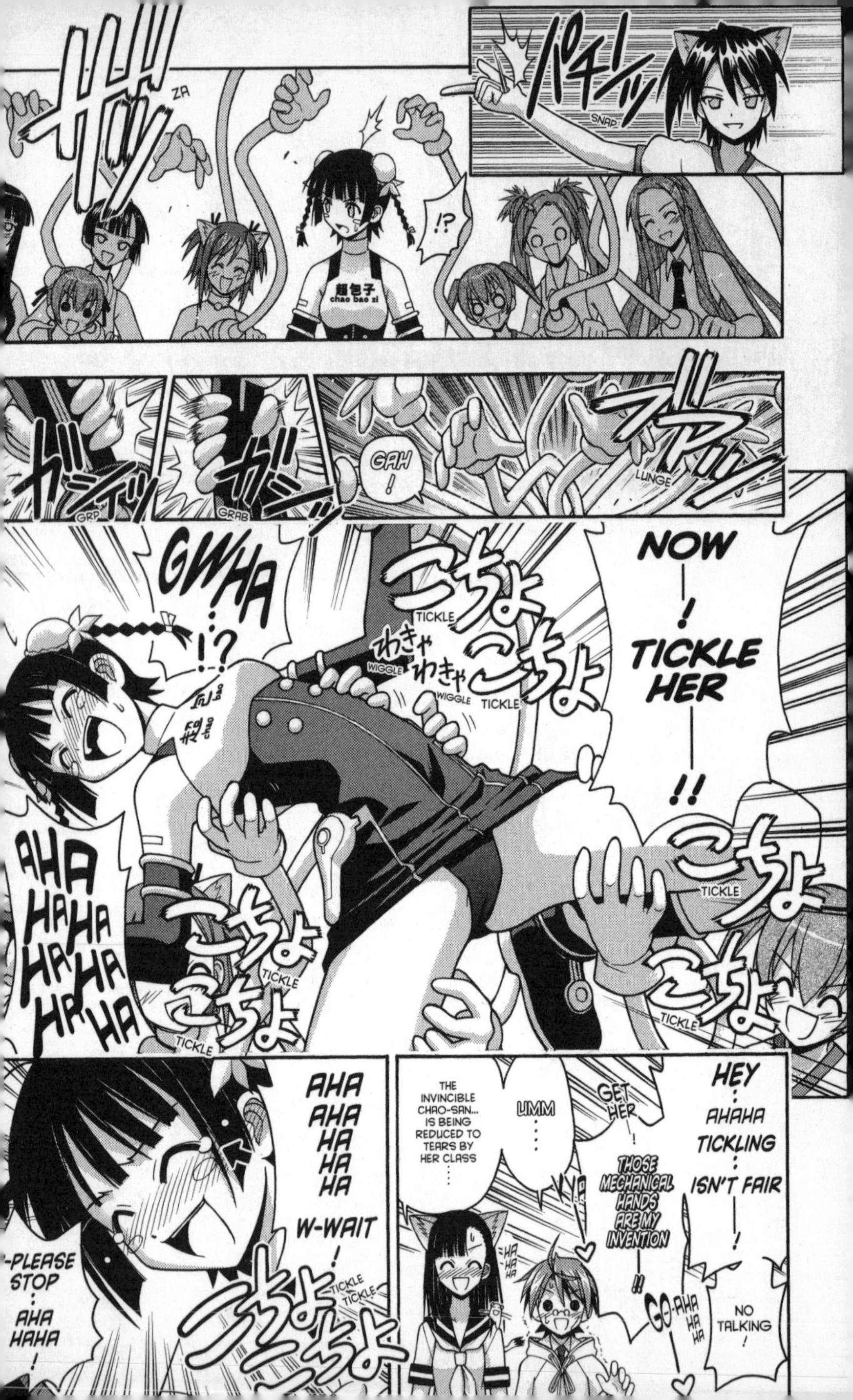

SNAP
ZA
!?
超包子 chao bao zi
LUNGE
GAH!
GRAB
GRP
NOW—! TICKLE HER—!!
GWHA...!?
TICKLE
WIGGLE
WIGGLE
TICKLE
超 chao 包 bao
TICKLE
TICKLE
AHA HA HA HA HA HA HA HA HA
TICKLE
TICKLE
HEY... AHAHA TICKLING... ISN'T FAIR—!
NO TALKING!
GET HER!
THOSE MECHANICAL HANDS ARE MY INVENTION!!
GO-AHA HA HA
KYA
UMM...
THE INVINCIBLE CHAO-SAN... IS BEING REDUCED TO TEARS BY HER CLASS...
HA HA HA
AHA AHA HA HA HA
W-WAIT!
TICKLE TICKLE
-PLEASE STOP... AHA HAHA!

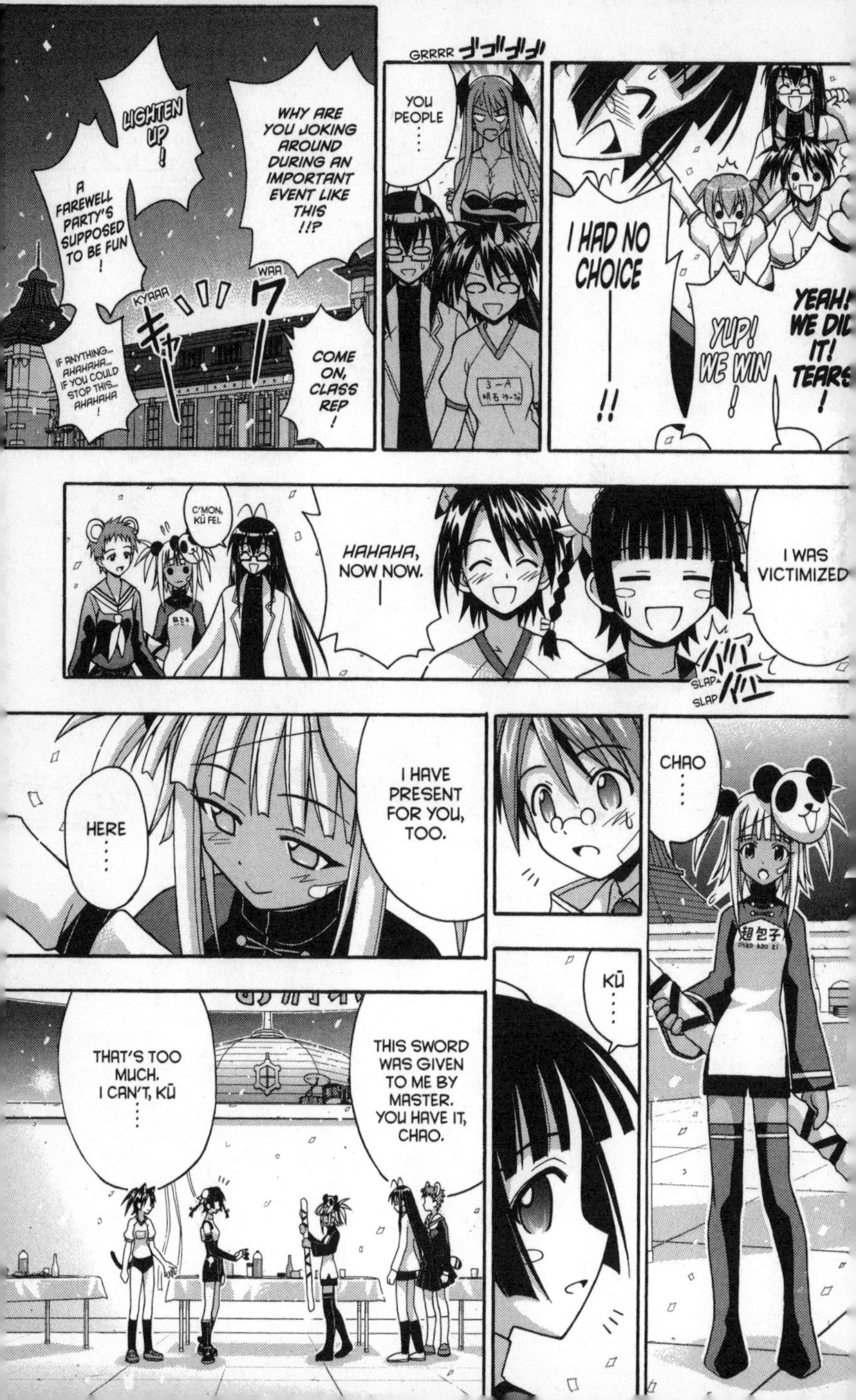
YEAH! WE DID IT! TEARS!
YUP! WE WIN!
I HAD NO CHOICE—!!
GRRRR
YOU PEOPLE...
WHY ARE YOU JOKING AROUND DURING AN IMPORTANT EVENT LIKE THIS!!?
LIGHTEN UP!
A FAREWELL PARTY'S SUPPOSED TO BE FUN!
WAA
KYAAA
COME ON, CLASS REP!
IF ANYTHING... AHAHAHA... IF YOU COULD STOP THIS... AHAHAHA!
I WAS VICTIMIZED
SLAP SLAP
HAHAHA, NOW NOW.
C'MON, KŪ FEI.
CHAO...
I HAVE PRESENT FOR YOU, TOO.
HERE...
KŪ...
THIS SWORD WAS GIVEN TO ME BY MASTER. YOU HAVE IT, CHAO.
THAT'S TOO MUCH. I CAN'T, KŪ...

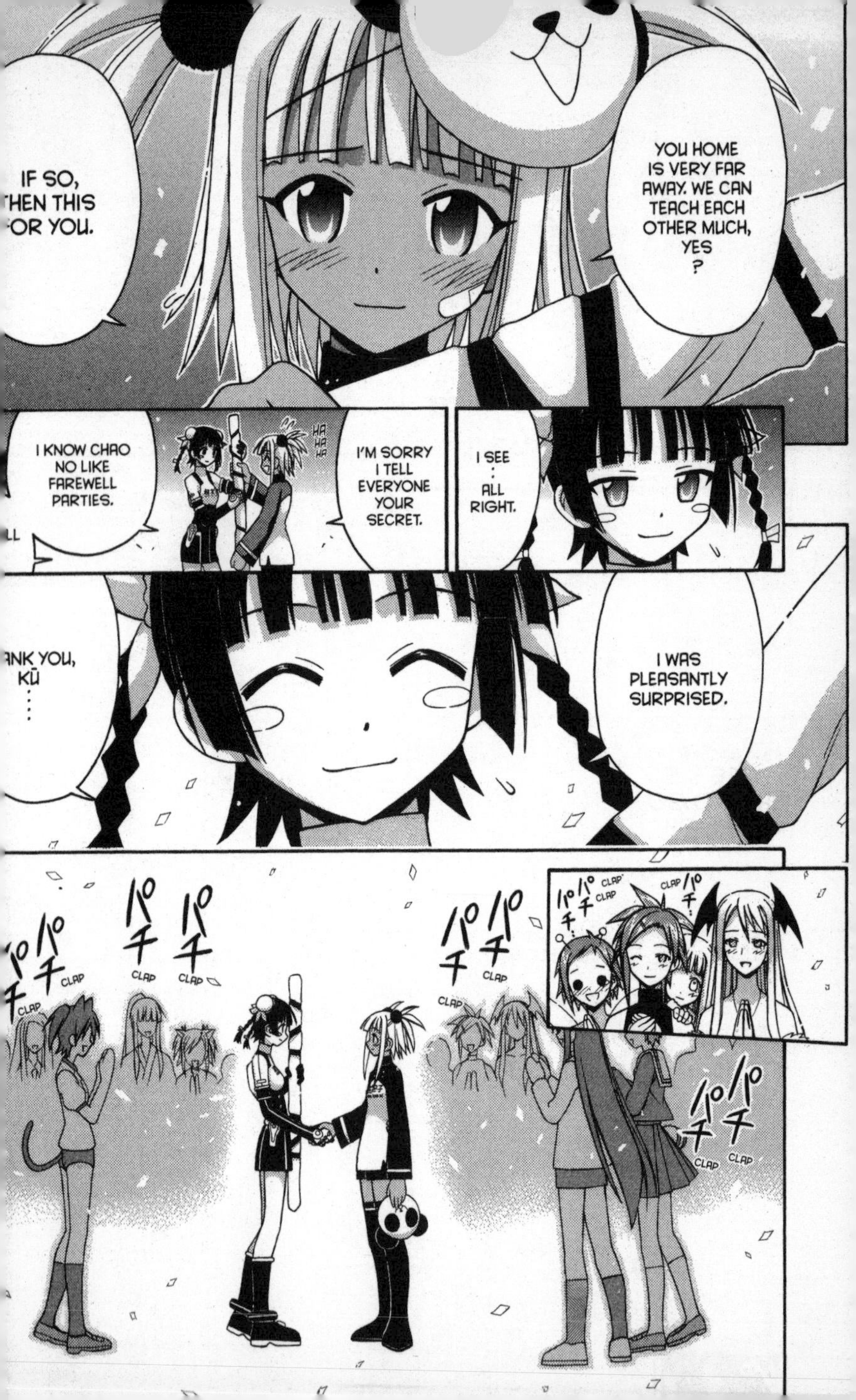

YOU HOME IS VERY FAR AWAY. WE CAN TEACH EACH OTHER MUCH, YES ?
IF SO, HEN THIS OR YOU.
I SEE : ALL RIGHT.
I'M SORRY I TELL EVERYONE YOUR SECRET.
HA HA HA
I KNOW CHAO NO LIKE FAREWELL PARTIES.
I WAS PLEASANTLY SURPRISED.
ANK YOU, KŪ ....
パチ CLAP
パチ CLAP
パチパチ CLAP CLAP
パチパチ CLAP CLAP
パチ CLAP
パチ CLAP
パチパチ CLAP
パチパチ CLAP CLAP

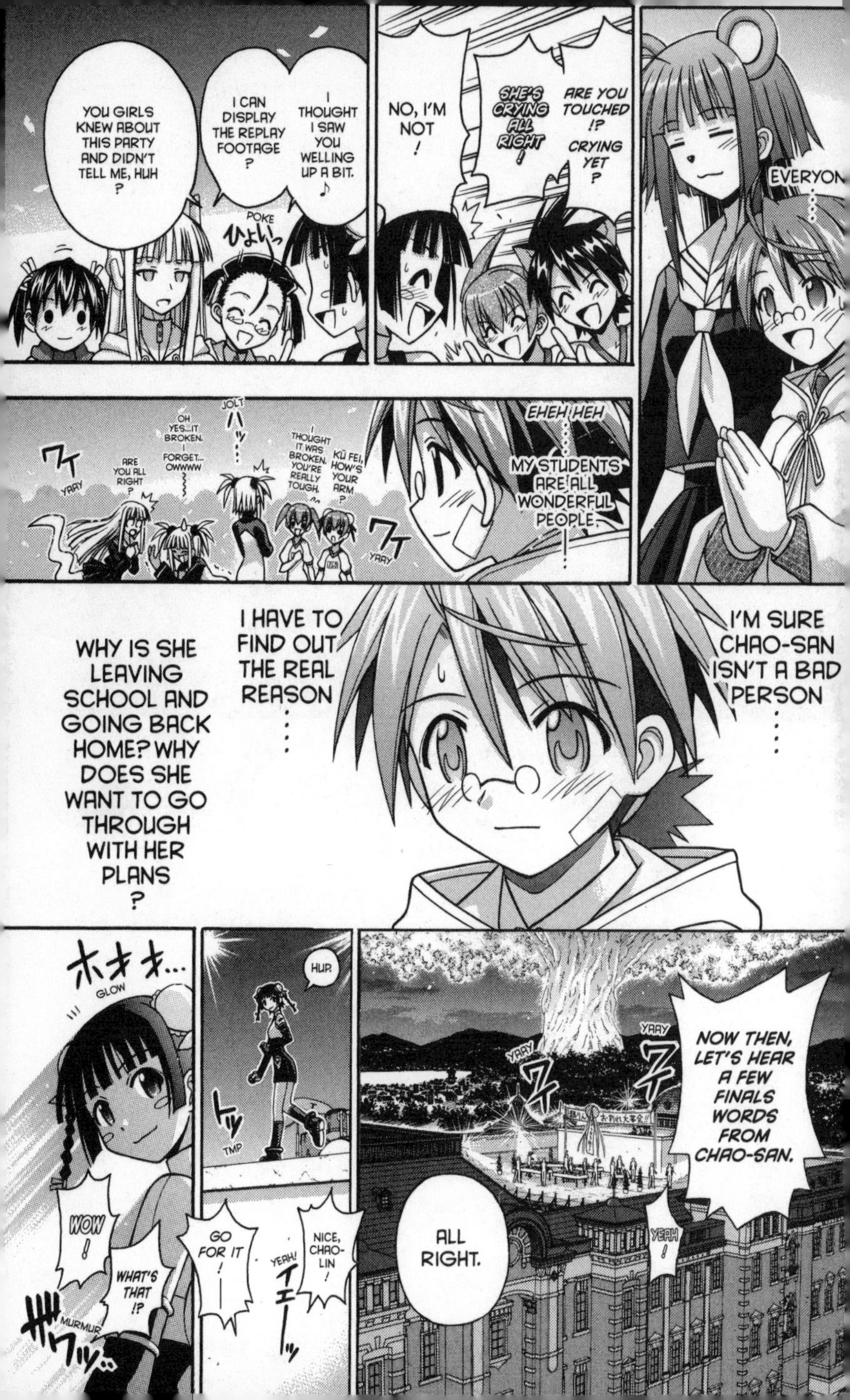
EVERYON...
ARE YOU TOUCHED!? CRYING YET?
SHE'S CRYING ALL RIGHT!
NO, I'M NOT!
I THOUGHT I SAW YOU WELLING UP A BIT. ♪
I CAN DISPLAY THE REPLAY FOOTAGE?
POKE ひょいっ
YOU GIRLS KNEW ABOUT THIS PARTY AND DIDN'T TELL ME, HUH?
EHEH HEH... MY STUDENTS ARE ALL WONDERFUL PEOPLE...!
KŪ FEI, HOW'S YOUR ARM?
I THOUGHT IT WAS BROKEN. YOU'RE REALLY TOUGH.
ワー YAAY
JOLT ハッ
OH YES...IT BROKEN. I FORGET... OWWWW
ARE YOU ALL RIGHT?
ワー YAAY
I'M SURE CHAO-SAN ISN'T A BAD PERSON...
I HAVE TO FIND OUT THE REAL REASON...
WHY IS SHE LEAVING SCHOOL AND GOING BACK HOME? WHY DOES SHE WANT TO GO THROUGH WITH HER PLANS?
NOW THEN, LET'S HEAR A FEW FINALS WORDS FROM CHAO-SAN.
YAAY ワ
YAAY ワ
YEAH!
ALL RIGHT.
HUP.
トッ TMP
NICE, CHAO-LIN!
YEAH! イエーッ
GO FOR IT!
ホオオ... GLOW
WOW!
WHAT'S THAT!?
ザワッ MURMUR

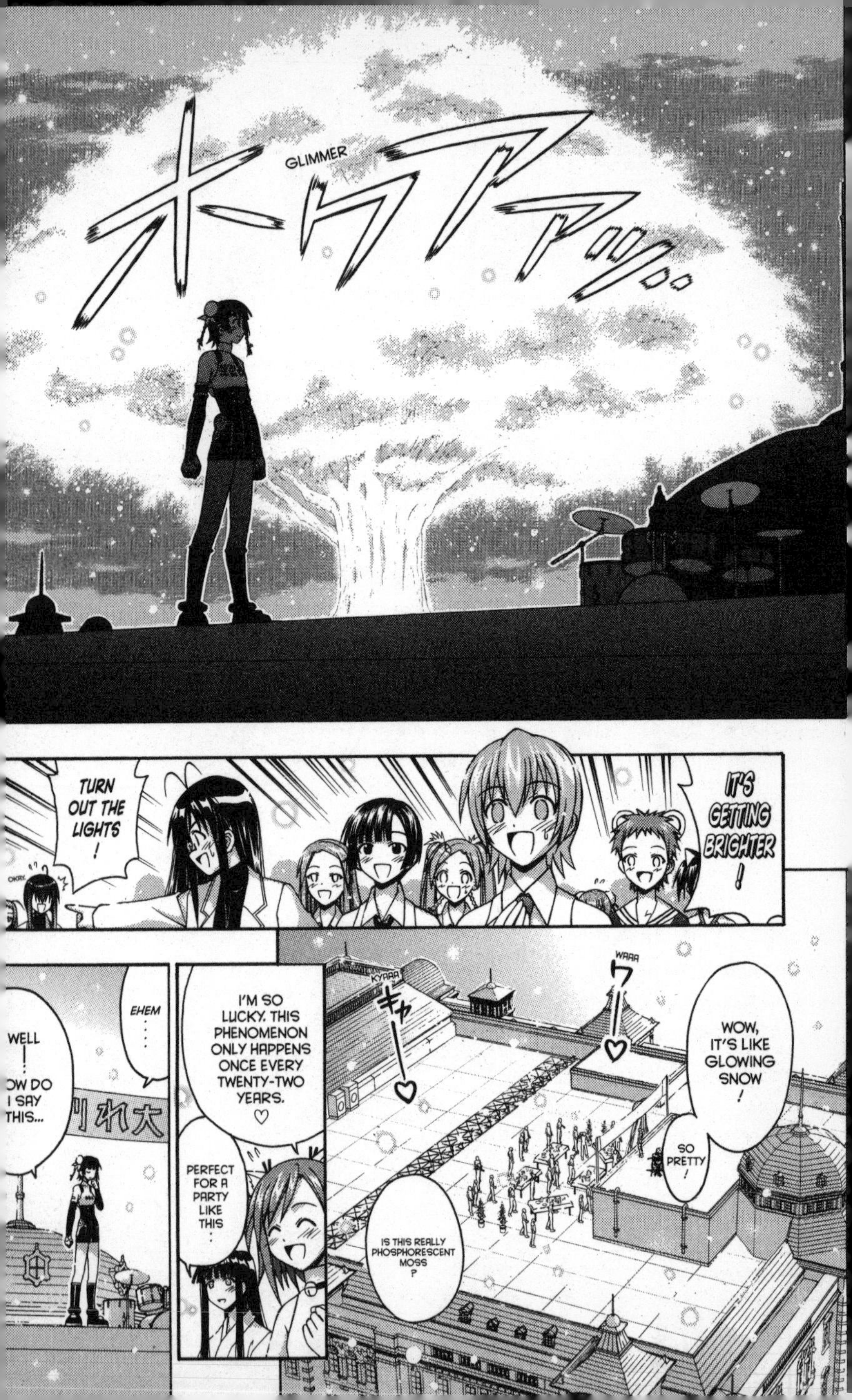
GLIMMER
IT'S GETTING BRIGHTER!
TURN OUT THE LIGHTS!
OKAY
WAAA
KYAAA
WOW, IT'S LIKE GLOWING SNOW!
SO PRETTY!
IS THIS REALLY PHOSPHORESCENT MOSS?
I'M SO LUCKY. THIS PHENOMENON ONLY HAPPENS ONCE EVERY TWENTY-TWO YEARS. ♡
PERFECT FOR A PARTY LIKE THIS...
EHEM...
WELL! OW DO I SAY THIS...

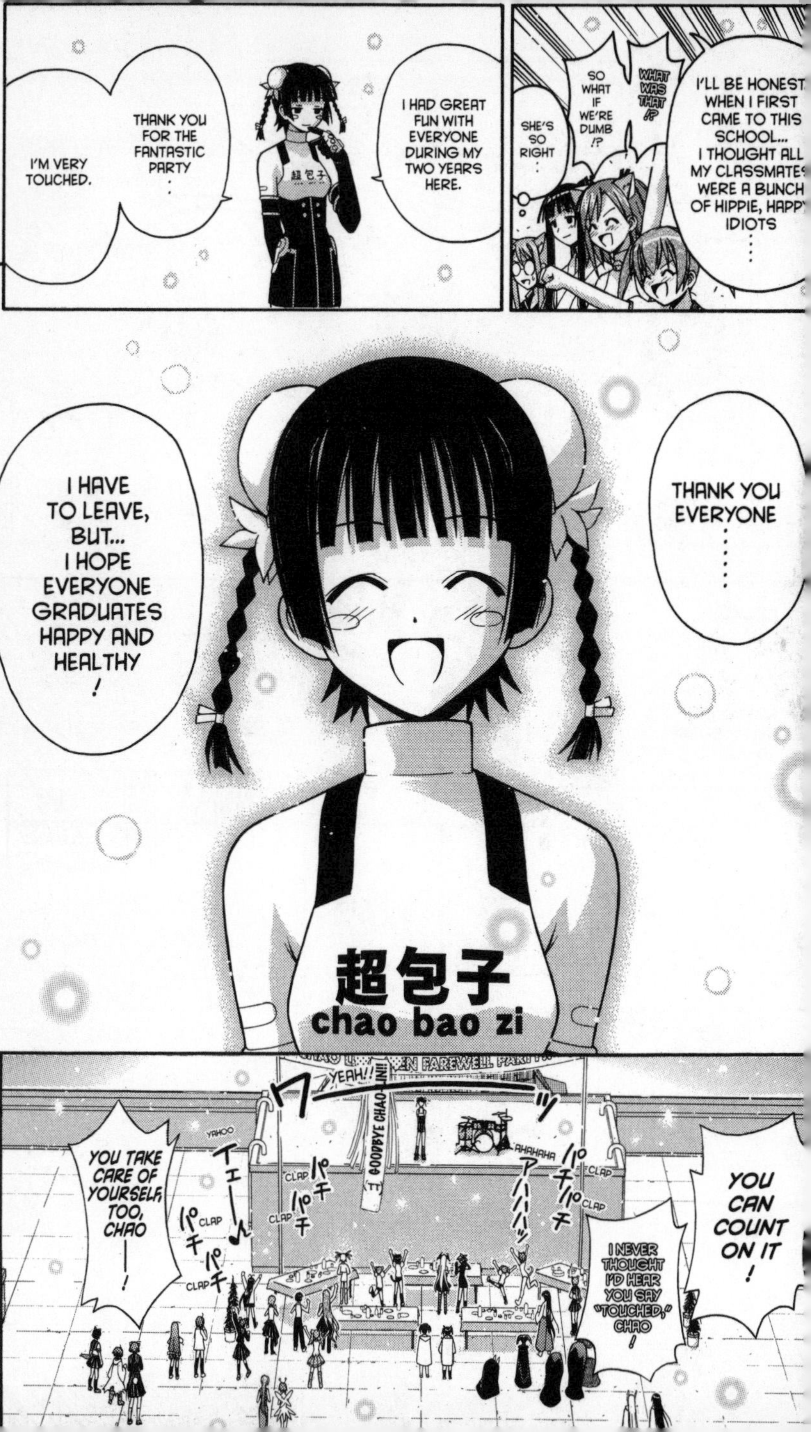
I'LL BE HONEST. WHEN I FIRST CAME TO THIS SCHOOL... I THOUGHT ALL MY CLASSMATES WERE A BUNCH OF HIPPIE, HAPPY IDIOTS ....
WHAT WAS THAT !?
SO WHAT IF WE'RE DUMB !?
SHE'S SO RIGHT ...
I HAD GREAT FUN WITH EVERYONE DURING MY TWO YEARS HERE.
THANK YOU FOR THE FANTASTIC PARTY ...
I'M VERY TOUCHED.
超包子
THANK YOU EVERYONE ......
I HAVE TO LEAVE, BUT... I HOPE EVERYONE GRADUATES HAPPY AND HEALTHY !
超包子
chao bao zi
FAREWELL PARTY
YEAH!!
GOODBYE CHAO LIN!!
ワーッ
YOU CAN COUNT ON IT !
I NEVER THOUGHT I'D HEAR YOU SAY "TOUCHED," CHAO !
パチパチ CLAP CLAP
アハハハ AHAHAHA
パチパチ CLAP CLAP
イエーイ YAHOO
パチパチ CLAP CLAP
YOU TAKE CARE OF YOURSELF, TOO, CHAO —— !

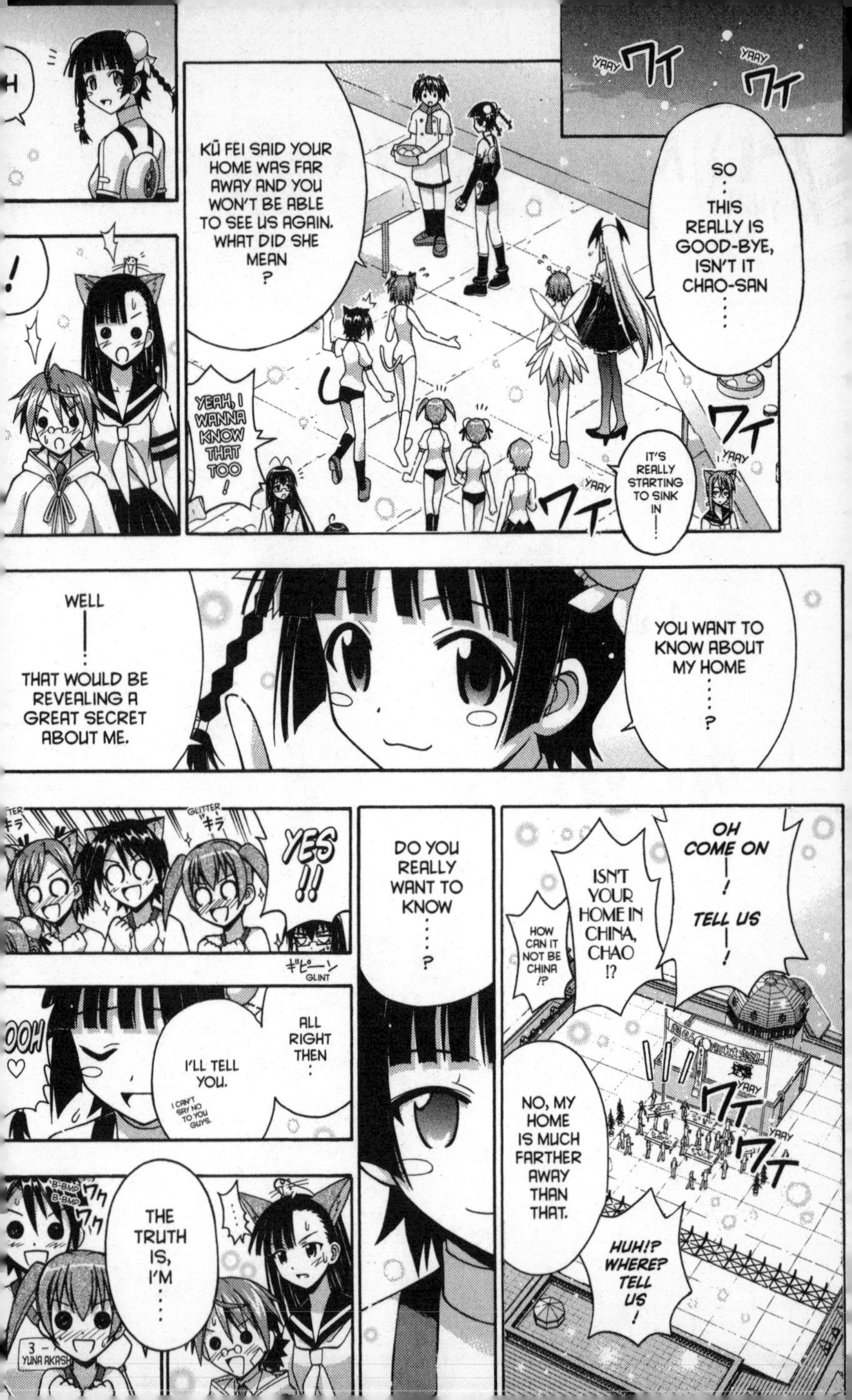
YAAY ワイ YAAY ワイ
SO... THIS REALLY IS GOOD-BYE, ISN'T IT CHAO-SAN...
ワイ YAAY
IT'S REALLY STARTING TO SINK IN—!
YAAY ワイ
KŪ FEI SAID YOUR HOME WAS FAR AWAY AND YOU WON'T BE ABLE TO SEE US AGAIN. WHAT DID SHE MEAN?
YEAH, I WANNA KNOW THAT TOO!
!
YOU WANT TO KNOW ABOUT MY HOME...?
WELL—. THAT WOULD BE REVEALING A GREAT SECRET ABOUT ME.
OH COME ON—! TELL US—!
ISN'T YOUR HOME IN CHINA, CHAO!?
HOW CAN IT NOT BE CHINA!?
YAAY ワイ YAAY ワイ
NO, MY HOME IS MUCH FARTHER AWAY THAN THAT.
HUH!? WHERE? TELL US!
DO YOU REALLY WANT TO KNOW...?
YES!!
GLITTER キラ
ギピーン GLINT
ALL RIGHT THEN...
I'LL TELL YOU.
I CAN'T SAY NO TO YOU GUYS.
OOH ♡
B-BMP ワク B-BMP ワク
THE TRUTH IS, I'M...
...
3 - YUNA AKASH

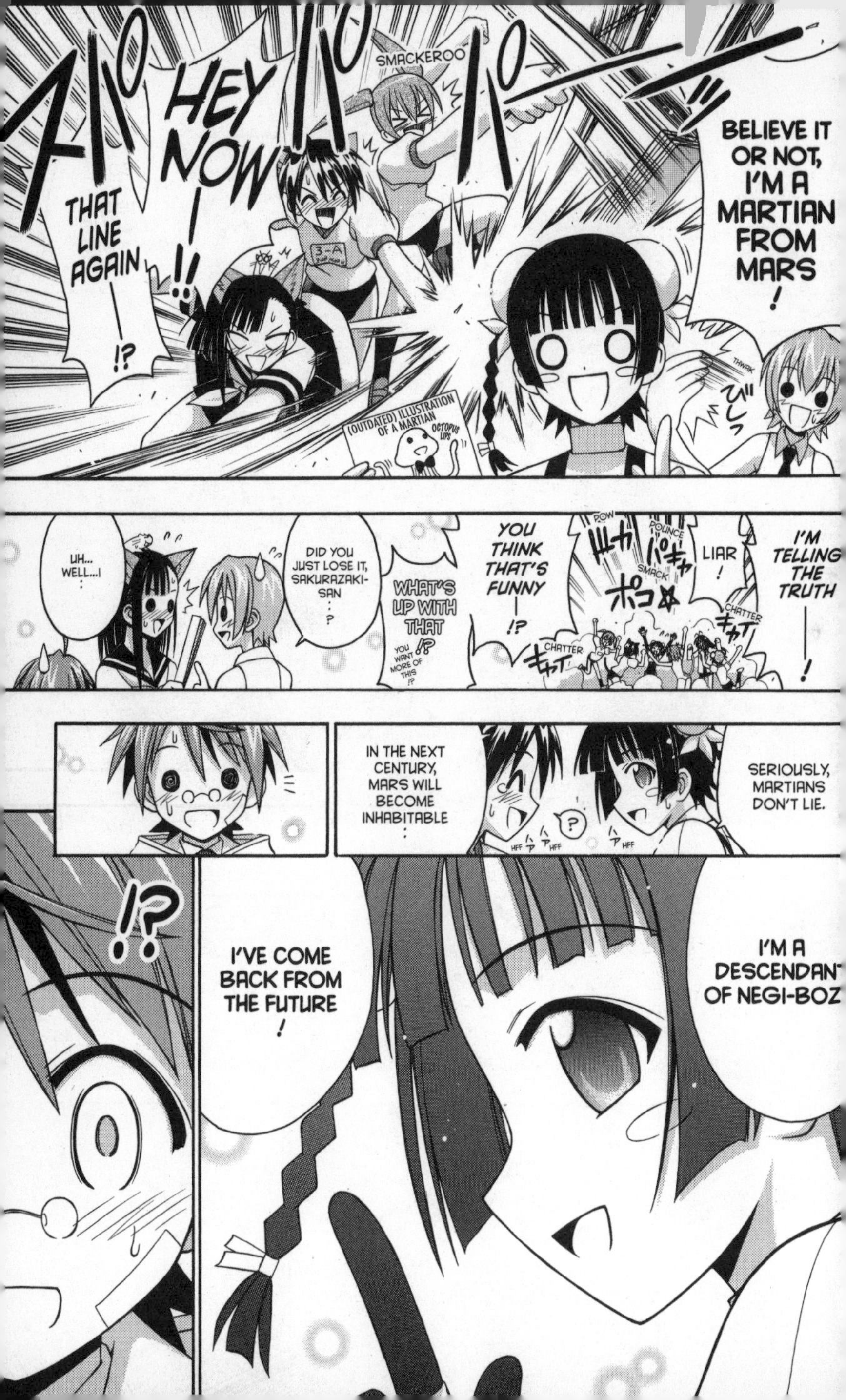
BELIEVE IT OR NOT, I'M A MARTIAN FROM MARS!
SMACKEROO
HEY NOW!!
THAT LINE AGAIN—!?
(OUTDATED) ILLUSTRATION OF A MARTIAN
OCTOPUS LIPS
THWAK
I'M TELLING THE TRUTH—!
LIAR!
POW
POUNCE
SMACK
CHATTER
CHATTER
YOU THINK THAT'S FUNNY—!?
WHAT'S UP WITH THAT!?
YOU WANT MORE OF THIS!?
DID YOU JUST LOSE IT, SAKURAZAKI-SAN...?
UH... WELL...I:
SERIOUSLY, MARTIANS DON'T LIE.
HFF HFF HFF
?
IN THE NEXT CENTURY, MARS WILL BECOME INHABITABLE:
I'M A DESCENDAN OF NEGI-BOZ
I'VE COME BACK FROM THE FUTURE!
!?

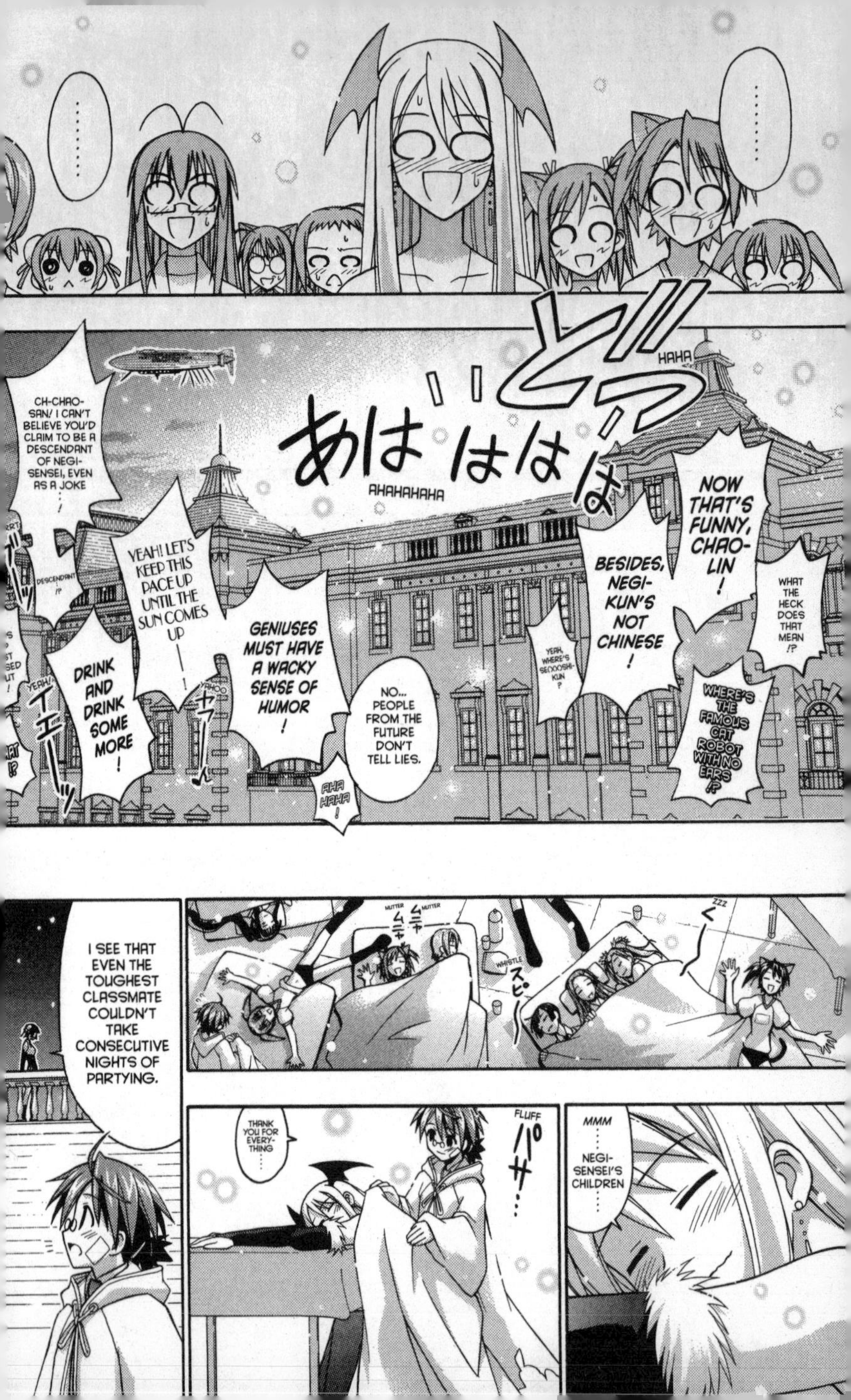
......
......
HAHA
NOW THAT'S FUNNY, CHAO-LIN!
WHAT THE HECK DOES THAT MEAN!?
WHERE'S THE FAMOUS CAT ROBOT WITH NO EARS!?
BESIDES, NEGI-KUN'S NOT CHINESE!
YEAH, WHERE'S SE(XX)SHI-KUN?
AHAHAHAHA
NO... PEOPLE FROM THE FUTURE DON'T TELL LIES.
AHA HAHA!
GENIUSES MUST HAVE A WACKY SENSE OF HUMOR!
YEAH! LET'S KEEP THIS PACE UP UNTIL THE SUN COMES UP—!
YAHOO
DRINK AND DRINK SOME MORE!
YEAH!
CH-CHAO-SAN! I CAN'T BELIEVE YOU'D CLAIM TO BE A DESCENDANT OF NEGI-SENSEI, EVEN AS A JOKE...!
DESCENDANT!?
ZZZ
WHISTLE
MUTTER MUTTER
I SEE THAT EVEN THE TOUGHEST CLASSMATE COULDN'T TAKE CONSECUTIVE NIGHTS OF PARTYING.
MMM... NEGI-SENSEI'S CHILDREN......
FLUFF
THANK YOU FOR EVERYTHING......

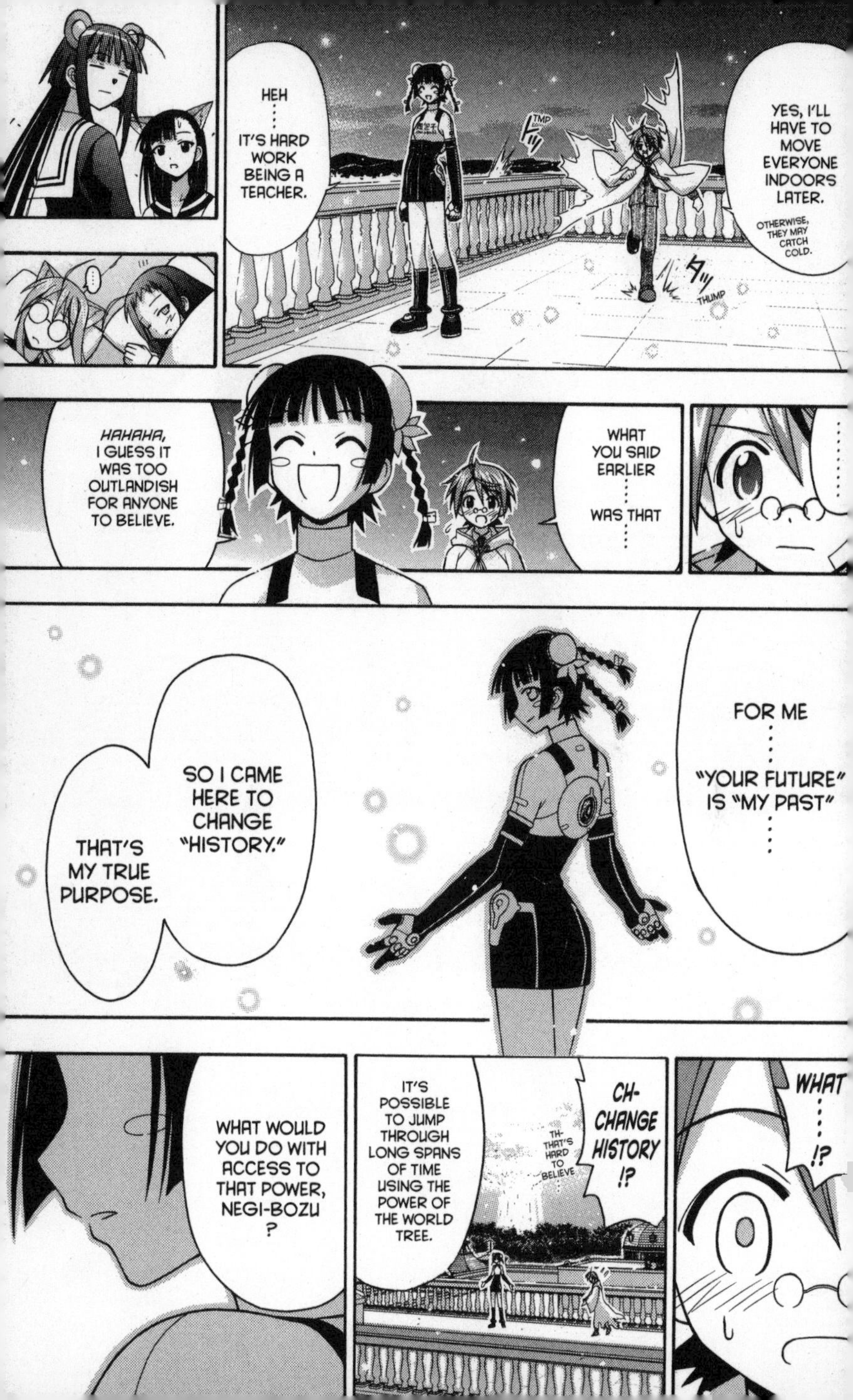
YES, I'LL HAVE TO MOVE EVERYONE INDOORS LATER.
OTHERWISE, THEY MAY CATCH COLD.
THUMP
TMP
HEH... IT'S HARD WORK BEING A TEACHER.
...
...
WHAT YOU SAID EARLIER... WAS THAT...
HAHAHA, I GUESS IT WAS TOO OUTLANDISH FOR ANYONE TO BELIEVE.
FOR ME... "YOUR FUTURE" IS "MY PAST"...
SO I CAME HERE TO CHANGE "HISTORY."
THAT'S MY TRUE PURPOSE.
WHAT...!?
CH-CHANGE HISTORY!?
TH-THAT'S HARD TO BELIEVE...
IT'S POSSIBLE TO JUMP THROUGH LONG SPANS OF TIME USING THE POWER OF THE WORLD TREE.
WHAT WOULD YOU DO WITH ACCESS TO THAT POWER, NEGI-BOZU?

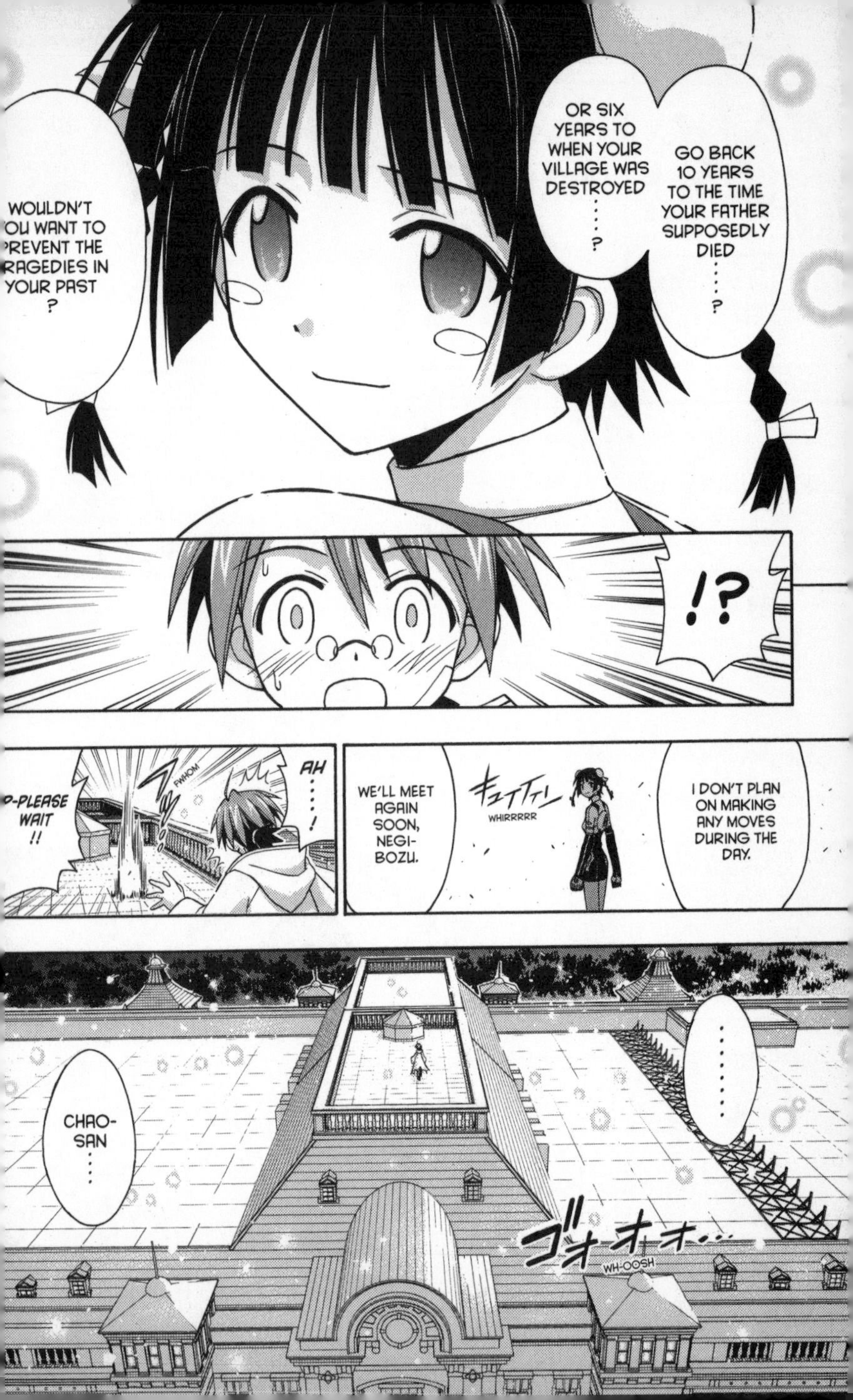
GO BACK 10 YEARS TO THE TIME YOUR FATHER SUPPOSEDLY DIED ....?
OR SIX YEARS TO WHEN YOUR VILLAGE WAS DESTROYED ....?
WOULDN'T OU WANT TO REVENT THE RAGEDIES IN YOUR PAST ?
!?
I DON'T PLAN ON MAKING ANY MOVES DURING THE DAY.
WHIRRRRR
WE'LL MEET AGAIN SOON, NEGI-BOZU.
AH ....!
FWHOM
-PLEASE WAIT !!
......
WH-OOSH
CHAO-SAN ....

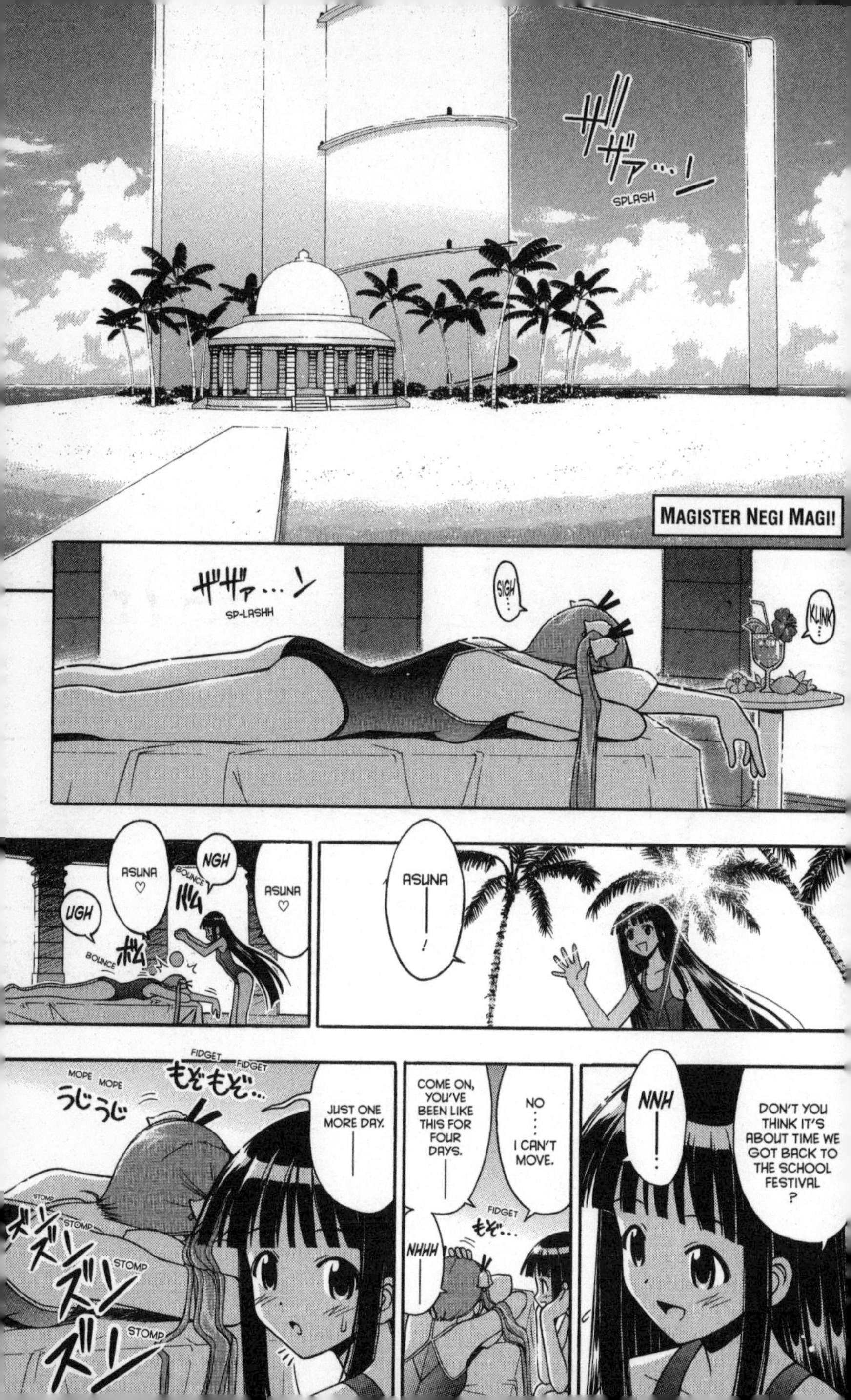
ザザァ…ン
SPLASH
MAGISTER NEGI MAGI!
KLINK…
SIGH…
ザザァ…ン
SP-LASHH
ASUNA —!
ASUNA ♡
NGH
バム
BOUNCE
ASUNA ♡
UGH
ボム
BOUNCE
DON'T YOU THINK IT'S ABOUT TIME WE GOT BACK TO THE SCHOOL FESTIVAL?
NNH —!
NO… I CAN'T MOVE.
COME ON, YOU'VE BEEN LIKE THIS FOR FOUR DAYS. —
もぞ…
FIDGET
NHHH —
JUST ONE MORE DAY. —
もぞもぞ…
FIDGET FIDGET
うじうじ
MOPE MOPE
ズン ズン ズン ズン
STOMP STOMP STOMP STOMP

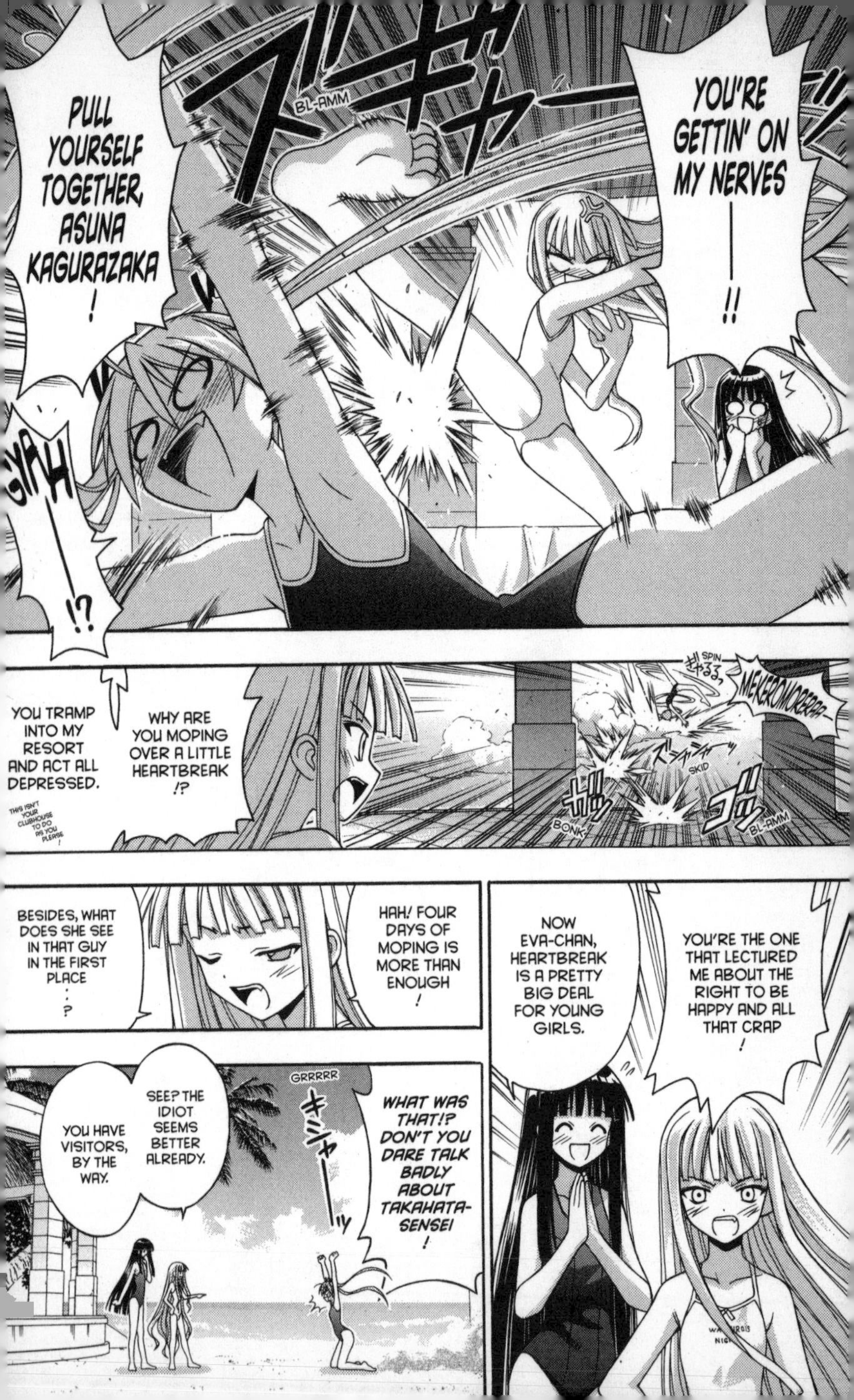

YOU'RE GETTIN' ON MY NERVES——!!
BL-AMM
PULL YOURSELF TOGETHER, ASUNA KAGURAZAKA!
GYAH——!?
SPIN
MEKEROMORERRR—
SKID
BONK
BL-AMM
WHY ARE YOU MOPING OVER A LITTLE HEARTBREAK!?
YOU TRAMP INTO MY RESORT AND ACT ALL DEPRESSED.
THIS ISN'T YOUR CLUBHOUSE TO DO AS YOU PLEASE!
YOU'RE THE ONE THAT LECTURED ME ABOUT THE RIGHT TO BE HAPPY AND ALL THAT CRAP!
NOW EVA-CHAN, HEARTBREAK IS A PRETTY BIG DEAL FOR YOUNG GIRLS.
HAH! FOUR DAYS OF MOPING IS MORE THAN ENOUGH!
BESIDES, WHAT DOES SHE SEE IN THAT GUY IN THE FIRST PLACE..?
GRRRRR
WHAT WAS THAT!? DON'T YOU DARE TALK BADLY ABOUT TAKAHATA-SENSEI!
SEE? THE IDIOT SEEMS BETTER ALREADY.
YOU HAVE VISITORS, BY THE WAY.

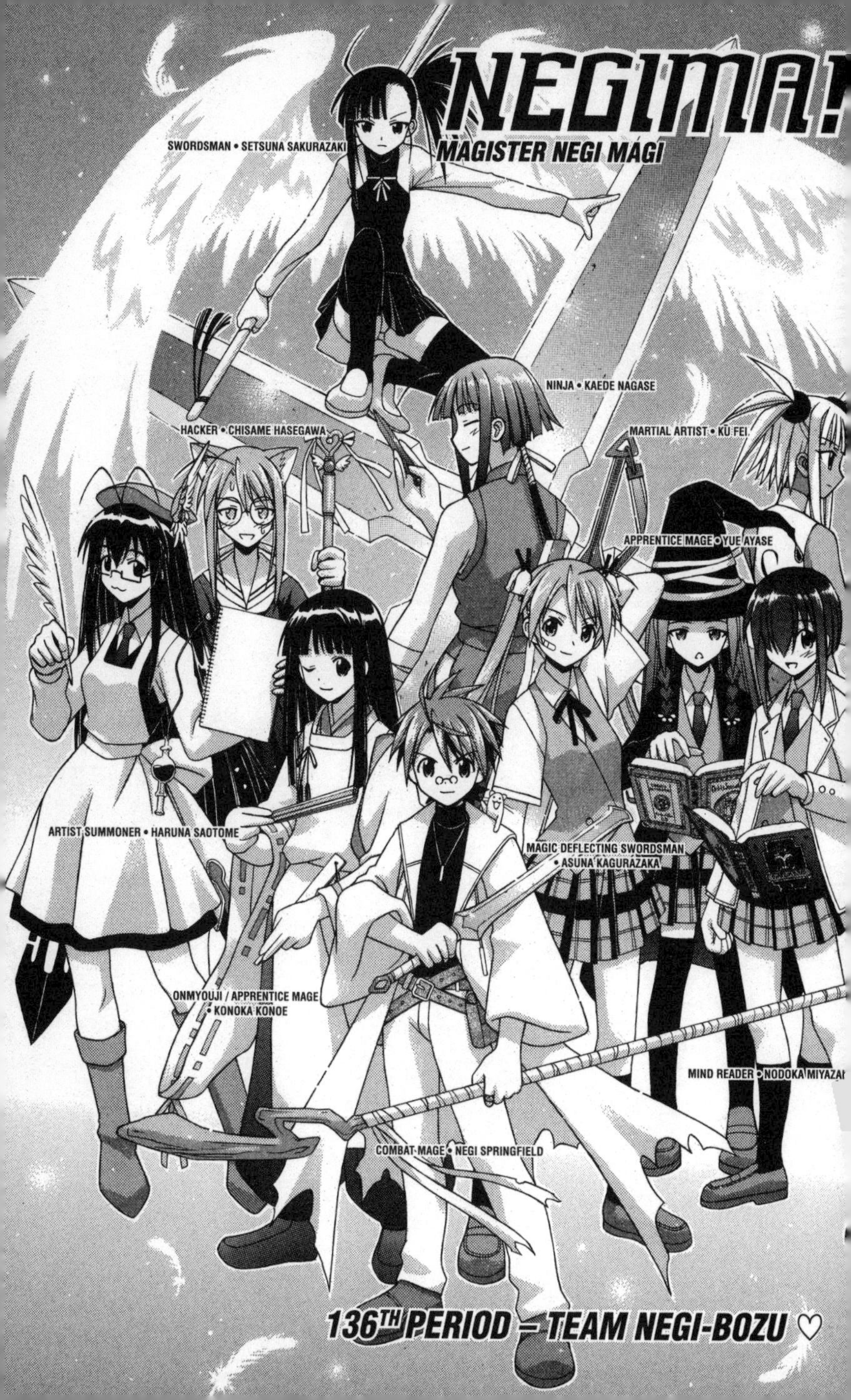
NEGIMA!
MAGISTER NEGI MAGI
SWORDSMAN • SETSUNA SAKURAZAKI
NINJA • KAEDE NAGASE
HACKER • CHISAME HASEGAWA
MARTIAL ARTIST • KU FEI
APPRENTICE MAGE • YUE AYASE
ARTIST SUMMONER • HARUNA SAOTOME
MAGIC DEFLECTING SWORDSMAN
• ASUNA KAGURAZAKA
ONMYOUJI / APPRENTICE MAGE
• KONOKA KONOE
MIND READER • NODOKA MIYAZA
COMBAT MAGE • NEGI SPRINGFIELD
136TH PERIOD – TEAM NEGI-BOZU ♡

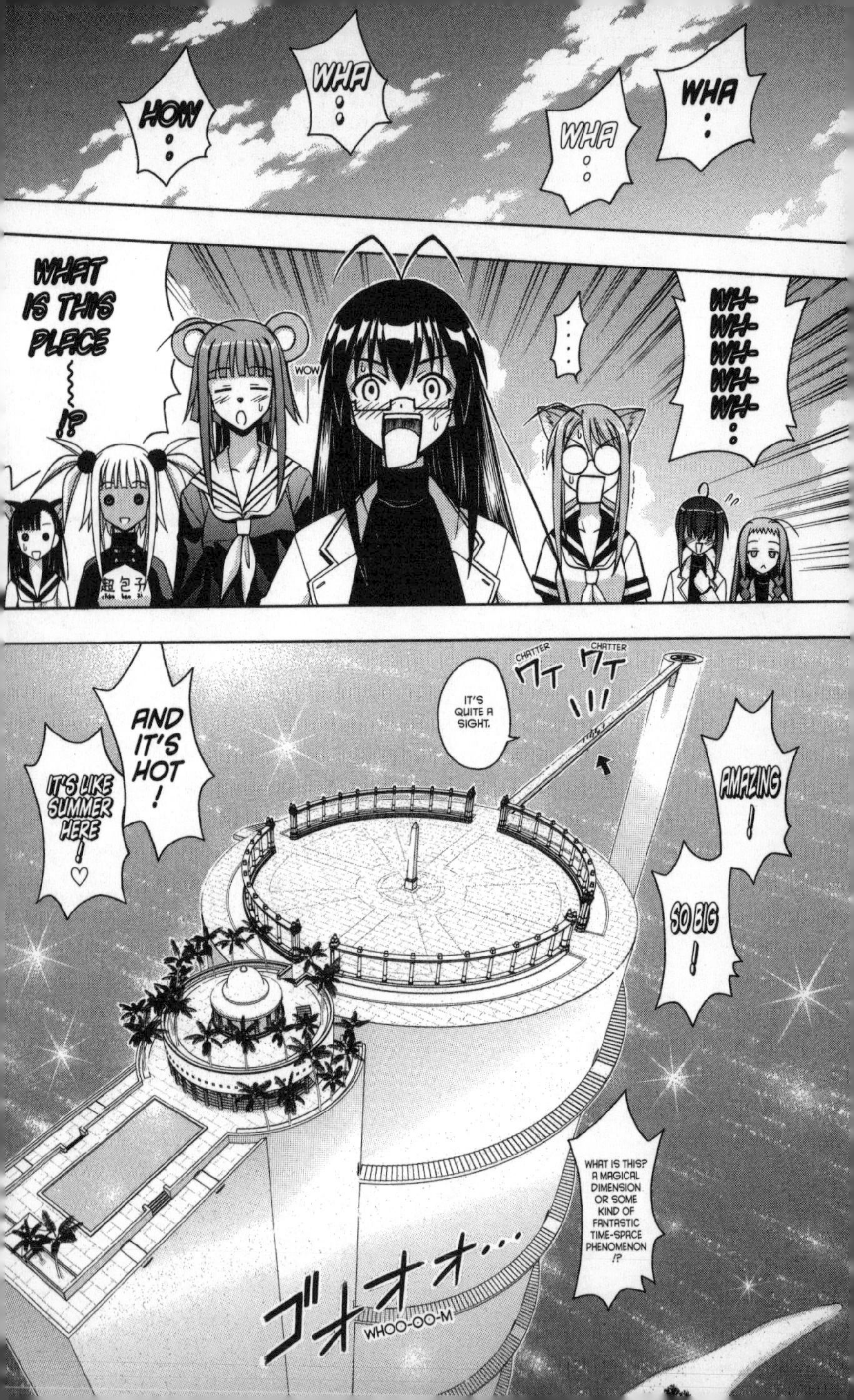
WHA . .
WHA . .
WHA . .
HOW . .
WH-WH-WH-WH-WH-. .
. . .
WOW
WHAT IS THIS PLACE ~~~ !?
超包子
CHATTER ワイ CHATTER ワイ
AMAZING!
SO BIG!
IT'S QUITE A SIGHT.
AND IT'S HOT!
IT'S LIKE SUMMER HERE! ♡
WHAT IS THIS? A MAGICAL DIMENSION OR SOME KIND OF FANTASTIC TIME-SPACE PHENOMENON !?
ゴオオ… WHOO-OO-M

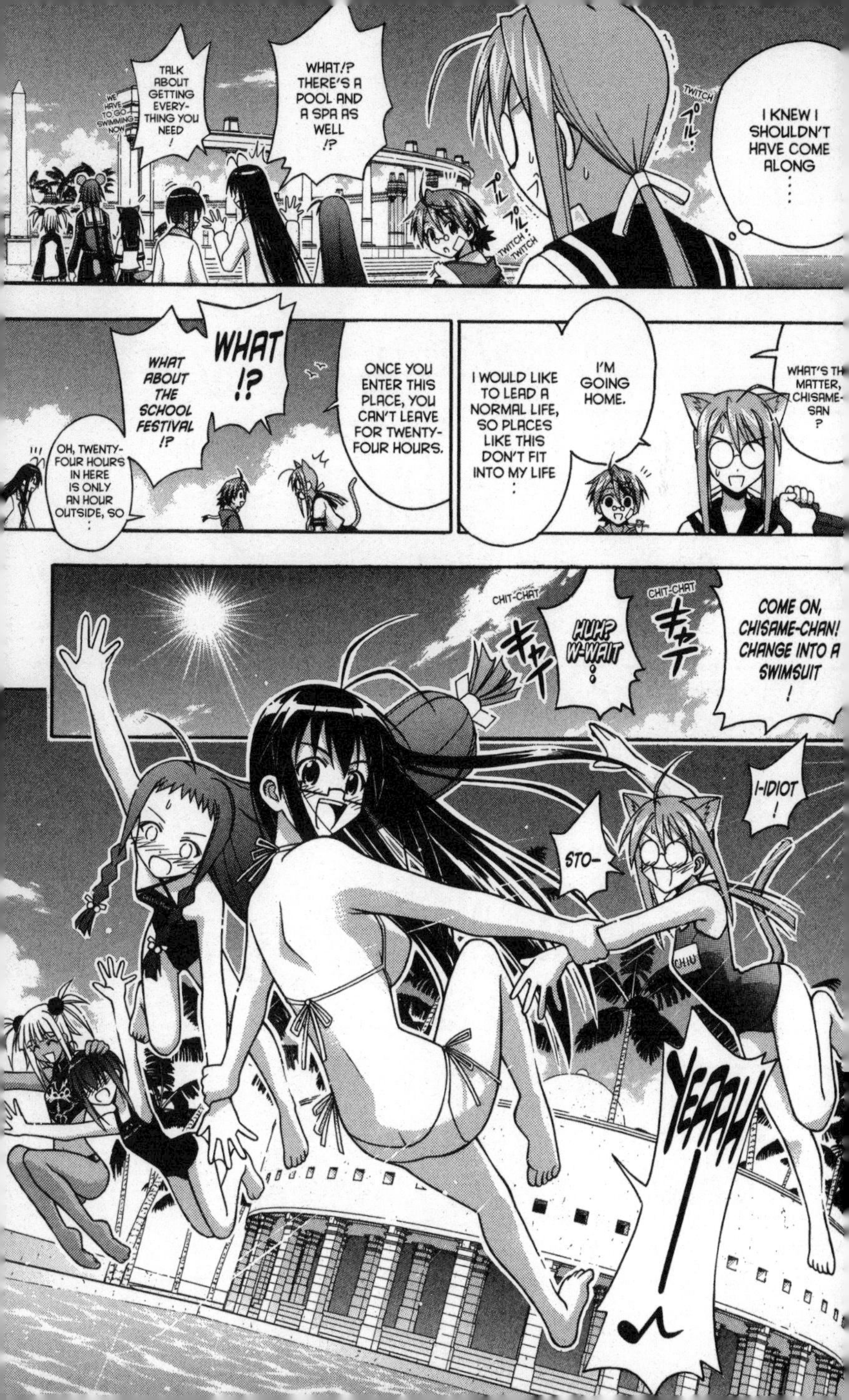

I KNEW I SHOULDN'T HAVE COME ALONG ....
TWITCH
TWITCH TWITCH
WHAT!? THERE'S A POOL AND A SPA AS WELL !?
TALK ABOUT GETTING EVERY-THING YOU NEED !
WE HAVE TO GO SWIMMING NOW
WHAT'S TH MATTER, CHISAME-SAN ?
I'M GOING HOME.
I WOULD LIKE TO LEAD A NORMAL LIFE, SO PLACES LIKE THIS DON'T FIT INTO MY LIFE :
ONCE YOU ENTER THIS PLACE, YOU CAN'T LEAVE FOR TWENTY-FOUR HOURS.
WHAT !?
WHAT ABOUT THE SCHOOL FESTIVAL !?
OH, TWENTY-FOUR HOURS IN HERE IS ONLY AN HOUR OUTSIDE, SO :
COME ON, CHISAME-CHAN! CHANGE INTO A SWIMSUIT !
CHIT-CHAT
HUH? W-WAIT ..
CHIT-CHAT
I-IDIOT !
STO-
YEAAH !

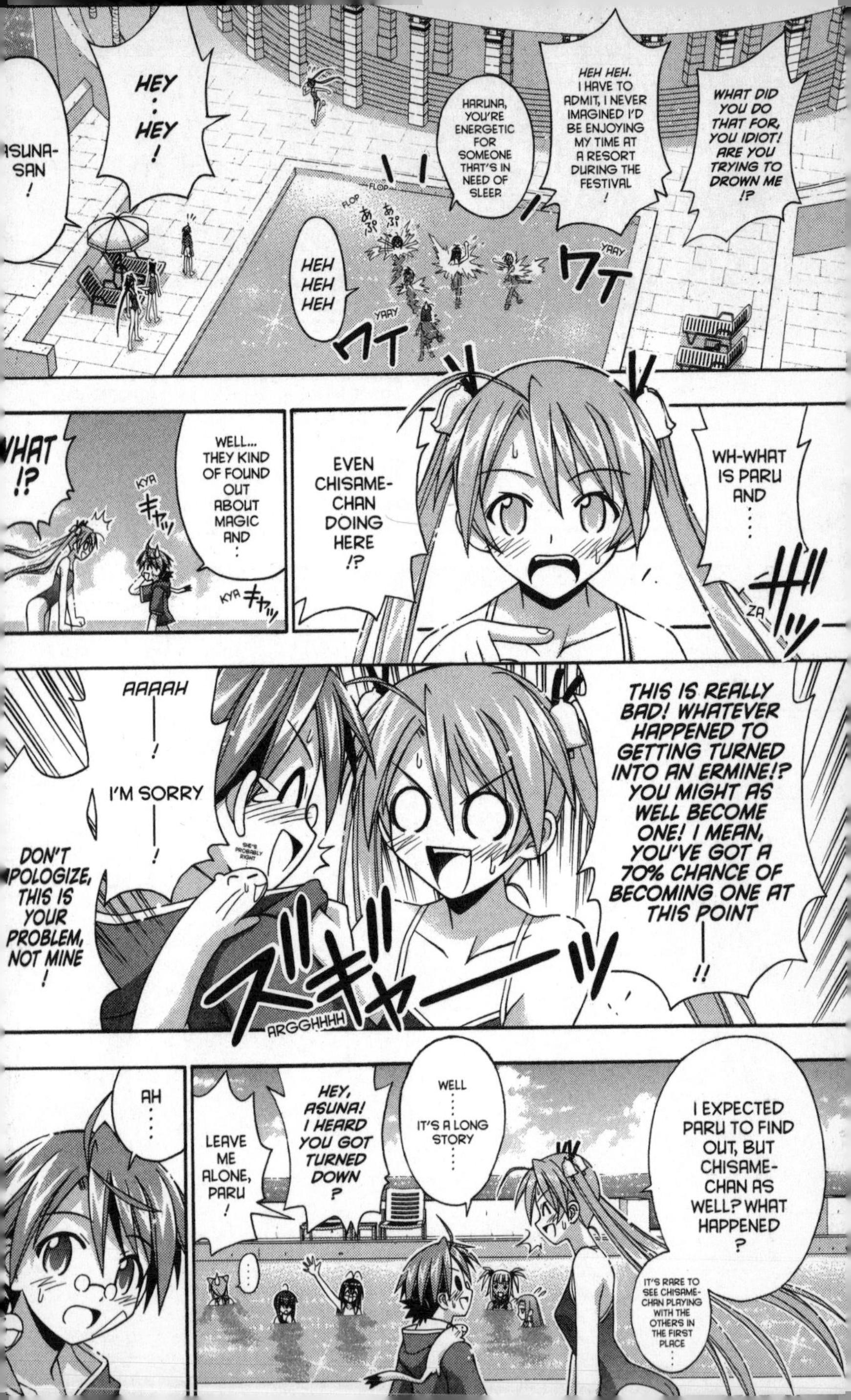
WHAT DID YOU DO THAT FOR, YOU IDIOT! ARE YOU TRYING TO DROWN ME !?
HEH HEH. I HAVE TO ADMIT, I NEVER IMAGINED I'D BE ENJOYING MY TIME AT A RESORT DURING THE FESTIVAL !
HARUNA, YOU'RE ENERGETIC FOR SOMEONE THAT'S IN NEED OF SLEEP.
YAAY
FLOP
FLOP
HEH HEH HEH
YAAY
HEY · HEY !
ASUNA-SAN !
WH-WHAT IS PARU AND ....
ZA
EVEN CHISAME-CHAN DOING HERE !?
WELL... THEY KIND OF FOUND OUT ABOUT MAGIC AND ...
KYA
KYA
WHAT !?
THIS IS REALLY BAD! WHATEVER HAPPENED TO GETTING TURNED INTO AN ERMINE!? YOU MIGHT AS WELL BECOME ONE! I MEAN, YOU'VE GOT A 70% CHANCE OF BECOMING ONE AT THIS POINT —!!
AAAAH —!
I'M SORRY —!
SHE'S PROBABLY RIGHT
DON'T APOLOGIZE, THIS IS YOUR PROBLEM, NOT MINE !
ARGGHHHH
I EXPECTED PARU TO FIND OUT, BUT CHISAME-CHAN AS WELL? WHAT HAPPENED ?
IT'S RARE TO SEE CHISAME-CHAN PLAYING WITH THE OTHERS IN THE FIRST PLACE ...
WELL ... IT'S A LONG STORY ...
HEY, ASUNA! I HEARD YOU GOT TURNED DOWN ?
LEAVE ME ALONE, PARU !
...
AH ...

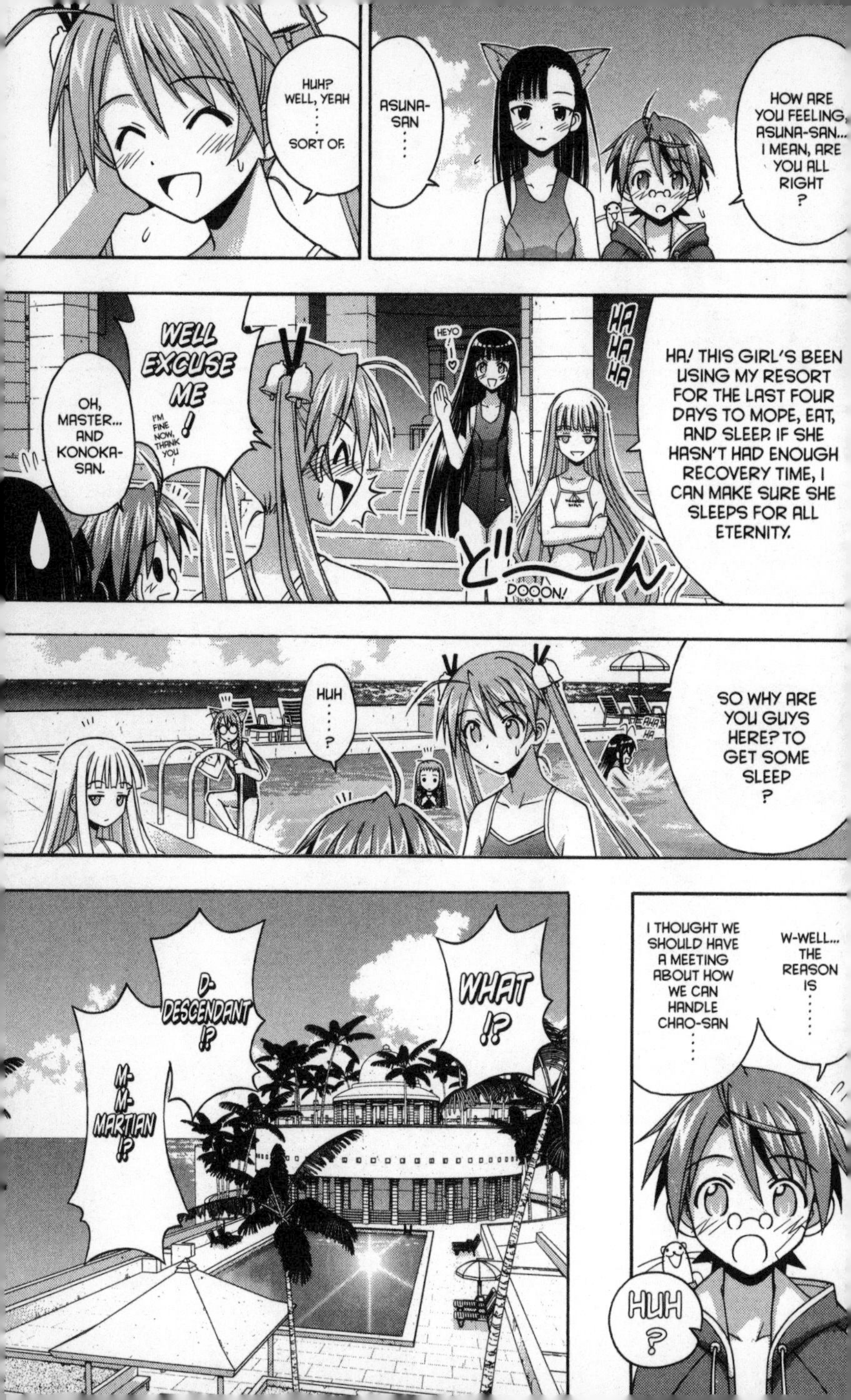
HOW ARE YOU FEELING, ASUNA-SAN... I MEAN, ARE YOU ALL RIGHT?
ASUNA-SAN.....
HUH? WELL, YEAH... SORT OF.
HA HA HA HA
HA! THIS GIRL'S BEEN USING MY RESORT FOR THE LAST FOUR DAYS TO MOPE, EAT, AND SLEEP. IF SHE HASN'T HAD ENOUGH RECOVERY TIME, I CAN MAKE SURE SHE SLEEPS FOR ALL ETERNITY.
HEYO ♥
DOOON!
WELL EXCUSE ME!
I'M FINE NOW, THANK YOU!
OH, MASTER... AND KONOKA-SAN.
SO WHY ARE YOU GUYS HERE? TO GET SOME SLEEP?
AHA HA
HUH...?
W-WELL... THE REASON IS......
I THOUGHT WE SHOULD HAVE A MEETING ABOUT HOW WE CAN HANDLE CHAO-SAN...
HUH?
WHAT!?
D-DESCENDANT!?
M-M-MARTIAN!?

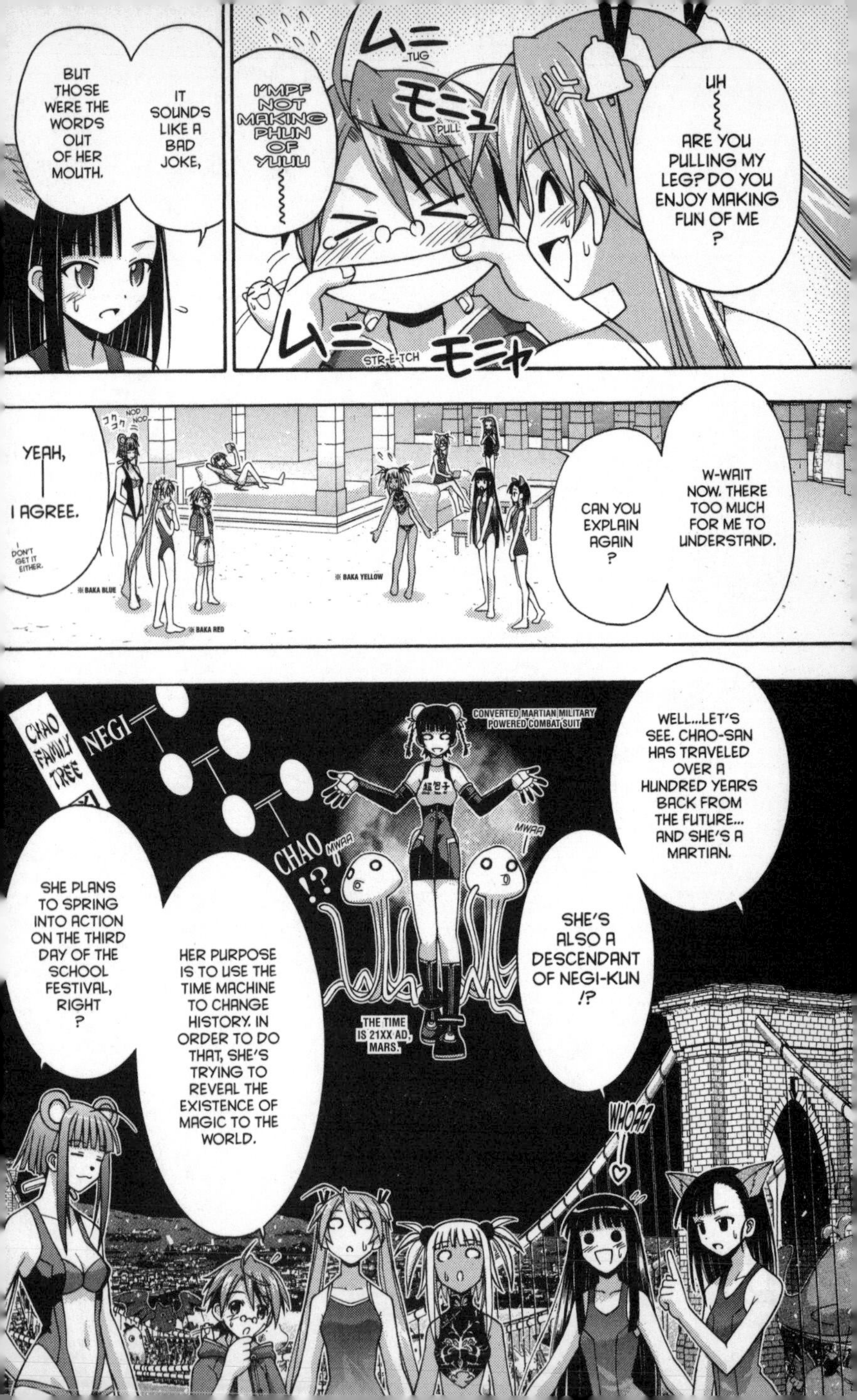
UH~ ARE YOU PULLING MY LEG? DO YOU ENJOY MAKING FUN OF ME?
ムニ
TUG
モニュ
PULL
I'MPF NOT MAKING PHUN OF YUUU~
ムニ
STR-E-TCH
モニャ
IT SOUNDS LIKE A BAD JOKE,
BUT THOSE WERE THE WORDS OUT OF HER MOUTH.
W-WAIT NOW. THERE TOO MUCH FOR ME TO UNDERSTAND.
CAN YOU EXPLAIN AGAIN?
※ BAKA YELLOW
コクコク
NOD NOD
YEAH, I AGREE.
I DON'T GET IT EITHER.
※ BAKA BLUE
※ BAKA RED
WELL...LET'S SEE. CHAO-SAN HAS TRAVELED OVER A HUNDRED YEARS BACK FROM THE FUTURE... AND SHE'S A MARTIAN.
CONVERTED MARTIAN MILITARY POWERED COMBAT SUIT
MWAA
MWAA
SHE'S ALSO A DESCENDANT OF NEGI-KUN!?
THE TIME IS 21XX AD, MARS.
CHAO FAMILY TREE
NEGI
CHAO!?
HER PURPOSE IS TO USE THE TIME MACHINE TO CHANGE HISTORY. IN ORDER TO DO THAT, SHE'S TRYING TO REVEAL THE EXISTENCE OF MAGIC TO THE WORLD.
SHE PLANS TO SPRING INTO ACTION ON THE THIRD DAY OF THE SCHOOL FESTIVAL, RIGHT?
WHOAA

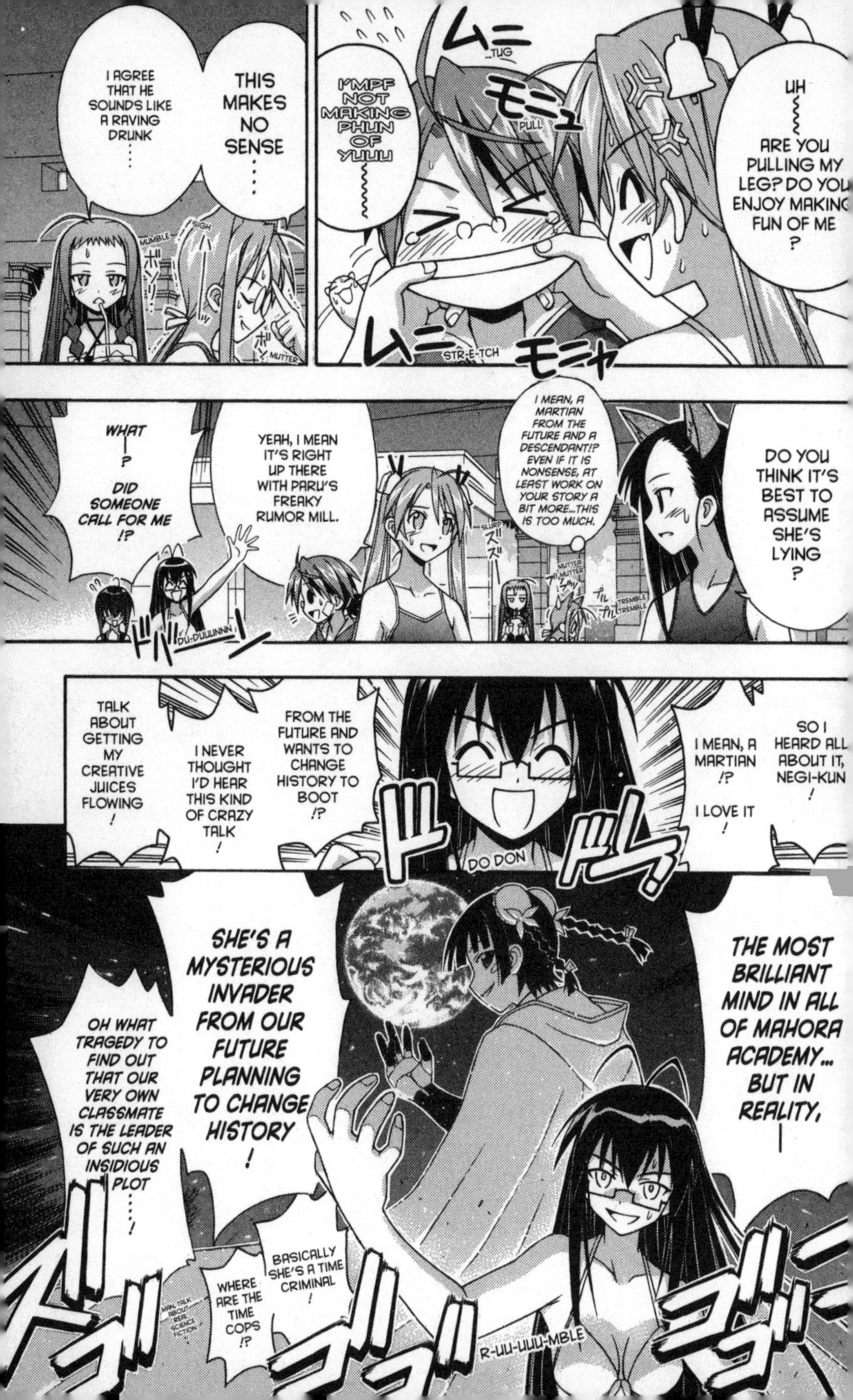
UH ~ ARE YOU PULLING MY LEG? DO YOU ENJOY MAKING FUN OF ME?
TUG
PULL
I'MPF NOT MAKING PHUN OF YUUU ~
STR-E-TCH
THIS MAKES NO SENSE...
I AGREE THAT HE SOUNDS LIKE A RAVING DRUNK...
SIGH
MUMBLE
MUTTER
DO YOU THINK IT'S BEST TO ASSUME SHE'S LYING?
I MEAN, A MARTIAN FROM THE FUTURE AND A DESCENDANT!? EVEN IF IT IS NONSENSE, AT LEAST WORK ON YOUR STORY A BIT MORE...THIS IS TOO MUCH.
TREMBLE TREMBLE
MUTTER MUTTER
SLURP
YEAH, I MEAN IT'S RIGHT UP THERE WITH PARU'S FREAKY RUMOR MILL.
WHAT!? DID SOMEONE CALL FOR ME!?
DU-DUUUNNN
SO I HEARD ALL ABOUT IT, NEGI-KUN!
I MEAN, A MARTIAN!? I LOVE IT!
DO DON
FROM THE FUTURE AND WANTS TO CHANGE HISTORY TO BOOT!?
I NEVER THOUGHT I'D HEAR THIS KIND OF CRAZY TALK!
TALK ABOUT GETTING MY CREATIVE JUICES FLOWING!
THE MOST BRILLIANT MIND IN ALL OF MAHORA ACADEMY... BUT IN REALITY, —
SHE'S A MYSTERIOUS INVADER FROM OUR FUTURE PLANNING TO CHANGE HISTORY!
OH WHAT TRAGEDY TO FIND OUT THAT OUR VERY OWN CLASSMATE IS THE LEADER OF SUCH AN INSIDIOUS PLOT...!
BASICALLY SHE'S A TIME CRIMINAL!
WHERE ARE THE TIME COPS!?
MAN, TALK ABOUT REAL SCIENCE FICTION
R-UU-UUU-MBLE

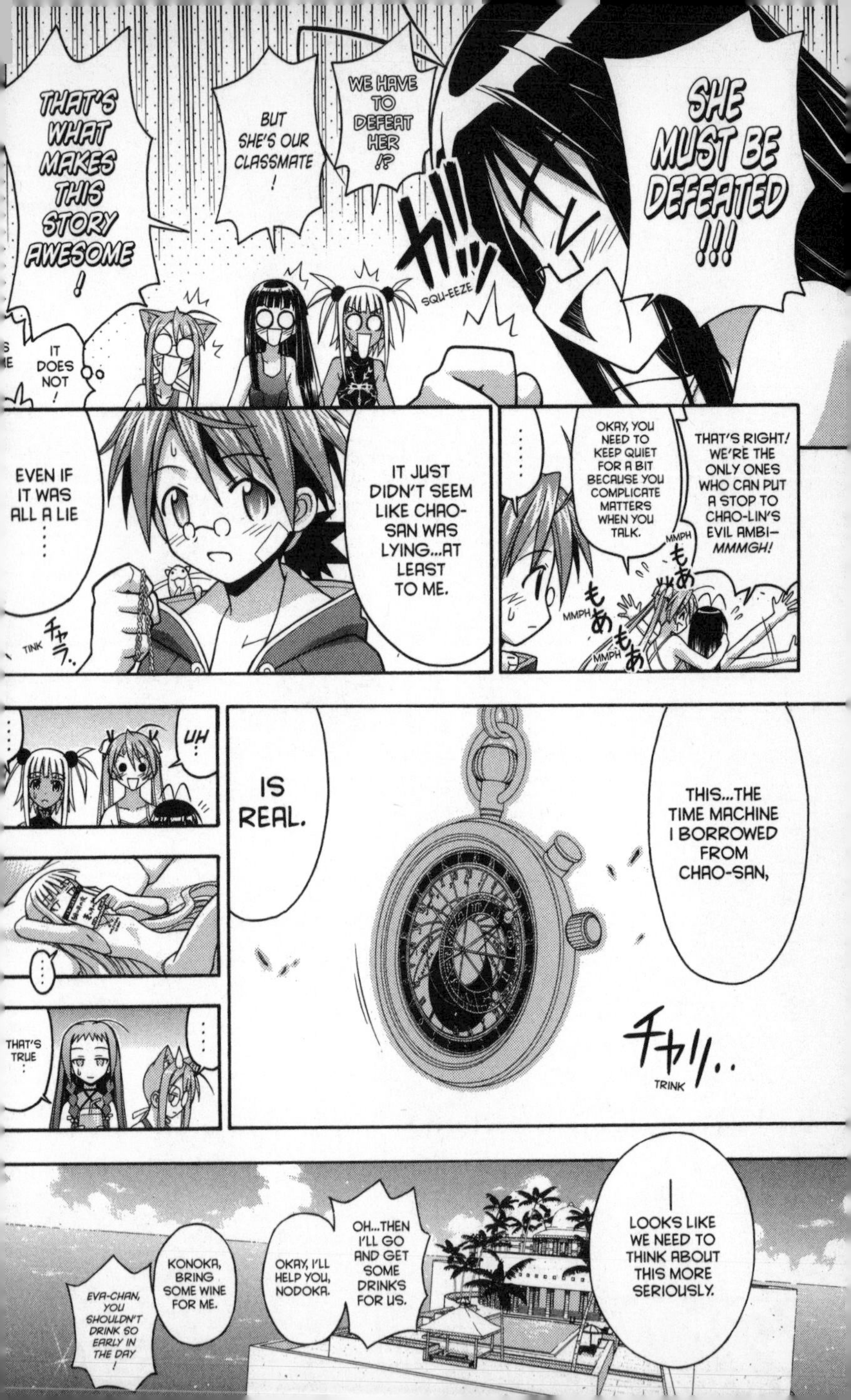
SHE MUST BE DEFEATED!!!
SQU-EEZE
WE HAVE TO DEFEAT HER!?
BUT SHE'S OUR CLASSMATE!
THAT'S WHAT MAKES THIS STORY AWESOME!
IT DOES NOT!
THAT'S RIGHT! WE'RE THE ONLY ONES WHO CAN PUT A STOP TO CHAO-LIN'S EVIL AMBI— MMMGH!
OKAY, YOU NEED TO KEEP QUIET FOR A BIT BECAUSE YOU COMPLICATE MATTERS WHEN YOU TALK.
......
MMPH
MMPH
MMPH
IT JUST DIDN'T SEEM LIKE CHAO-SAN WAS LYING...AT LEAST TO ME.
EVEN IF IT WAS ALL A LIE......
TINK
THIS...THE TIME MACHINE I BORROWED FROM CHAO-SAN,
IS REAL.
TRINK
UH...
......
......
......
THAT'S TRUE...
LOOKS LIKE WE NEED TO THINK ABOUT THIS MORE SERIOUSLY.
OH...THEN I'LL GO AND GET SOME DRINKS FOR US.
OKAY, I'LL HELP YOU, NODOKA.
KONOKA, BRING SOME WINE FOR ME.
EVA-CHAN, YOU SHOULDN'T DRINK SO EARLY IN THE DAY!

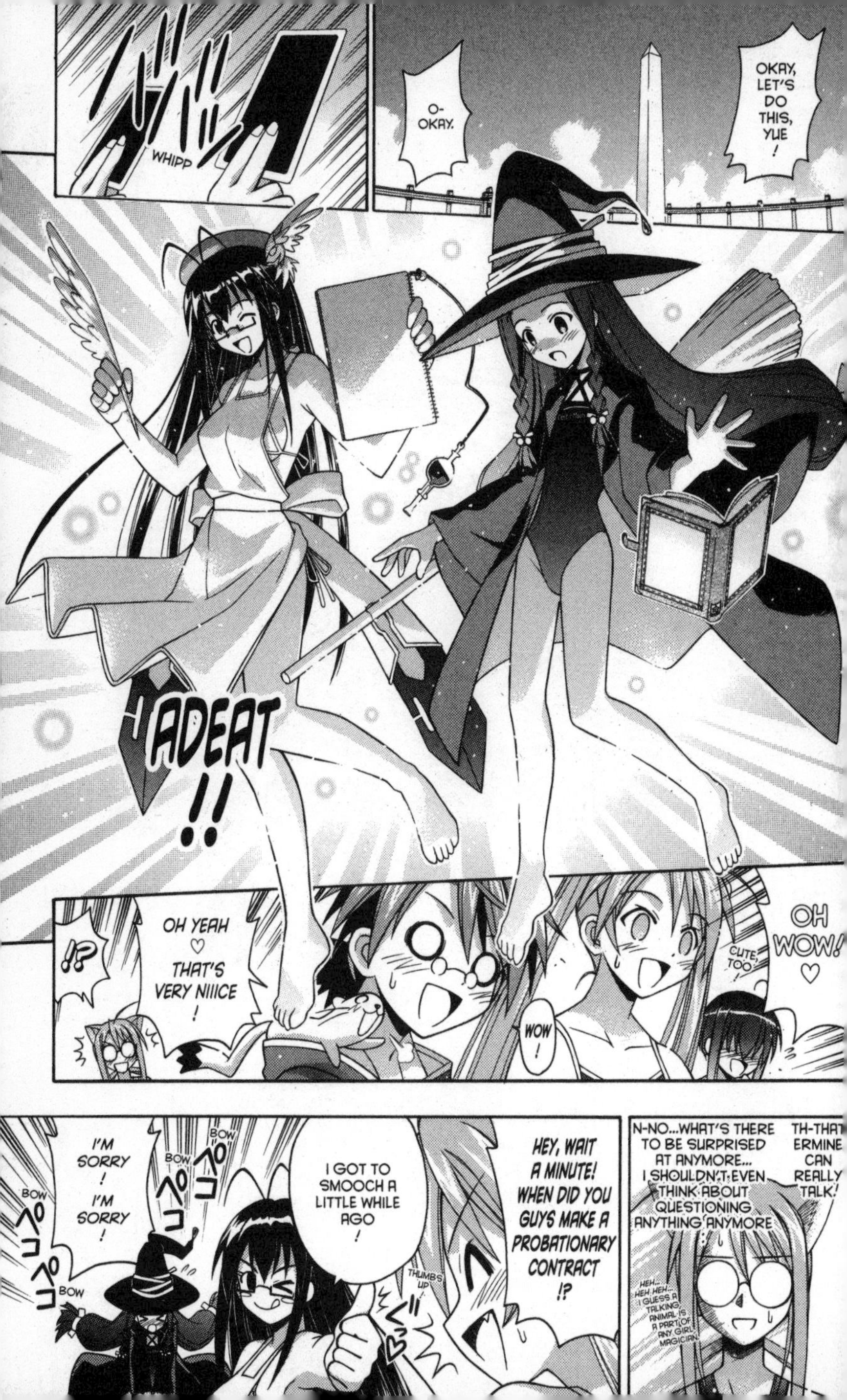
OKAY, LET'S DO THIS, YUE!
O-OKAY.
WHIPP
ADEAT!!
OH WOW! ♡
CUTE, TOO
WOW!
OH YEAH ♡ THAT'S VERY NIIICE!
!?
TH-THAT ERMINE CAN REALLY TALK!
N-NO...WHAT'S THERE TO BE SURPRISED AT ANYMORE... I SHOULDN'T EVEN THINK ABOUT QUESTIONING ANYTHING ANYMORE
HEH... HEH HEH... I GUESS A TALKING ANIMAL IS A PART OF ANY GIRL MAGICIAN
HEY, WAIT A MINUTE! WHEN DID YOU GUYS MAKE A PROBATIONARY CONTRACT!?
THUMBS UP
I GOT TO SMOOCH A LITTLE WHILE AGO!
BOW
BOW
I'M SORRY! I'M SORRY!
BOW
BOW

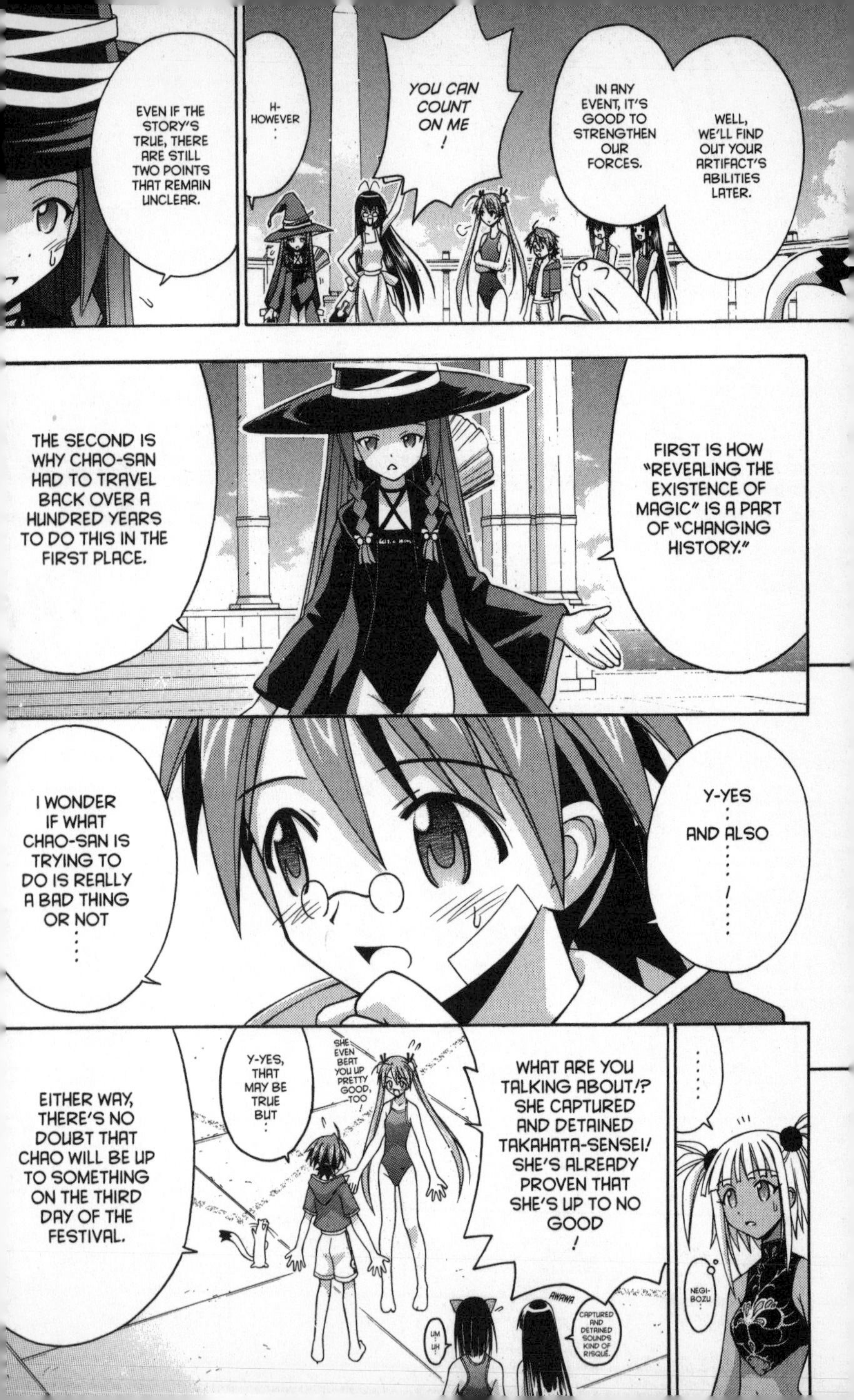
WELL, WE'LL FIND OUT YOUR ARTIFACT'S ABILITIES LATER.
IN ANY EVENT, IT'S GOOD TO STRENGTHEN OUR FORCES.
YOU CAN COUNT ON ME!
H-HOWEVER...
EVEN IF THE STORY'S TRUE, THERE ARE STILL TWO POINTS THAT REMAIN UNCLEAR.
FIRST IS HOW "REVEALING THE EXISTENCE OF MAGIC" IS A PART OF "CHANGING HISTORY."
THE SECOND IS WHY CHAO-SAN HAD TO TRAVEL BACK OVER A HUNDRED YEARS TO DO THIS IN THE FIRST PLACE.
Y-YES... AND ALSO......!....
I WONDER IF WHAT CHAO-SAN IS TRYING TO DO IS REALLY A BAD THING OR NOT...
......
NEGI-BOZU...
WHAT ARE YOU TALKING ABOUT!? SHE CAPTURED AND DETAINED TAKAHATA-SENSEI! SHE'S ALREADY PROVEN THAT SHE'S UP TO NO GOOD!
SHE EVEN BEAT YOU UP PRETTY GOOD, TOO!
Y-YES, THAT MAY BE TRUE BUT
EITHER WAY, THERE'S NO DOUBT THAT CHAO WILL BE UP TO SOMETHING ON THE THIRD DAY OF THE FESTIVAL.
AWAWA
CAPTURED AND DETAINED SOUNDS KIND OF RISQUÉ.
UM UH

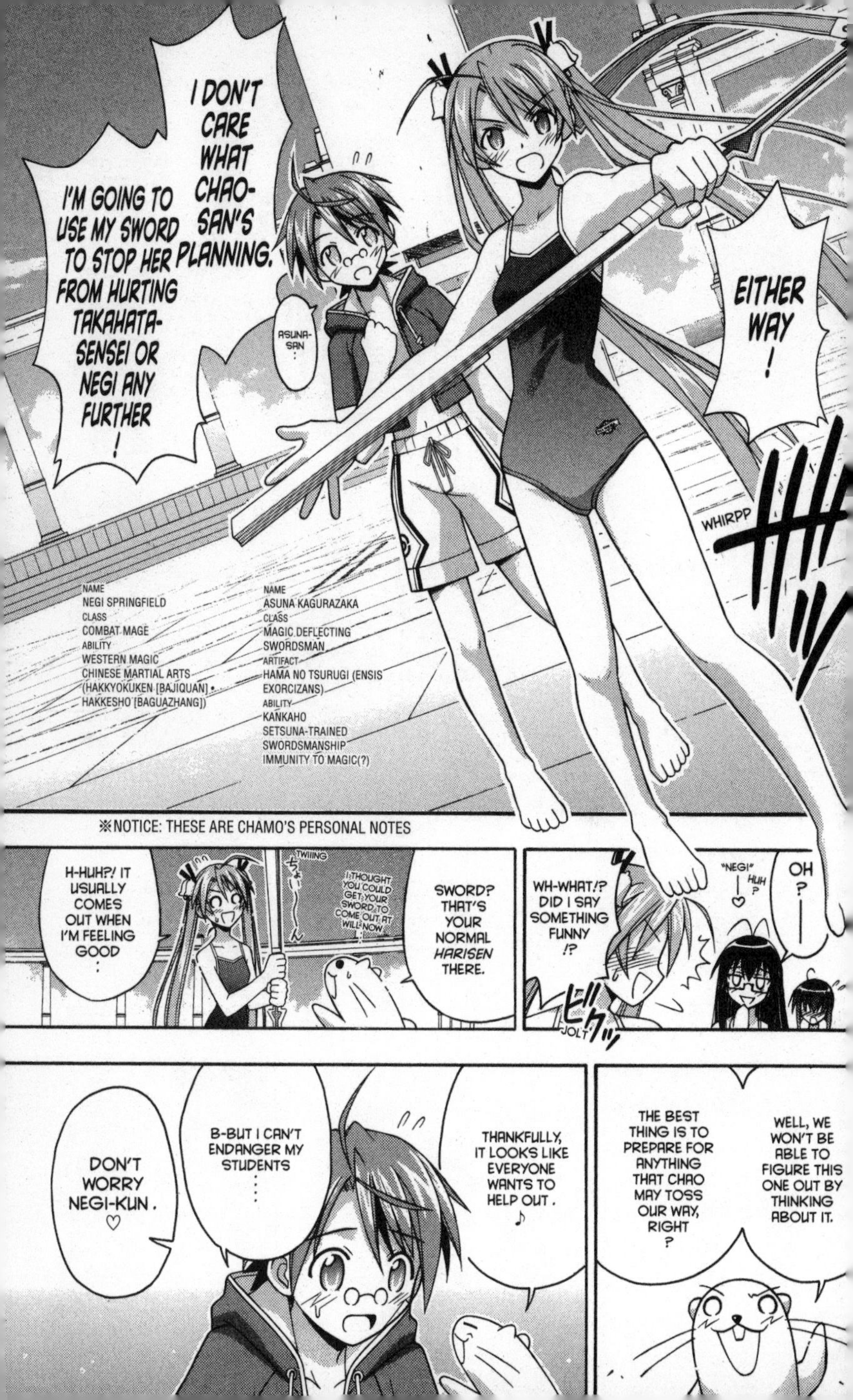
I DON'T CARE WHAT CHAO-SAN'S PLANNING.
I'M GOING TO USE MY SWORD TO STOP HER FROM HURTING TAKAHATA-SENSEI OR NEGI ANY FURTHER!
EITHER WAY!
ASUNA-SAN...
WHIRPP
NAME
NEGI SPRINGFIELD
CLASS
COMBAT MAGE
ABILITY
WESTERN MAGIC
CHINESE MARTIAL ARTS (HAKKYOKUKEN [BAJIQUAN] • HAKKESHO [BAGUAZHANG])
NAME
ASUNA KAGURAZAKA
CLASS
MAGIC DEFLECTING SWORDSMAN
ARTIFACT
HAMA NO TSURUGI (ENSIS EXORCIZANS)
ABILITY
KANKAHO
SETSUNA-TRAINED SWORDSMANSHIP
IMMUNITY TO MAGIC(?)
※NOTICE: THESE ARE CHAMO'S PERSONAL NOTES
OH?
"NEGI" HUH? ♡
WH-WHAT!? DID I SAY SOMETHING FUNNY!?
JOLT
SWORD? THAT'S YOUR NORMAL HARISEN THERE.
I THOUGHT YOU COULD GET YOUR SWORD TO COME OUT AT WILL NOW
TWIIING
H-HUH?! IT USUALLY COMES OUT WHEN I'M FEELING GOOD...
WELL, WE WON'T BE ABLE TO FIGURE THIS ONE OUT BY THINKING ABOUT IT.
THE BEST THING IS TO PREPARE FOR ANYTHING THAT CHAO MAY TOSS OUR WAY, RIGHT?
THANKFULLY, IT LOOKS LIKE EVERYONE WANTS TO HELP OUT. ♪
B-BUT I CAN'T ENDANGER MY STUDENTS...
DON'T WORRY NEGI-KUN. ♡

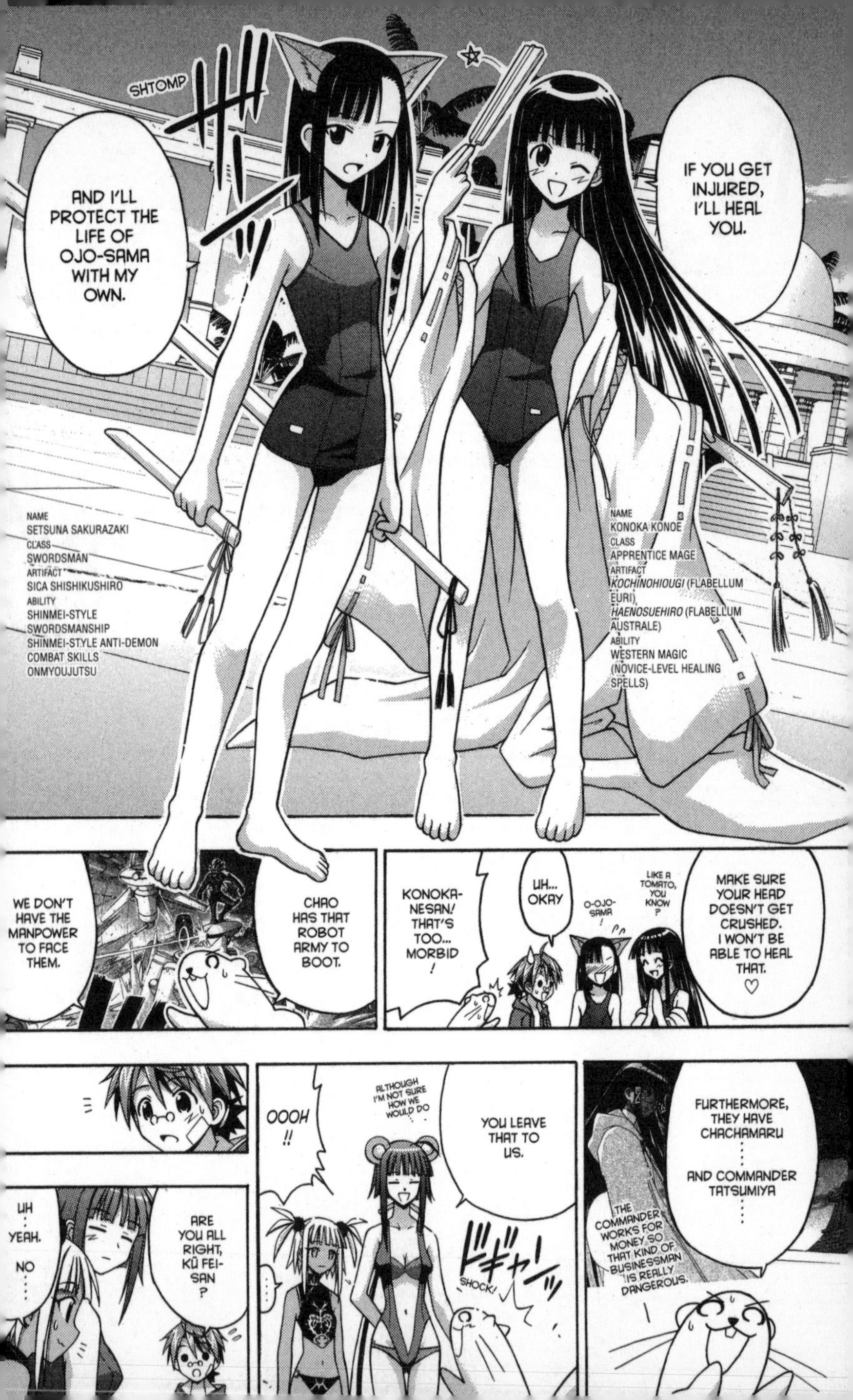
IF YOU GET INJURED, I'LL HEAL YOU.
SHTOMP
AND I'LL PROTECT THE LIFE OF OJO-SAMA WITH MY OWN.
NAME
KONOKA KONOE
CLASS
APPRENTICE MAGE
ARTIFACT
KOCHINOHIOUGI (FLABELLUM EURI), *HAENOSUEHIRO* (FLABELLUM AUSTRALE)
ABILITY
WESTERN MAGIC (NOVICE-LEVEL HEALING SPELLS)
NAME
SETSUNA SAKURAZAKI
CLASS
SWORDSMAN
ARTIFACT
SICA SHISHIKUSHIRO
ABILITY
SHINMEI-STYLE SWORDSMANSHIP
SHINMEI-STYLE ANTI-DEMON COMBAT SKILLS
ONMYOUJUTSU
MAKE SURE YOUR HEAD DOESN'T GET CRUSHED. I WON'T BE ABLE TO HEAL THAT. ♡
LIKE A TOMATO, YOU KNOW?
O-OJO-SAMA!
UH... OKAY
KONOKA-NESAN! THAT'S TOO... MORBID!
CHAO HAS THAT ROBOT ARMY TO BOOT.
WE DON'T HAVE THE MANPOWER TO FACE THEM.
FURTHERMORE, THEY HAVE CHACHAMARU......
AND COMMANDER TATSUMIYA......
THE COMMANDER WORKS FOR MONEY SO THAT KIND OF BUSINESSMAN IS REALLY DANGEROUS.
YOU LEAVE THAT TO US.
ALTHOUGH I'M NOT SURE HOW WE WOULD DO...
OOOH!!
SHOCK!
ARE YOU ALL RIGHT, KŪ FEI-SAN?
UH... YEAH.
NO......

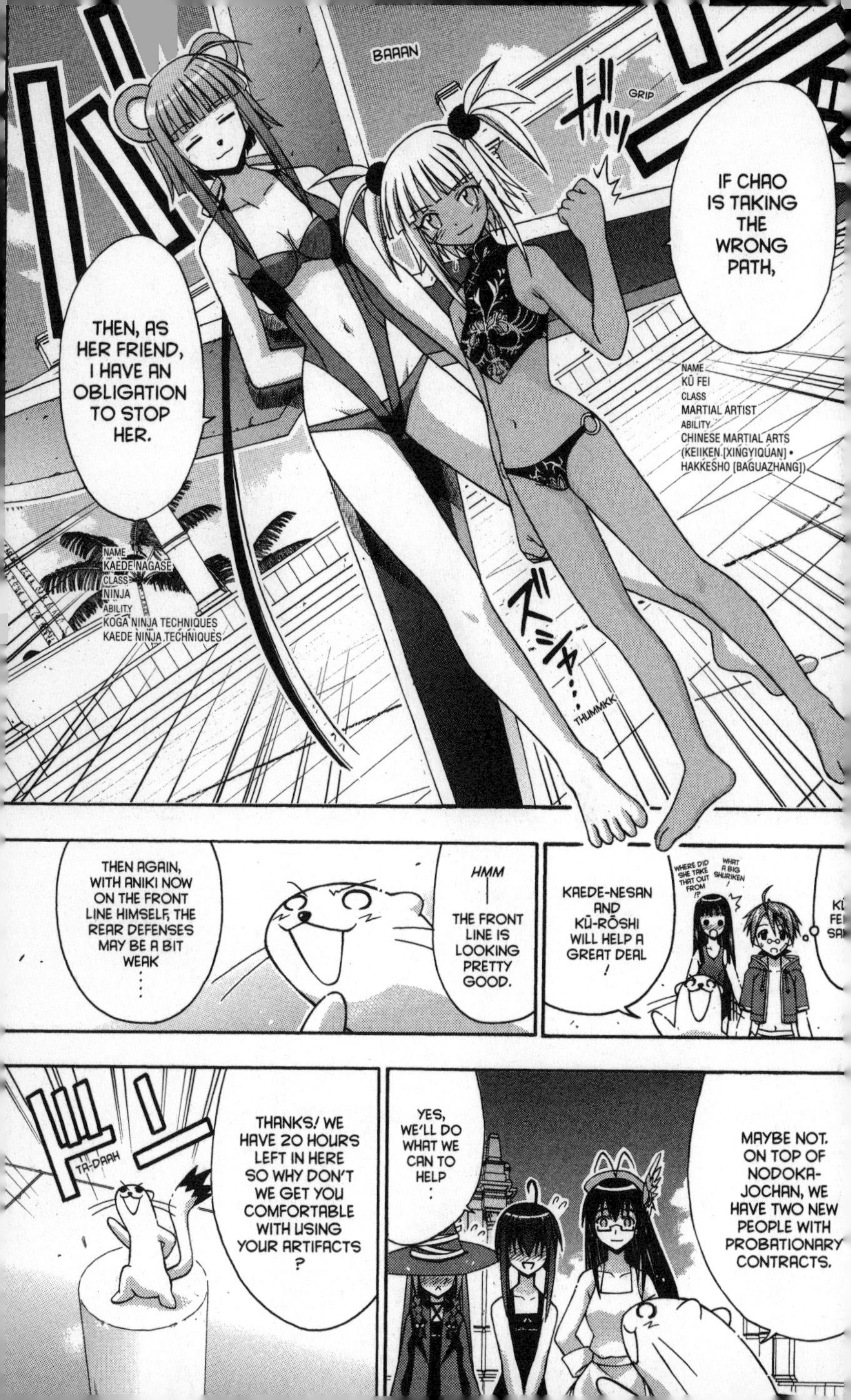
BAAAN
GRIP
IF CHAO IS TAKING THE WRONG PATH,
THEN, AS HER FRIEND, I HAVE AN OBLIGATION TO STOP HER.
NAME KŪ FEI CLASS MARTIAL ARTIST ABILITY CHINESE MARTIAL ARTS (KEIIKEN [XINGYIQUAN] • HAKKESHO [BAGUAZHANG])
NAME KAEDE NAGASE CLASS NINJA ABILITY KOGA NINJA TECHNIQUES KAEDE NINJA TECHNIQUES
THUMMKK
WHERE DID SHE TAKE THAT OUT FROM !?
WHAT A BIG SHURIKEN !
KAEDE-NESAN AND KŪ-RŌSHI WILL HELP A GREAT DEAL !
HMM
THE FRONT LINE IS LOOKING PRETTY GOOD.
THEN AGAIN, WITH ANIKI NOW ON THE FRONT LINE HIMSELF, THE REAR DEFENSES MAY BE A BIT WEAK ...
MAYBE NOT. ON TOP OF NODOKA-JOCHAN, WE HAVE TWO NEW PEOPLE WITH PROBATIONARY CONTRACTS.
YES, WE'LL DO WHAT WE CAN TO HELP :
THANKS! WE HAVE 20 HOURS LEFT IN HERE SO WHY DON'T WE GET YOU COMFORTABLE WITH USING YOUR ARTIFACTS ?
TA-DAAH

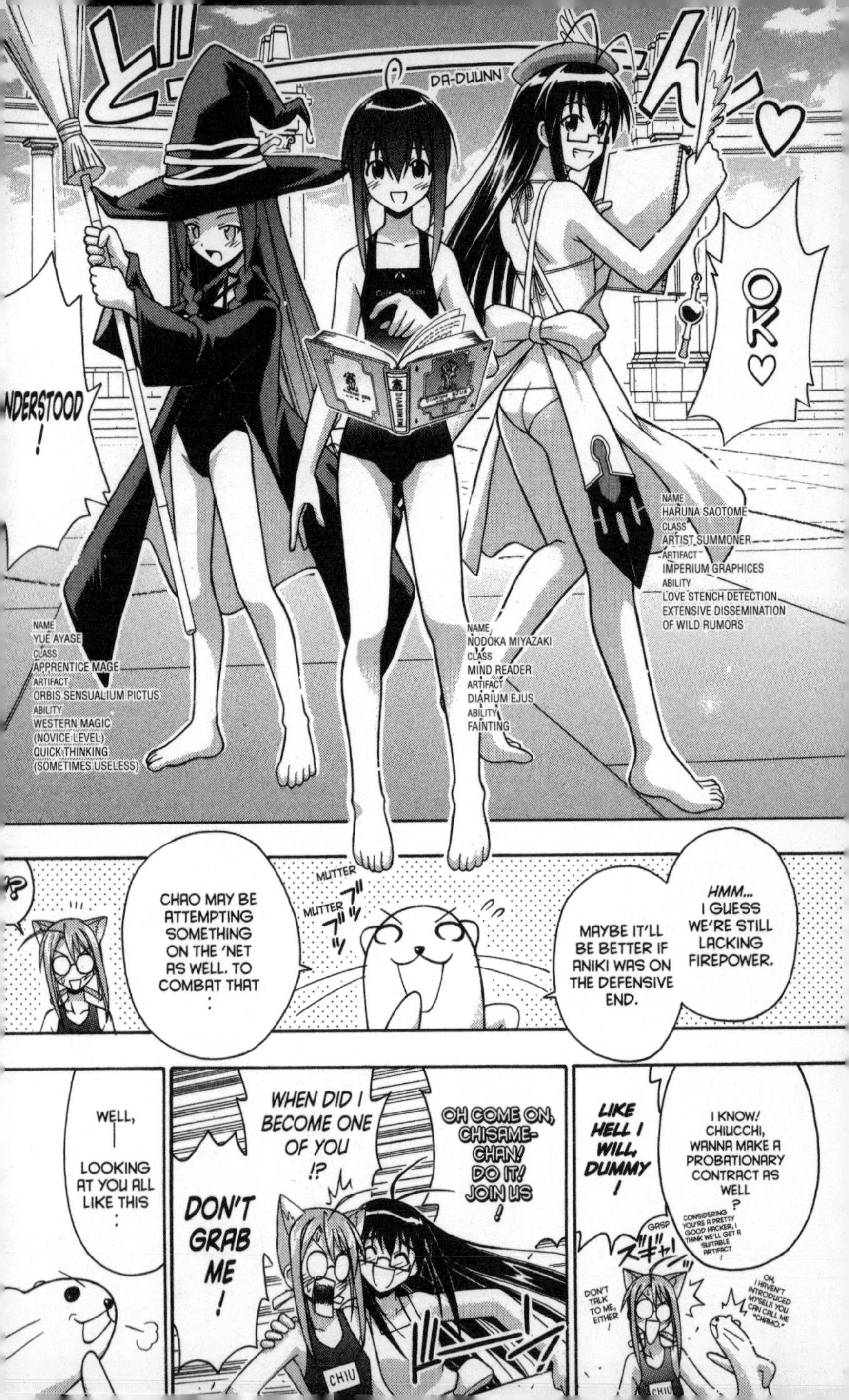
OK ♥
NAME HARUNA SAOTOME CLASS ARTIST SUMMONER ARTIFACT IMPERIUM GRAPHICES ABILITY LOVE STENCH DETECTION EXTENSIVE DISSEMINATION OF WILD RUMORS
DA-DUUNN
NAME NODOKA MIYAZAKI CLASS MIND READER ARTIFACT DIARIUM EJUS ABILITY FAINTING
NDERSTOOD !
NAME YUE AYASE CLASS APPRENTICE MAGE ARTIFACT ORBIS SENSUALIUM PICTUS ABILITY WESTERN MAGIC (NOVICE LEVEL) QUICK THINKING (SOMETIMES USELESS)
HMM... I GUESS WE'RE STILL LACKING FIREPOWER.
MAYBE IT'LL BE BETTER IF ANIKI WAS ON THE DEFENSIVE END.
MUTTER MUTTER
CHAO MAY BE ATTEMPTING SOMETHING ON THE 'NET AS WELL. TO COMBAT THAT :
!?
I KNOW! CHIUCCHI, WANNA MAKE A PROBATIONARY CONTRACT AS WELL ?
CONSIDERING YOU'RE A PRETTY GOOD HACKER, I THINK WE'LL GET A SUITABLE ARTIFACT !
LIKE HELL I WILL, DUMMY !
GASP
OH, I HAVEN'T INTRODUCED MYSELF. YOU CAN CALL ME "CHAMO."
DON'T TALK TO ME, EITHER !
CHIU
OH COME ON, CHISAME-CHAN! DO IT! JOIN US !
WHEN DID I BECOME ONE OF YOU !?
DON'T GRAB ME !
CHIU
WELL, LOOKING AT YOU ALL LIKE THIS :

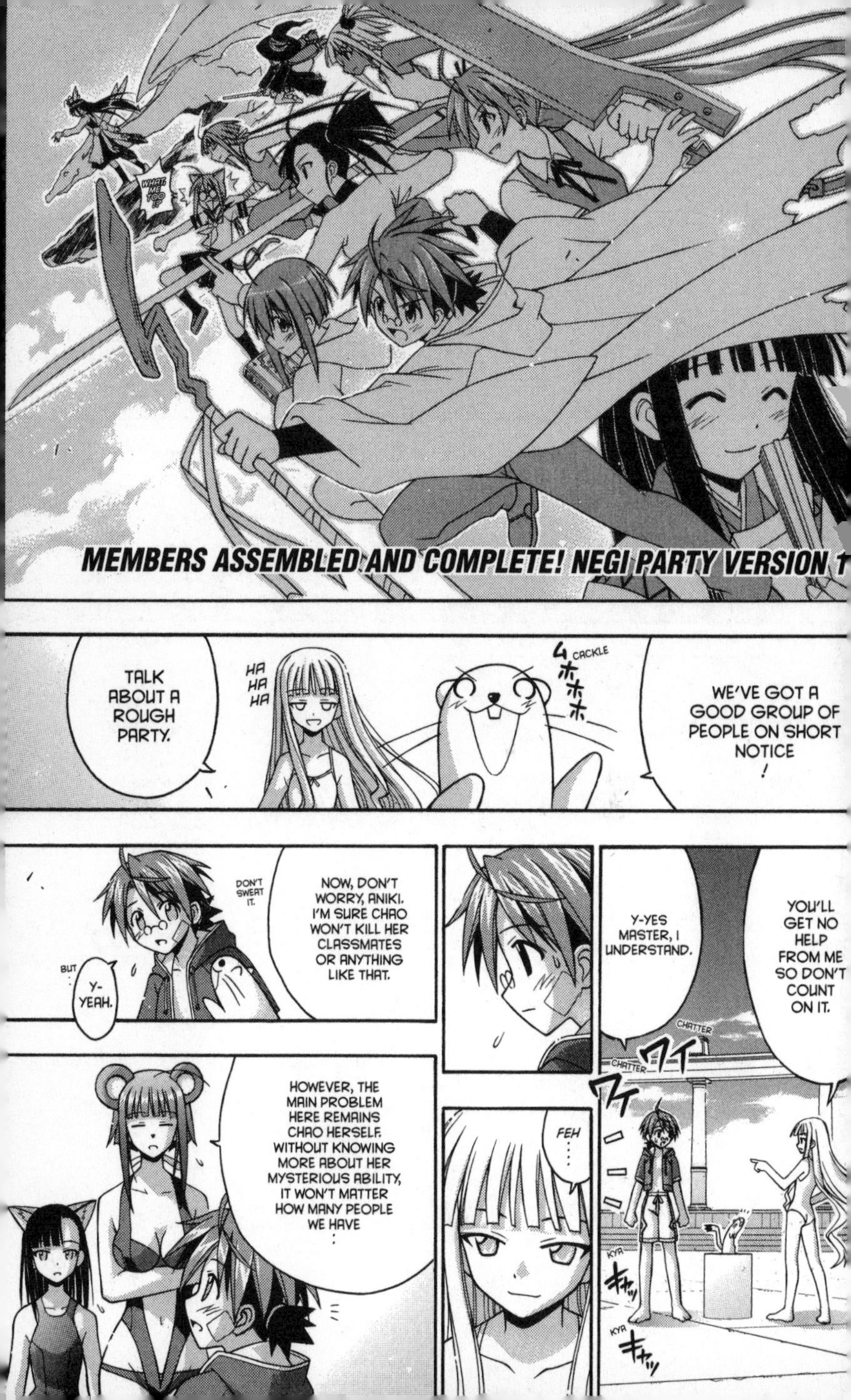
WHAT ME TOO!?
MEMBERS ASSEMBLED AND COMPLETE! NEGI PARTY VERSION 1
WE'VE GOT A GOOD GROUP OF PEOPLE ON SHORT NOTICE!
CACKLE
HA HA HA
TALK ABOUT A ROUGH PARTY.
YOU'LL GET NO HELP FROM ME SO DON'T COUNT ON IT.
Y-YES MASTER, I UNDERSTAND.
CHATTER
CHATTER
KYA
KYA
NOW, DON'T WORRY, ANIKI. I'M SURE CHAO WON'T KILL HER CLASSMATES OR ANYTHING LIKE THAT.
DON'T SWEAT IT.
BUT...
Y-YEAH.
FEH...
HOWEVER, THE MAIN PROBLEM HERE REMAINS CHAO HERSELF. WITHOUT KNOWING MORE ABOUT HER MYSTERIOUS ABILITY, IT WON'T MATTER HOW MANY PEOPLE WE HAVE...

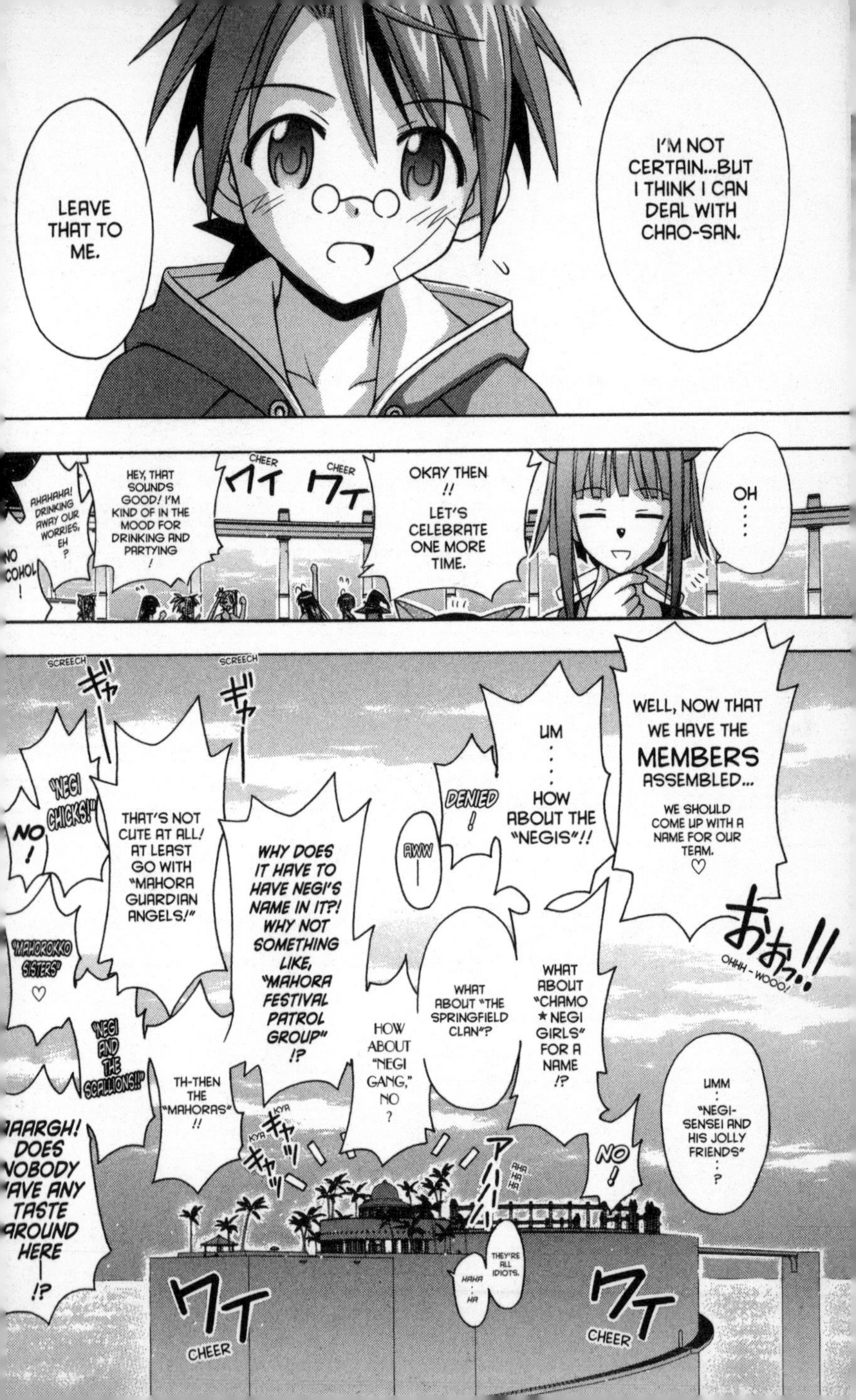
I'M NOT CERTAIN...BUT I THINK I CAN DEAL WITH CHAO-SAN.
LEAVE THAT TO ME.
OH ...
OKAY THEN!! LET'S CELEBRATE ONE MORE TIME.
ワイ CHEER
ワイ CHEER
HEY, THAT SOUNDS GOOD! I'M KIND OF IN THE MOOD FOR DRINKING AND PARTYING!
AHAHAHA! DRINKING AWAY OUR WORRIES, EH?
NO COHOL!
WELL, NOW THAT WE HAVE THE MEMBERS ASSEMBLED... WE SHOULD COME UP WITH A NAME FOR OUR TEAM. ♡
おおっ!! OHHH - WOOO!
UM... HOW ABOUT THE "NEGIS"!!
DENIED!
AWW—
WHAT ABOUT "CHAMO★NEGI GIRLS" FOR A NAME!?
WHAT ABOUT "THE SPRINGFIELD CLAN"?
WHY DOES IT HAVE TO HAVE NEGI'S NAME IN IT?! WHY NOT SOMETHING LIKE, "MAHORA FESTIVAL PATROL GROUP"!?
THAT'S NOT CUTE AT ALL! AT LEAST GO WITH "MAHORA GUARDIAN ANGELS!"
ギャー SCREECH
ギャー SCREECH
"NEGI CHICKS!"
NO!
"MAHOROKKO SISTERS" ♡
UMM: "NEGI-SENSEI AND HIS JOLLY FRIENDS"..?
NO!
HOW ABOUT "NEGI GANG," NO?
"NEGI AND THE SCALLIONS!!"
TH-THEN THE "MAHORAS"!!
ギャッ ギャッ KYA KYA
アハハハ AHAHAHA
THEY'RE ALL IDIOTS.
HAHA.. HA
AARGH! DOES NOBODY HAVE ANY TASTE AROUND HERE—!?
ワイ CHEER
ワイ CHEER

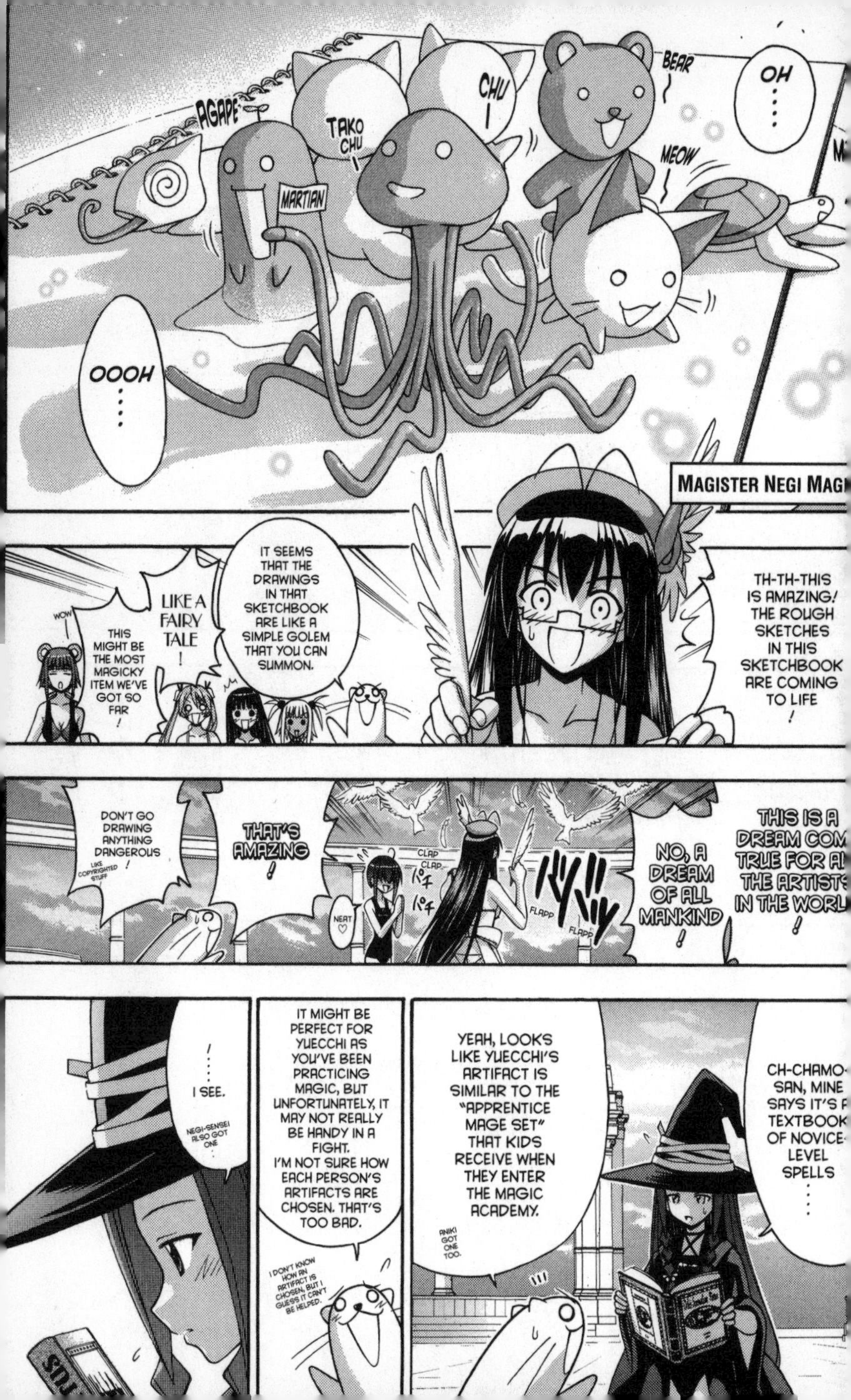
OH ....
BEAR ~
CHU !
MEOW ~
TAKO CHU !
AGAPE
MARTIAN
OOOH ....
TH-TH-THIS IS AMAZING! THE ROUGH SKETCHES IN THIS SKETCHBOOK ARE COMING TO LIFE!
IT SEEMS THAT THE DRAWINGS IN THAT SKETCHBOOK ARE LIKE A SIMPLE GOLEM THAT YOU CAN SUMMON.
LIKE A FAIRY TALE!
THIS MIGHT BE THE MOST MAGICKY ITEM WE'VE GOT SO FAR!
WOW!
THIS IS A DREAM COM TRUE FOR AL THE ARTISTS IN THE WORL!
NO, A DREAM OF ALL MANKIND!
FLAPP FLAPP
CLAP CLAP パチ パチ
NEAT ♡
THAT'S AMAZING!
DON'T GO DRAWING ANYTHING DANGEROUS!
LIKE COPYRIGHTED STUFF
CH-CHAMO-SAN, MINE SAYS IT'S A TEXTBOOK OF NOVICE-LEVEL SPELLS ....
YEAH, LOOKS LIKE YUECCHI'S ARTIFACT IS SIMILAR TO THE "APPRENTICE MAGE SET" THAT KIDS RECEIVE WHEN THEY ENTER THE MAGIC ACADEMY.
ANIKI GOT ONE TOO.
IT MIGHT BE PERFECT FOR YUECCHI AS YOU'VE BEEN PRACTICING MAGIC, BUT UNFORTUNATELY, IT MAY NOT REALLY BE HANDY IN A FIGHT. I'M NOT SURE HOW EACH PERSON'S ARTIFACTS ARE CHOSEN. THAT'S TOO BAD.
I DON'T KNOW HOW AN ARTIFACT IS CHOSEN, BUT I GUESS IT CAN'T BE HELPED.
....! I SEE.
NEGI-SENSEI ALSO GOT ONE...

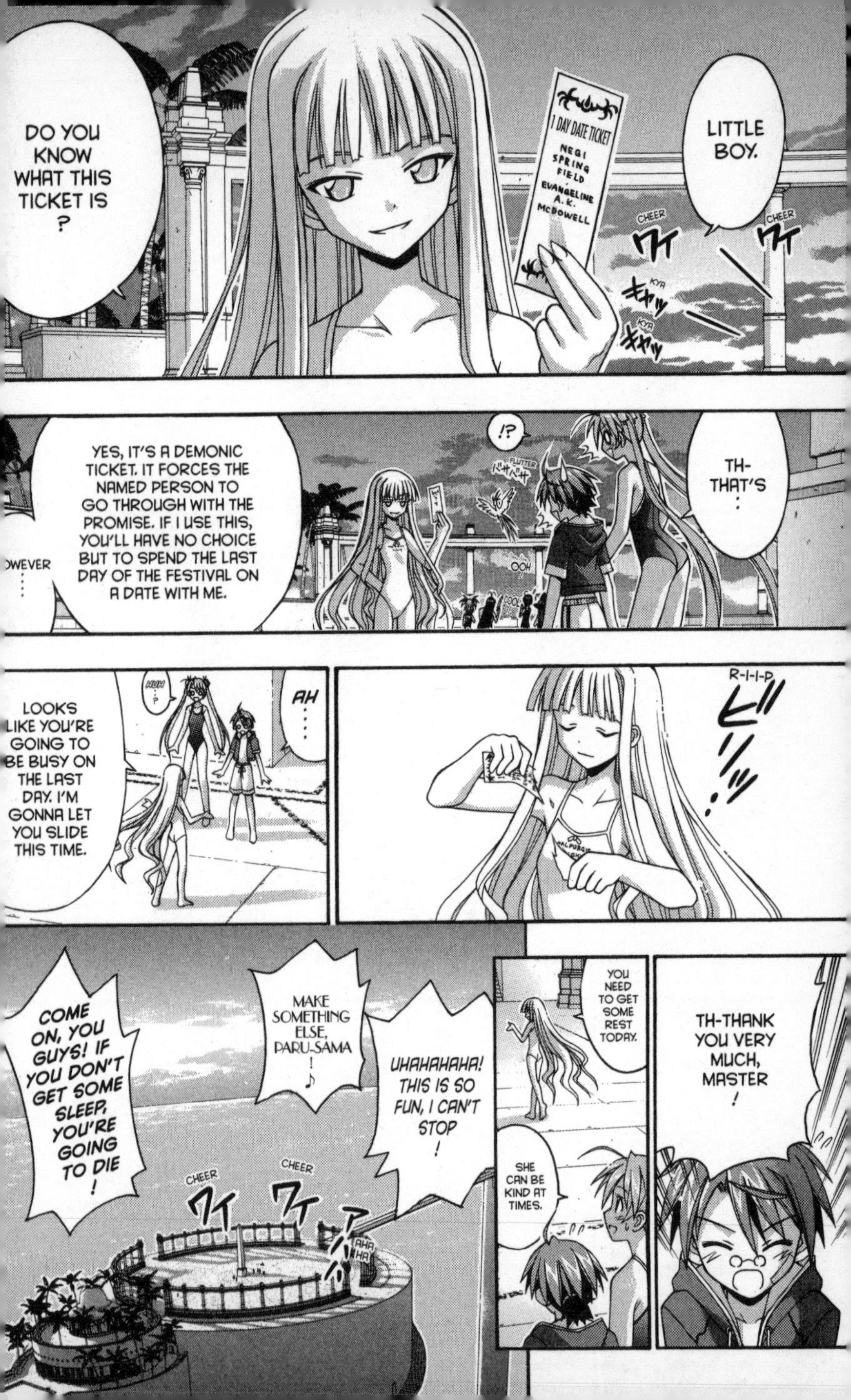
LITTLE BOY.
CHEER
CHEER
1 DAY DATE TICKET
NEGI SPRING FIELD
EVANGELINE A.K. McDOWELL
DO YOU KNOW WHAT THIS TICKET IS?
KYA
KYA
TH-THAT'S...
!?
FLUTTER
YES, IT'S A DEMONIC TICKET. IT FORCES THE NAMED PERSON TO GO THROUGH WITH THE PROMISE. IF I USE THIS, YOU'LL HAVE NO CHOICE BUT TO SPEND THE LAST DAY OF THE FESTIVAL ON A DATE WITH ME.
OOH
OWEVER...
R-I-I-P
AH...
HUH...?
LOOKS LIKE YOU'RE GOING TO BE BUSY ON THE LAST DAY. I'M GONNA LET YOU SLIDE THIS TIME.
TH-THANK YOU VERY MUCH, MASTER!
YOU NEED TO GET SOME REST TODAY.
SHE CAN BE KIND AT TIMES.
UHAHAHAHA! THIS IS SO FUN, I CAN'T STOP!
MAKE SOMETHING ELSE, PARU-SAMA!♪
COME ON, YOU GUYS! IF YOU DON'T GET SOME SLEEP, YOU'RE GOING TO DIE!
CHEER
CHEER
AHA HA

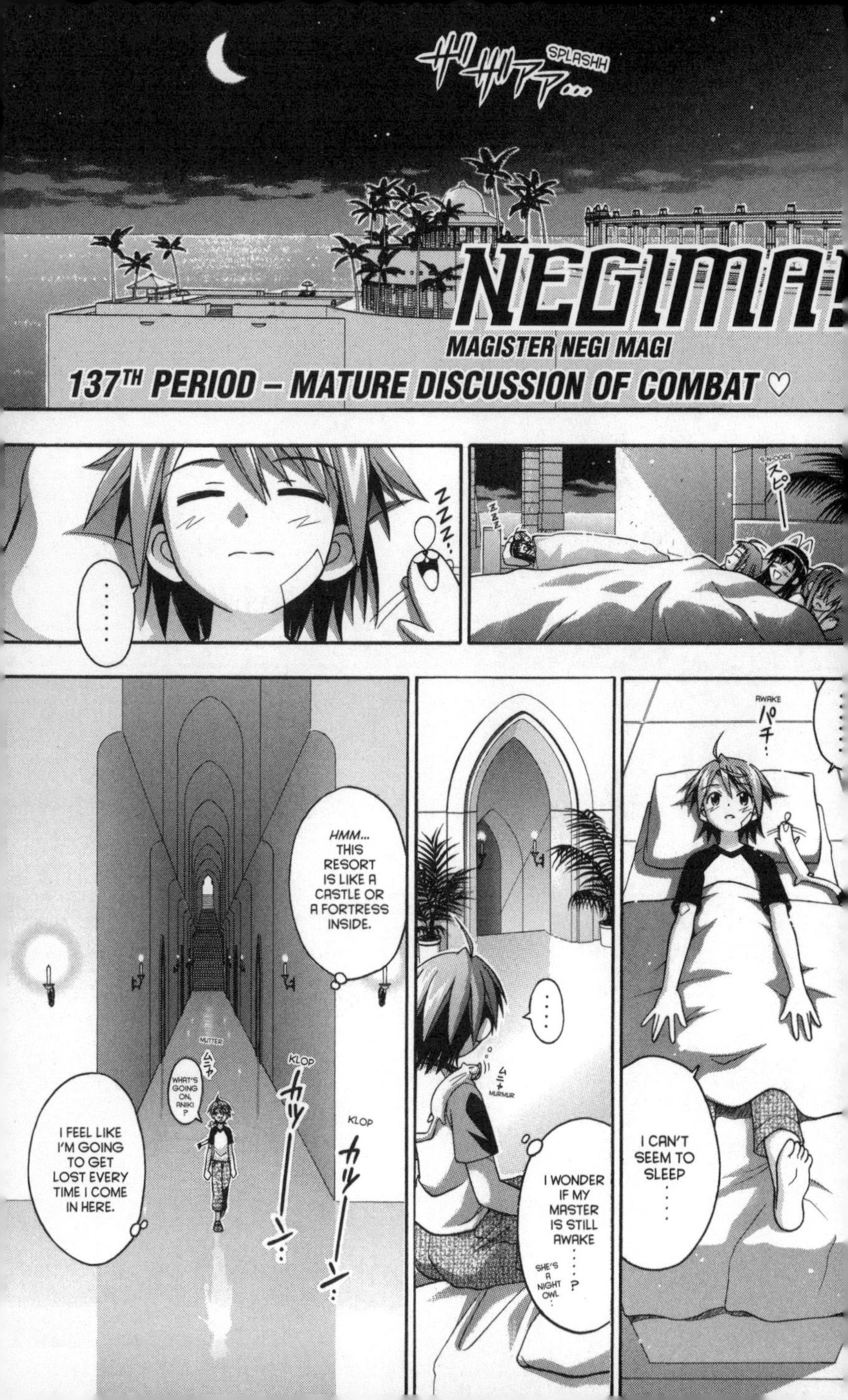
SPLASHH
NEGIMA!
MAGISTER NEGI MAGI
137TH PERIOD – MATURE DISCUSSION OF COMBAT ♡
S-N-ORE
スピー
ZZZ...
......
AWAKE
パチ...
I CAN'T SEEM TO SLEEP ......
....
MURMUR
I WONDER IF MY MASTER IS STILL AWAKE ....?
SHE'S A NIGHT OWL...
HMM... THIS RESORT IS LIKE A CASTLE OR A FORTRESS INSIDE.
KLOP
KLOP
MUTTER
WHAT'S GOING ON, ANIKI?
I FEEL LIKE I'M GOING TO GET LOST EVERY TIME I COME IN HERE.

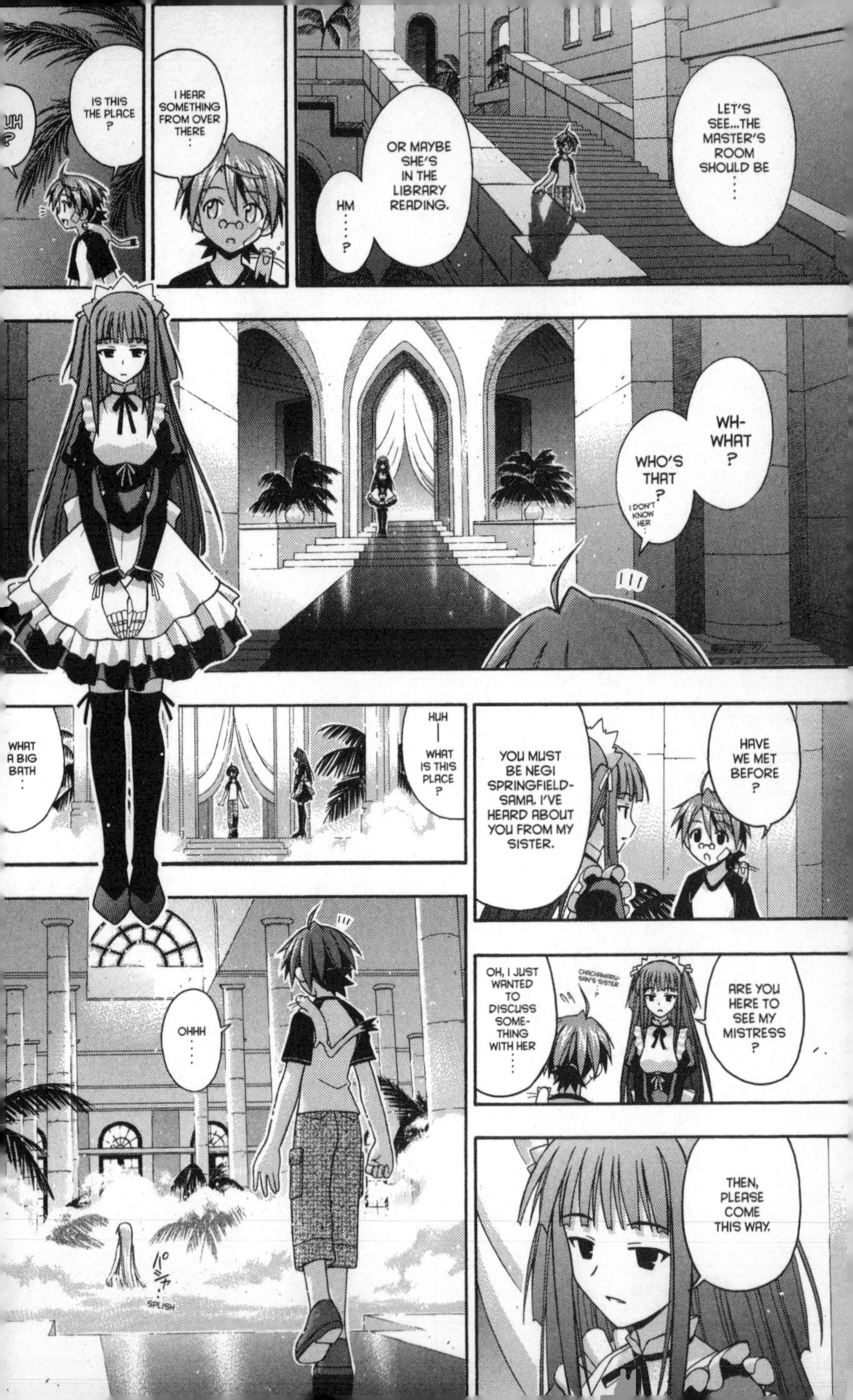
LET'S SEE...THE MASTER'S ROOM SHOULD BE ...
OR MAYBE SHE'S IN THE LIBRARY READING.
HM ...?
I HEAR SOMETHING FROM OVER THERE ...
IS THIS THE PLACE?
WH-WHAT?
WHO'S THAT?
I DON'T KNOW HER ...
HAVE WE MET BEFORE?
YOU MUST BE NEGI SPRINGFIELD-SAMA. I'VE HEARD ABOUT YOU FROM MY SISTER.
HUH — WHAT IS THIS PLACE?
WHAT A BIG BATH ...
ARE YOU HERE TO SEE MY MISTRESS?
CHACHAMARU-SAN'S SISTER?
OH, I JUST WANTED TO DISCUSS SOMETHING WITH HER ...
THEN, PLEASE COME THIS WAY.
OHHH ...
SPLISH

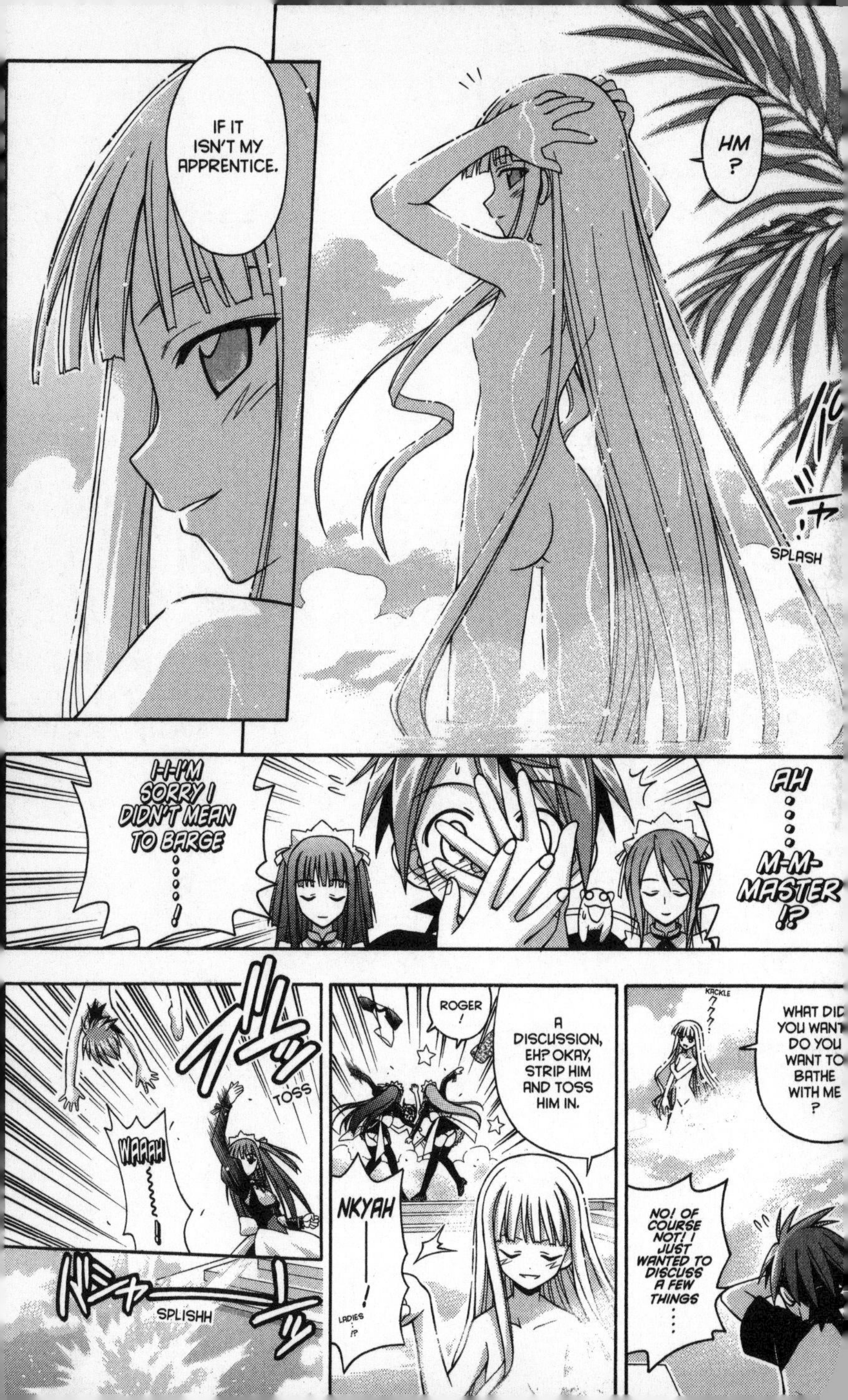
HM?
SPLASH
IF IT ISN'T MY APPRENTICE.
AH.... M-M-MASTER!?
I-I-I'M SORRY I DIDN'T MEAN TO BARGE.....!
KACKLE
WHAT DID YOU WANT DO YOU WANT TO BATHE WITH ME?
NO! OF COURSE NOT! I JUST WANTED TO DISCUSS A FEW THINGS....
A DISCUSSION, EH? OKAY, STRIP HIM AND TOSS HIM IN.
ROGER!
NKYAH!
LADIES!?
TOSS
WAAAH~!
SPLISHH

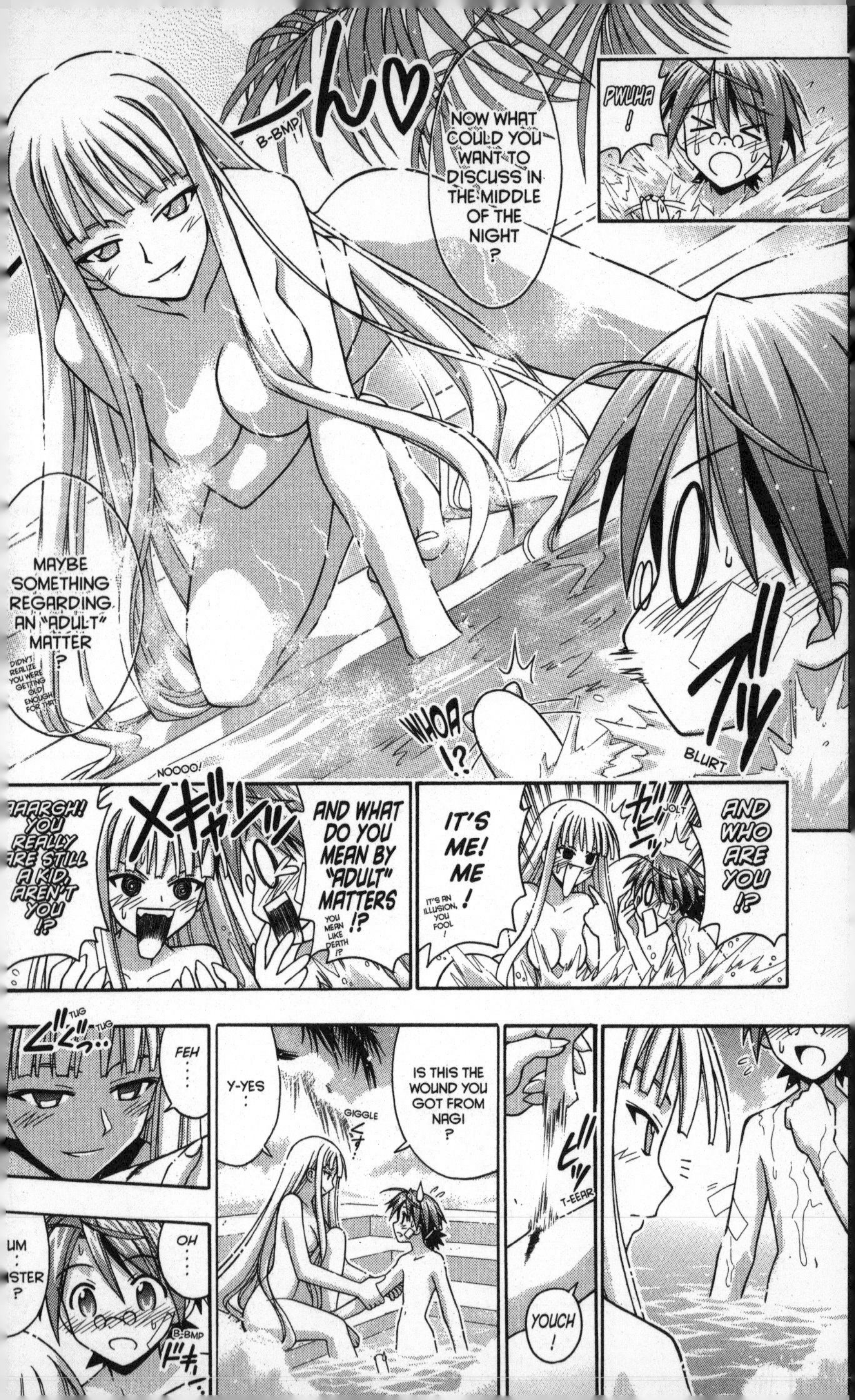
PWUHA !
NOW WHAT COULD YOU WANT TO DISCUSS IN THE MIDDLE OF THE NIGHT ?
B-BMP
MAYBE SOMETHING REGARDING AN "ADULT" MATTER ?
DIDN'T REALIZE YOU WERE GETTING OLD ENOUGH FOR THAT
BLURT
WHOA !?
AND WHO ARE YOU !?
JOLT
IT'S ME! ME !
IT'S AN ILLUSION, YOU FOOL !
AND WHAT DO YOU MEAN BY "ADULT" MATTERS !?
YOU MEAN LIKE DEATH !?
AAARGH! YOU REALLY ARE STILL A KID, AREN'T YOU !?
NOOOO!
T-EEAR
YOUCH !
IS THIS THE WOUND YOU GOT FROM NAGI ?
GIGGLE
Y-YES . . .
TUG TUG
FEH . . .
OH
UM . . .
ISTER ?
B-BMP

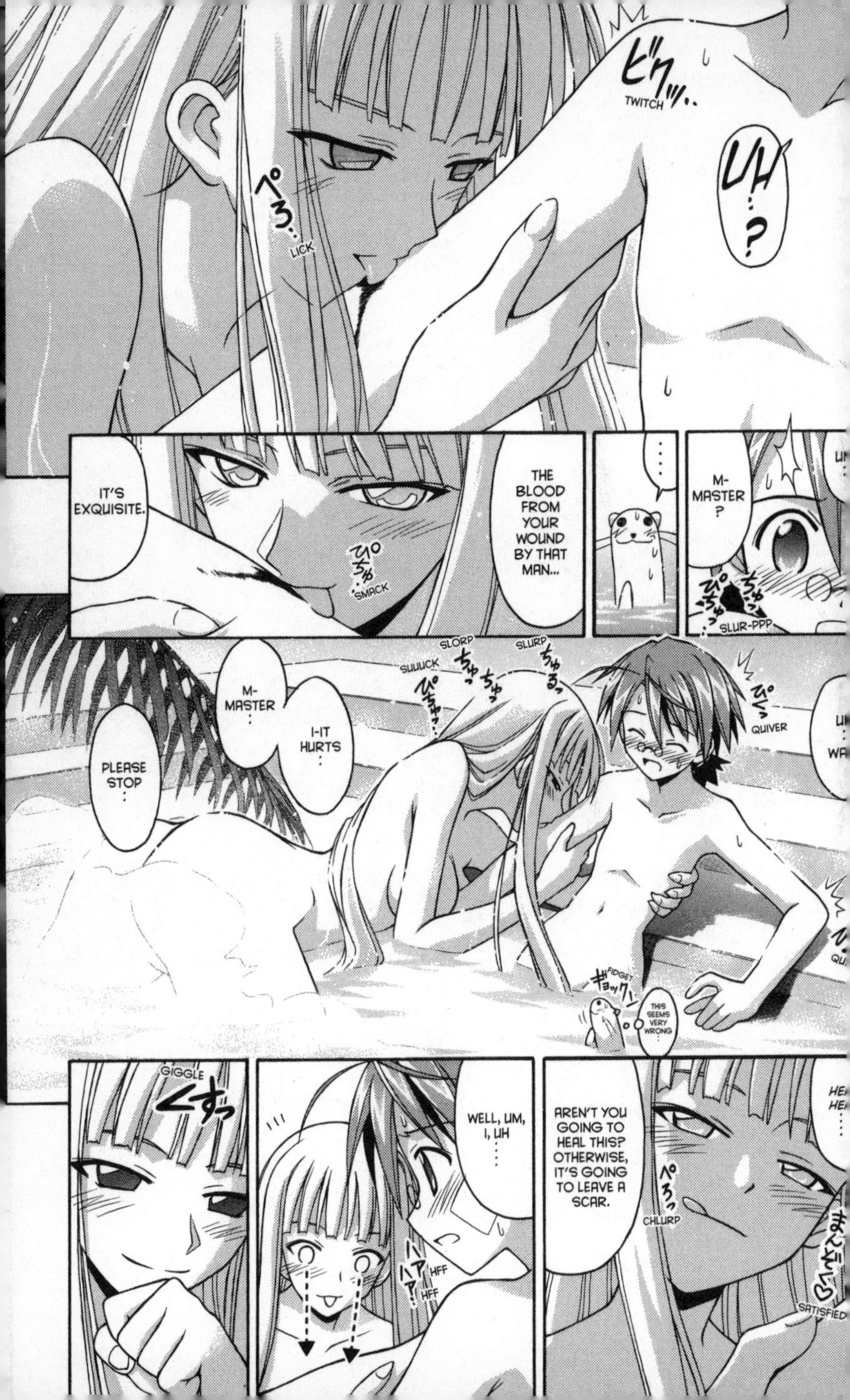
TWITCH
UH...?
LICK
M-MASTER?
SLUR-PPP
....
THE BLOOD FROM YOUR WOUND BY THAT MAN...
SMACK
IT'S EXQUISITE.
QUIVER
SLURP
SLORP
SUUUCK
M-MASTER...
I-IT HURTS...
PLEASE STOP...
FIDGET
THIS SEEMS VERY WRONG...
CHLURP
SATISFIED
AREN'T YOU GOING TO HEAL THIS? OTHERWISE, IT'S GOING TO LEAVE A SCAR.
WELL, UM, I, UH....
HFF HFF
GIGGLE

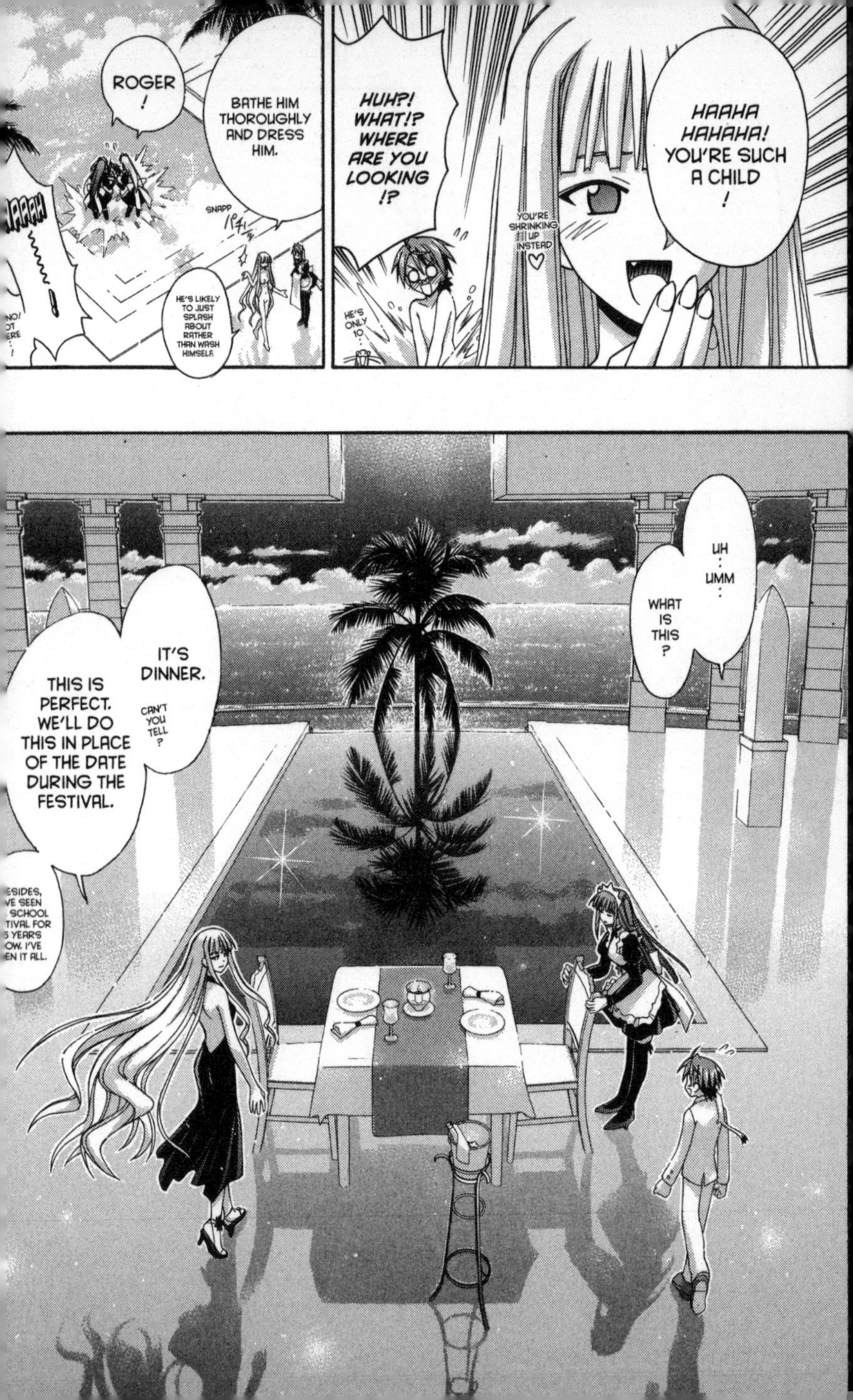
HAAHA HAHAHA! YOU'RE SUCH A CHILD!
YOU'RE SHRINKING UP INSTEAD
HUH?! WHAT!? WHERE ARE YOU LOOKING!?
HE'S ONLY 10...
BATHE HIM THOROUGHLY AND DRESS HIM.
ROGER!
SNAPP
HE'S LIKELY TO JUST SPLASH ABOUT RATHER THAN WASH HIMSELF.
UH... UMM... WHAT IS THIS?
IT'S DINNER.
CAN'T YOU TELL?
THIS IS PERFECT. WE'LL DO THIS IN PLACE OF THE DATE DURING THE FESTIVAL.

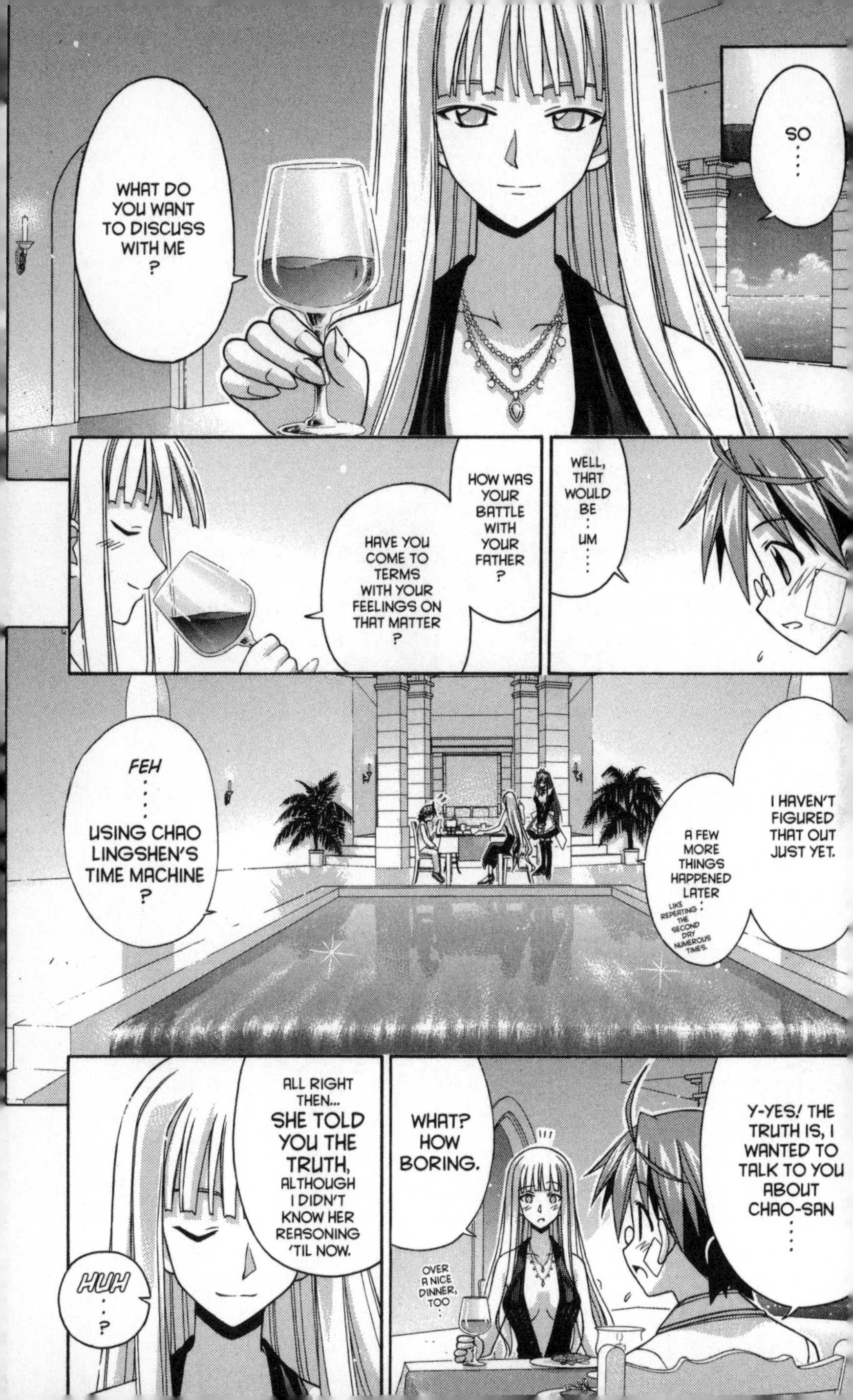
SO...
WHAT DO YOU WANT TO DISCUSS WITH ME?
WELL, THAT WOULD BE... UM...
HOW WAS YOUR BATTLE WITH YOUR FATHER?
HAVE YOU COME TO TERMS WITH YOUR FEELINGS ON THAT MATTER?
I HAVEN'T FIGURED THAT OUT JUST YET.
A FEW MORE THINGS HAPPENED LATER:
LIKE REPEATING THE SECOND DAY NUMEROUS TIMES.
FEH... USING CHAO LINGSHEN'S TIME MACHINE?
Y-YES! THE TRUTH IS, I WANTED TO TALK TO YOU ABOUT CHAO-SAN...
WHAT? HOW BORING.
OVER A NICE DINNER, TOO...
ALL RIGHT THEN... SHE TOLD YOU THE TRUTH, ALTHOUGH I DIDN'T KNOW HER REASONING 'TIL NOW.
HUH...?

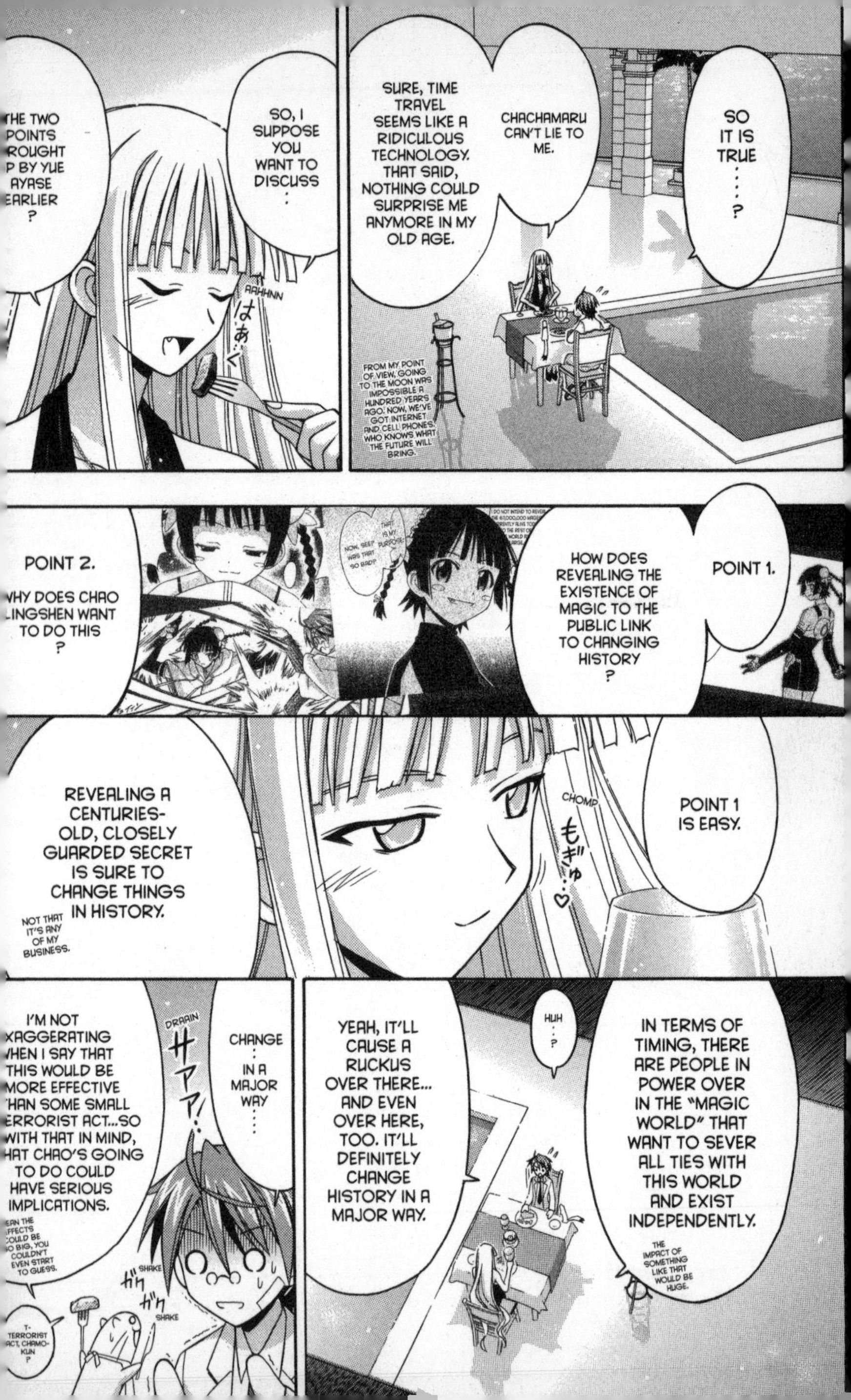
SO IT IS TRUE....?
CHACHAMARU CAN'T LIE TO ME.
SURE, TIME TRAVEL SEEMS LIKE A RIDICULOUS TECHNOLOGY. THAT SAID, NOTHING COULD SURPRISE ME ANYMORE IN MY OLD AGE.
FROM MY POINT OF VIEW, GOING TO THE MOON WAS IMPOSSIBLE A HUNDRED YEARS AGO. NOW, WE'VE GOT INTERNET AND CELL PHONES. WHO KNOWS WHAT THE FUTURE WILL BRING.
AHHHNN
はあ…く
SO, I SUPPOSE YOU WANT TO DISCUSS...
THE TWO POINTS ROUGHT P BY YUE AYASE EARLIER ?
POINT 1.
HOW DOES REVEALING THE EXISTENCE OF MAGIC TO THE PUBLIC LINK TO CHANGING HISTORY ?
THAT IS MY PURPOSE.
NOW, SEE? WAS THAT SO BAD?
POINT 2.
VHY DOES CHAO INGSHEN WANT TO DO THIS ?
POINT 1 IS EASY.
CHOMP
もぎゅ…♡
REVEALING A CENTURIES-OLD, CLOSELY GUARDED SECRET IS SURE TO CHANGE THINGS IN HISTORY.
NOT THAT IT'S ANY OF MY BUSINESS.
IN TERMS OF TIMING, THERE ARE PEOPLE IN POWER OVER IN THE "MAGIC WORLD" THAT WANT TO SEVER ALL TIES WITH THIS WORLD AND EXIST INDEPENDENTLY.
THE IMPACT OF SOMETHING LIKE THAT WOULD BE HUGE.
HUH...?
YEAH, IT'LL CAUSE A RUCKUS OVER THERE... AND EVEN OVER HERE, TOO. IT'LL DEFINITELY CHANGE HISTORY IN A MAJOR WAY.
CHANGE... IN A MAJOR WAY...
DRAAIN
サァア
I'M NOT XAGGERATING VHEN I SAY THAT THIS WOULD BE MORE EFFECTIVE HAN SOME SMALL ERRORIST ACT...SO WITH THAT IN MIND, HAT CHAO'S GOING TO DO COULD HAVE SERIOUS IMPLICATIONS.
EAN THE FFECTS COULD BE O BIG, YOU COULDN'T EVEN START TO GUESS.
SHAKE
ガク
ガク
SHAKE
T-TERRORIST ACT, CHAMO-KUN ?

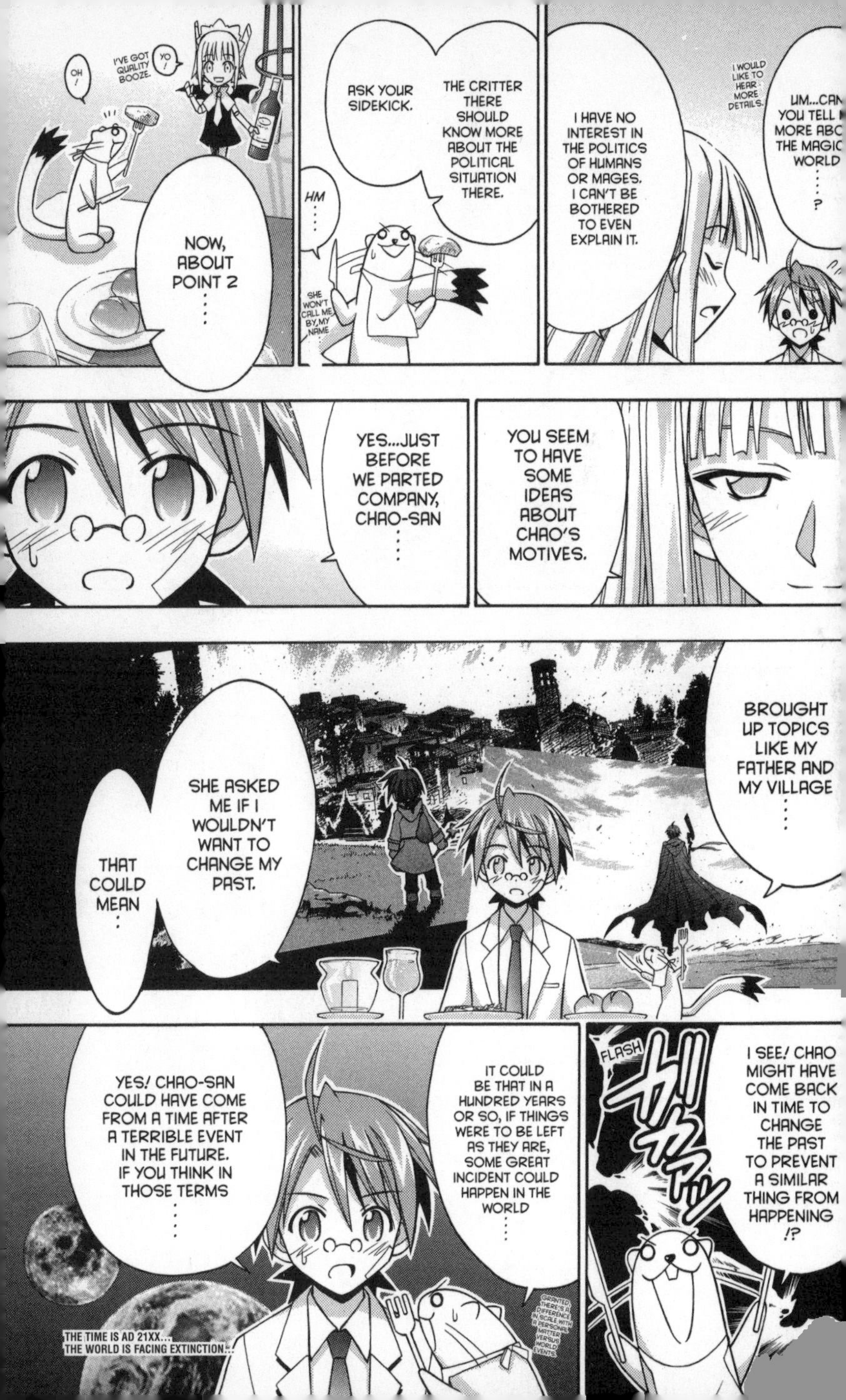
UM...CAN YOU TELL M MORE ABO THE MAGIC WORLD ...?
I WOULD LIKE TO HEAR MORE DETAILS.
I HAVE NO INTEREST IN THE POLITICS OF HUMANS OR MAGES. I CAN'T BE BOTHERED TO EVEN EXPLAIN IT.
THE CRITTER THERE SHOULD KNOW MORE ABOUT THE POLITICAL SITUATION THERE.
ASK YOUR SIDEKICK.
HM...
SHE WON'T CALL ME BY MY NAME
YO!
I'VE GOT QUALITY BOOZE.
OH!
NOW, ABOUT POINT 2...
YOU SEEM TO HAVE SOME IDEAS ABOUT CHAO'S MOTIVES.
YES...JUST BEFORE WE PARTED COMPANY, CHAO-SAN...
BROUGHT UP TOPICS LIKE MY FATHER AND MY VILLAGE...
SHE ASKED ME IF I WOULDN'T WANT TO CHANGE MY PAST.
THAT COULD MEAN...
FLASH
I SEE! CHAO MIGHT HAVE COME BACK IN TIME TO CHANGE THE PAST TO PREVENT A SIMILAR THING FROM HAPPENING!?
IT COULD BE THAT IN A HUNDRED YEARS OR SO, IF THINGS WERE TO BE LEFT AS THEY ARE, SOME GREAT INCIDENT COULD HAPPEN IN THE WORLD...
YES! CHAO-SAN COULD HAVE COME FROM A TIME AFTER A TERRIBLE EVENT IN THE FUTURE. IF YOU THINK IN THOSE TERMS...
GRANTED, THERE'S A DIFFERENCE IN SCALE WITH A PERSONAL MATTER VERSUS WORLD EVENTS.
THE TIME IS AD 21XX... THE WORLD IS FACING EXTINCTION...

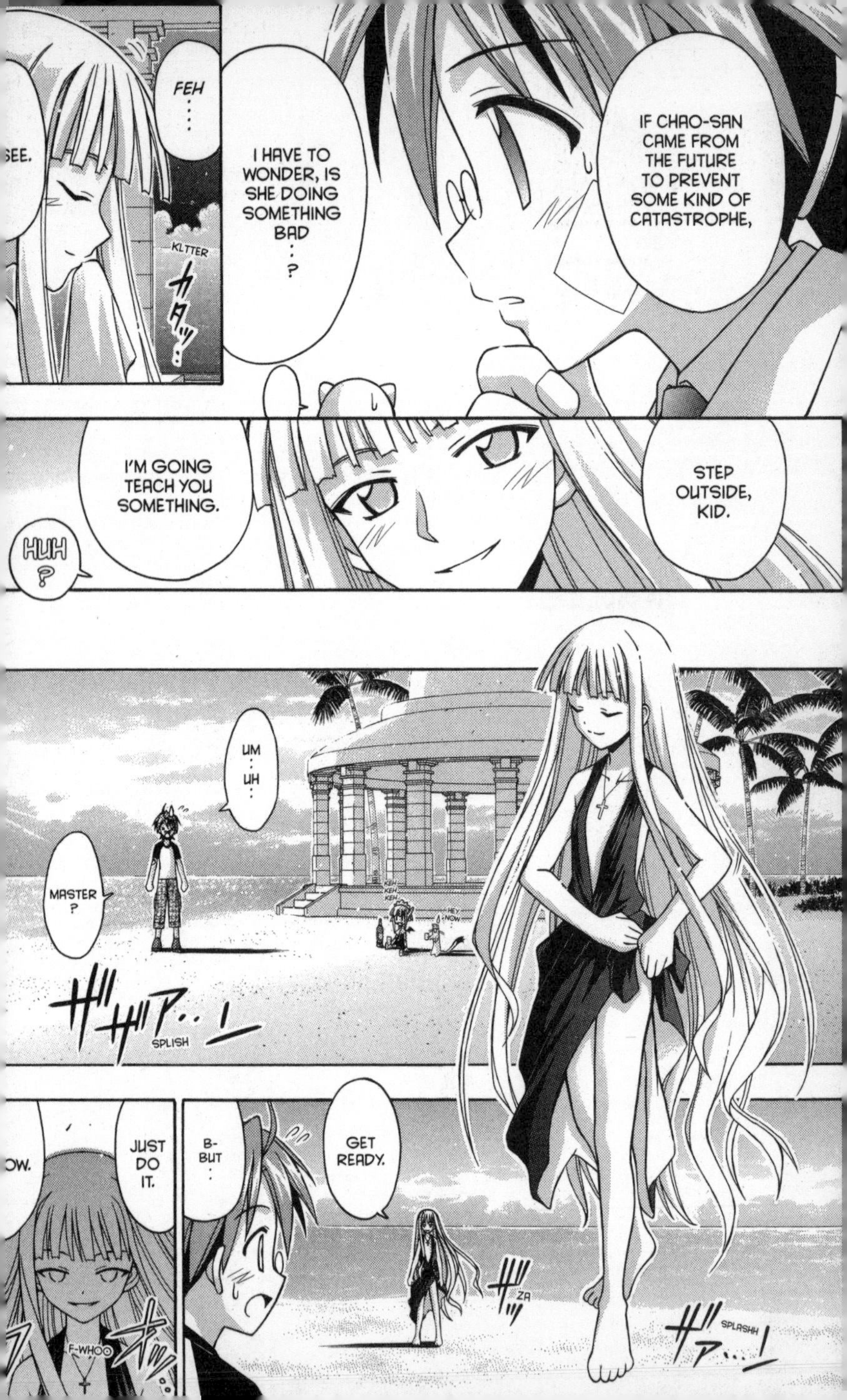
IF CHAO-SAN CAME FROM THE FUTURE TO PREVENT SOME KIND OF CATASTROPHE,
I HAVE TO WONDER, IS SHE DOING SOMETHING BAD...?
FEH...
SEE.
KLTTER
カタッ
STEP OUTSIDE, KID.
I'M GOING TEACH YOU SOMETHING.
HUH?
UM... UH...
MASTER?
KEH KEH KEH
HEY NOW
ザザァ...!
SPLISH
ザァ...!
SPLASHH
ザッ
ZA
GET READY.
B-BUT...
JUST DO IT.
OW.
F-WHOO

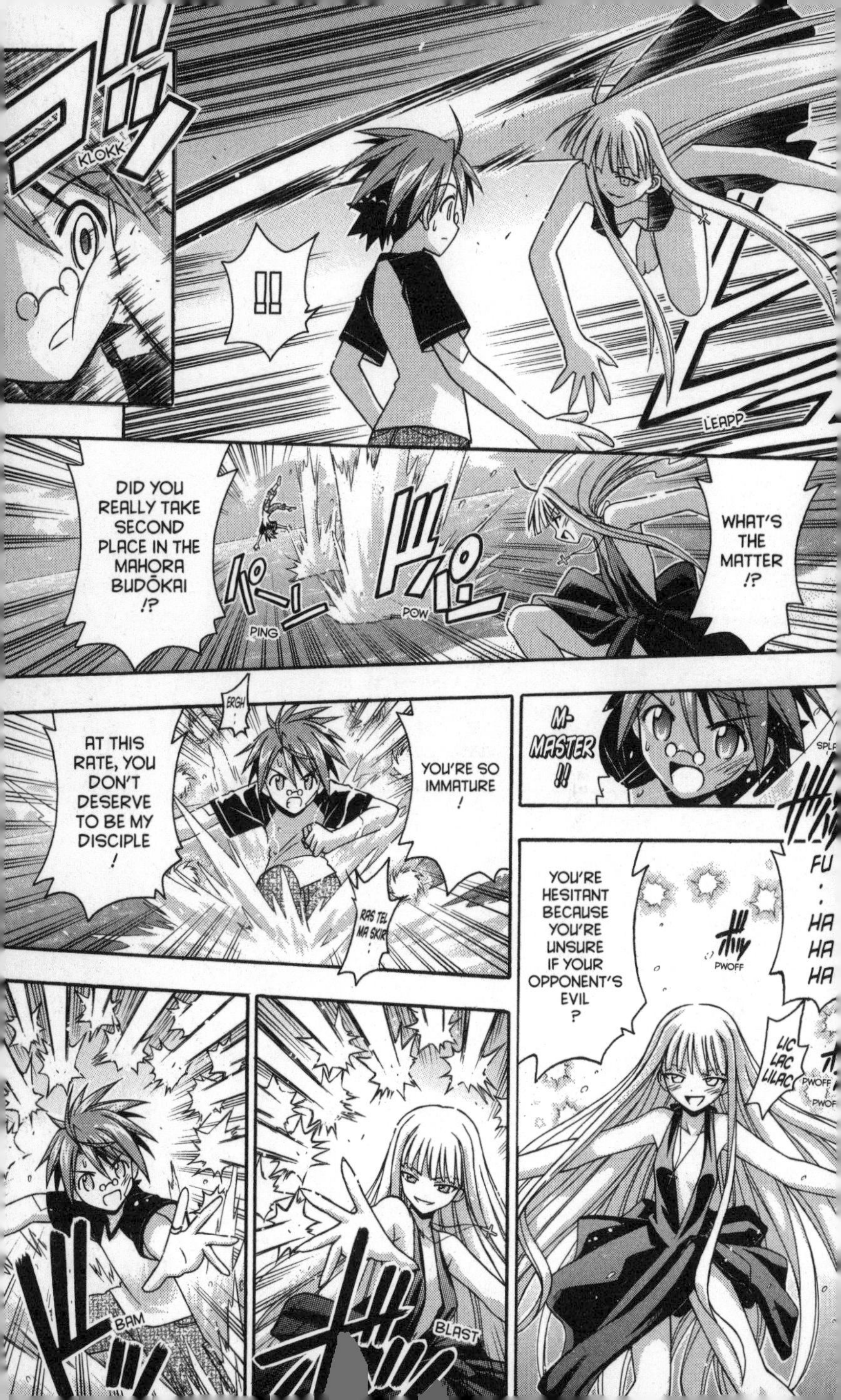

!!
LEAPP
KLOKK
WHAT'S THE MATTER !?
POW
PING
DID YOU REALLY TAKE SECOND PLACE IN THE MAHORA BUDŌKAI !?
M-MASTER !!
ERGH...
YOU'RE SO IMMATURE!
AT THIS RATE, YOU DON'T DESERVE TO BE MY DISCIPLE!
RAS TEL MA SKIR...
FU... HA HA HA
YOU'RE HESITANT BECAUSE YOU'RE UNSURE IF YOUR OPPONENT'S EVIL?
PWOFF
LIC LAC LILAC
PWOFF
PWOFF
BLAST
BAM

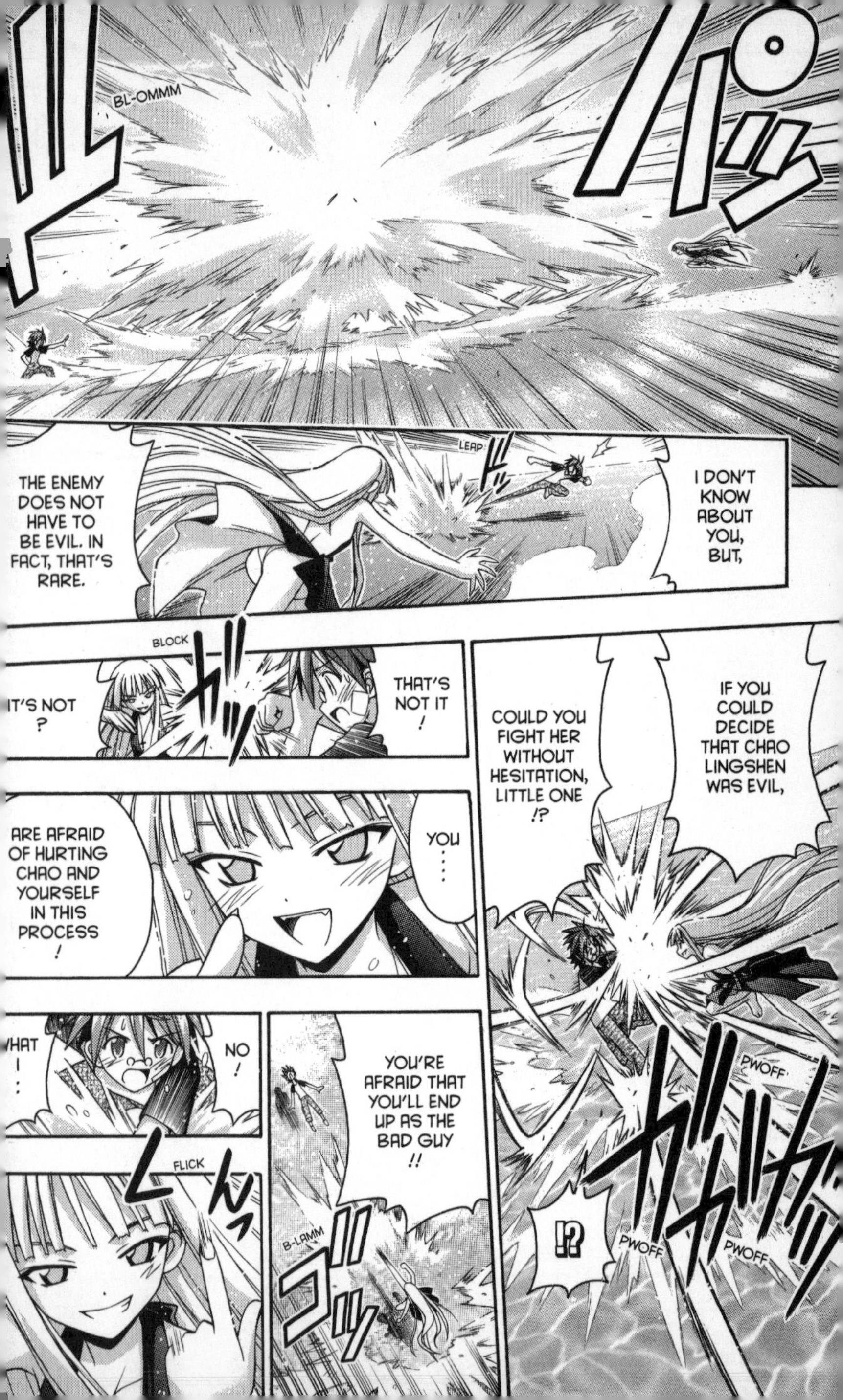
BL-OMMM
I DON'T KNOW ABOUT YOU, BUT,
LEAP
THE ENEMY DOES NOT HAVE TO BE EVIL. IN FACT, THAT'S RARE.
IF YOU COULD DECIDE THAT CHAO LINGSHEN WAS EVIL,
COULD YOU FIGHT HER WITHOUT HESITATION, LITTLE ONE!?
PWOFF
!?
PWOFF
PWOFF
BLOCK
THAT'S NOT IT!
IT'S NOT?
YOU....
ARE AFRAID OF HURTING CHAO AND YOURSELF IN THIS PROCESS!
YOU'RE AFRAID THAT YOU'LL END UP AS THE BAD GUY!!
B-LAMM
NO!
WHAT!..
FLICK

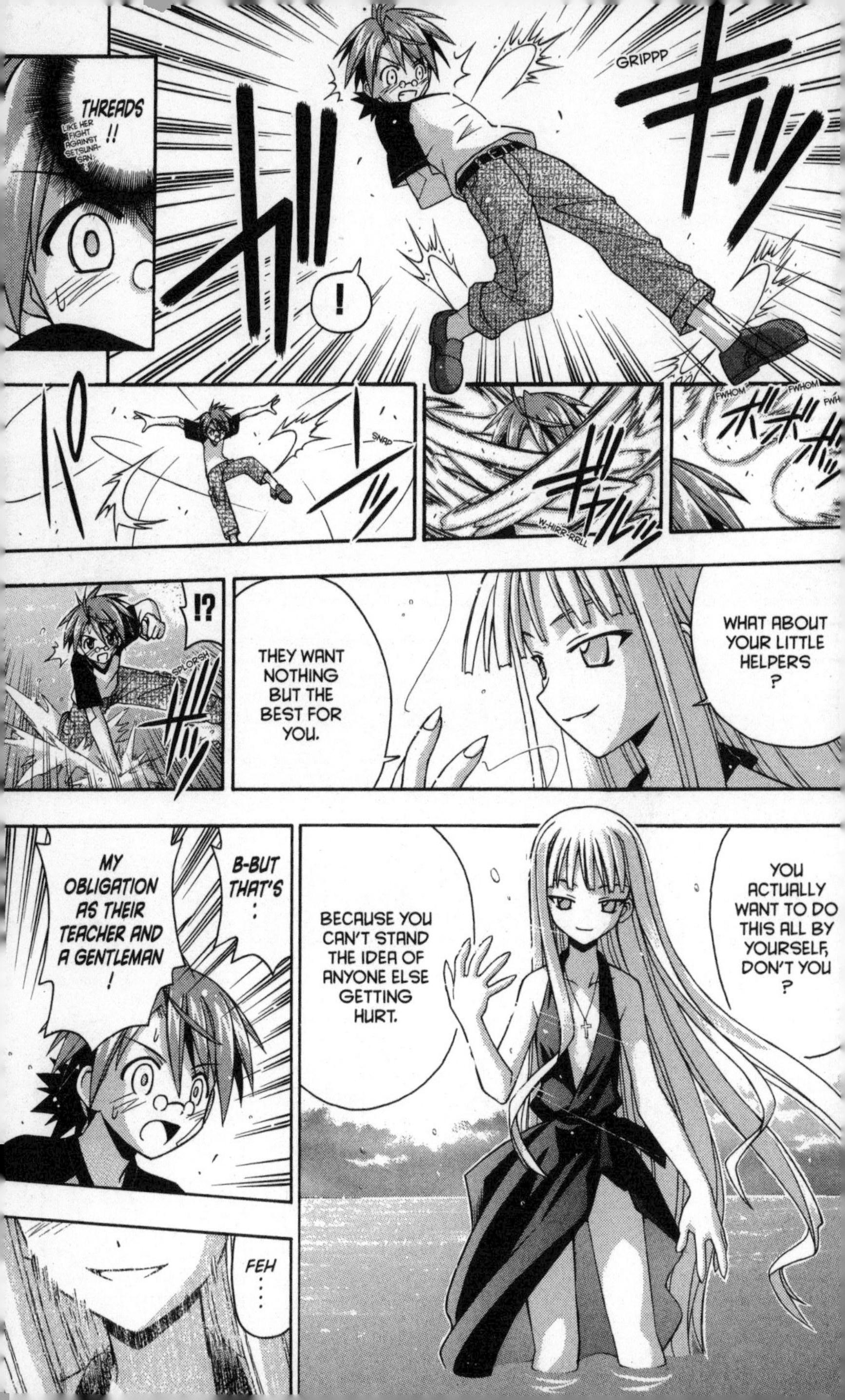
GRIPPP
!
THREADS !!
LIKE HER FIGHT AGAINST SETSUNA-SAN
FWHOM FWHOM FWH
W-HIRR-RRLL
SNAP
WHAT ABOUT YOUR LITTLE HELPERS ?
THEY WANT NOTHING BUT THE BEST FOR YOU.
!?
SPLORSH
YOU ACTUALLY WANT TO DO THIS ALL BY YOURSELF, DON'T YOU ?
BECAUSE YOU CAN'T STAND THE IDEA OF ANYONE ELSE GETTING HURT.
B-BUT THAT'S :
MY OBLIGATION AS THEIR TEACHER AND A GENTLEMAN !
FEH....

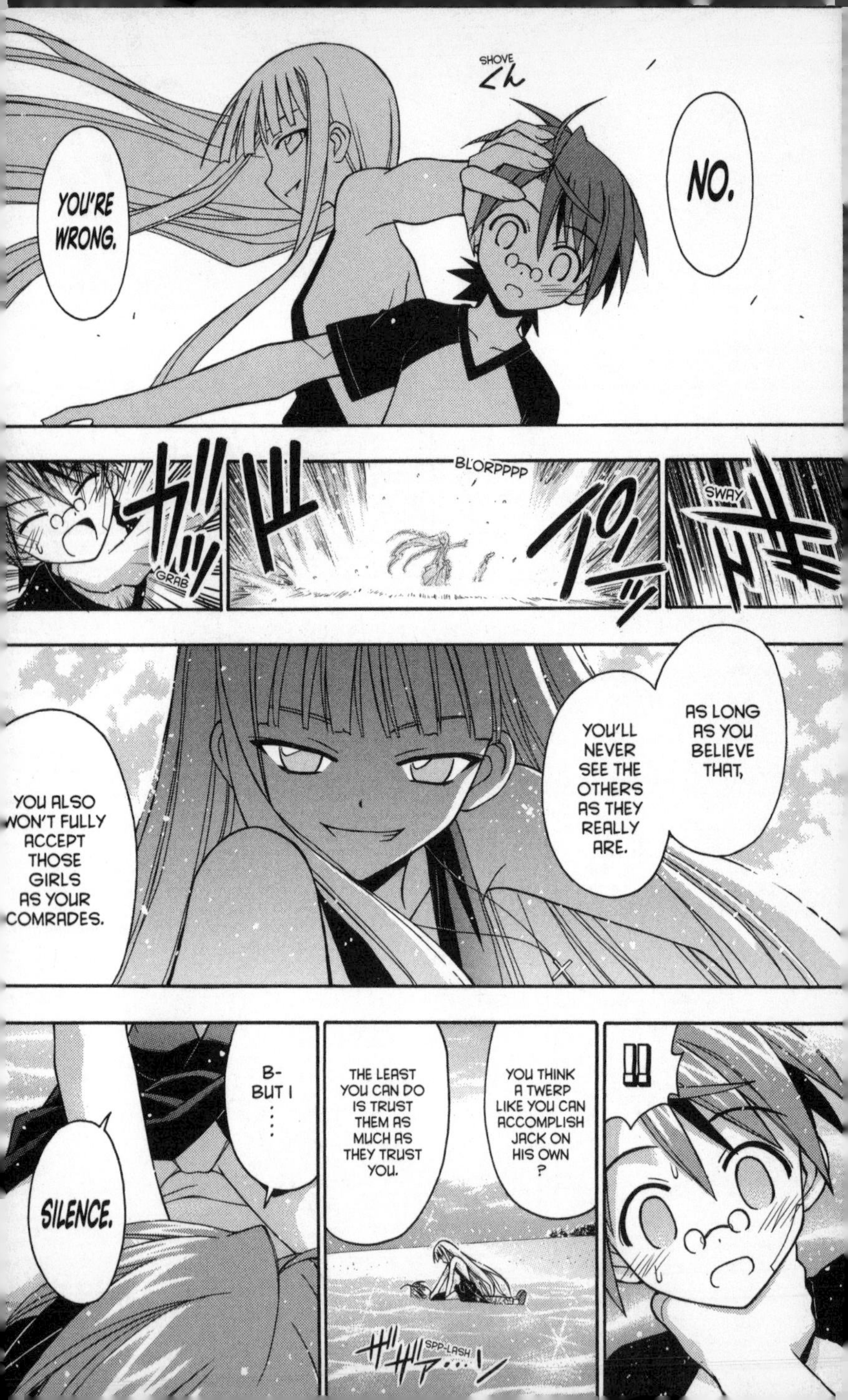

SHOVE
くん
NO.
YOU'RE WRONG.
SWAY
BLORPPPP
GRAB
AS LONG AS YOU BELIEVE THAT,
YOU'LL NEVER SEE THE OTHERS AS THEY REALLY ARE.
YOU ALSO WON'T FULLY ACCEPT THOSE GIRLS AS YOUR COMRADES.
!!
YOU THINK A TWERP LIKE YOU CAN ACCOMPLISH JACK ON HIS OWN?
THE LEAST YOU CAN DO IS TRUST THEM AS MUCH AS THEY TRUST YOU.
SPP-LASH
B- BUT I ....
SILENCE.

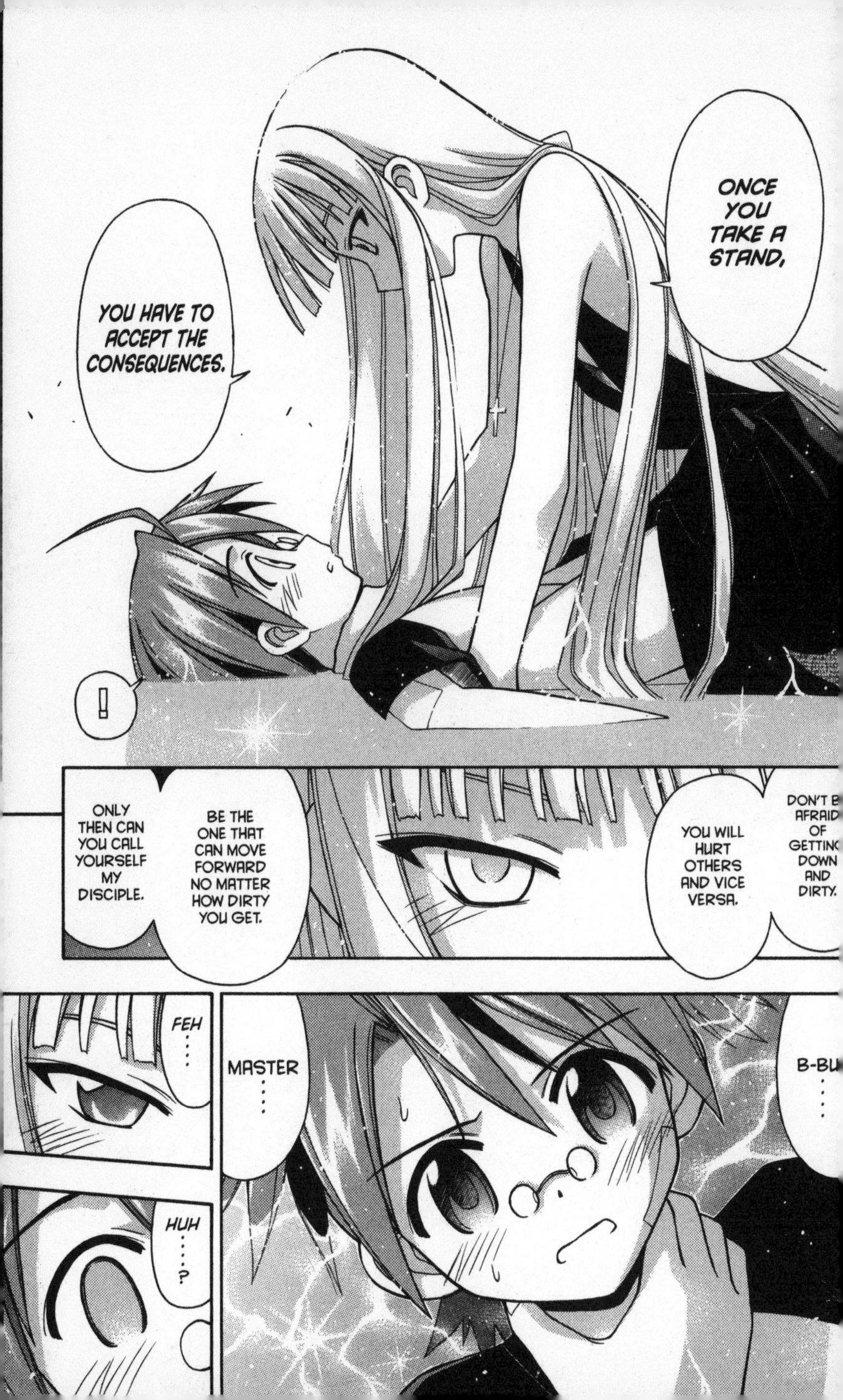
ONCE YOU TAKE A STAND,
YOU HAVE TO ACCEPT THE CONSEQUENCES.
!
DON'T B AFRAID OF GETTING DOWN AND DIRTY.
YOU WILL HURT OTHERS AND VICE VERSA.
BE THE ONE THAT CAN MOVE FORWARD NO MATTER HOW DIRTY YOU GET.
ONLY THEN CAN YOU CALL YOURSELF MY DISCIPLE.
B-BU...
MASTER...
FEH...
HUH...?

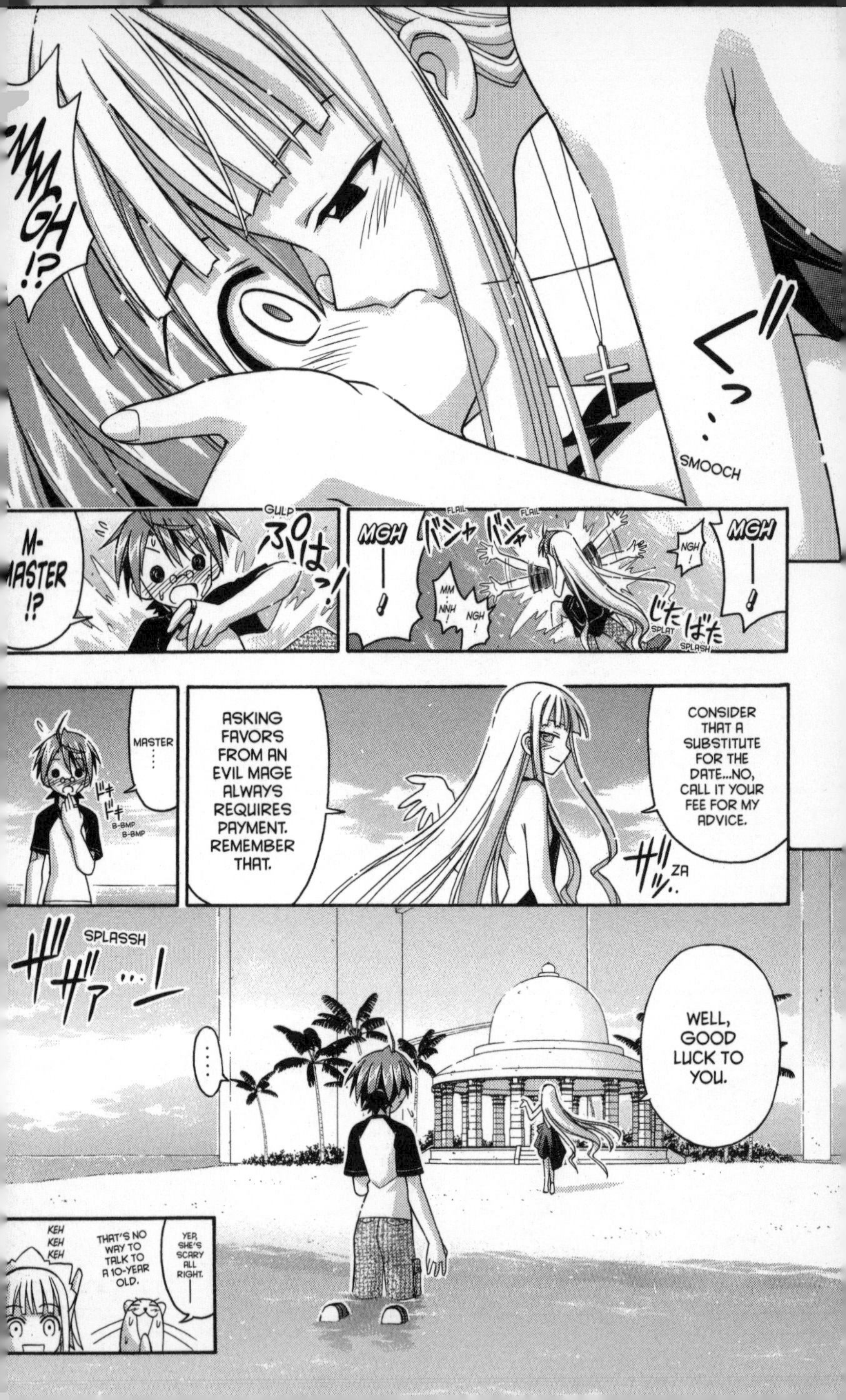
SMOOCH
MMMGH!?
MGH—!
NGH!
MM...NNH!
NGH!
FLAIL
FLAIL
SPLAT
SPLASH
MGH—!
GULP
M-MASTER!?
CONSIDER THAT A SUBSTITUTE FOR THE DATE...NO, CALL IT YOUR FEE FOR MY ADVICE.
ZA
ASKING FAVORS FROM AN EVIL MAGE ALWAYS REQUIRES PAYMENT. REMEMBER THAT.
MASTER.....
B-BMP B-BMP
SPLASSH
WELL, GOOD LUCK TO YOU.
....
YEP, SHE'S SCARY ALL RIGHT.
THAT'S NO WAY TO TALK TO A 10-YEAR OLD.
KEH KEH KEH

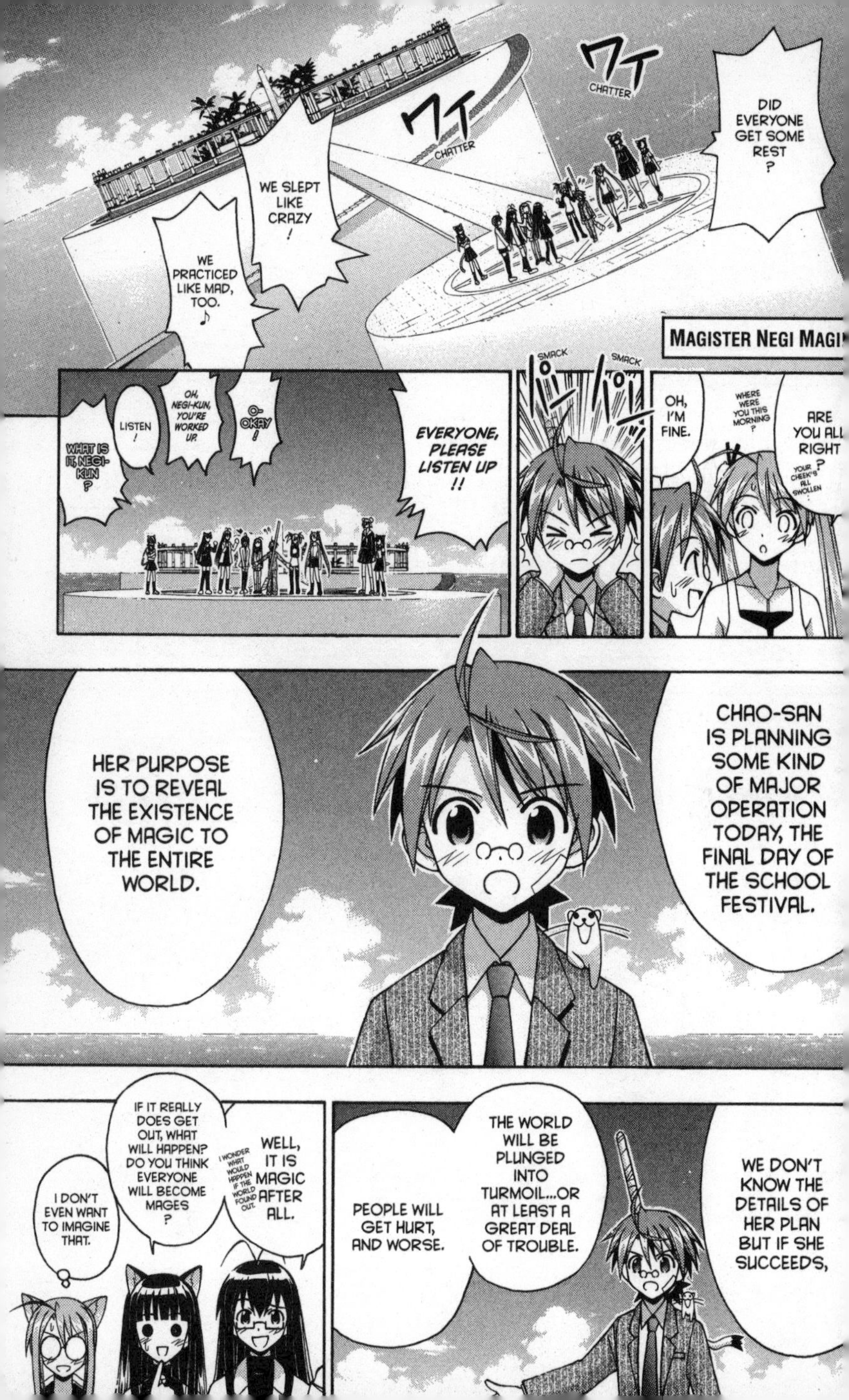
CHATTER
DID EVERYONE GET SOME REST?
CHATTER
WE SLEPT LIKE CRAZY!
WE PRACTICED LIKE MAD, TOO. ♪
MAGISTER NEGI MAGI!
ARE YOU ALL RIGHT?
YOUR CHEEK'S ALL SWOLLEN
WHERE WERE YOU THIS MORNING?
OH, I'M FINE.
SMACK
SMACK
EVERYONE, PLEASE LISTEN UP!!
O-OKAY!
OH, NEGI-KUN, YOU'RE WORKED UP.
LISTEN!
WHAT IS IT, NEGI-KUN?
CHAO-SAN IS PLANNING SOME KIND OF MAJOR OPERATION TODAY, THE FINAL DAY OF THE SCHOOL FESTIVAL.
HER PURPOSE IS TO REVEAL THE EXISTENCE OF MAGIC TO THE ENTIRE WORLD.
WE DON'T KNOW THE DETAILS OF HER PLAN BUT IF SHE SUCCEEDS,
THE WORLD WILL BE PLUNGED INTO TURMOIL...OR AT LEAST A GREAT DEAL OF TROUBLE.
PEOPLE WILL GET HURT, AND WORSE.
WELL, IT IS MAGIC AFTER ALL.
I WONDER WHAT WOULD HAPPEN IF THE WORLD FOUND OUT.
IF IT REALLY DOES GET OUT, WHAT WILL HAPPEN? DO YOU THINK EVERYONE WILL BECOME MAGES?
I DON'T EVEN WANT TO IMAGINE THAT.

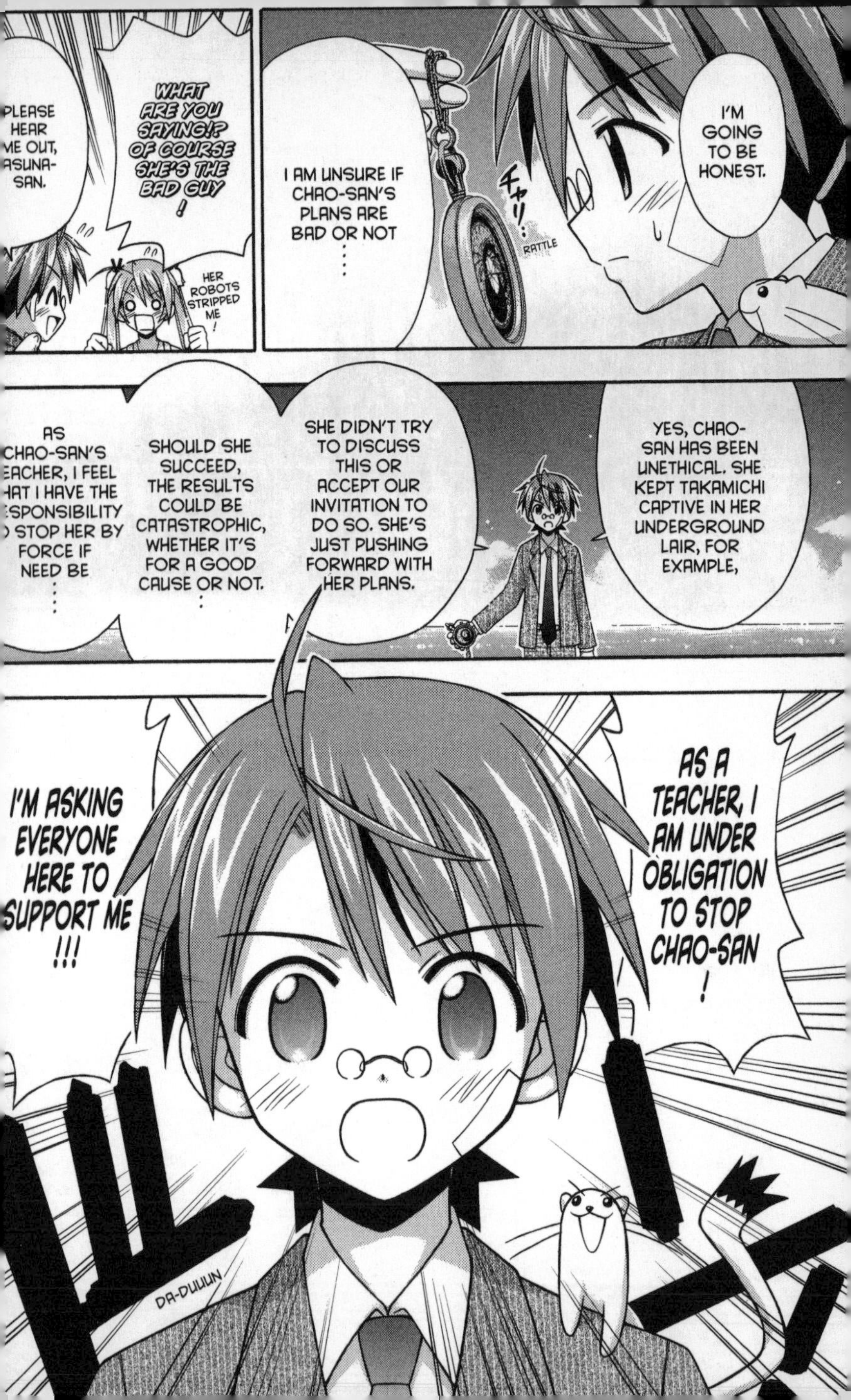
I'M GOING TO BE HONEST.
チャリ
RATTLE
I AM UNSURE IF CHAO-SAN'S PLANS ARE BAD OR NOT ...
WHAT ARE YOU SAYING!? OF COURSE SHE'S THE BAD GUY!
PLEASE HEAR ME OUT, ASUNA-SAN.
HER ROBOTS STRIPPED ME!
YES, CHAO-SAN HAS BEEN UNETHICAL. SHE KEPT TAKAMICHI CAPTIVE IN HER UNDERGROUND LAIR, FOR EXAMPLE,
SHE DIDN'T TRY TO DISCUSS THIS OR ACCEPT OUR INVITATION TO DO SO. SHE'S JUST PUSHING FORWARD WITH HER PLANS.
SHOULD SHE SUCCEED, THE RESULTS COULD BE CATASTROPHIC, WHETHER IT'S FOR A GOOD CAUSE OR NOT. ...
AS CHAO-SAN'S TEACHER, I FEEL THAT I HAVE THE RESPONSIBILITY TO STOP HER BY FORCE IF NEED BE ...
AS A TEACHER, I AM UNDER OBLIGATION TO STOP CHAO-SAN!
I'M ASKING EVERYONE HERE TO SUPPORT ME!!!
DA-DUUUN

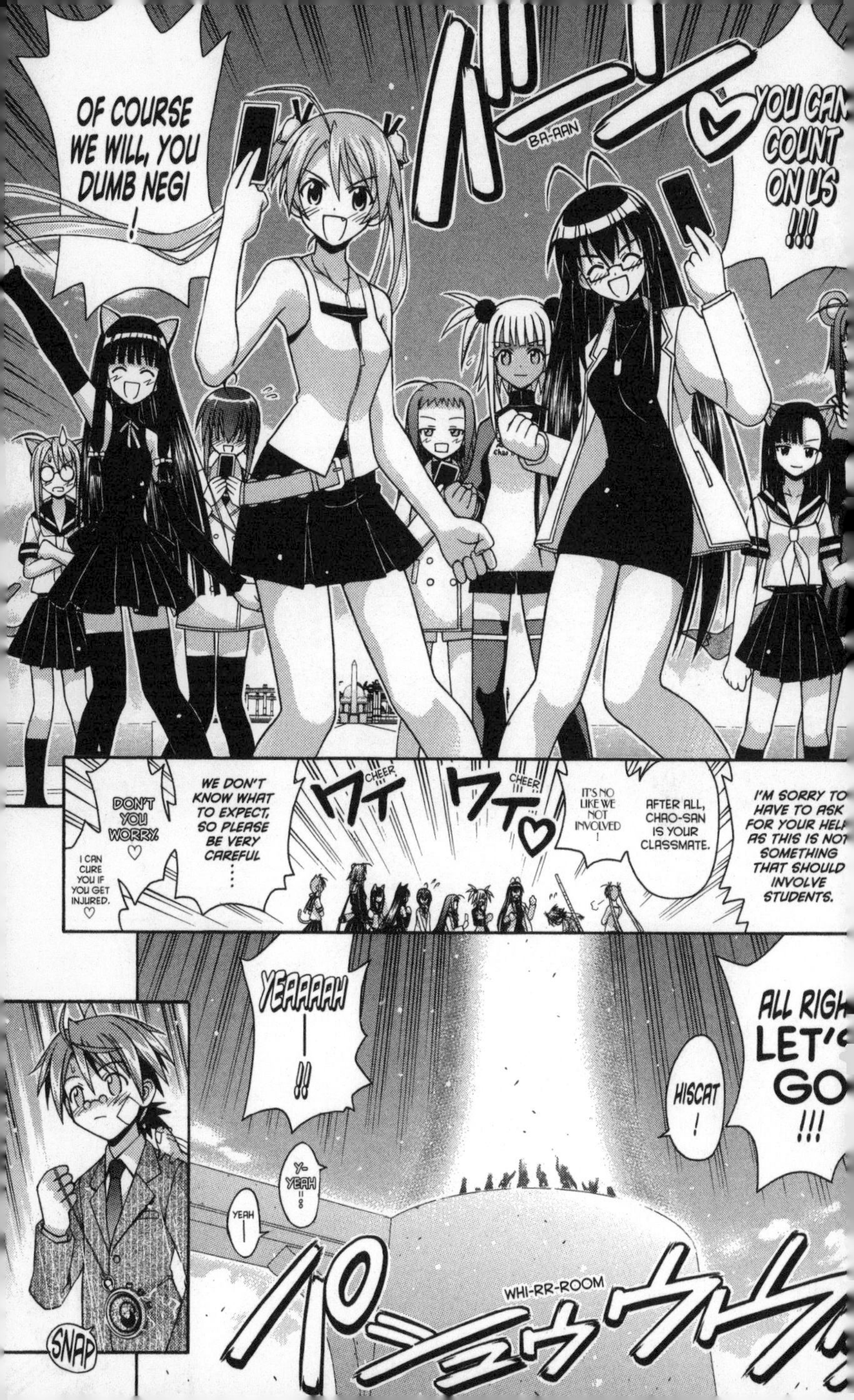

YOU CAN COUNT ON US!!!
BA-AAN
OF COURSE WE WILL, YOU DUMB NEGI!
I'M SORRY TO HAVE TO ASK FOR YOUR HEL AS THIS IS NOT SOMETHING THAT SHOULD INVOLVE STUDENTS.
AFTER ALL, CHAO-SAN IS YOUR CLASSMATE.
IT'S NO LIKE WE NOT INVOLVED!
CHEER
CHEER
WE DON'T KNOW WHAT TO EXPECT, SO PLEASE BE VERY CAREFUL....
DON'T YOU WORRY. ♡
I CAN CURE YOU IF YOU GET INJURED. ♡
ALL RIGH LET'S GO!!!
HISCAT!
YEAAAAH—!!
Y-YEAH!!?
YEAH—
WHI-RR-ROOM
SNAP

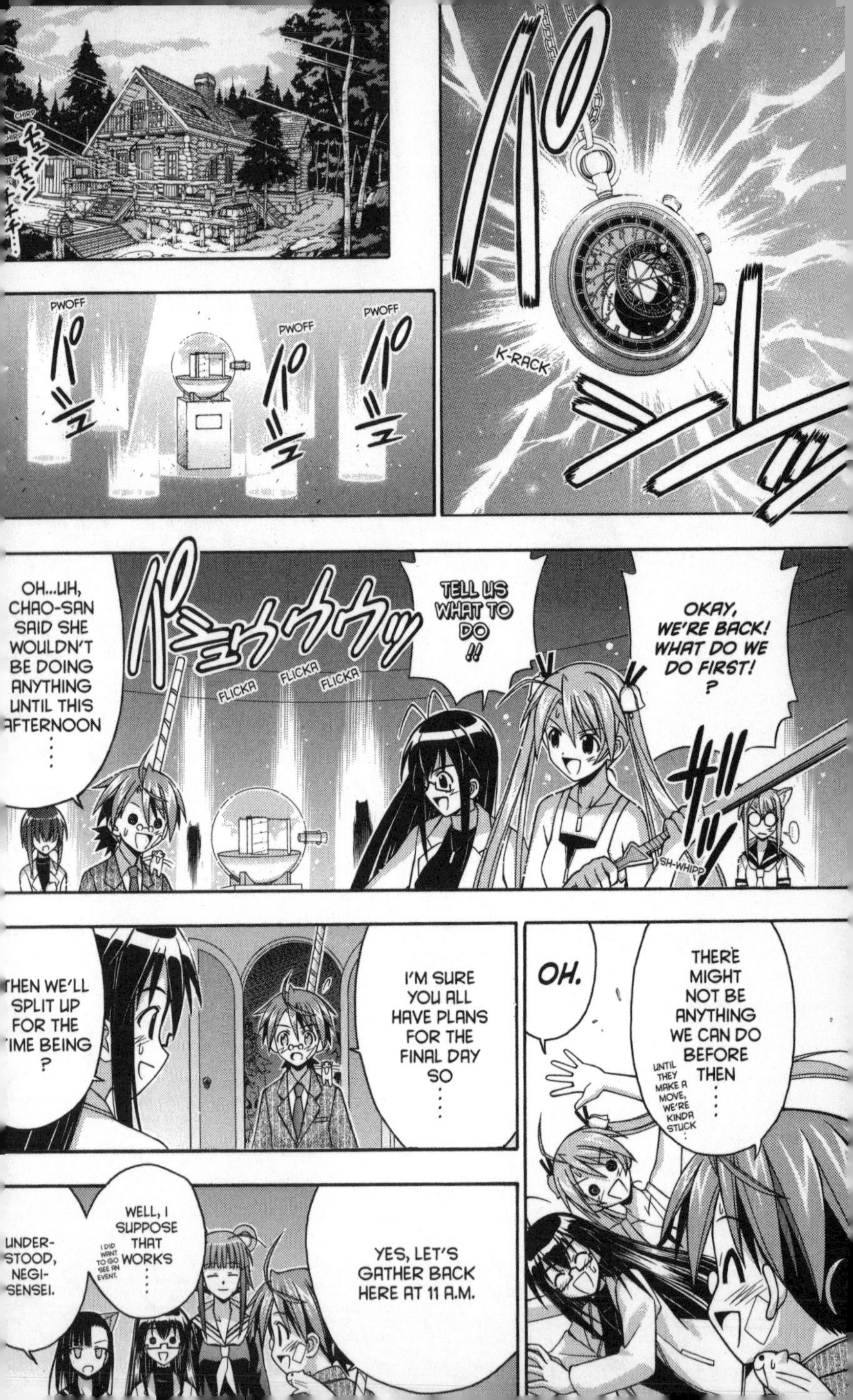
K-RACK
CHIRP
CHIRP
PWOFF
PWOFF
PWOFF
OKAY, WE'RE BACK! WHAT DO WE DO FIRST!?
SH-WHIPP
TELL US WHAT TO DO!!
FLICKA
FLICKA
FLICKA
OH...UH, CHAO-SAN SAID SHE WOULDN'T BE DOING ANYTHING UNTIL THIS AFTERNOON....
THERE MIGHT NOT BE ANYTHING WE CAN DO BEFORE THEN...
UNTIL THEY MAKE A MOVE, WE'RE KINDA STUCK...
OH.
I'M SURE YOU ALL HAVE PLANS FOR THE FINAL DAY SO....
THEN WE'LL SPLIT UP FOR THE TIME BEING?
YES, LET'S GATHER BACK HERE AT 11 A.M.
WELL, I SUPPOSE THAT WORKS....
I DID WANT TO GO SEE AN EVENT.
UNDERSTOOD, NEGI-SENSEI.

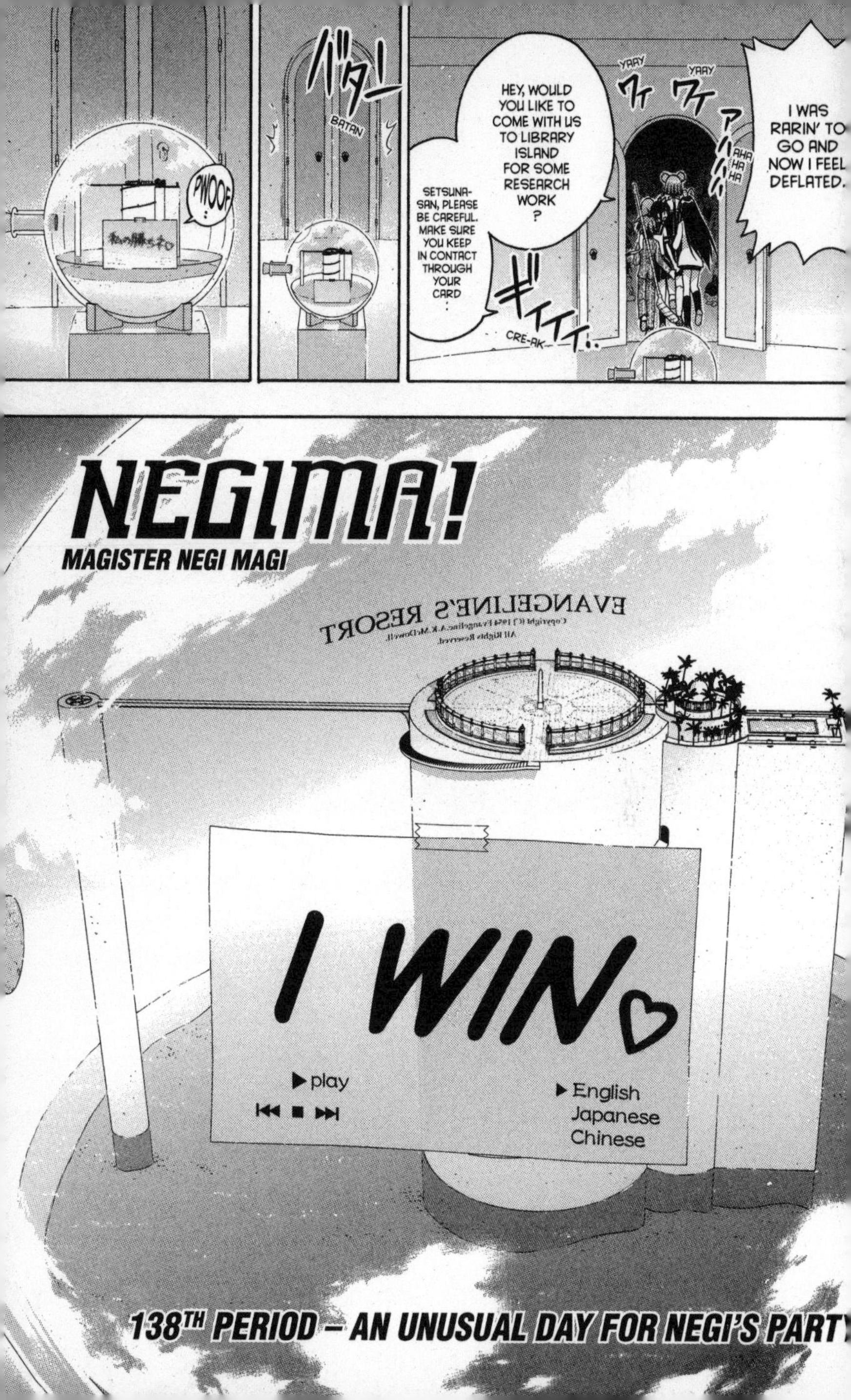
I WAS RARIN' TO GO AND NOW I FEEL DEFLATED.
YAAY
YAAY
AHA HA HA
HEY, WOULD YOU LIKE TO COME WITH US TO LIBRARY ISLAND FOR SOME RESEARCH WORK?
SETSUNA-SAN, PLEASE BE CAREFUL. MAKE SURE YOU KEEP IN CONTACT THROUGH YOUR CARD.
CRE-AK
BATAN
PWOOF
NEGIMA!
MAGISTER NEGI MAGI
EVANGELINE'S RESORT
I WIN
▶ play
▶ English
Japanese
Chinese
138TH PERIOD – AN UNUSUAL DAY FOR NEGI'S PARTY

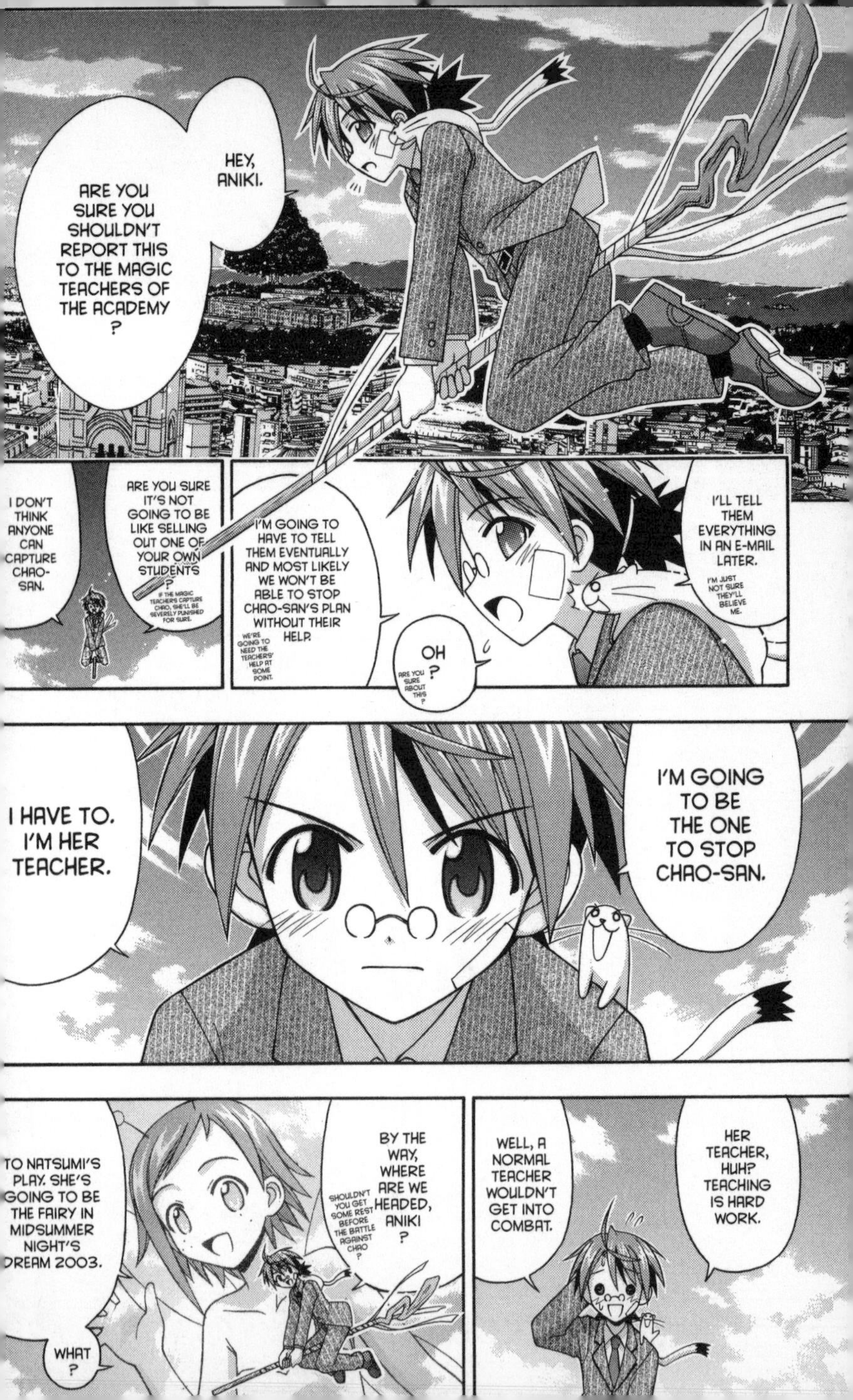

HEY, ANIKI.
ARE YOU SURE YOU SHOULDN'T REPORT THIS TO THE MAGIC TEACHERS OF THE ACADEMY?
I'LL TELL THEM EVERYTHING IN AN E-MAIL LATER.
I'M JUST NOT SURE THEY'LL BELIEVE ME.
OH?
ARE YOU SURE ABOUT THIS?
I'M GOING TO HAVE TO TELL THEM EVENTUALLY AND MOST LIKELY WE WON'T BE ABLE TO STOP CHAO-SAN'S PLAN WITHOUT THEIR HELP.
WE'RE GOING TO NEED THE TEACHERS' HELP AT SOME POINT.
ARE YOU SURE IT'S NOT GOING TO BE LIKE SELLING OUT ONE OF YOUR OWN STUDENTS?
IF THE MAGIC TEACHERS CAPTURE CHAO, SHE'LL BE SEVERELY PUNISHED FOR SURE.
I DON'T THINK ANYONE CAN CAPTURE CHAO-SAN.
I'M GOING TO BE THE ONE TO STOP CHAO-SAN.
I HAVE TO. I'M HER TEACHER.
HER TEACHER, HUH? TEACHING IS HARD WORK.
WELL, A NORMAL TEACHER WOULDN'T GET INTO COMBAT.
BY THE WAY, WHERE ARE WE HEADED, ANIKI?
SHOULDN'T YOU GET SOME REST BEFORE THE BATTLE AGAINST CHAO?
TO NATSUMI'S PLAY. SHE'S GOING TO BE THE FAIRY IN MIDSUMMER NIGHT'S DREAM 2003.
WHAT?

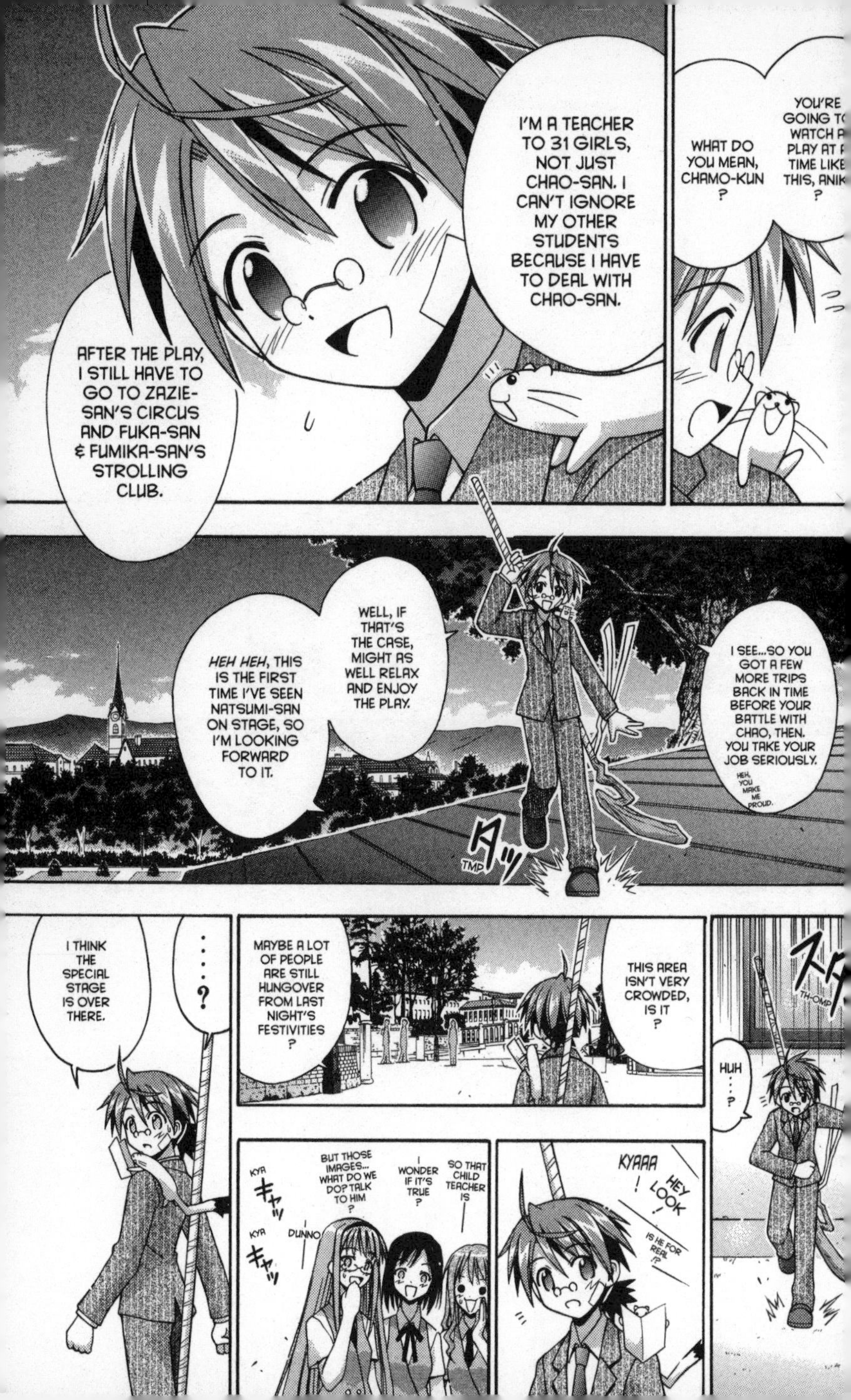
YOU'RE GOING T WATCH A PLAY AT TIME LIKE THIS, ANIK ?
WHAT DO YOU MEAN, CHAMO-KUN?
I'M A TEACHER TO 31 GIRLS, NOT JUST CHAO-SAN. I CAN'T IGNORE MY OTHER STUDENTS BECAUSE I HAVE TO DEAL WITH CHAO-SAN.
AFTER THE PLAY, I STILL HAVE TO GO TO ZAZIE-SAN'S CIRCUS AND FUKA-SAN & FUMIKA-SAN'S STROLLING CLUB.
I SEE...SO YOU GOT A FEW MORE TRIPS BACK IN TIME BEFORE YOUR BATTLE WITH CHAO, THEN. YOU TAKE YOUR JOB SERIOUSLY.
HEH, YOU MAKE ME PROUD.
WELL, IF THAT'S THE CASE, MIGHT AS WELL RELAX AND ENJOY THE PLAY.
HEH HEH, THIS IS THE FIRST TIME I'VE SEEN NATSUMI-SAN ON STAGE, SO I'M LOOKING FORWARD TO IT.
TMP
TH-OMP
HUH...?
THIS AREA ISN'T VERY CROWDED, IS IT?
MAYBE A LOT OF PEOPLE ARE STILL HUNGOVER FROM LAST NIGHT'S FESTIVITIES?
KYAAA!
HEY LOOK!
IS HE FOR REAL!?
SO THAT CHILD TEACHER IS
I WONDER IF IT'S TRUE?
BUT THOSE IMAGES... WHAT DO WE DO? TALK TO HIM?
I DUNNO
KYA
KYA
...?
I THINK THE SPECIAL STAGE IS OVER THERE.

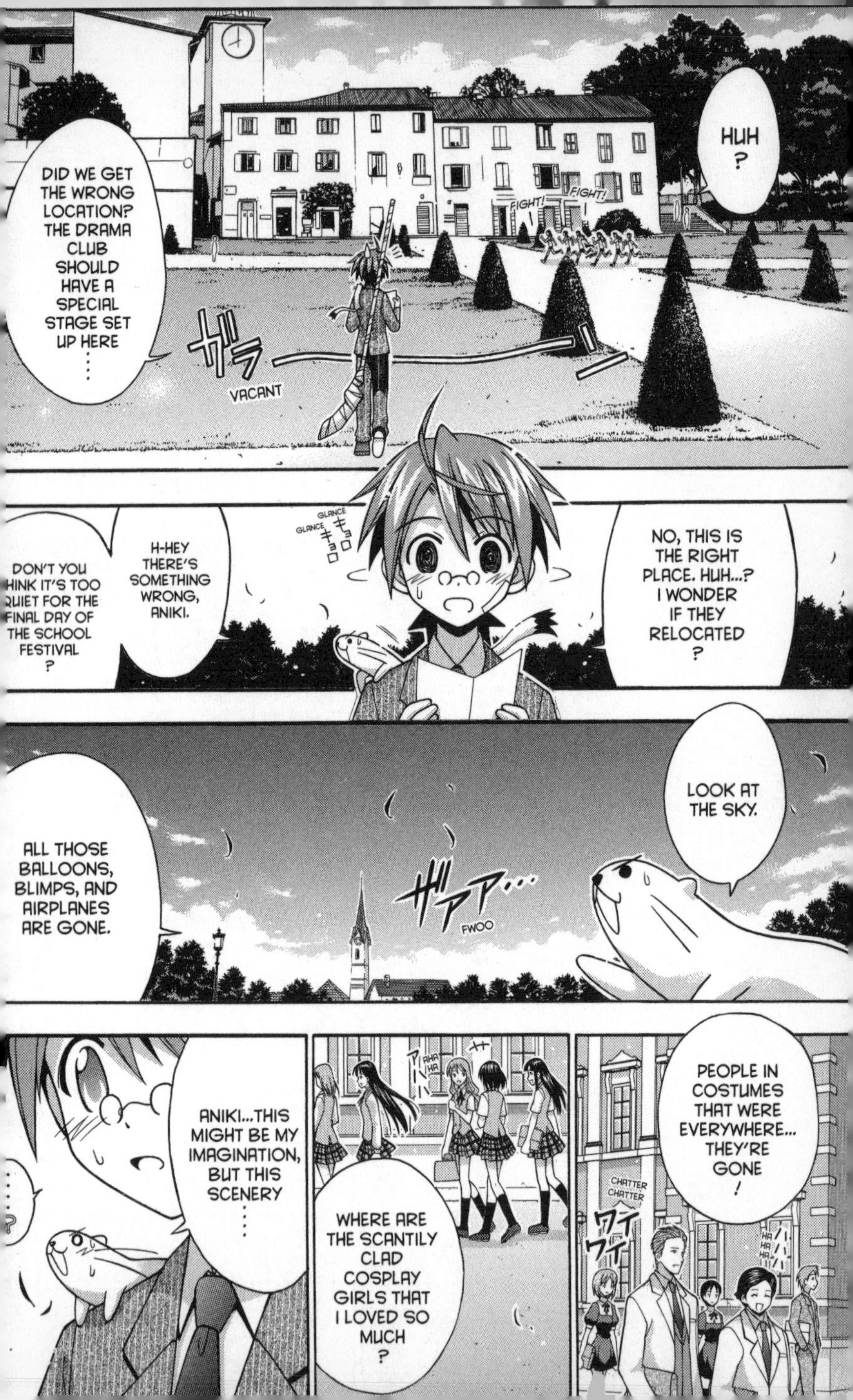
HUH ?
FIGHT! FIGHT!
DID WE GET THE WRONG LOCATION? THE DRAMA CLUB SHOULD HAVE A SPECIAL STAGE SET UP HERE ....
ガラ
VACANT
NO, THIS IS THE RIGHT PLACE. HUH...? I WONDER IF THEY RELOCATED ?
GLANCE GLANCE
キョロキョロ
H-HEY THERE'S SOMETHING WRONG, ANIKI.
DON'T YOU HINK IT'S TOO UIET FOR THE INAL DAY OF THE SCHOOL FESTIVAL ?
LOOK AT THE SKY.
ザァア...
FWOO
ALL THOSE BALLOONS, BLIMPS, AND AIRPLANES ARE GONE.
PEOPLE IN COSTUMES THAT WERE EVERYWHERE... THEY'RE GONE !
CHATTER CHATTER
ワイワイ
HA HA HA
ハハハ
AHA HA
アハハ
WHERE ARE THE SCANTILY CLAD COSPLAY GIRLS THAT I LOVED SO MUCH ?
ANIKI...THIS MIGHT BE MY IMAGINATION, BUT THIS SCENERY ....
....?

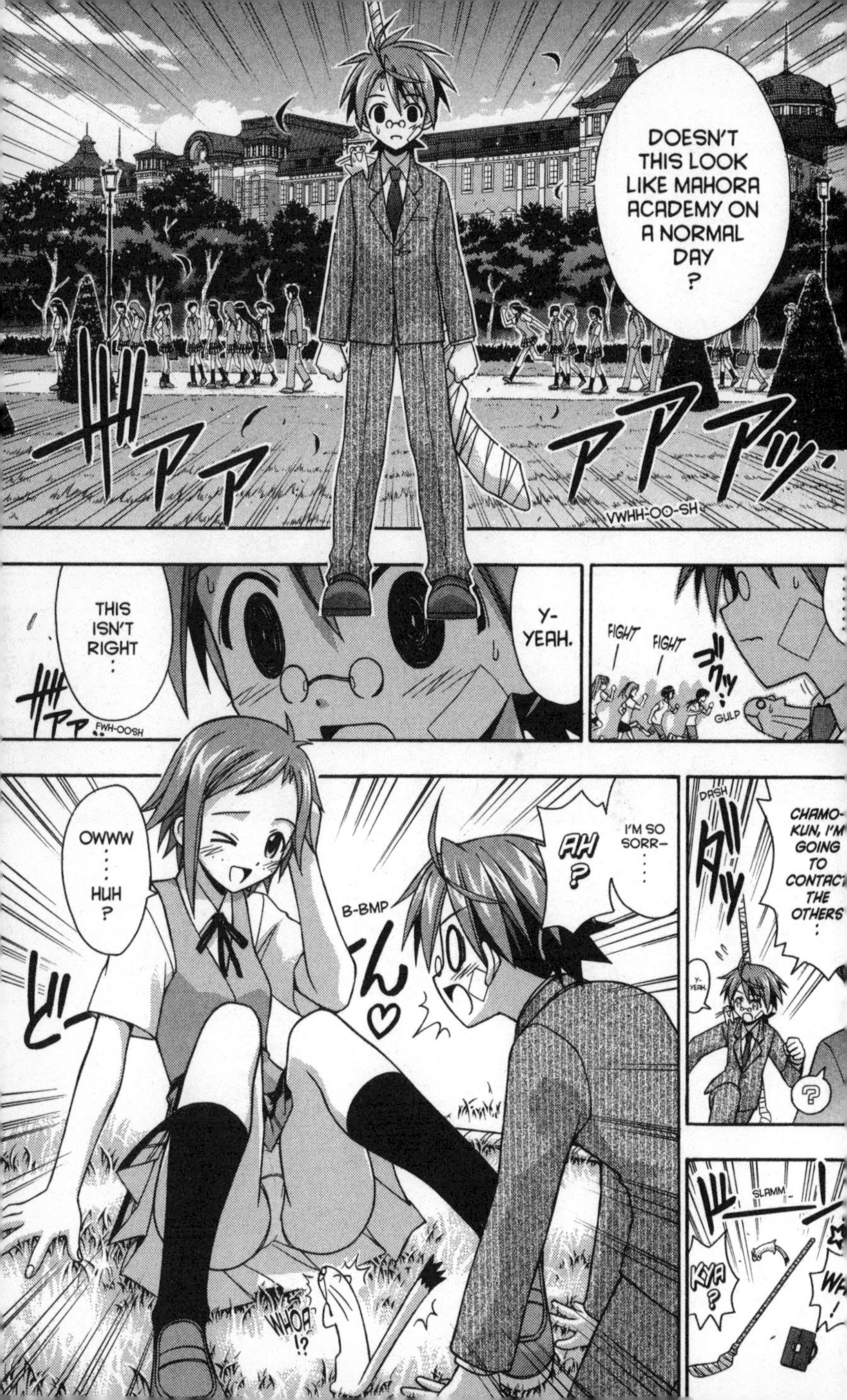
DOESN'T THIS LOOK LIKE MAHORA ACADEMY ON A NORMAL DAY ?
VWHH-OO-SH
FIGHT
FIGHT
GULP
Y- YEAH.
THIS ISN'T RIGHT :
FWH-OOSH
DASH
CHAMO-KUN, I'M GOING TO CONTACT THE OTHERS ...
Y- YEAH.
SLAMM
WA !
KYA ?
AH ?
I'M SO SORR- ....
B-BMP
OWWW ... HUH ?
WHOA !?

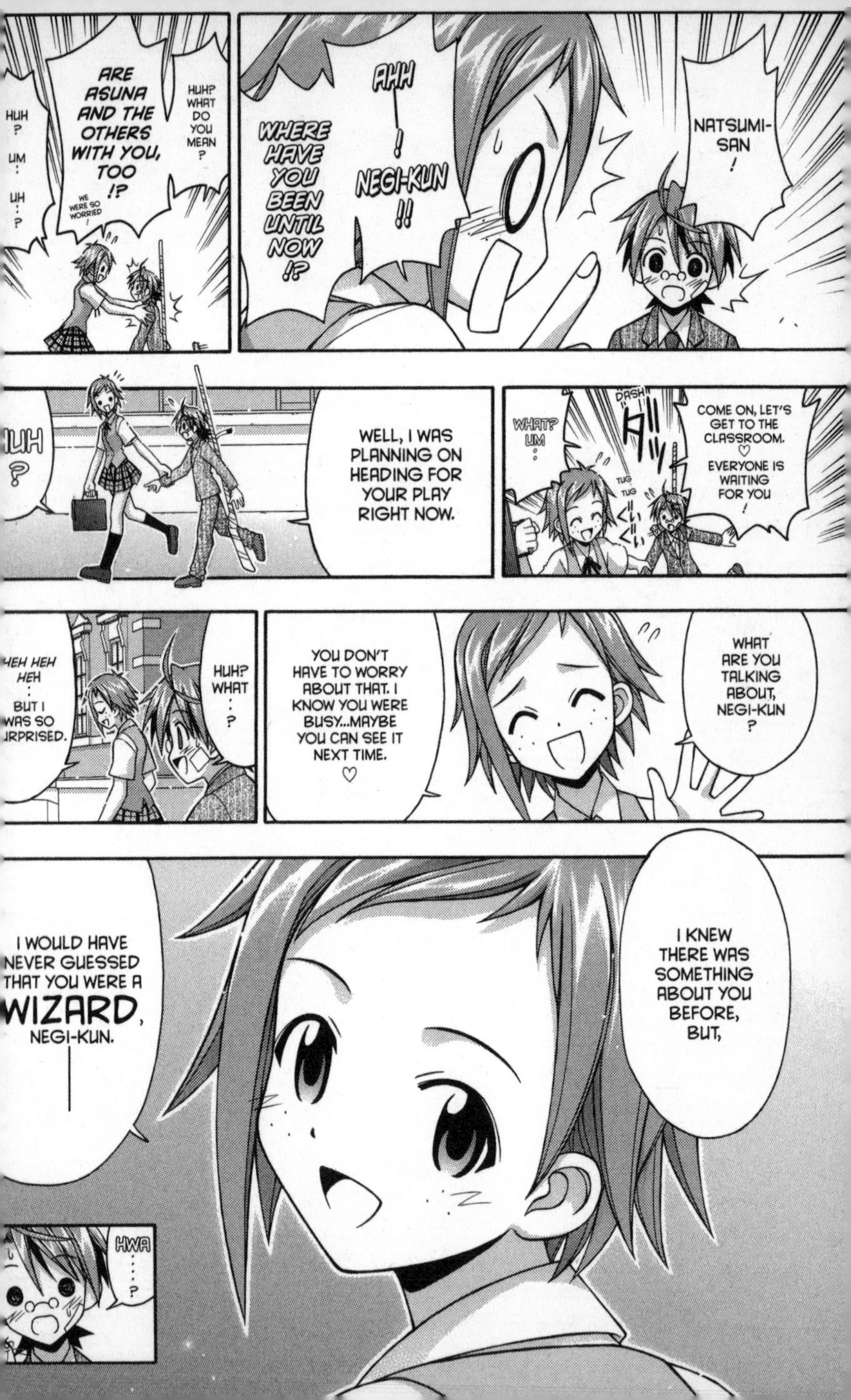
NATSUMI-SAN!
AHH! NEGI-KUN!!
WHERE HAVE YOU BEEN UNTIL NOW!?
HUH? WHAT DO YOU MEAN?
ARE ASUNA AND THE OTHERS WITH YOU, TOO!?
WE WERE SO WORRIED!
HUH? UM... UH..?
COME ON, LET'S GET TO THE CLASSROOM. ♡ EVERYONE IS WAITING FOR YOU!
DASH
TUG TUG
WHAT? UM..
WELL, I WAS PLANNING ON HEADING FOR YOUR PLAY RIGHT NOW.
UH ?
WHAT ARE YOU TALKING ABOUT, NEGI-KUN?
YOU DON'T HAVE TO WORRY ABOUT THAT. I KNOW YOU WERE BUSY...MAYBE YOU CAN SEE IT NEXT TIME. ♡
HUH? WHAT...?
EH HEH HEH... BUT I WAS SO URPRISED.
I KNEW THERE WAS SOMETHING ABOUT YOU BEFORE, BUT,
I WOULD HAVE NEVER GUESSED THAT YOU WERE A WIZARD, NEGI-KUN.
HWA...?

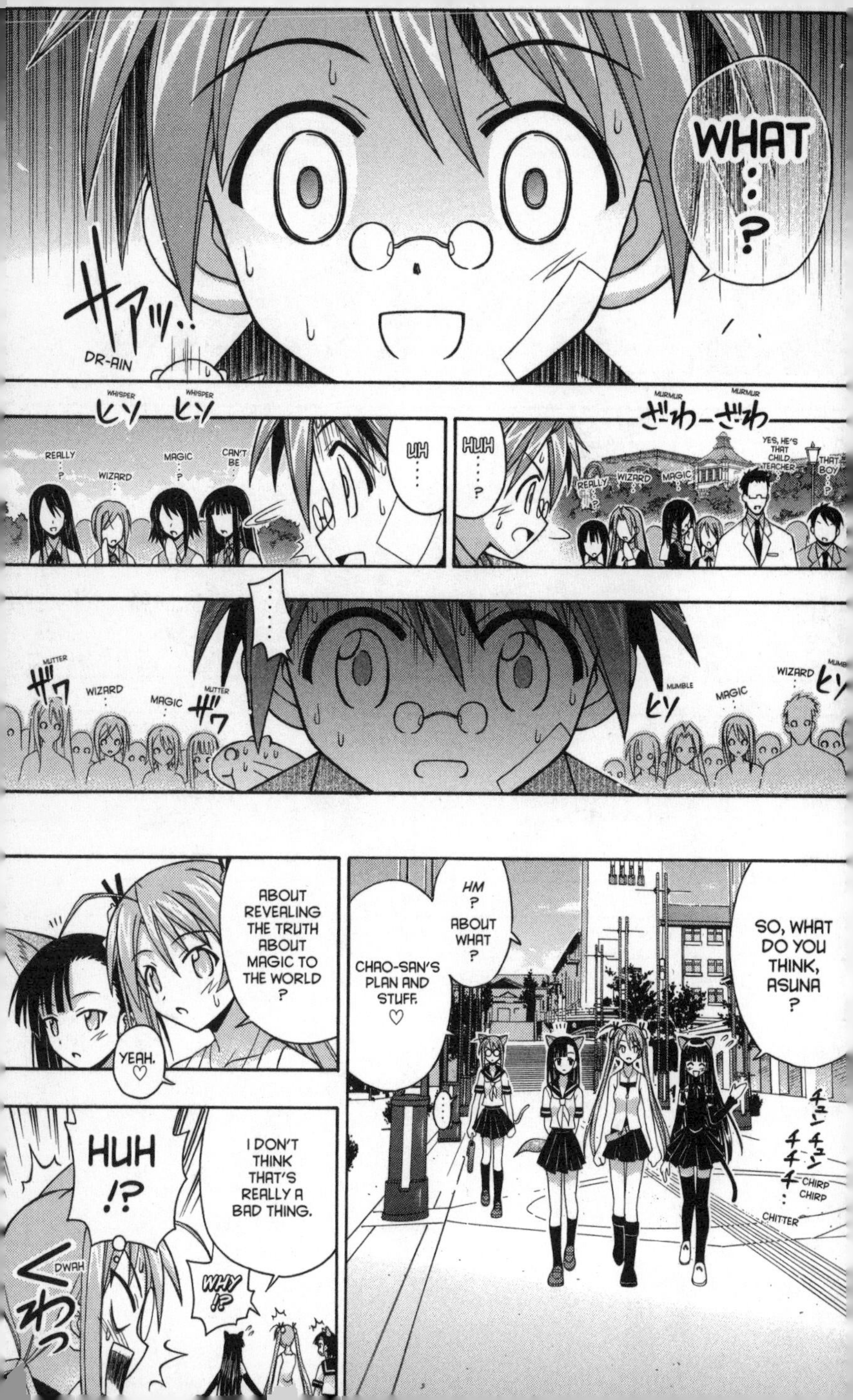
WHAT..?
サァッ..
DR-AIN
HUH....?
ざわーざわ
MURMUR MURMUR
YES, HE'S THAT CHILD TEACHER
THAT BOY..?
REALLY..?
WIZARD
MAGIC
UH....
ヒソ ヒソ
WHISPER WHISPER
CAN'T BE
MAGIC..?
WIZARD
REALLY..?
......
ヒソ
MUMBLE
WIZARD
MAGIC
ヒソ
MUMBLE
ザワ
MUTTER
MAGIC
WIZARD
ザワ
MUTTER
SO, WHAT DO YOU THINK, ASUNA?
HM? ABOUT WHAT?
CHAO-SAN'S PLAN AND STUFF. ♡
...
チュン チュン チチチ..
CHIRP CHIRP
CHITTER
ABOUT REVEALING THE TRUTH ABOUT MAGIC TO THE WORLD?
YEAH. ♡
I DON'T THINK THAT'S REALLY A BAD THING.
HUH!?
WHY!?
くわっ
DWAH

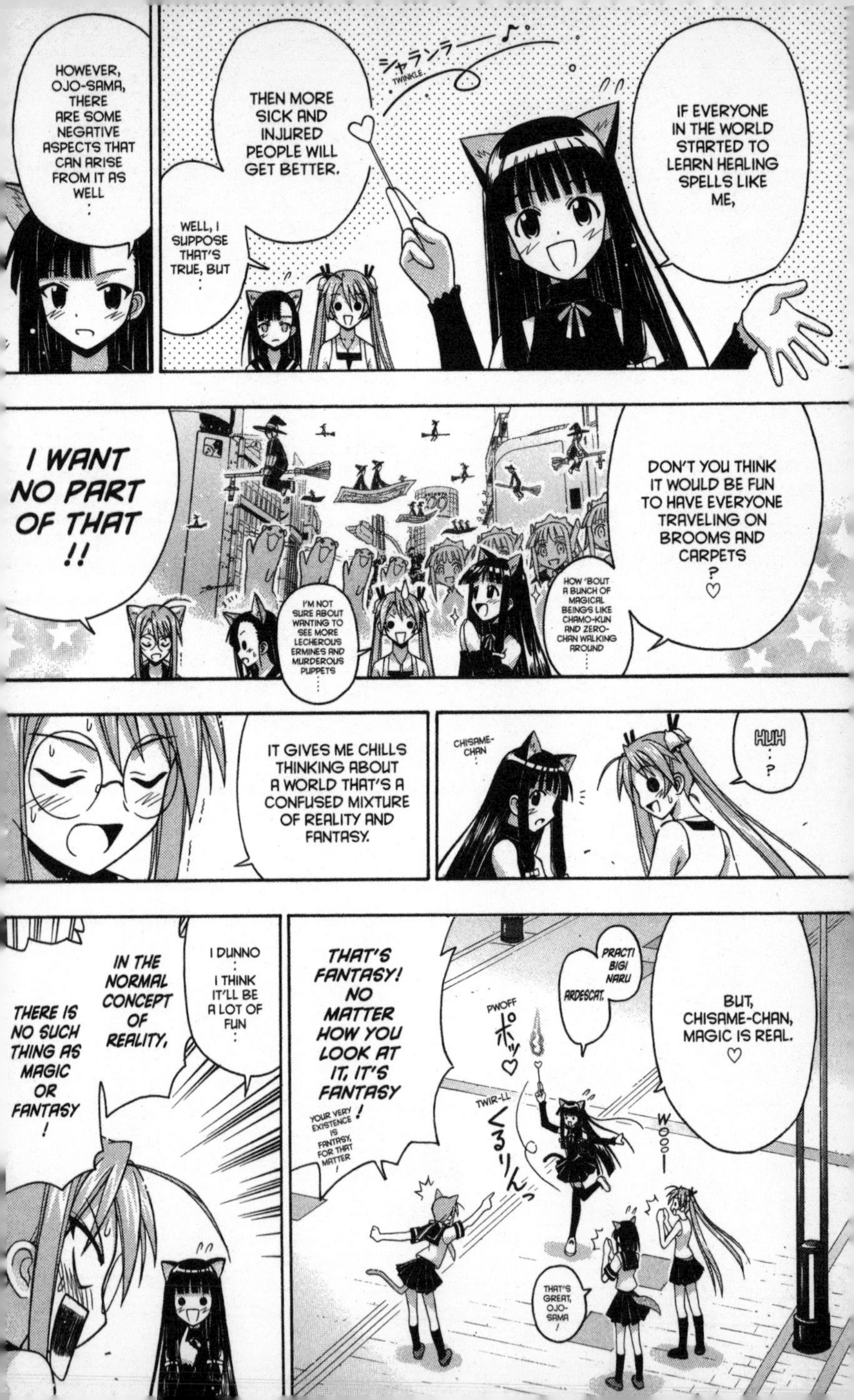
IF EVERYONE IN THE WORLD STARTED TO LEARN HEALING SPELLS LIKE ME,
シャランラー♪
TWINKLE.
THEN MORE SICK AND INJURED PEOPLE WILL GET BETTER.
WELL, I SUPPOSE THAT'S TRUE, BUT ...
HOWEVER, OJO-SAMA, THERE ARE SOME NEGATIVE ASPECTS THAT CAN ARISE FROM IT AS WELL ...
DON'T YOU THINK IT WOULD BE FUN TO HAVE EVERYONE TRAVELING ON BROOMS AND CARPETS? ♡
HOW 'BOUT A BUNCH OF MAGICAL BEINGS LIKE CHAMO-KUN AND ZERO-CHAN WALKING AROUND ...
I'M NOT SURE ABOUT WANTING TO SEE MORE LECHEROUS ERMINES AND MURDEROUS PUPPETS ...
I WANT NO PART OF THAT !!
HUH ...?
CHISAME-CHAN ...
IT GIVES ME CHILLS THINKING ABOUT A WORLD THAT'S A CONFUSED MIXTURE OF REALITY AND FANTASY.
BUT, CHISAME-CHAN, MAGIC IS REAL. ♡
PRACTI BIGI NARU ARDESCAT.
PWOFF
ポッ♡
TWIR-LL
くるりんっ
WOOO—
THAT'S GREAT, OJO-SAMA!
THAT'S FANTASY! NO MATTER HOW YOU LOOK AT IT, IT'S FANTASY!
YOUR VERY EXISTENCE IS FANTASY, FOR THAT MATTER!
I DUNNO ... I THINK IT'LL BE A LOT OF FUN ...
IN THE NORMAL CONCEPT OF REALITY,
THERE IS NO SUCH THING AS MAGIC OR FANTASY!

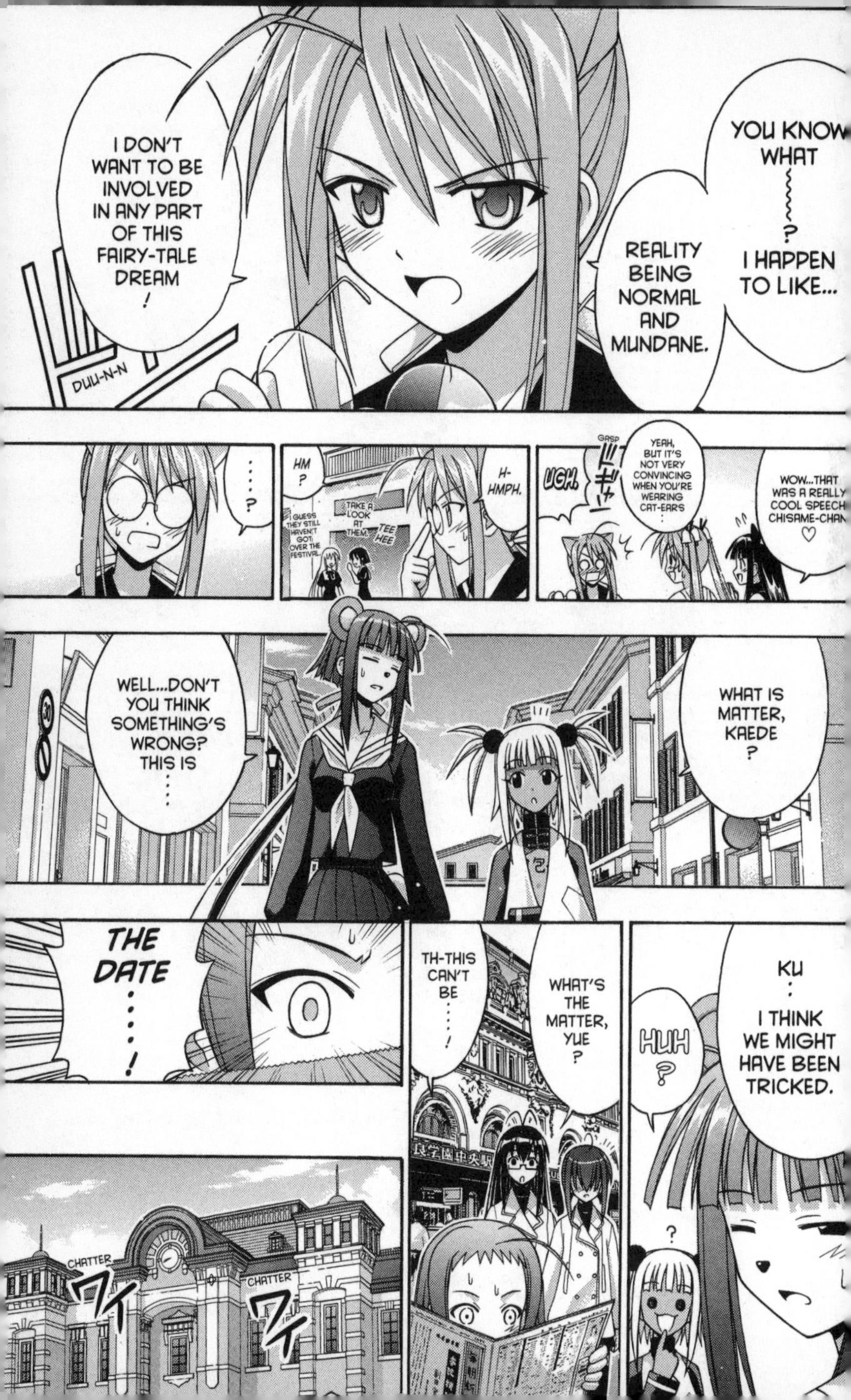
YOU KNOW WHAT ~~~~~?
I HAPPEN TO LIKE...
REALITY BEING NORMAL AND MUNDANE.
I DON'T WANT TO BE INVOLVED IN ANY PART OF THIS FAIRY-TALE DREAM!
DUU-N-N
WOW...THAT WAS A REALLY COOL SPEECH CHISAME-CHAN ♡
YEAH, BUT IT'S NOT VERY CONVINCING WHEN YOU'RE WEARING CAT-EARS...
GASP
UGH.
H-HMPH.
TEE HEE
TAKE A LOOK AT THEM.
I GUESS THEY STILL HAVEN'T GOT OVER THE FESTIVAL.
HM?
...?
WHAT IS MATTER, KAEDE?
WELL...DON'T YOU THINK SOMETHING'S WRONG? THIS IS....
KU... I THINK WE MIGHT HAVE BEEN TRICKED.
HUH?
?
WHAT'S THE MATTER, YUE?
TH-THIS CAN'T BE....!
THE DATE.....!
CHATTER
CHATTER

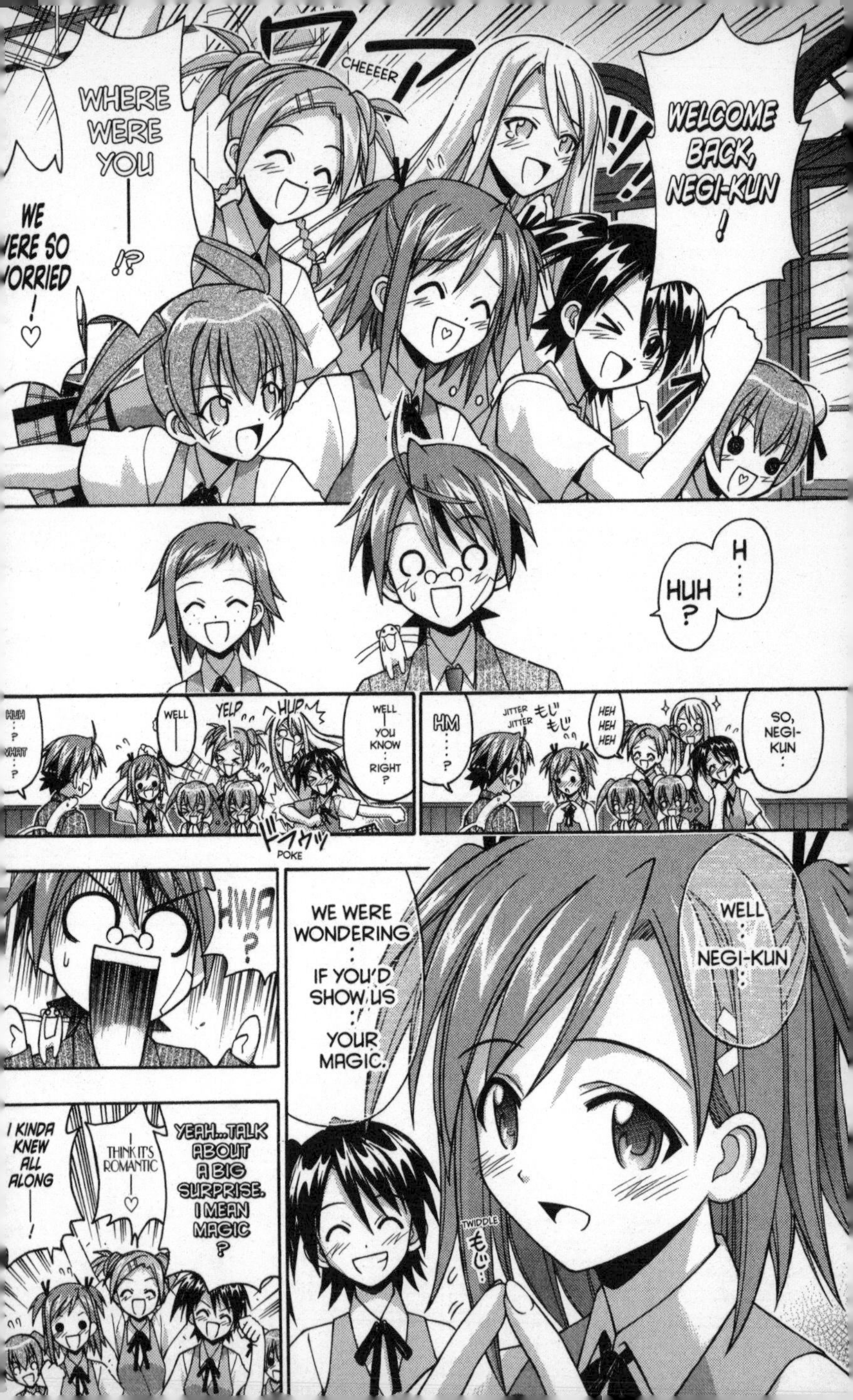
WELCOME BACK, NEGI-KUN!
!!
CHEEEER
WHERE WERE YOU—!?
WE ERE SO ORRIED! ♡
H....
HUH?
SO, NEGI-KUN...
HEH HEH HEH
JITTER JITTER もじもじ
HM....?
WELL I YOU KNOW... RIGHT?
HUP
YELP!
WELL—
HUH? WHAT...?
POKE
WELL... NEGI-KUN...
WE WERE WONDERING... IF YOU'D SHOW US... YOUR MAGIC.
TWIDDLE もじ...
HWA?
YEAH...TALK ABOUT A BIG SURPRISE. I MEAN MAGIC?
I THINK IT'S ROMANTIC—♡
I KINDA KNEW ALL ALONG—!

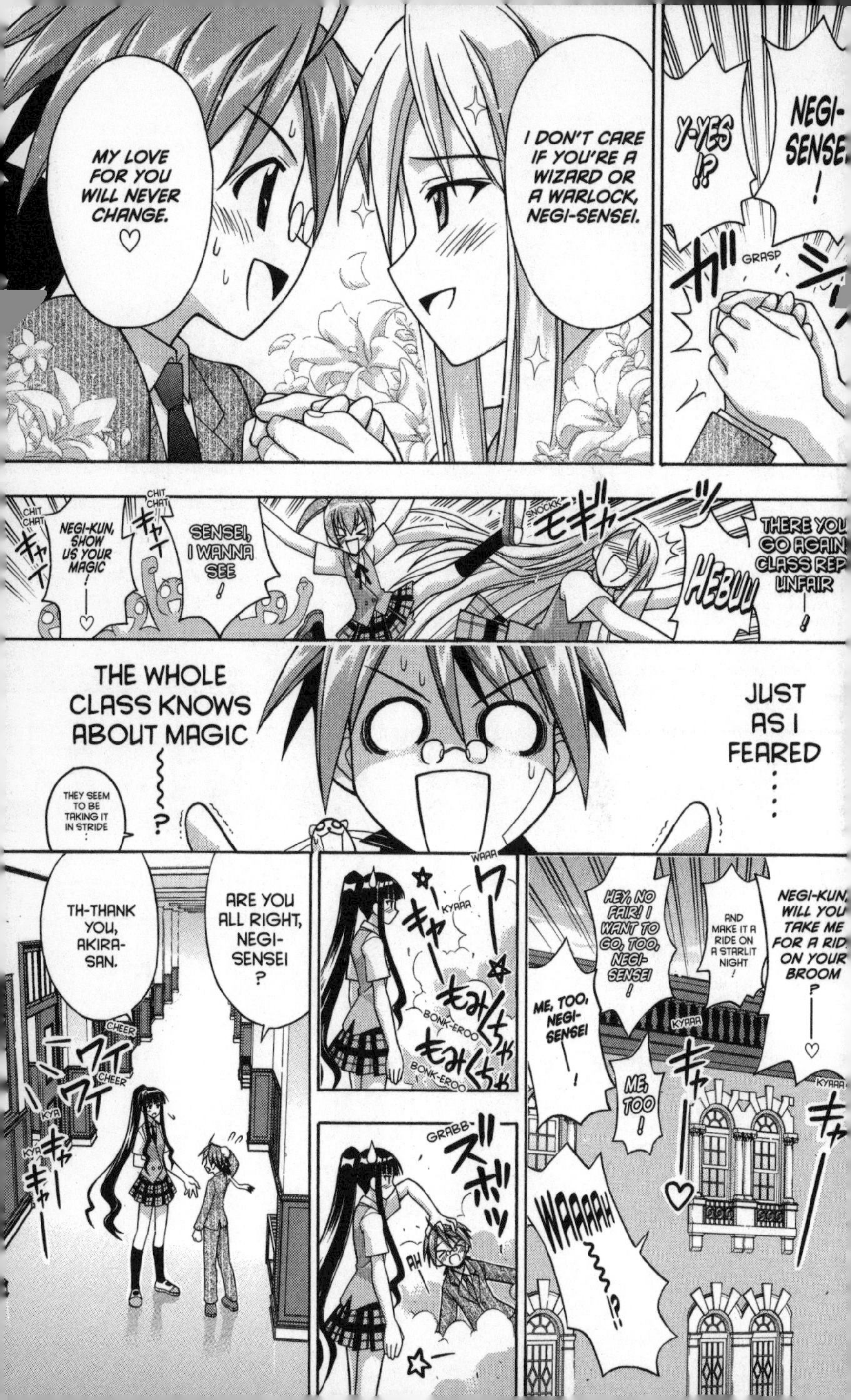
NEGI-SENSEI !
Y-YES !?
GRASP
I DON'T CARE IF YOU'RE A WIZARD OR A WARLOCK, NEGI-SENSEI.
MY LOVE FOR YOU WILL NEVER CHANGE. ♡
THERE YOU GO AGAIN CLASS REP UNFAIR !
HEBUU
SNOCKK
SENSEI, I WANNA SEE !
CHIT CHAT
NEGI-KUN, SHOW US YOUR MAGIC ! ♡
CHIT CHAT
JUST AS I FEARED ....
THE WHOLE CLASS KNOWS ABOUT MAGIC ~~~?
THEY SEEM TO BE TAKING IT IN STRIDE :
NEGI-KUN, WILL YOU TAKE ME FOR A RIDE ON YOUR BROOM ? ♡
AND MAKE IT A RIDE ON A STARLIT NIGHT !
HEY, NO FAIR! I WANT TO GO, TOO, NEGI-SENSEI !
ME, TOO, NEGI-SENSEI !
KYAAA
ME, TOO !
KYAAA
WAAAAH ~~~?!
WAAA
KYAAA
BONK-EROO
BONK-EROO
GRABB-
AH
ARE YOU ALL RIGHT, NEGI-SENSEI ?
TH-THANK YOU, AKIRA-SAN.
CHEER
CHEER
KYA
KYA

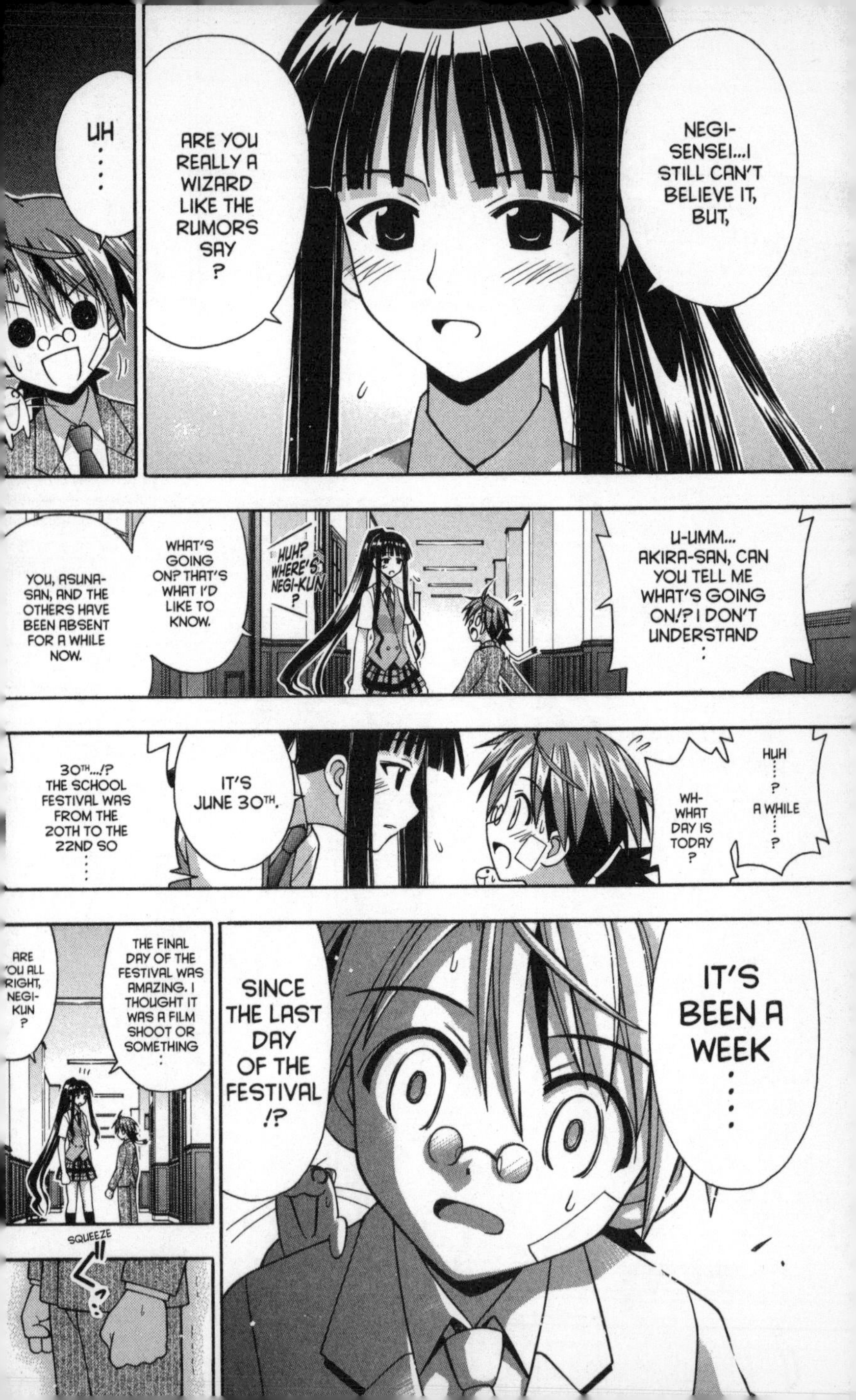

NEGI-SENSEI...I STILL CAN'T BELIEVE IT, BUT,
ARE YOU REALLY A WIZARD LIKE THE RUMORS SAY?
UH ....
U-UMM... AKIRA-SAN, CAN YOU TELL ME WHAT'S GOING ON!? I DON'T UNDERSTAND :
HUH? WHERE'S NEGI-KUN?
WHAT'S GOING ON? THAT'S WHAT I'D LIKE TO KNOW.
YOU, ASUNA-SAN, AND THE OTHERS HAVE BEEN ABSENT FOR A WHILE NOW.
HUH...? A WHILE...?
WH-WHAT DAY IS TODAY?
IT'S JUNE 30TH.
30TH...!? THE SCHOOL FESTIVAL WAS FROM THE 20TH TO THE 22ND SO ....
IT'S BEEN A WEEK ....
SINCE THE LAST DAY OF THE FESTIVAL!?
THE FINAL DAY OF THE FESTIVAL WAS AMAZING. I THOUGHT IT WAS A FILM SHOOT OR SOMETHING :
ARE YOU ALL RIGHT, NEGI-KUN?
SQUEEZE

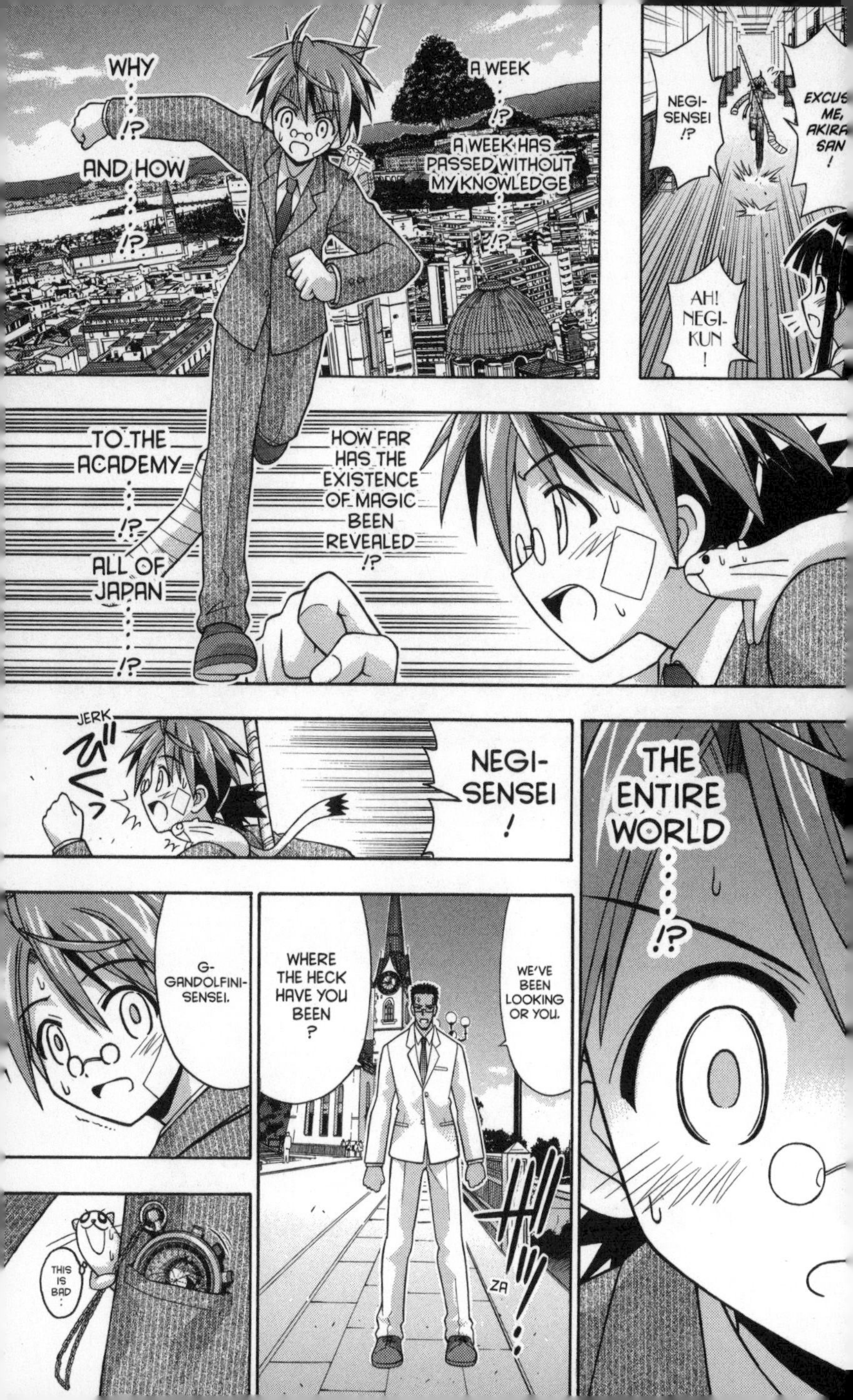

EXCUS ME, AKIRA SAN !
NEGI-SENSEI !?
AH! NEGI-KUN !
A WEEK ...!?
A WEEK HAS PASSED WITHOUT MY KNOWLEDGE ...!?
WHY ...!?
AND HOW ...!?
HOW FAR HAS THE EXISTENCE OF MAGIC BEEN REVEALED !?
TO THE ACADEMY ...!?
ALL OF JAPAN ...!?
THE ENTIRE WORLD ......!?
NEGI-SENSEI !
JERK
びくっ
WE'VE BEEN LOOKING OR YOU.
WHERE THE HECK HAVE YOU BEEN ?
G-GANDOLFINI-SENSEI.
ZA
THIS IS BAD...

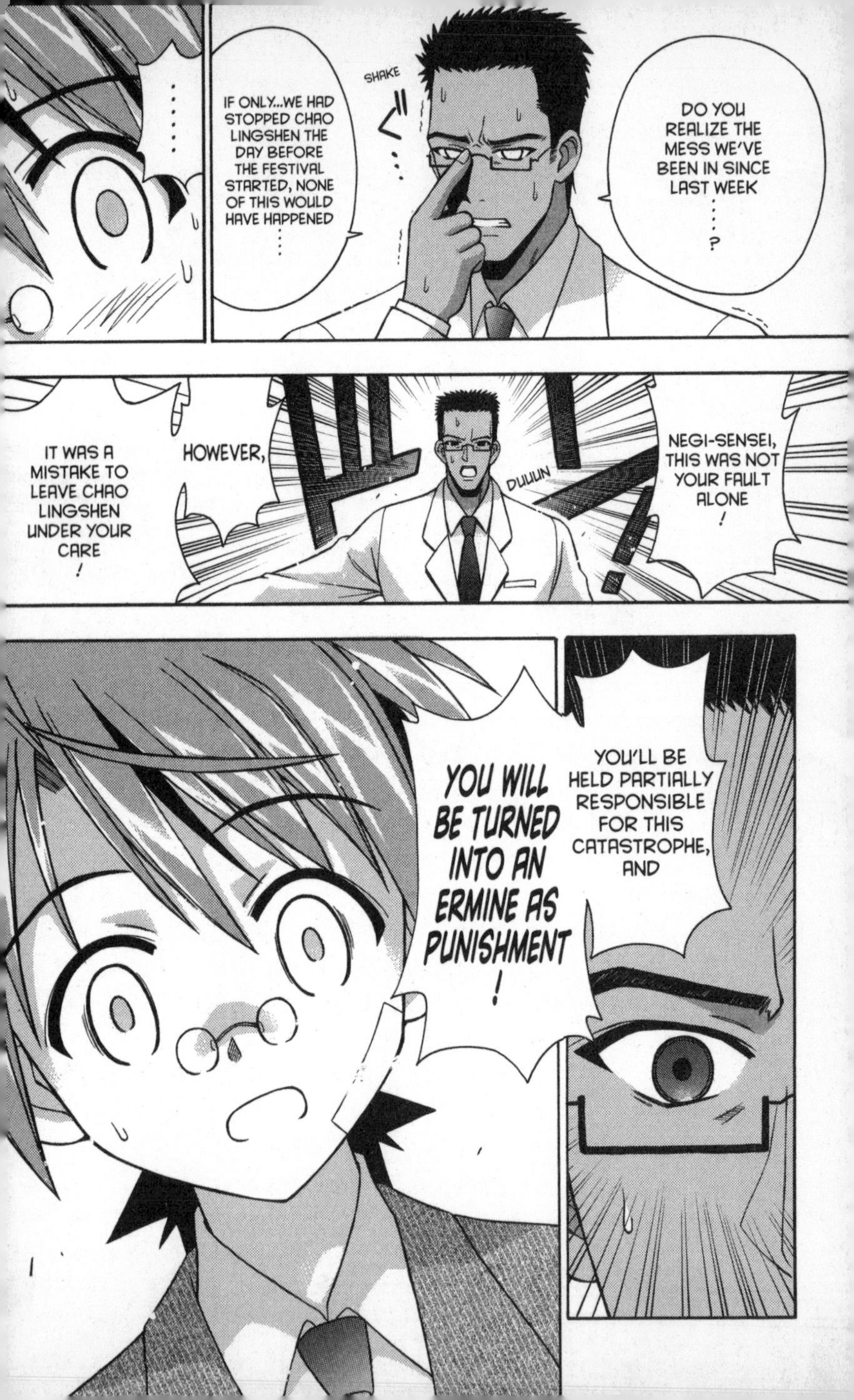
DO YOU REALIZE THE MESS WE'VE BEEN IN SINCE LAST WEEK...?
SHAKE
IF ONLY...WE HAD STOPPED CHAO LINGSHEN THE DAY BEFORE THE FESTIVAL STARTED, NONE OF THIS WOULD HAVE HAPPENED...
...
NEGI-SENSEI, THIS WAS NOT YOUR FAULT ALONE!
DUUUN
HOWEVER,
IT WAS A MISTAKE TO LEAVE CHAO LINGSHEN UNDER YOUR CARE!
YOU'LL BE HELD PARTIALLY RESPONSIBLE FOR THIS CATASTROPHE, AND
YOU WILL BE TURNED INTO AN ERMINE AS PUNISHMENT!

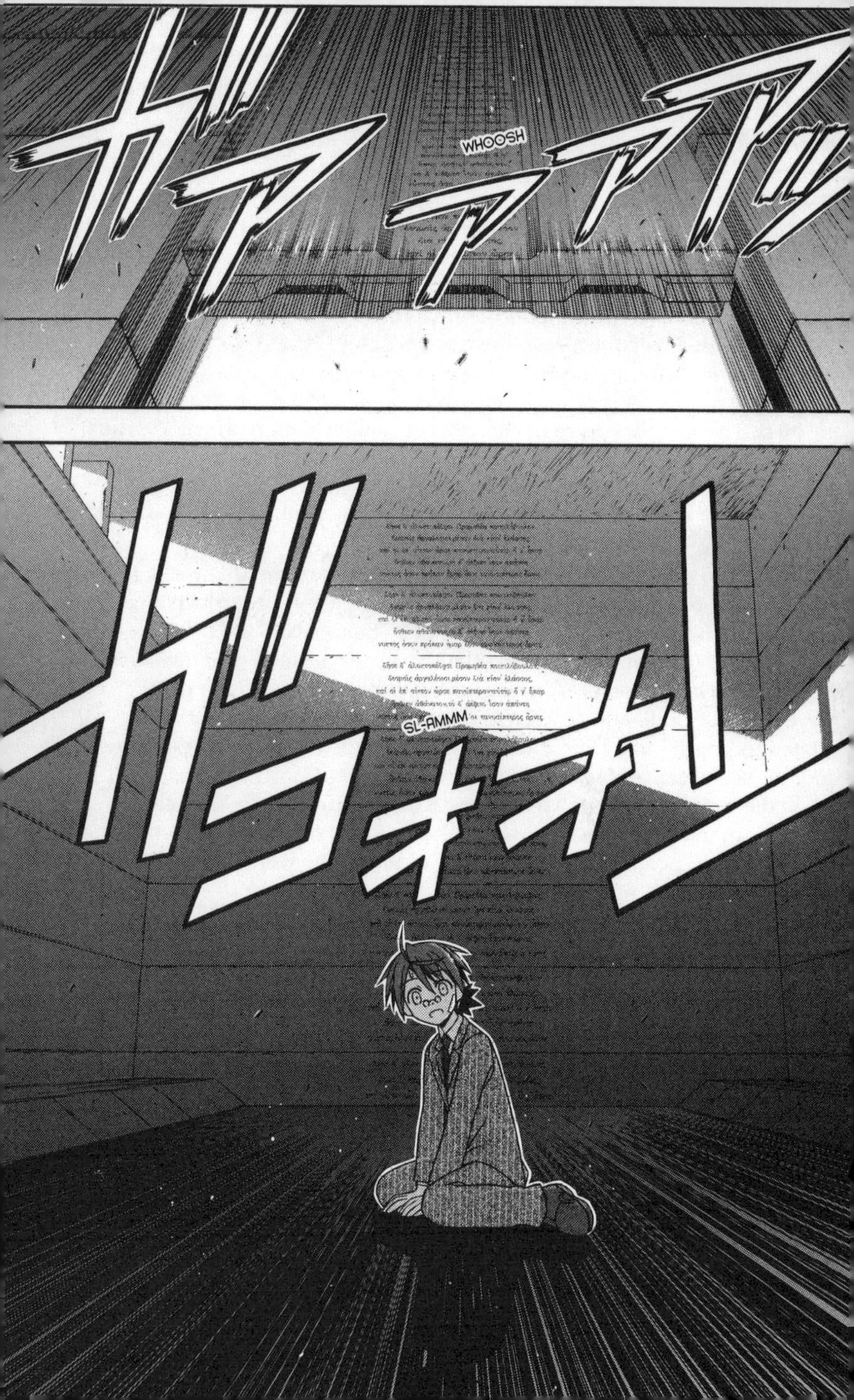
ガアアアアッ
WHOOSH
ガコォオン
SL-AMMM

LEXICON MAGICUM NEGIMARUM

■マギステース
(μαγιστής)

MAGISTER

The English words "mage," "magician," "magic," etc. are derived from the the Latin word *magus,* which means "wizard." The root of the Latin word comes from an ancient Greek word μάγος and the ancient Persian word *magu**. An excerpt from Herodotus's *The Histories,* volume ı, chapter ıoı, reads: "The Median tribes are these: the Busae, the Paretaceni, the Struchates, the Arizanti, the Budii, the Magi [μάγοι]. Their tribes are this many." The μάγος, magus, mage, etc. were originally one of the tribes of the Mede Empire. They were in charge of dream divination, astrology, ritual sacrifices, and other priestly duties. (In chapter ıo7 of the same book, there is a record of a μάγος performing a dream divination, and in chapter ı32 are records of ritual sacrifice. In volume 7, chapter 37, there is a record of the observations and interpretations of a solar eclipse.)

Magic and magic users exist in various cultures around the world. For example, in Latin: *incantator* (a person who can cast a spell, "enchanter" in English), *pharmacus* (maker of medicines, "pharmacist" in English), *praecantator* (one who can see the future), *sortilegus* (one who divinates with raffle tickets, "sorcerer" in English), *theurgus* (one who see the movements of God), and *venefiscus* ("apothecary" in English) were all related to "magic" in a Latin dictionary. "Magicians" were the priests, artists, doctors, scientists, and teachers of various cultures.

In the world of *Negima!,* the mages are called μαγιστής. The usage is similar to the Median and Persian cultures' word for magic. The ending ‐ιστής means "people who do/use." For example, the word "artist" is *artista* in Latin and τεχνιστής in Greek.

* Ancient Persian characters cannot be depicted so they have been Latinized.

■魔法界

MAGIANITAS

This word means "the Society of the Mages." The Society of the Mages has its own systems of law, economy, transportation, communication, and education. Even so, looking over the long history of human civilization, nearly all pre-modern societies can be seen to have been based in magic and mysticism. However, the arrival of the major world religions, such as Islam and Christianity, pushed aside much of the mysticism found in ancient societies and played a role, beginning in Europe in the Middle Ages, in creating modern culture.

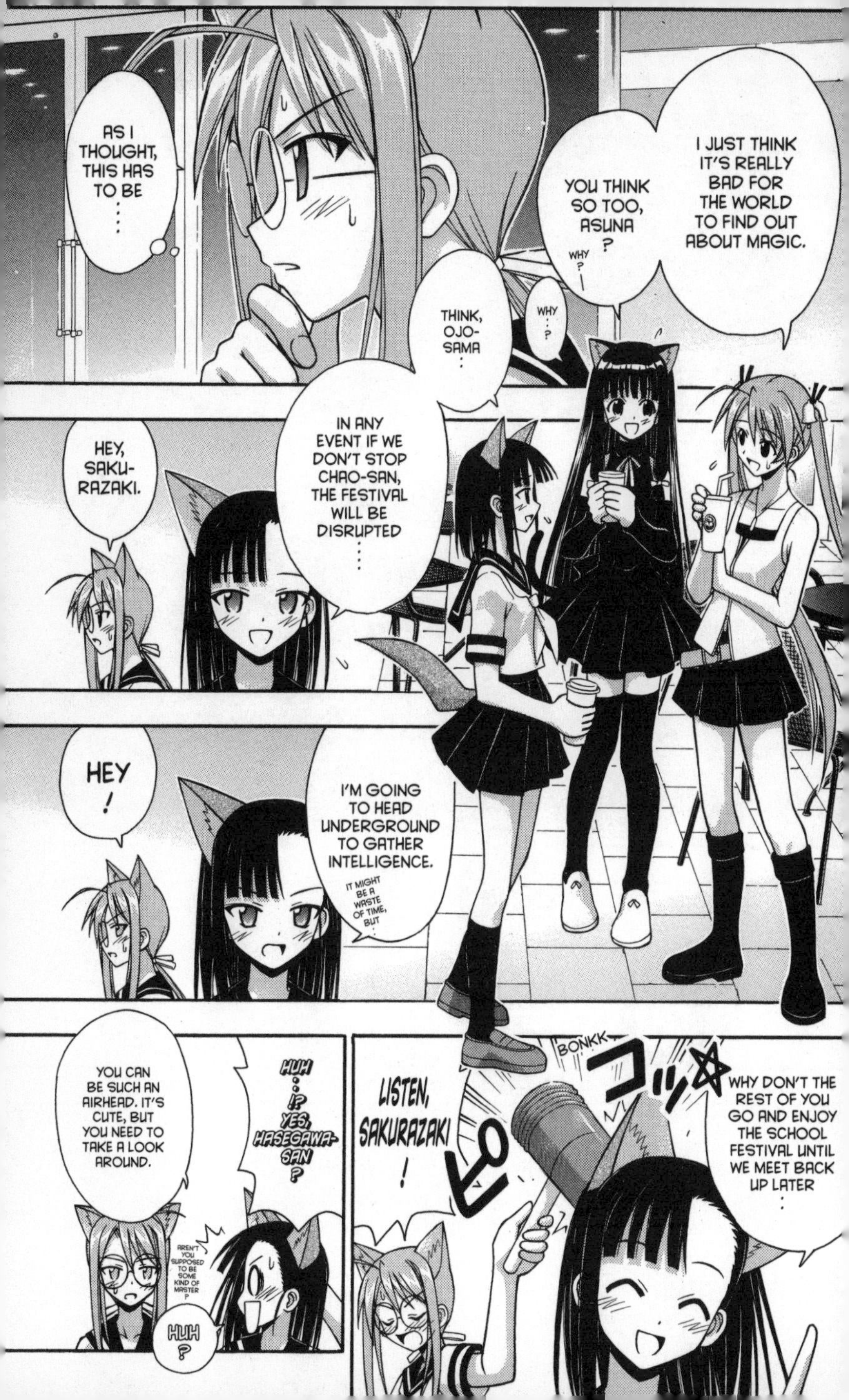
I JUST THINK IT'S REALLY BAD FOR THE WORLD TO FIND OUT ABOUT MAGIC.
YOU THINK SO TOO, ASUNA?
WHY?!
WHY..?
THINK, OJO-SAMA..
AS I THOUGHT, THIS HAS TO BE...
IN ANY EVENT IF WE DON'T STOP CHAO-SAN, THE FESTIVAL WILL BE DISRUPTED...
HEY, SAKURAZAKI.
I'M GOING TO HEAD UNDERGROUND TO GATHER INTELLIGENCE.
IT MIGHT BE A WASTE OF TIME, BUT..
HEY!
WHY DON'T THE REST OF YOU GO AND ENJOY THE SCHOOL FESTIVAL UNTIL WE MEET BACK UP LATER..
BONKK
LISTEN, SAKURAZAKI!
HUH..!? YES, HASEGAWA-SAN?
YOU CAN BE SUCH AN AIRHEAD. IT'S CUTE, BUT YOU NEED TO TAKE A LOOK AROUND.
AREN'T YOU SUPPOSED TO BE SOME KIND OF MASTER?
HUH?

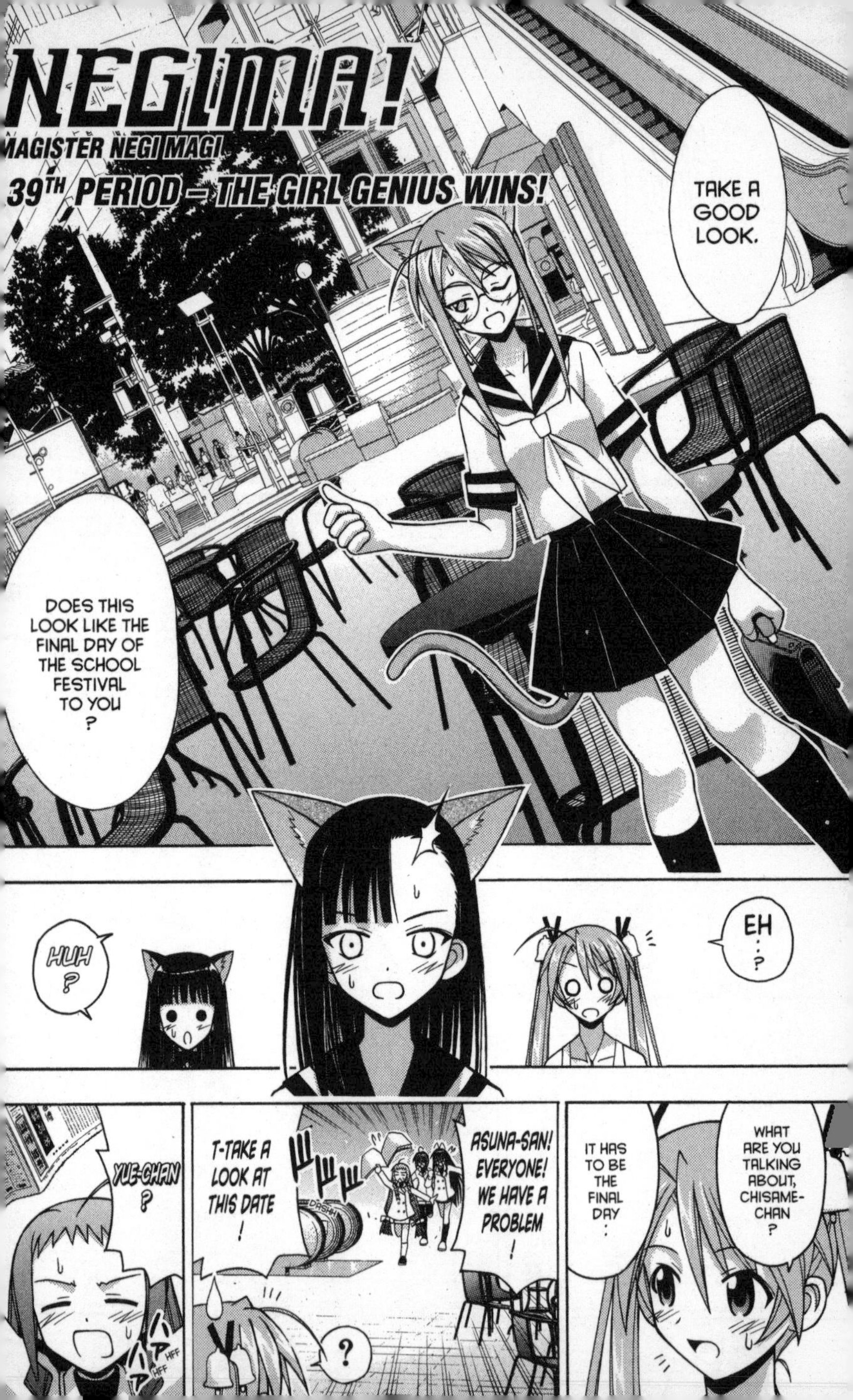
NEGIMA!
MAGISTER NEGI MAGI
39TH PERIOD – THE GIRL GENIUS WINS!
TAKE A GOOD LOOK.
DOES THIS LOOK LIKE THE FINAL DAY OF THE SCHOOL FESTIVAL TO YOU ?
EH ..?
HUH ?
WHAT ARE YOU TALKING ABOUT, CHISAME-CHAN ?
IT HAS TO BE THE FINAL DAY :
ASUNA-SAN! EVERYONE! WE HAVE A PROBLEM !
T-TAKE A LOOK AT THIS DATE !
DRSHH
?
YUE-CHAN ?
HFF
HFF

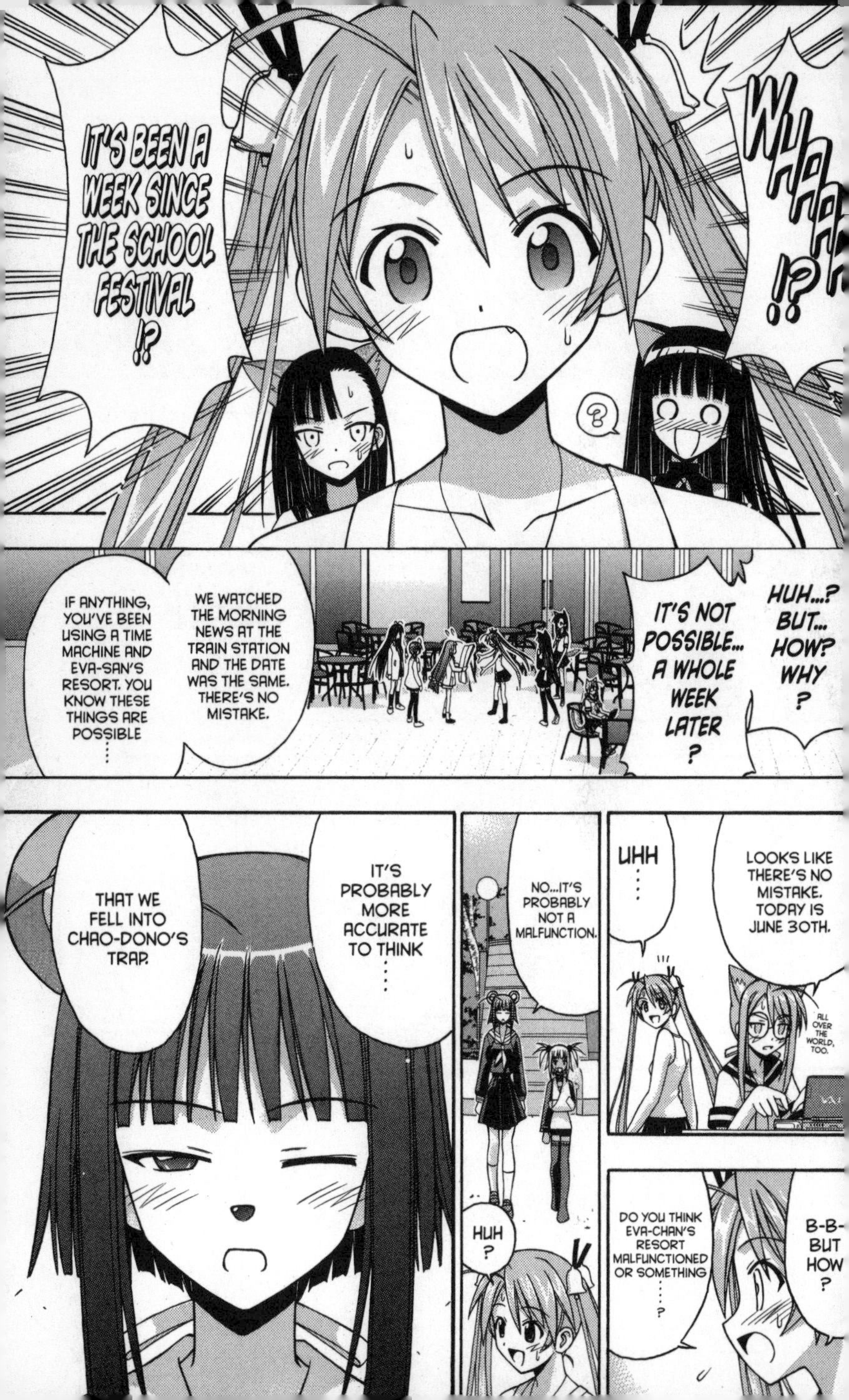

WHAAA...!?
IT'S BEEN A WEEK SINCE THE SCHOOL FESTIVAL!?
?
HUH...? BUT... HOW? WHY?
IT'S NOT POSSIBLE... A WHOLE WEEK LATER?
WE WATCHED THE MORNING NEWS AT THE TRAIN STATION AND THE DATE WAS THE SAME. THERE'S NO MISTAKE.
IF ANYTHING, YOU'VE BEEN USING A TIME MACHINE AND EVA-SAN'S RESORT. YOU KNOW THESE THINGS ARE POSSIBLE...
LOOKS LIKE THERE'S NO MISTAKE. TODAY IS JUNE 30TH.
ALL OVER THE WORLD, TOO.
UHH...
B-B-BUT HOW?
DO YOU THINK EVA-CHAN'S RESORT MALFUNCTIONED OR SOMETHING....?
NO...IT'S PROBABLY NOT A MALFUNCTION.
HUH?
IT'S PROBABLY MORE ACCURATE TO THINK...
THAT WE FELL INTO CHAO-DONO'S TRAP.

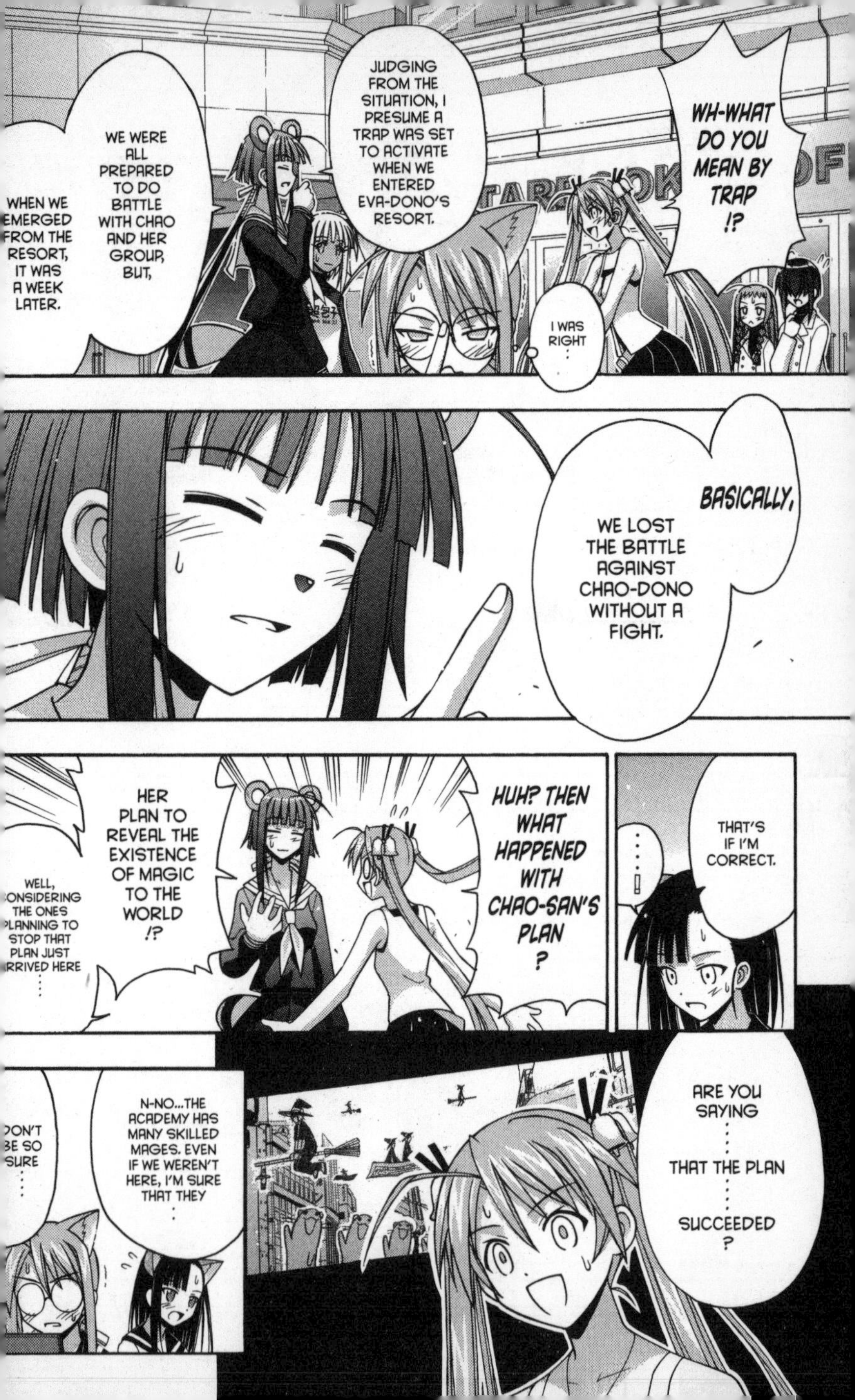

WH-WHAT DO YOU MEAN BY TRAP !?
JUDGING FROM THE SITUATION, I PRESUME A TRAP WAS SET TO ACTIVATE WHEN WE ENTERED EVA-DONO'S RESORT.
I WAS RIGHT ...
WE WERE ALL PREPARED TO DO BATTLE WITH CHAO AND HER GROUP, BUT,
WHEN WE EMERGED FROM THE RESORT, IT WAS A WEEK LATER.
BASICALLY,
WE LOST THE BATTLE AGAINST CHAO-DONO WITHOUT A FIGHT.
THAT'S IF I'M CORRECT.
.....!
HUH? THEN WHAT HAPPENED WITH CHAO-SAN'S PLAN ?
HER PLAN TO REVEAL THE EXISTENCE OF MAGIC TO THE WORLD !?
WELL, CONSIDERING THE ONES PLANNING TO STOP THAT PLAN JUST ARRIVED HERE ...
ARE YOU SAYING ... THAT THE PLAN ... SUCCEEDED ?
N-NO...THE ACADEMY HAS MANY SKILLED MAGES. EVEN IF WE WEREN'T HERE, I'M SURE THAT THEY ...
DON'T BE SO SURE ...

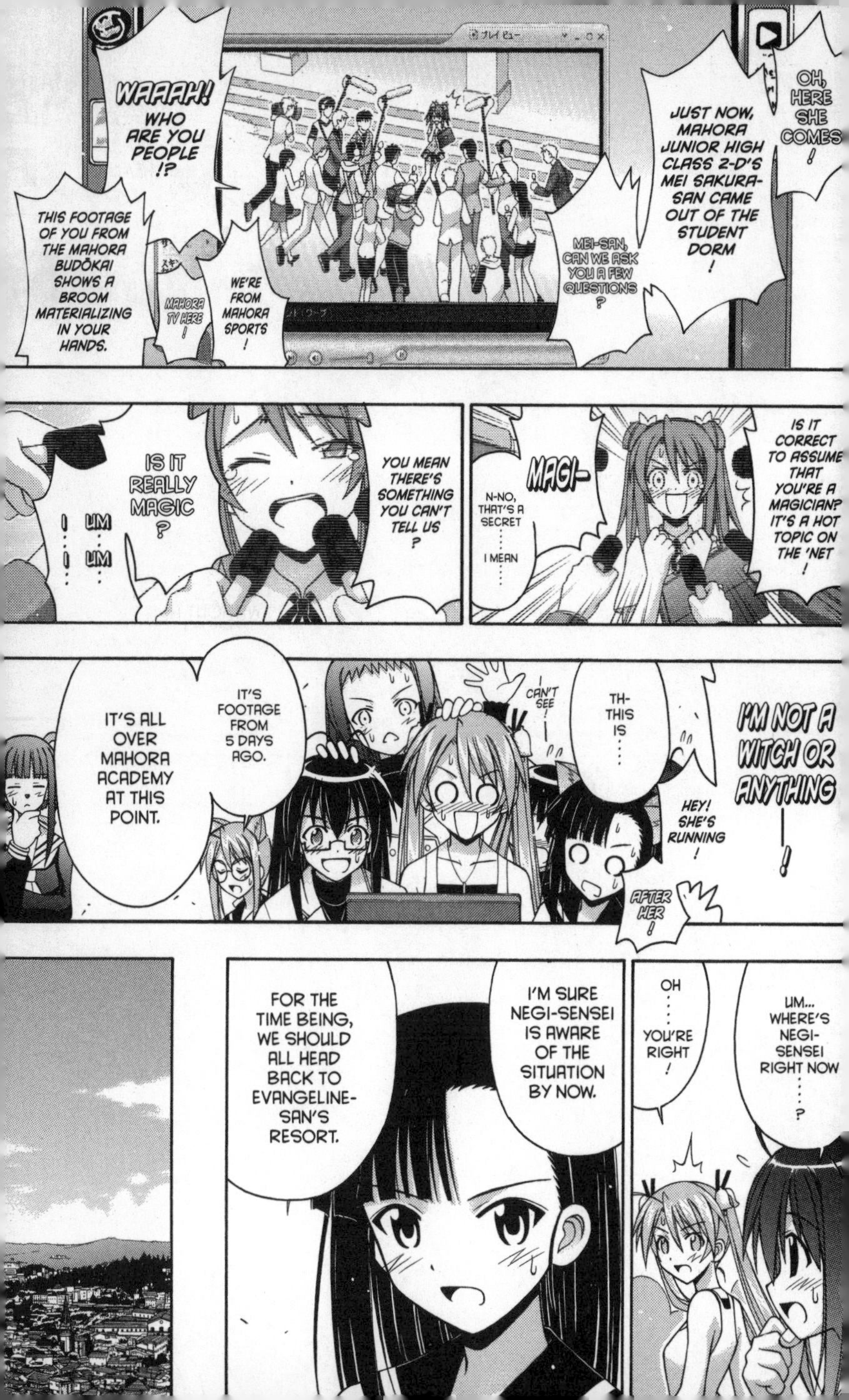
OH, HERE SHE COMES!
JUST NOW, MAHORA JUNIOR HIGH CLASS 2-D'S MEI SAKURA-SAN CAME OUT OF THE STUDENT DORM!
MEI-SAN, CAN WE ASK YOU A FEW QUESTIONS?
WAAAH! WHO ARE YOU PEOPLE!?
WE'RE FROM MAHORA SPORTS!
MAHORA TV HERE!
THIS FOOTAGE OF YOU FROM THE MAHORA BUDŌKAI SHOWS A BROOM MATERIALIZING IN YOUR HANDS.
IS IT CORRECT TO ASSUME THAT YOU'RE A MAGICIAN? IT'S A HOT TOPIC ON THE 'NET!
MAGI-
N-NO, THAT'S A SECRET...... I MEAN
YOU MEAN THERE'S SOMETHING YOU CAN'T TELL US?
IS IT REALLY MAGIC?
UM... UM...
I... I...
I'M NOT A WITCH OR ANYTHING—!
HEY! SHE'S RUNNING!
AFTER HER!
TH-THIS IS....
I CAN'T SEE!
IT'S FOOTAGE FROM 5 DAYS AGO.
IT'S ALL OVER MAHORA ACADEMY AT THIS POINT.
UM... WHERE'S NEGI-SENSEI RIGHT NOW....?
OH.... YOU'RE RIGHT!
I'M SURE NEGI-SENSEI IS AWARE OF THE SITUATION BY NOW.
FOR THE TIME BEING, WE SHOULD ALL HEAD BACK TO EVANGELINE-SAN'S RESORT.

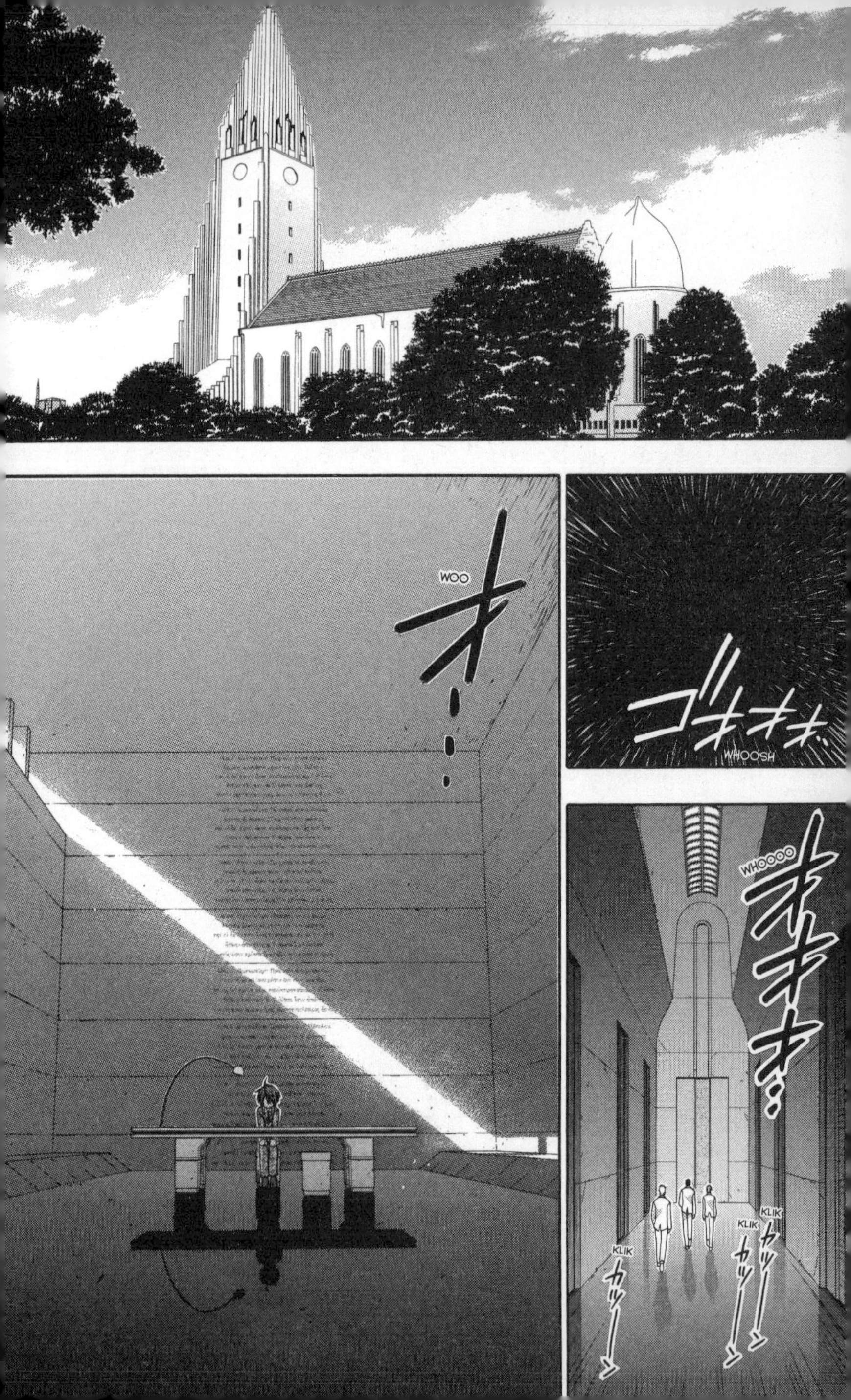

ゴォォォ…
WHOOSH
オォォォ…
WHOOOO
KLIK
カツー
KLIK
カツー
KLIK
カツー
WOO
オー…

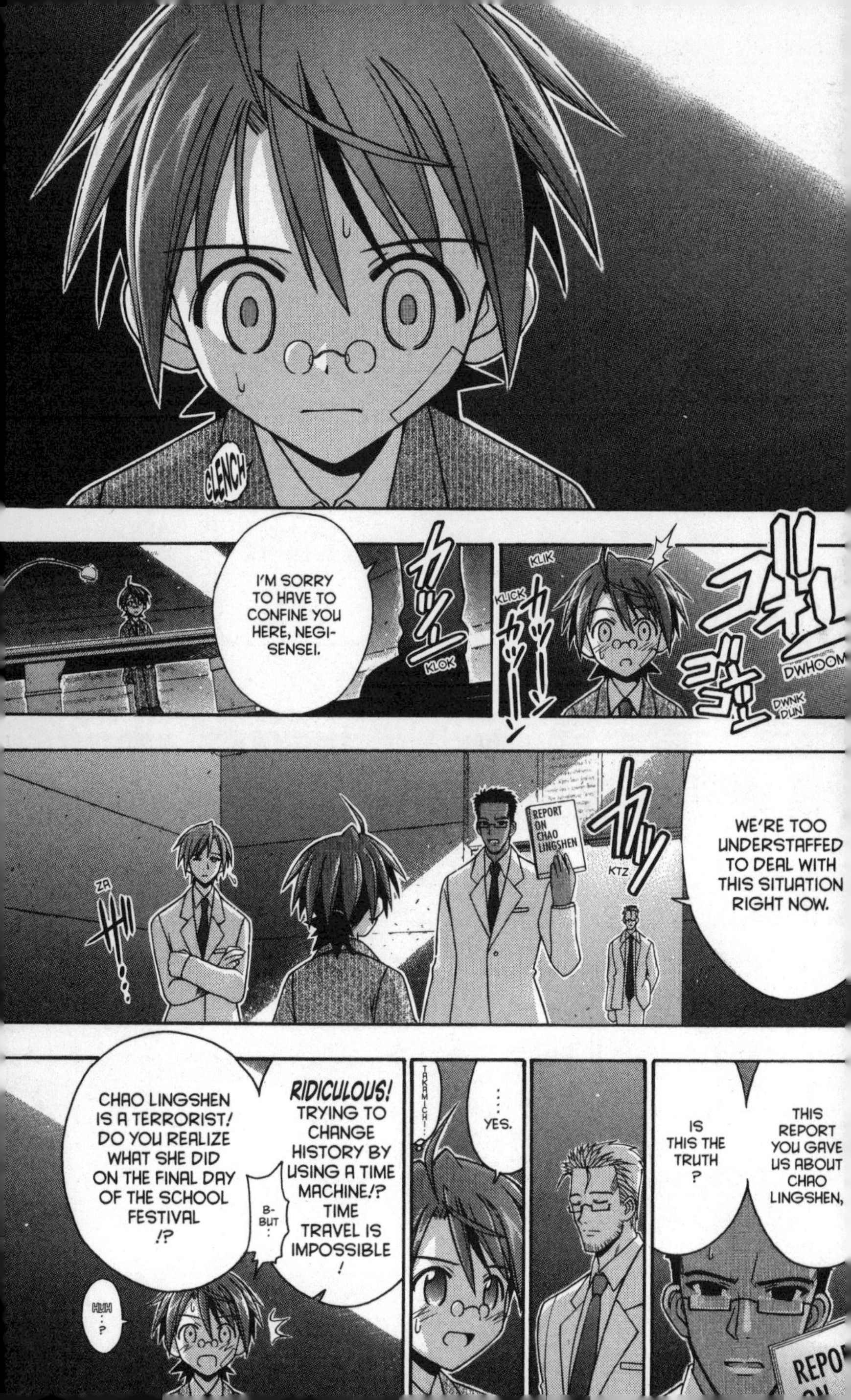
CLENCH
DWHOOM
DWNK DUN
KLIK
KLICK
KLOK
I'M SORRY TO HAVE TO CONFINE YOU HERE, NEGI-SENSEI.
WE'RE TOO UNDERSTAFFED TO DEAL WITH THIS SITUATION RIGHT NOW.
KTZ
REPORT ON CHAO LINGSHEN
ZA
THIS REPORT YOU GAVE US ABOUT CHAO LINGSHEN,
IS THIS THE TRUTH?
REPORT
...YES.
TAKAMICHI!...
RIDICULOUS! TRYING TO CHANGE HISTORY BY USING A TIME MACHINE!? TIME TRAVEL IS IMPOSSIBLE!
B-BUT...
CHAO LINGSHEN IS A TERRORIST! DO YOU REALIZE WHAT SHE DID ON THE FINAL DAY OF THE SCHOOL FESTIVAL!?
HUH...?

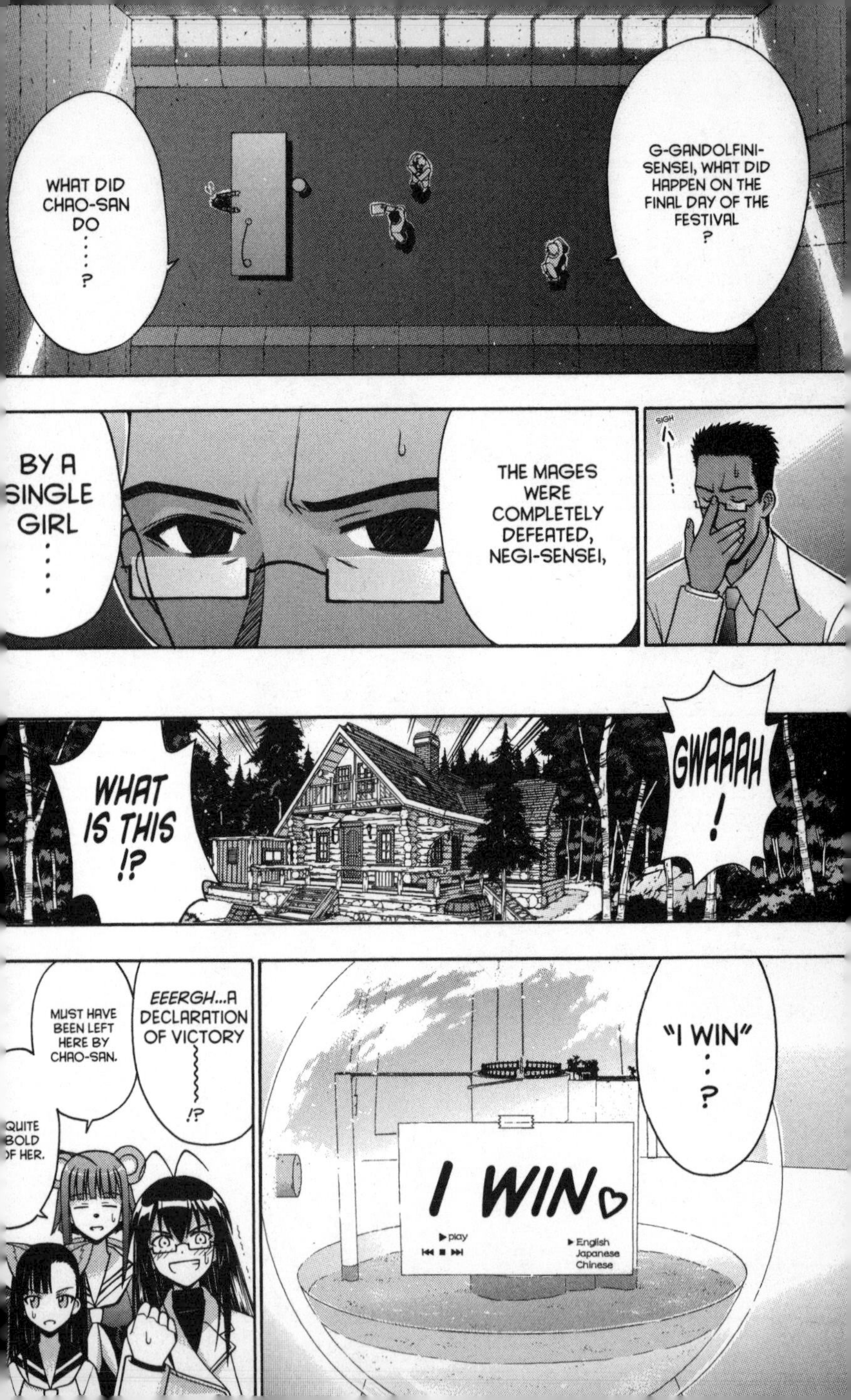
G-GANDOLFINI-SENSEI, WHAT DID HAPPEN ON THE FINAL DAY OF THE FESTIVAL ?
WHAT DID CHAO-SAN DO.....?
SIGH
THE MAGES WERE COMPLETELY DEFEATED, NEGI-SENSEI,
BY A SINGLE GIRL.....
GWAAAH!
WHAT IS THIS!?
"I WIN"..?
I WIN ♡
▶play
▶English
Japanese
Chinese
EEERGH...A DECLARATION OF VICTORY~!?
MUST HAVE BEEN LEFT HERE BY CHAO-SAN.
QUITE BOLD OF HER.

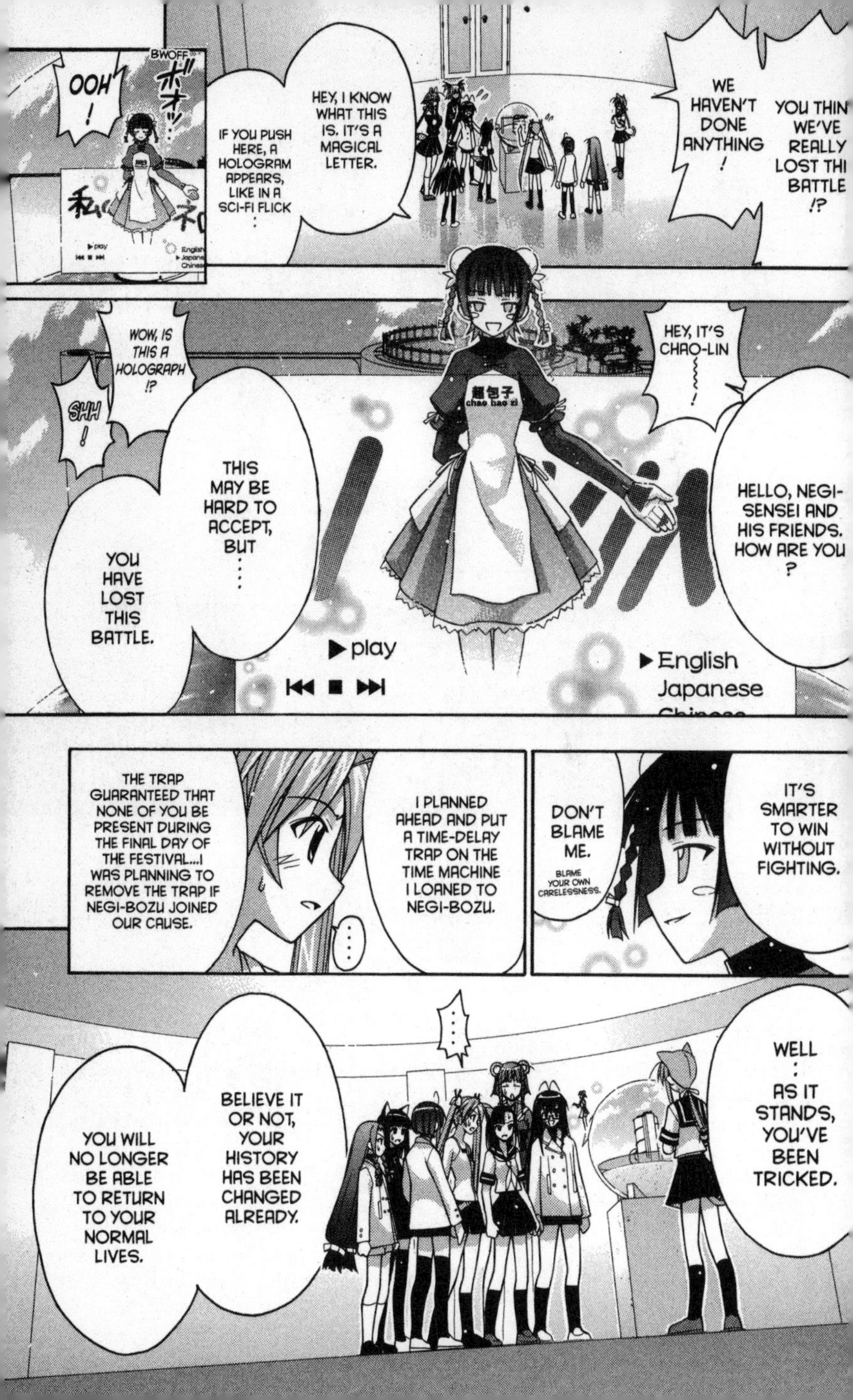
YOU THIN WE'VE REALLY LOST THI BATTLE !?
WE HAVEN'T DONE ANYTHING !
HEY, I KNOW WHAT THIS IS. IT'S A MAGICAL LETTER.
IF YOU PUSH HERE, A HOLOGRAM APPEARS, LIKE IN A SCI-FI FLICK :
BWOFF
OOH !
HEY, IT'S CHAO-LIN ~ !
HELLO, NEGI-SENSEI AND HIS FRIENDS. HOW ARE YOU ?
WOW, IS THIS A HOLOGRAPH !?
SHH !
THIS MAY BE HARD TO ACCEPT, BUT ....
YOU HAVE LOST THIS BATTLE.
超包子
chao bao zi
▶ play
▶ English
Japanese
IT'S SMARTER TO WIN WITHOUT FIGHTING.
DON'T BLAME ME.
BLAME YOUR OWN CARELESSNESS.
I PLANNED AHEAD AND PUT A TIME-DELAY TRAP ON THE TIME MACHINE I LOANED TO NEGI-BOZU.
THE TRAP GUARANTEED THAT NONE OF YOU BE PRESENT DURING THE FINAL DAY OF THE FESTIVAL...I WAS PLANNING TO REMOVE THE TRAP IF NEGI-BOZU JOINED OUR CAUSE.
....
WELL : AS IT STANDS, YOU'VE BEEN TRICKED.
....!
BELIEVE IT OR NOT, YOUR HISTORY HAS BEEN CHANGED ALREADY.
YOU WILL NO LONGER BE ABLE TO RETURN TO YOUR NORMAL LIVES.

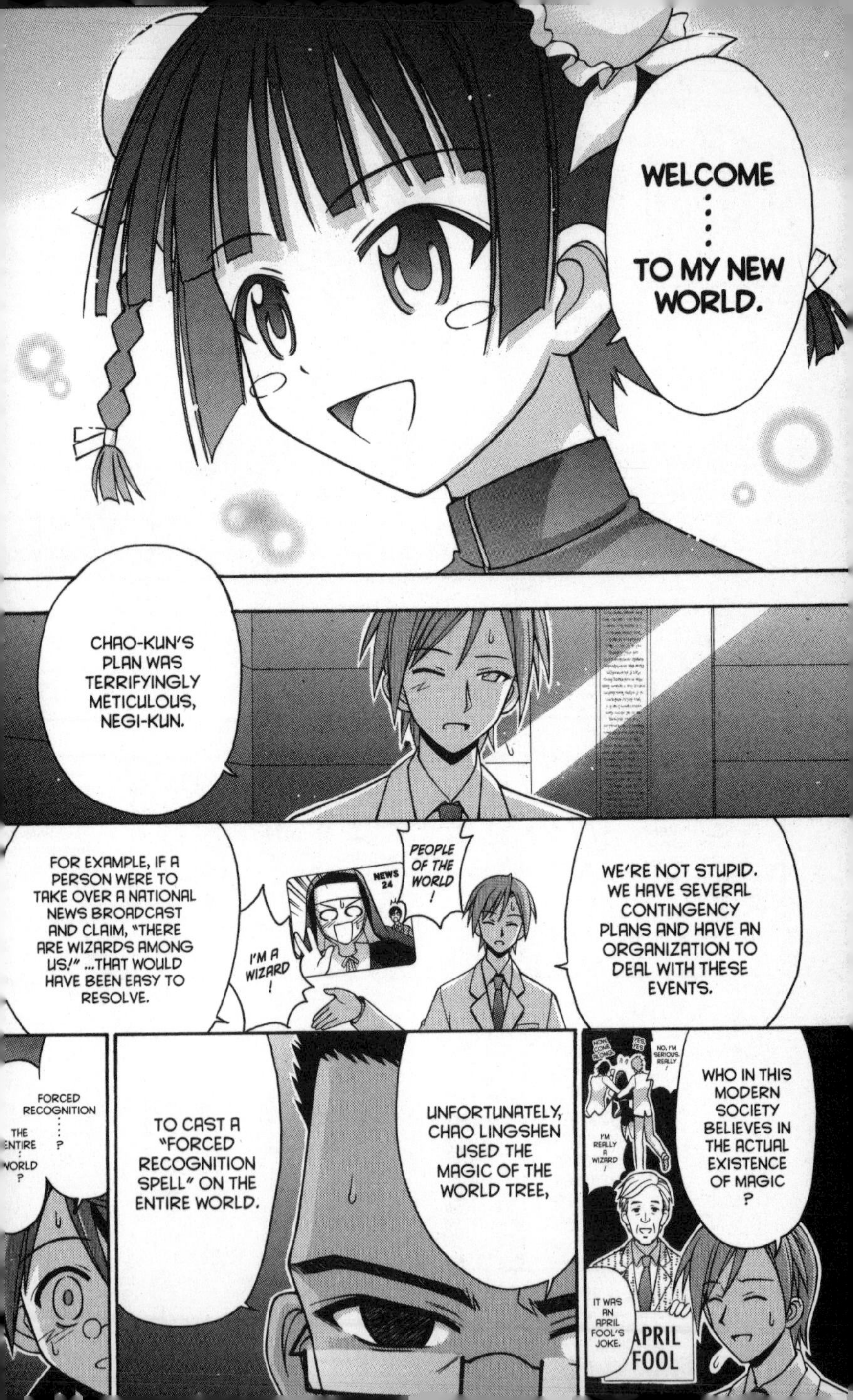
WELCOME ... TO MY NEW WORLD.
CHAO-KUN'S PLAN WAS TERRIFYINGLY METICULOUS, NEGI-KUN.
WE'RE NOT STUPID. WE HAVE SEVERAL CONTINGENCY PLANS AND HAVE AN ORGANIZATION TO DEAL WITH THESE EVENTS.
PEOPLE OF THE WORLD!
NEWS 24
FOR EXAMPLE, IF A PERSON WERE TO TAKE OVER A NATIONAL NEWS BROADCAST AND CLAIM, "THERE ARE WIZARDS AMONG US!" ...THAT WOULD HAVE BEEN EASY TO RESOLVE.
I'M A WIZARD!
WHO IN THIS MODERN SOCIETY BELIEVES IN THE ACTUAL EXISTENCE OF MAGIC?
NO, I'M SERIOUS. REALLY!
YES YES
NOW, COME ALONG.
I'M REALLY A WIZARD!
IT WAS AN APRIL FOOL'S JOKE.
APRIL FOOL
UNFORTUNATELY, CHAO LINGSHEN USED THE MAGIC OF THE WORLD TREE,
TO CAST A "FORCED RECOGNITION SPELL" ON THE ENTIRE WORLD.
FORCED RECOGNITION ...?
THE ENTIRE : WORLD ?

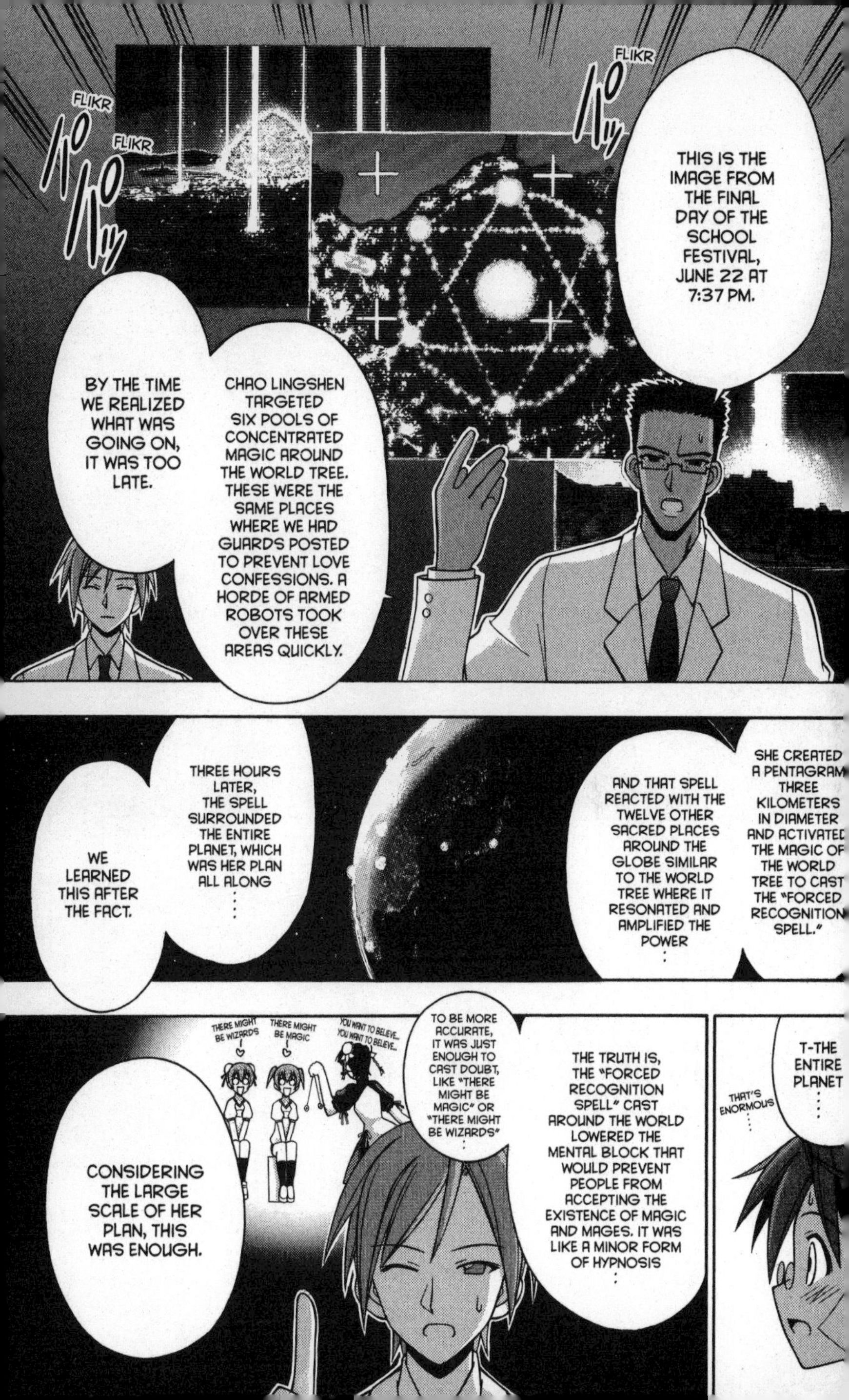
FLIKR
THIS IS THE IMAGE FROM THE FINAL DAY OF THE SCHOOL FESTIVAL, JUNE 22 AT 7:37 PM.
FLIKR
FLIKR
CHAO LINGSHEN TARGETED SIX POOLS OF CONCENTRATED MAGIC AROUND THE WORLD TREE. THESE WERE THE SAME PLACES WHERE WE HAD GUARDS POSTED TO PREVENT LOVE CONFESSIONS. A HORDE OF ARMED ROBOTS TOOK OVER THESE AREAS QUICKLY.
BY THE TIME WE REALIZED WHAT WAS GOING ON, IT WAS TOO LATE.
SHE CREATED A PENTAGRAM THREE KILOMETERS IN DIAMETER AND ACTIVATED THE MAGIC OF THE WORLD TREE TO CAST THE "FORCED RECOGNITION SPELL."
AND THAT SPELL REACTED WITH THE TWELVE OTHER SACRED PLACES AROUND THE GLOBE SIMILAR TO THE WORLD TREE WHERE IT RESONATED AND AMPLIFIED THE POWER...
THREE HOURS LATER, THE SPELL SURROUNDED THE ENTIRE PLANET, WHICH WAS HER PLAN ALL ALONG...
WE LEARNED THIS AFTER THE FACT.
T-THE ENTIRE PLANET...
THAT'S ENORMOUS...
THE TRUTH IS, THE "FORCED RECOGNITION SPELL" CAST AROUND THE WORLD LOWERED THE MENTAL BLOCK THAT WOULD PREVENT PEOPLE FROM ACCEPTING THE EXISTENCE OF MAGIC AND MAGES. IT WAS LIKE A MINOR FORM OF HYPNOSIS...
TO BE MORE ACCURATE, IT WAS JUST ENOUGH TO CAST DOUBT, LIKE "THERE MIGHT BE MAGIC" OR "THERE MIGHT BE WIZARDS"...
YOU WANT TO BELIEVE... YOU WANT TO BELIEVE...
THERE MIGHT BE MAGIC
THERE MIGHT BE WIZARDS
CONSIDERING THE LARGE SCALE OF HER PLAN, THIS WAS ENOUGH.

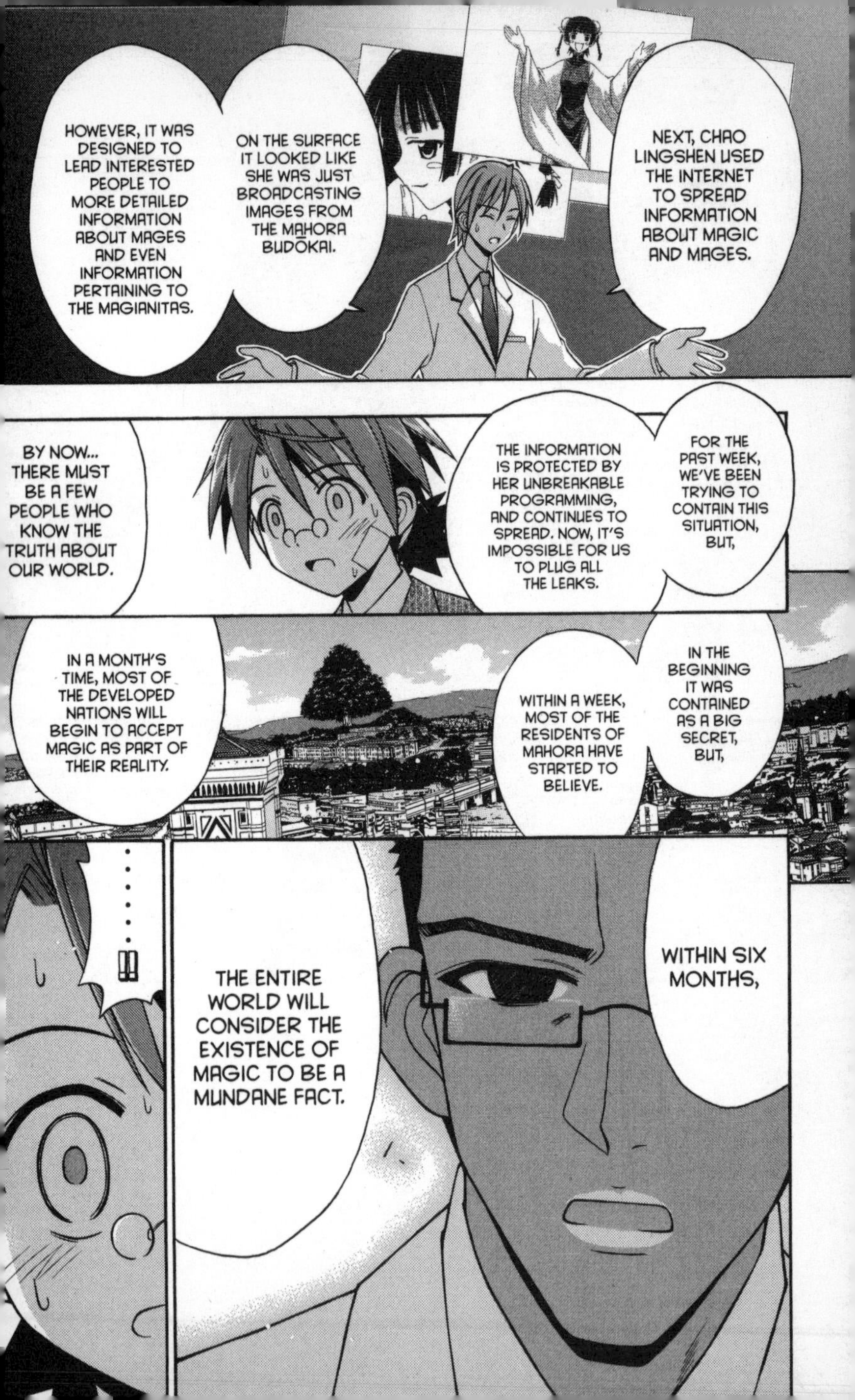
NEXT, CHAO LINGSHEN USED THE INTERNET TO SPREAD INFORMATION ABOUT MAGIC AND MAGES.
ON THE SURFACE IT LOOKED LIKE SHE WAS JUST BROADCASTING IMAGES FROM THE MAHORA BUDŌKAI.
HOWEVER, IT WAS DESIGNED TO LEAD INTERESTED PEOPLE TO MORE DETAILED INFORMATION ABOUT MAGES AND EVEN INFORMATION PERTAINING TO THE MAGIANITAS.
FOR THE PAST WEEK, WE'VE BEEN TRYING TO CONTAIN THIS SITUATION, BUT,
THE INFORMATION IS PROTECTED BY HER UNBREAKABLE PROGRAMMING, AND CONTINUES TO SPREAD. NOW, IT'S IMPOSSIBLE FOR US TO PLUG ALL THE LEAKS.
BY NOW... THERE MUST BE A FEW PEOPLE WHO KNOW THE TRUTH ABOUT OUR WORLD.
IN THE BEGINNING IT WAS CONTAINED AS A BIG SECRET, BUT,
WITHIN A WEEK, MOST OF THE RESIDENTS OF MAHORA HAVE STARTED TO BELIEVE.
IN A MONTH'S TIME, MOST OF THE DEVELOPED NATIONS WILL BEGIN TO ACCEPT MAGIC AS PART OF THEIR REALITY.
WITHIN SIX MONTHS,
THE ENTIRE WORLD WILL CONSIDER THE EXISTENCE OF MAGIC TO BE A MUNDANE FACT.
.......!!

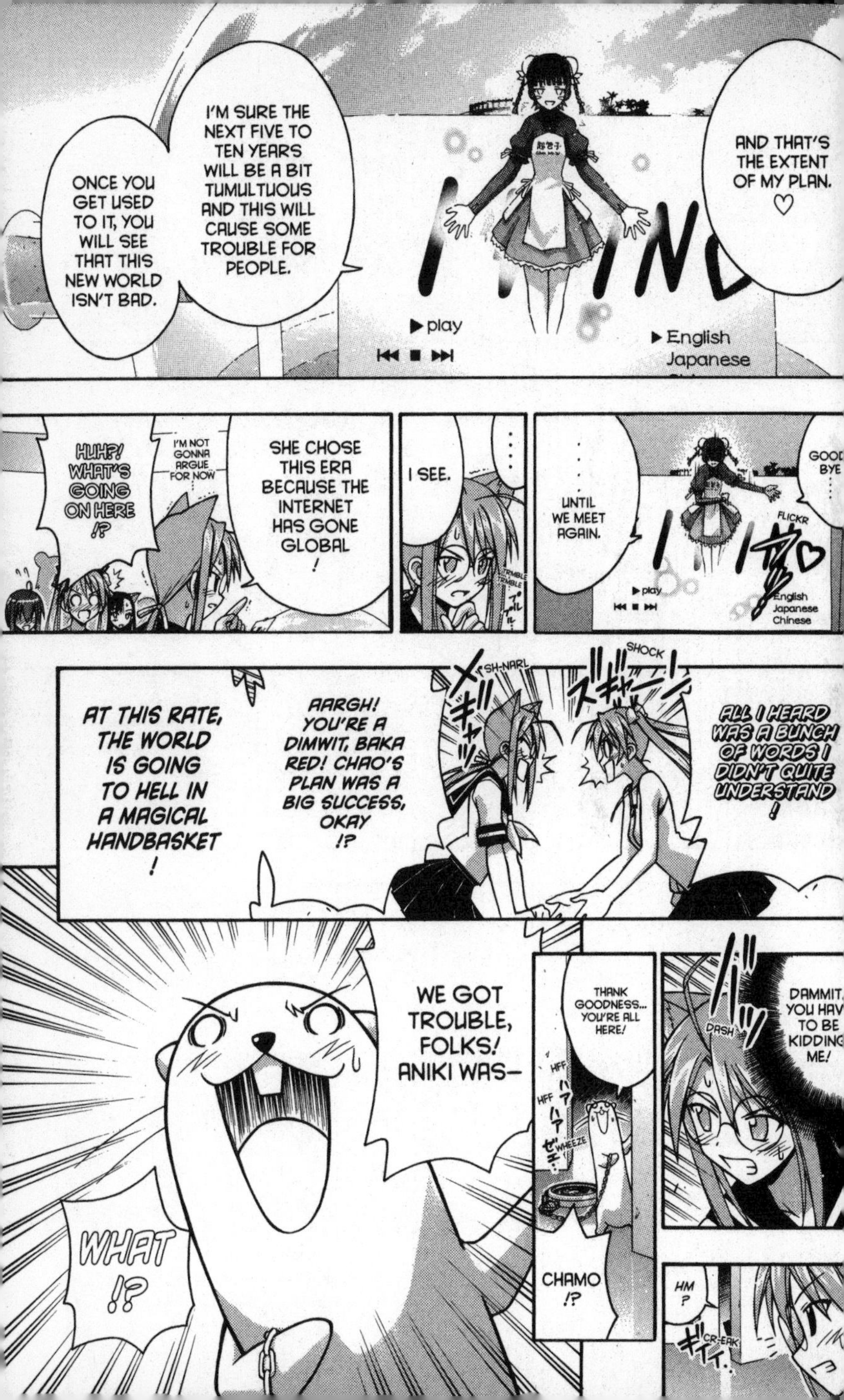
AND THAT'S THE EXTENT OF MY PLAN. ♡
I'M SURE THE NEXT FIVE TO TEN YEARS WILL BE A BIT TUMULTUOUS AND THIS WILL CAUSE SOME TROUBLE FOR PEOPLE.
ONCE YOU GET USED TO IT, YOU WILL SEE THAT THIS NEW WORLD ISN'T BAD.
▶play
▶English
Japanese
GOOD BYE...
...UNTIL WE MEET AGAIN.
FLICKR
▶play
English
Japanese
Chinese
...
I SEE.
TREMBLE TREMBLE
SHE CHOSE THIS ERA BECAUSE THE INTERNET HAS GONE GLOBAL!
I'M NOT GONNA ARGUE FOR NOW
HUH?! WHAT'S GOING ON HERE!?
ALL I HEARD WAS A BUNCH OF WORDS I DIDN'T QUITE UNDERSTAND!
SHOCK
SH-NARL
AARGH! YOU'RE A DIMWIT, BAKA RED! CHAO'S PLAN WAS A BIG SUCCESS, OKAY!?
AT THIS RATE, THE WORLD IS GOING TO HELL IN A MAGICAL HANDBASKET!
DAMMIT, YOU HAV TO BE KIDDING ME!
DASH
HM?
CR-EAK
THANK GOODNESS... YOU'RE ALL HERE!
HFF HFF
WHEEZE
CHAMO!?
WE GOT TROUBLE, FOLKS! ANIKI WAS—
WHAT!?

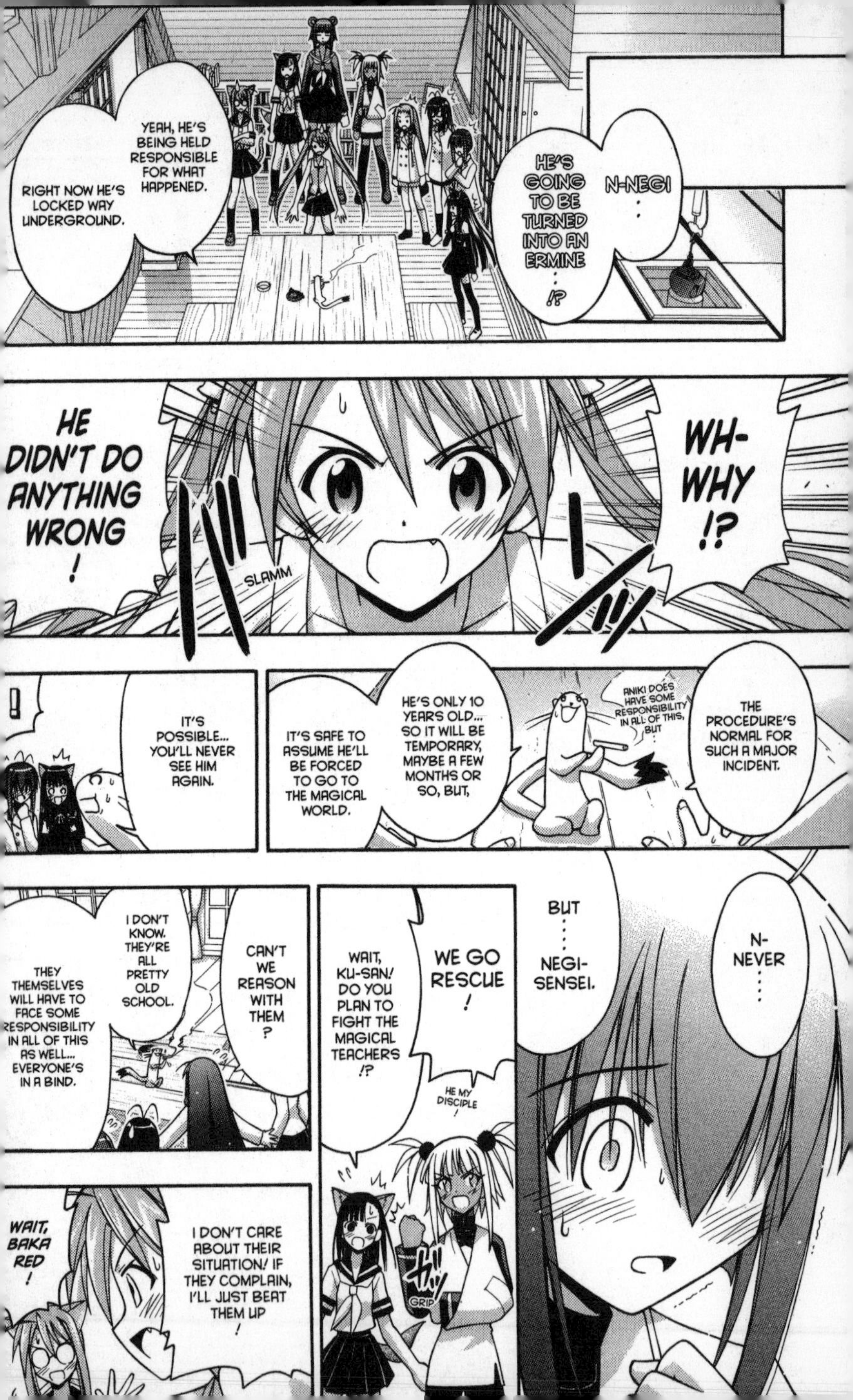
N-NEGI . . .
HE'S GOING TO BE TURNED INTO AN ERMINE . . . !?
YEAH, HE'S BEING HELD RESPONSIBLE FOR WHAT HAPPENED.
RIGHT NOW HE'S LOCKED WAY UNDERGROUND.
WH-WHY !?
SLAMM
HE DIDN'T DO ANYTHING WRONG !
THE PROCEDURE'S NORMAL FOR SUCH A MAJOR INCIDENT.
ANIKI DOES HAVE SOME RESPONSIBILITY IN ALL OF THIS, BUT . . .
HE'S ONLY 10 YEARS OLD... SO IT WILL BE TEMPORARY, MAYBE A FEW MONTHS OR SO, BUT,
IT'S SAFE TO ASSUME HE'LL BE FORCED TO GO TO THE MAGICAL WORLD.
IT'S POSSIBLE... YOU'LL NEVER SEE HIM AGAIN.
!
N-NEVER . . . . .
BUT . . . . NEGI-SENSEI.
WE GO RESCUE !
HE MY DISCIPLE !
GRIP
WAIT, KU-SAN! DO YOU PLAN TO FIGHT THE MAGICAL TEACHERS !?
CAN'T WE REASON WITH THEM ?
I DON'T KNOW. THEY'RE ALL PRETTY OLD SCHOOL.
THEY THEMSELVES WILL HAVE TO FACE SOME RESPONSIBILITY IN ALL OF THIS AS WELL... EVERYONE'S IN A BIND.
I DON'T CARE ABOUT THEIR SITUATION! IF THEY COMPLAIN, I'LL JUST BEAT THEM UP !
WAIT, BAKA RED !

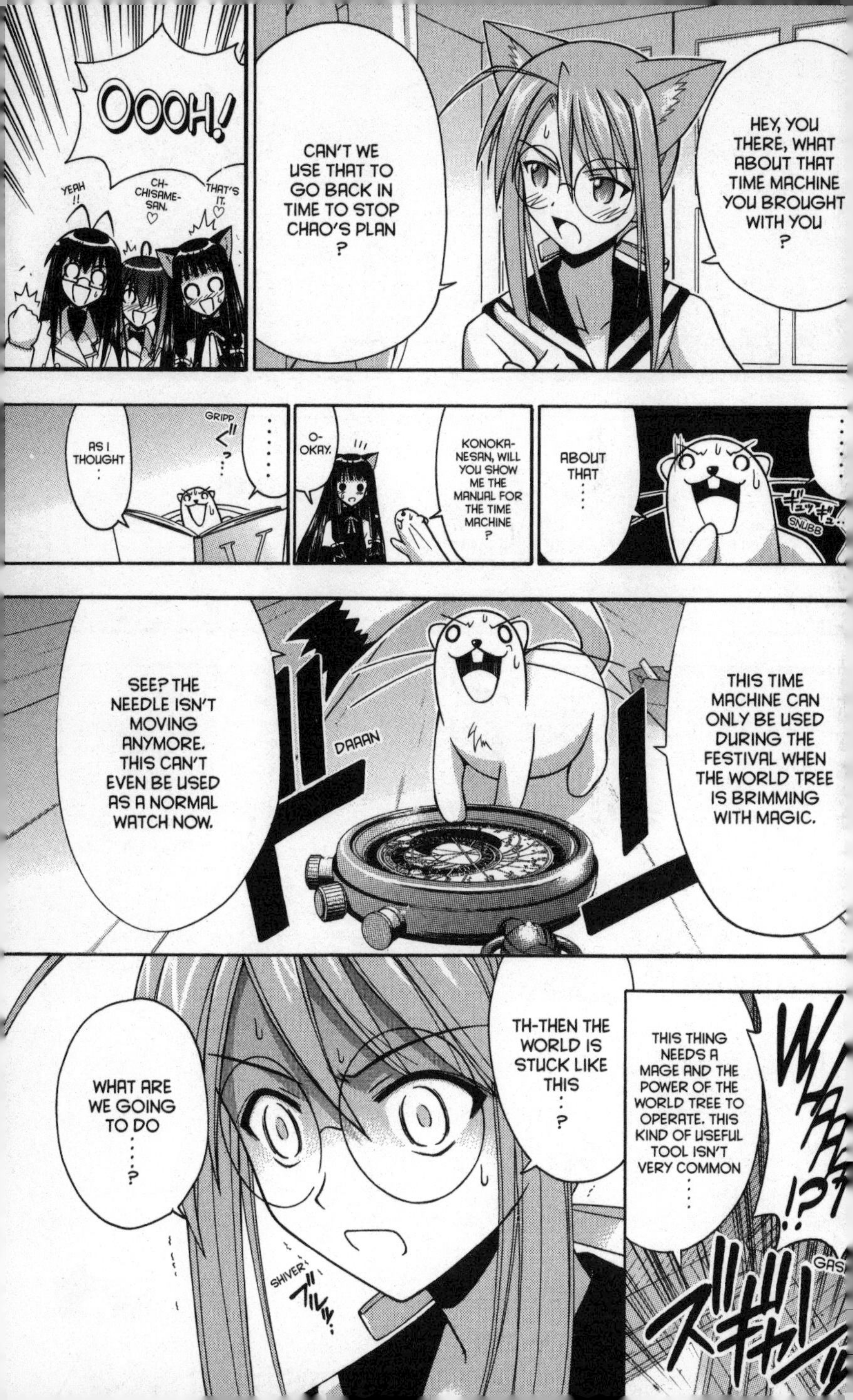

HEY, YOU THERE, WHAT ABOUT THAT TIME MACHINE YOU BROUGHT WITH YOU?
CAN'T WE USE THAT TO GO BACK IN TIME TO STOP CHAO'S PLAN?
OOOH!
THAT'S IT. ♡
CH-CHISAME-SAN. ♡
YEAH!!
......
SNUBB
ABOUT THAT...
KONOKA-NESAN, WILL YOU SHOW ME THE MANUAL FOR THE TIME MACHINE?
O-OKAY.
......
GRIPP
AS I THOUGHT...
THIS TIME MACHINE CAN ONLY BE USED DURING THE FESTIVAL WHEN THE WORLD TREE IS BRIMMING WITH MAGIC.
DAAAN
SEE? THE NEEDLE ISN'T MOVING ANYMORE. THIS CAN'T EVEN BE USED AS A NORMAL WATCH NOW.
THIS THING NEEDS A MAGE AND THE POWER OF THE WORLD TREE TO OPERATE. THIS KIND OF USEFUL TOOL ISN'T VERY COMMON...
!?
TH-THEN THE WORLD IS STUCK LIKE THIS...?
WHAT ARE WE GOING TO DO...?
SHIVER

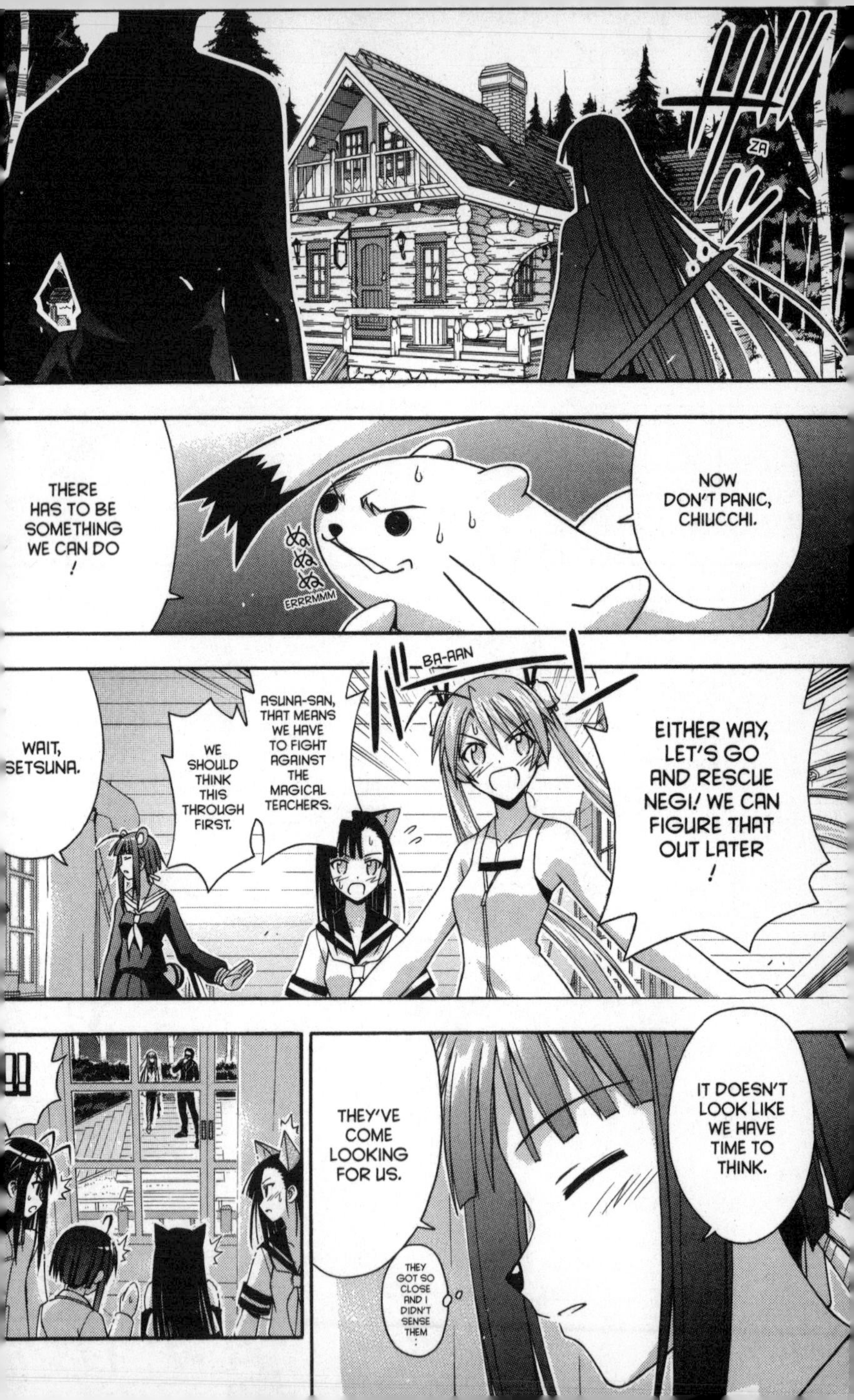
ZA
NOW DON'T PANIC, CHIUCCHI.
THERE HAS TO BE SOMETHING WE CAN DO!
ぬぬぬ
ERRRMMM
BA-AAN
EITHER WAY, LET'S GO AND RESCUE NEGI! WE CAN FIGURE THAT OUT LATER!
ASUNA-SAN, THAT MEANS WE HAVE TO FIGHT AGAINST THE MAGICAL TEACHERS.
WE SHOULD THINK THIS THROUGH FIRST.
WAIT, SETSUNA.
IT DOESN'T LOOK LIKE WE HAVE TIME TO THINK.
THEY'VE COME LOOKING FOR US.
THEY GOT SO CLOSE AND I DIDN'T SENSE THEM...
!!

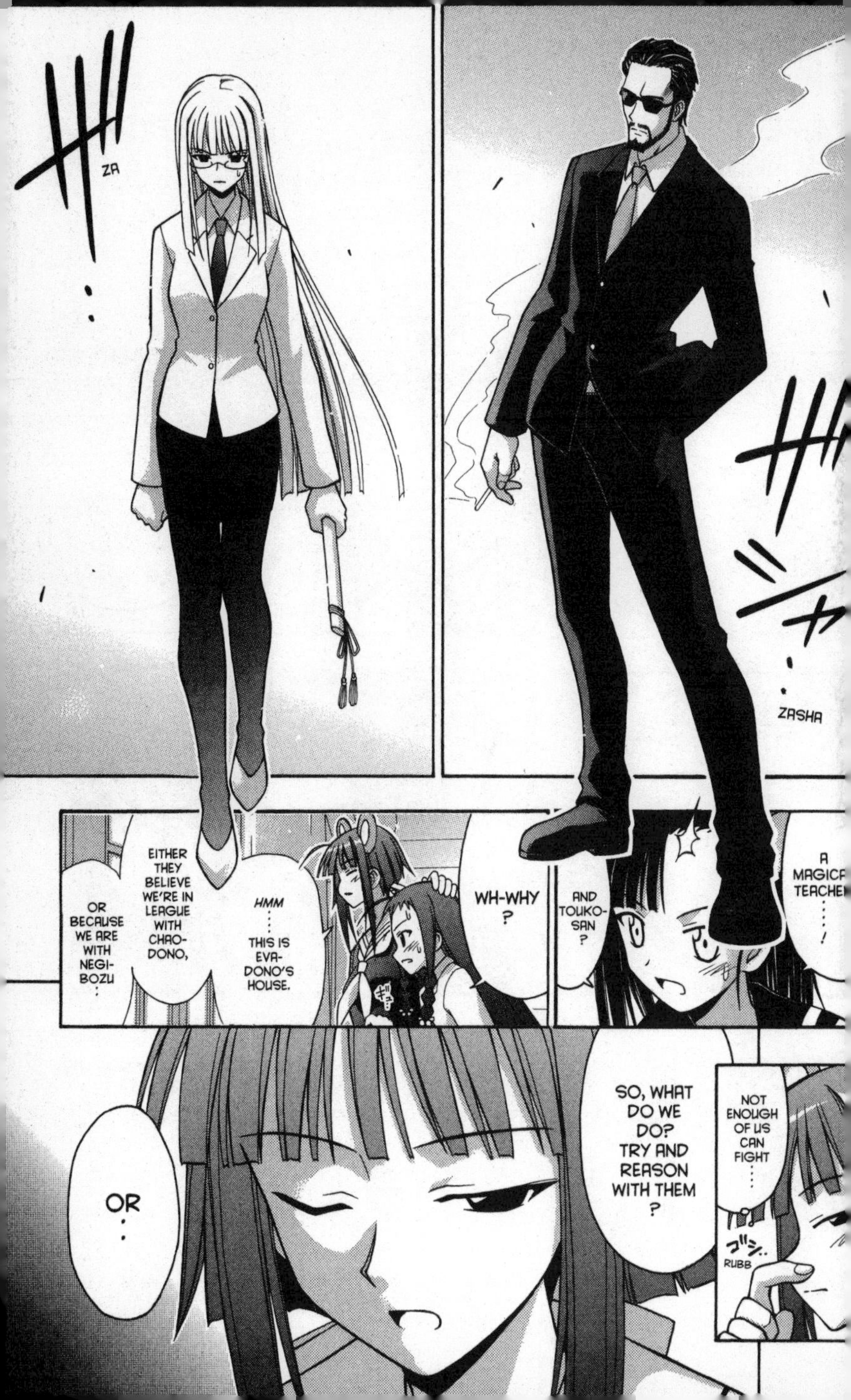
ZASHA
ZA
A MAGICA TEACHE ....!
AND TOUKO-SAN?
WH-WHY?
HMM... THIS IS EVA-DONO'S HOUSE.
EITHER THEY BELIEVE WE'RE IN LEAGUE WITH CHAO-DONO,
OR BECAUSE WE ARE WITH NEGI-BOZU...
NOT ENOUGH OF US CAN FIGHT.....
RUBB
SO, WHAT DO WE DO? TRY AND REASON WITH THEM?
OR..

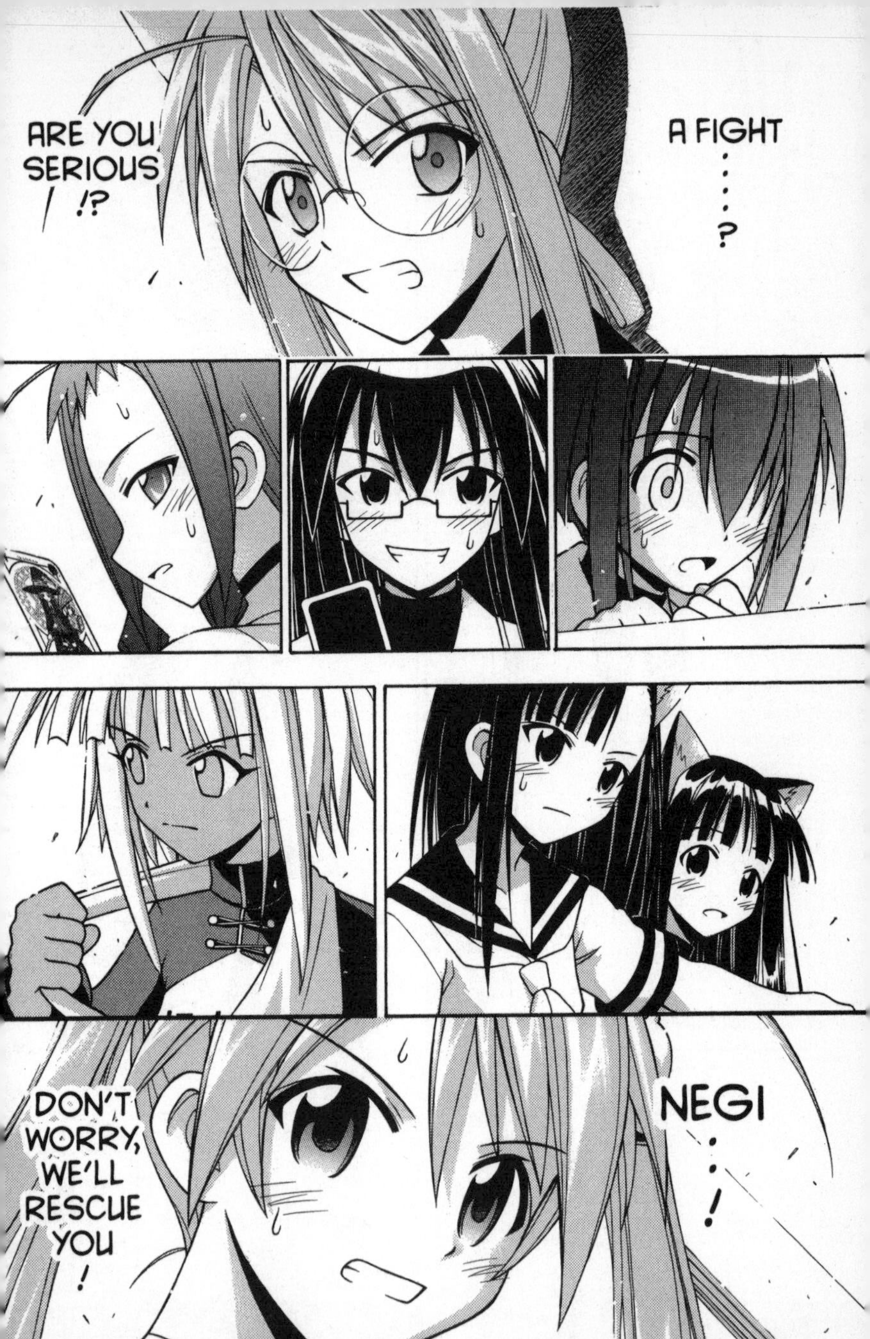
A FIGHT ...?
ARE YOU SERIOUS !?
NEGI ...!
DON'T WORRY, WE'LL RESCUE YOU !

TO BE CONTINUED IN *NEGIMA!* VOLUME 16.

-STAFF-

Ken Akamatsu

Takashi Takemoto

Kenichi Nakamura

Masaki Ohyama

Keiichi Yamashita

Tadashi Maki

Tohru Mitsuhashi

Thanks to
Ran Ayanaga

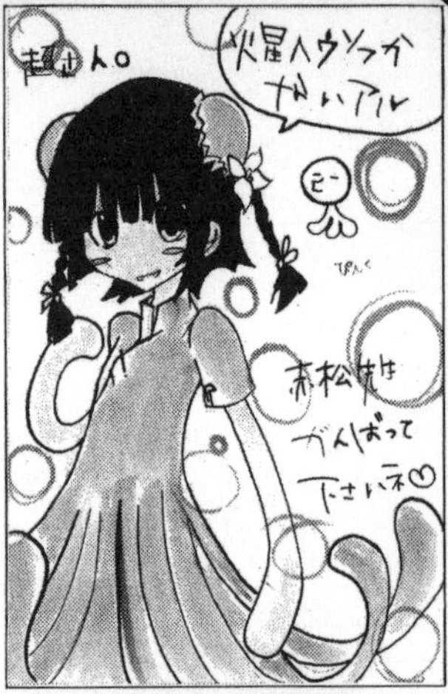
火星人ウソつかないアル
赤松先生
がんばって
下さいネ♡

MARTIAN = OCTOPUS? (LAUGHS)

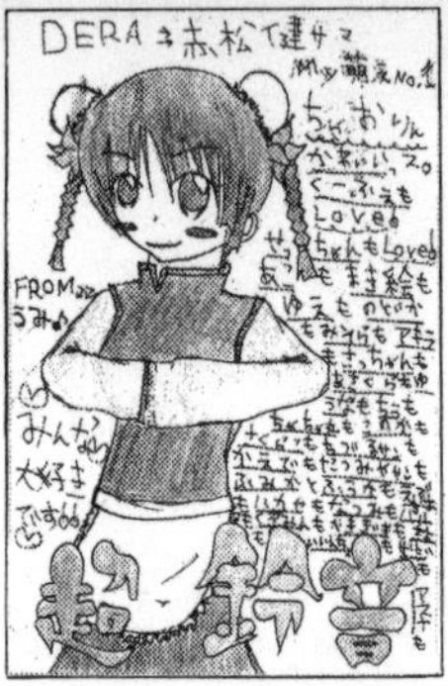
DERAさ赤松健サマ
超鈴音

A REALLY ENERGETIC CHAO!

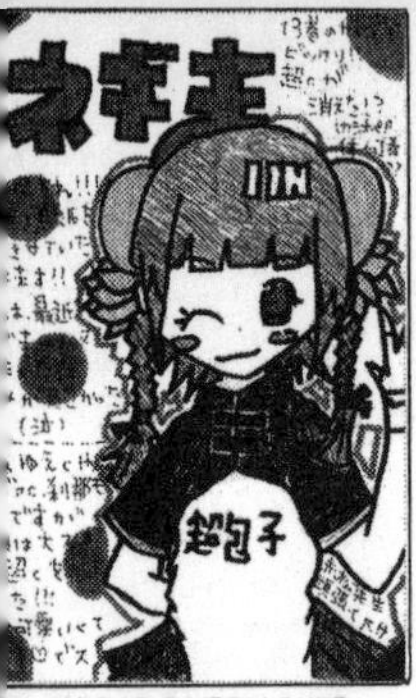
ネギま

THIS IS A VERY CUTE-LOOKING CHAO.

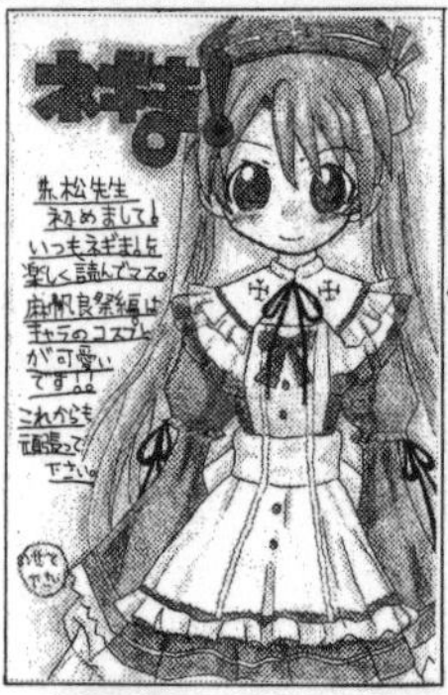
ネギま!
赤松先生
初めまして!
いつもネギま!を
楽しく読んでマス。
麻帆良祭編は
キャラのコスプレ
が可愛い
です!!
これからも
頑張って
下さい。

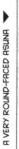

A VERY ROUND-FACED ASUNA

NEGIMA! FAN ART CORNER

AS USUAL, WE WELCOME ALL ILLUSTRATIONS SENT IN BY THE FANS! IT'S NICE TO SEE MORE PICTURES OF CHAO COMING IN AS HER STORYLINE UNFOLDS. ★

SETSUNA PICTURES HAVE MAINTAINED THEIR POPULARITY. ★

IF YOU SEND IN PICTURES OF MINOR CHARACTERS TO GIVE THEM EXPOSURE, MAYBE THEY'LL GET THEIR OWN STORY LINE! WE LOOK FORWARD TO SEEING MORE OF YOUR ILLUSTRATIONS!

YOU CAN SEND YOUR ILLUSTRATIONS TO THE EDITORIAL OFFICES OF "KODANSHA COMICS."

TEXT: ASS'T MAX

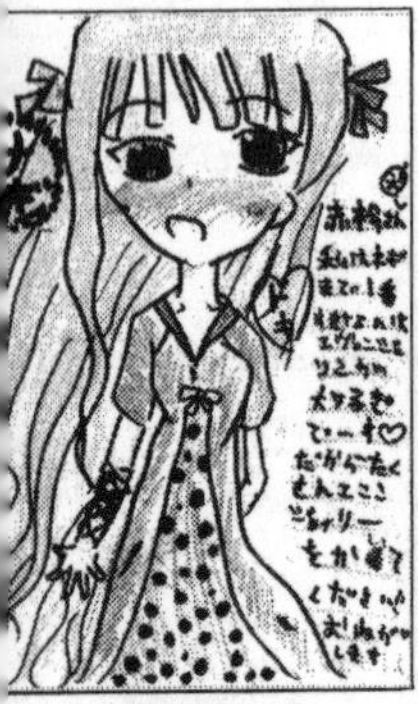

WE CAN FEEL THE ANTICIPATION IN HER EXPRESSION!

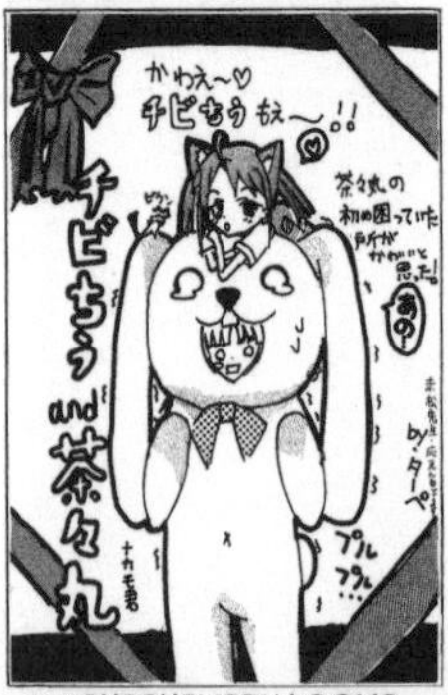
チビちう
and
茶々丸

CHACHAMARU LOOKS CUTE IN HER COSTUME!

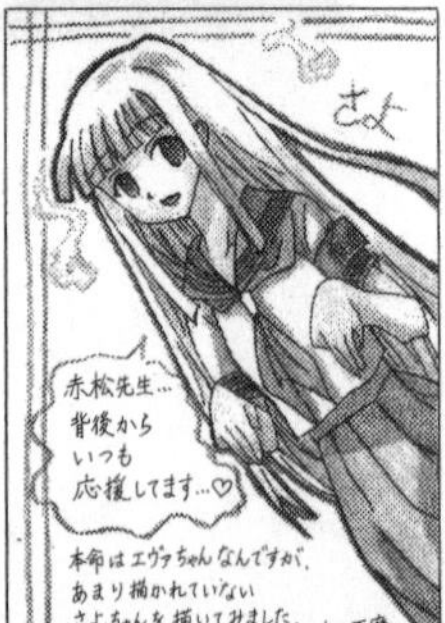
赤松先生…
背後から
いつも
応援してます…♡
本命はエヴァちゃんなんですが、
あまり描かれていない
さよちゃんを描いてみました。 by 天魔

SHE SEEM TO BE COMING OUT OF THE PAPER. I LIKE IT! (LAUGHS)

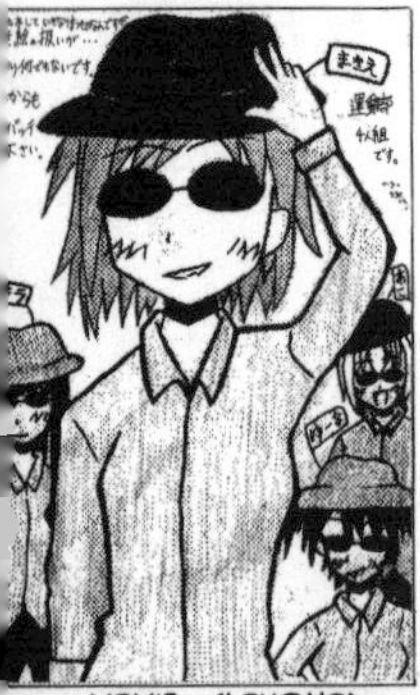

MAKIE... (LAUGHS)
[NOTE: THIS ONE IS A PUN ON HER NAME. THE "E" HERE IS THE KANJI FOR PICTURE. SO IT'S LITERALLY "MAKI-PICTURE"]

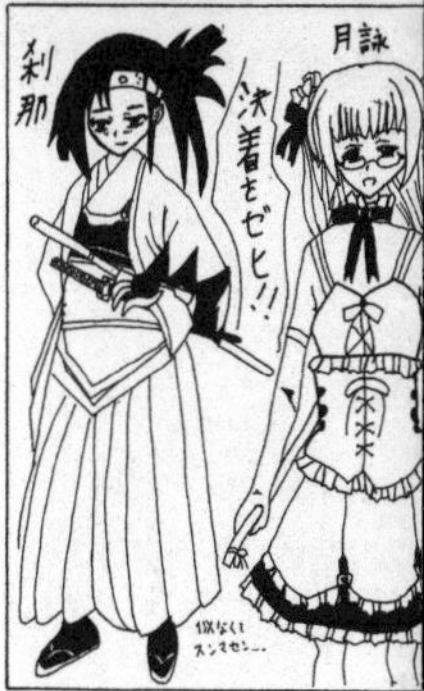
刹那
月詠
決着をぜひ!!

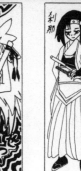

▲ WE'D ALSO LOVE TO SEE A REMATCH.

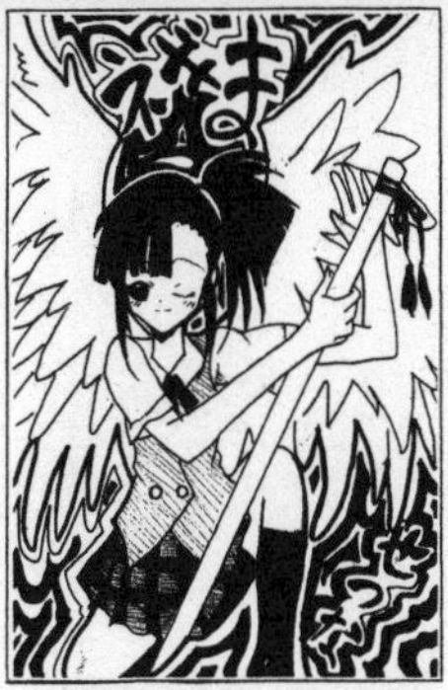

▲ THE PICTURE GIVES OFF A VERY WONDERFUL FEELING.

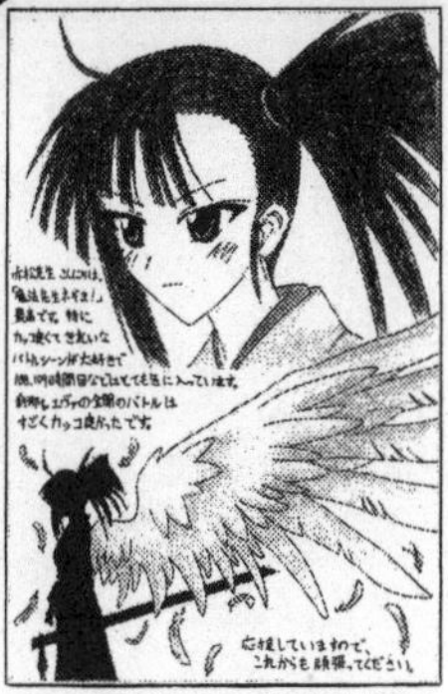

▲ SETSUNA LOOKS VERY SHARP!

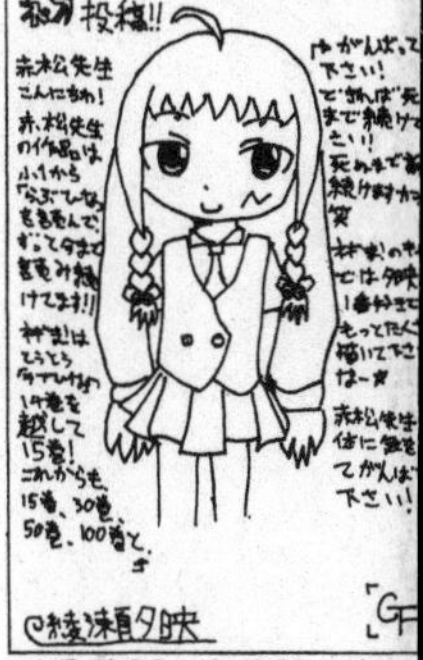
初投稿!!
綾瀬夕映

▲ WE ALSO WONDER WHAT'S GOING TO HAPPEN WITH YUE...

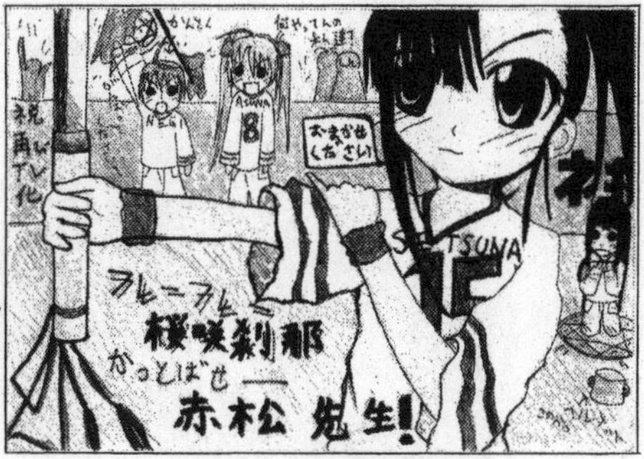
SETSUNA
桜咲刹那
かっとばせー
赤松 先生!

▲ SETSUNA LOOKS VERY STRONG AND DEPENDABLE.

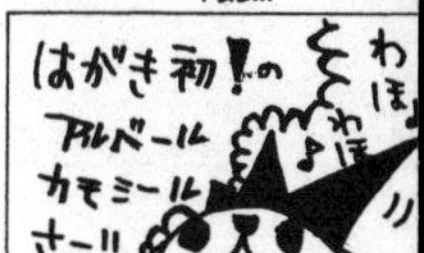
はがき初!の
アルベール
カモミール
さー!!
初!

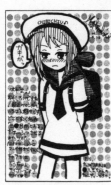

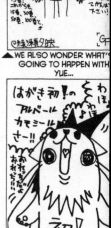

▲ HE'S PUTTING UP A VERY TOUGH FRONT. (LAUGHS)

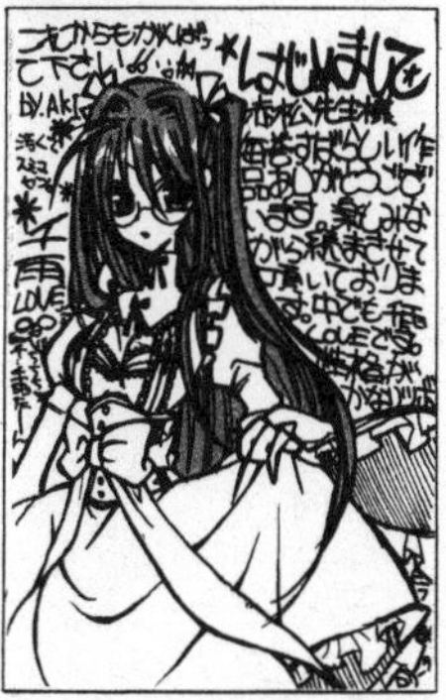
はじめまして

▲ WHAT A VERY PRETTY CHIU!

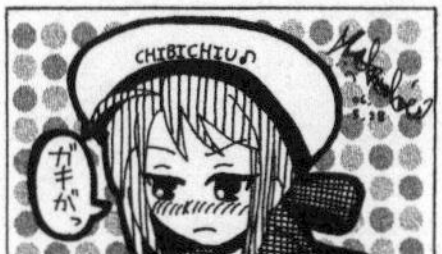
CHIBICHIU♪
ガキがっ

▲ CHIBI-CHIU IS SO POPULAR!

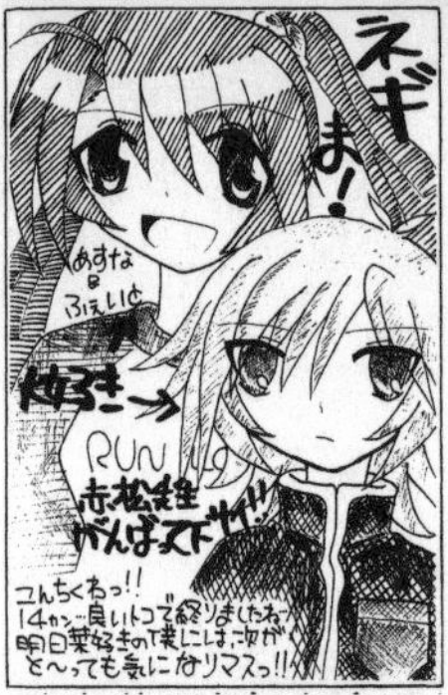
ネギま!
あすな
ふぇいと
RUN
赤松先生がんばって下サイ!!

▲ ASUNA LOOKS ENERGETIC!

THEY LOOK VERY CLOSE! ▶

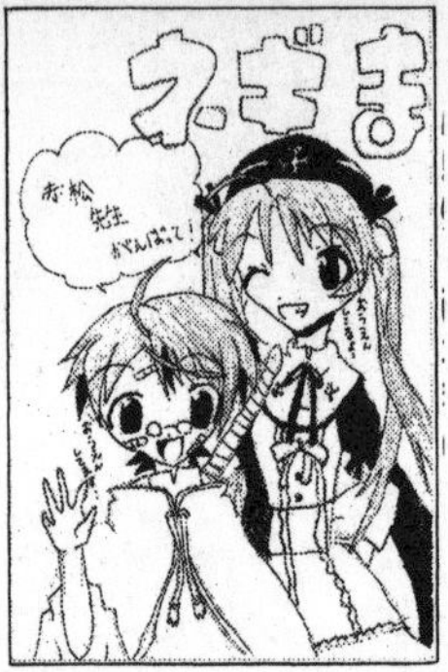
ネギま

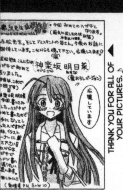

THANK YOU FOR ALL OF YOUR PICTURES.♪ ▶

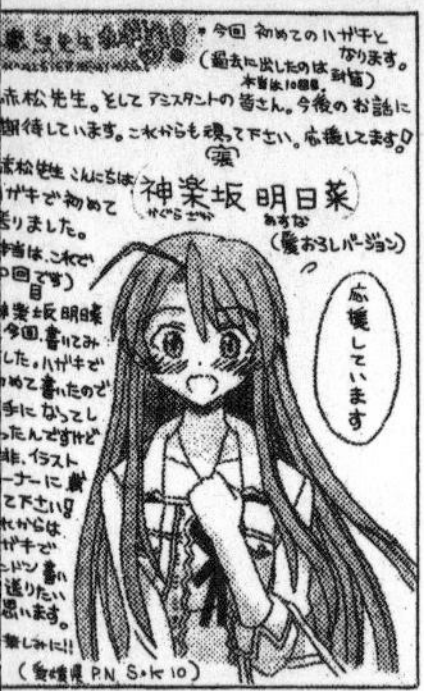
神楽坂 明日菜
応援しています

THE BOOKSTORE GIRL LOOKS SMART HERE. ▶

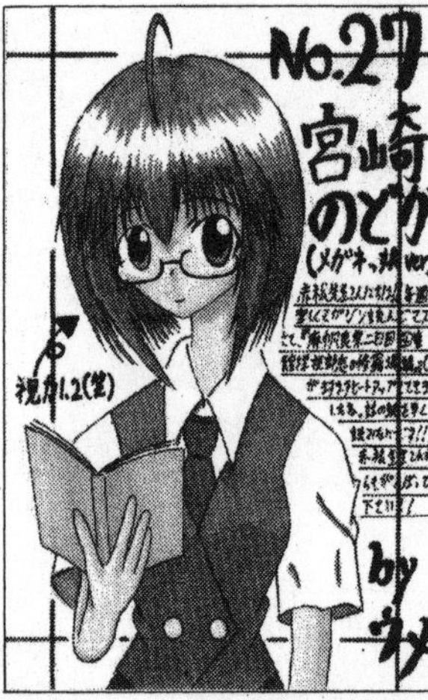
No.27
宮崎のどか
by ウメ

THANK YOU SO MUCH.♪ ▶

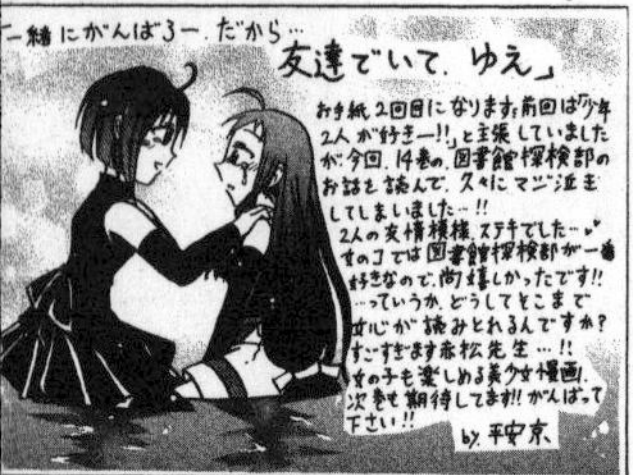
友達でいて、ゆえ」
by.平安京.

SO THEY'RE THE WINNING GROUP, HUH? (LAUGHS) ▶

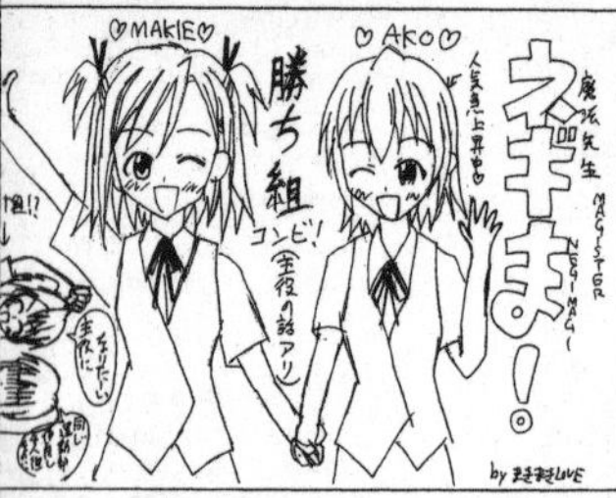
MAKIE
AKO
勝ち組
コンビ!
ネギま!
MAGISTER NEGI MAGI

WHOA! WE CAN FEEL YOUR LOVE FOR HIM! ▼

EISHUN! VERY NICE. ▶

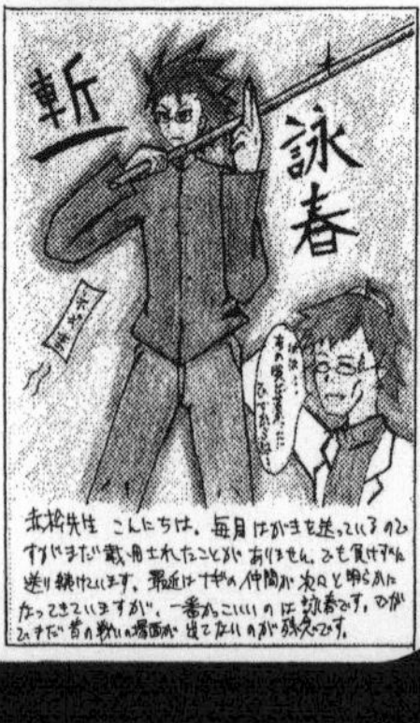
斬
詠春

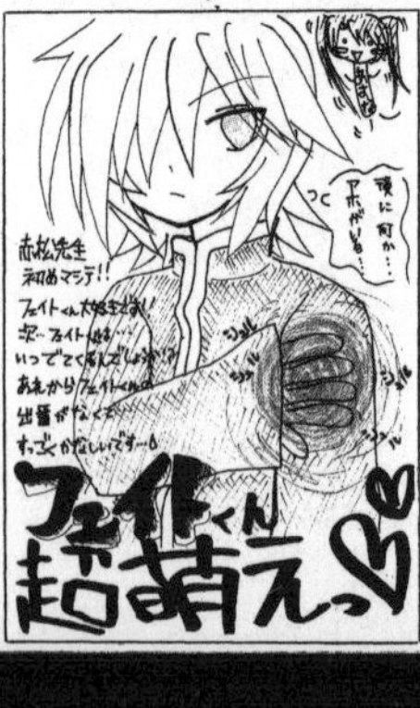
フェイトくん超萌えっ

WE WANT TO SAY THANK YOU, TOO! ▶

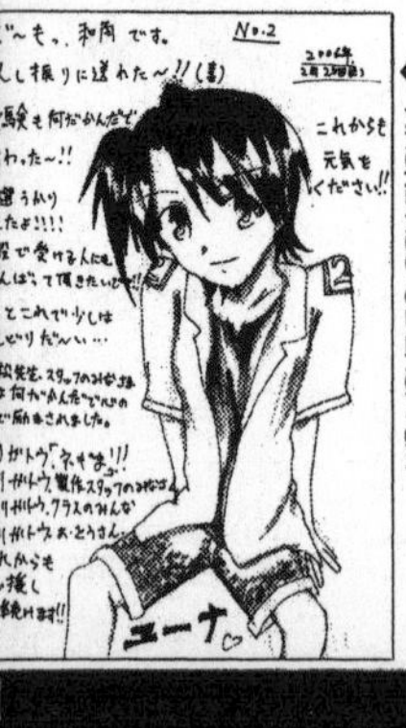
No.2
ユーナ

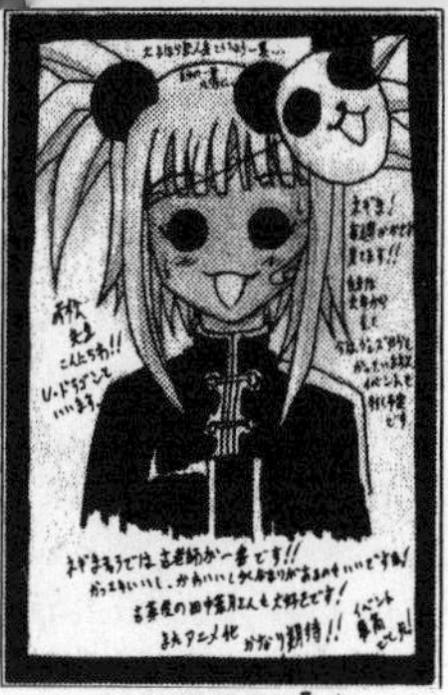

▲ MASTER KŪ.♪

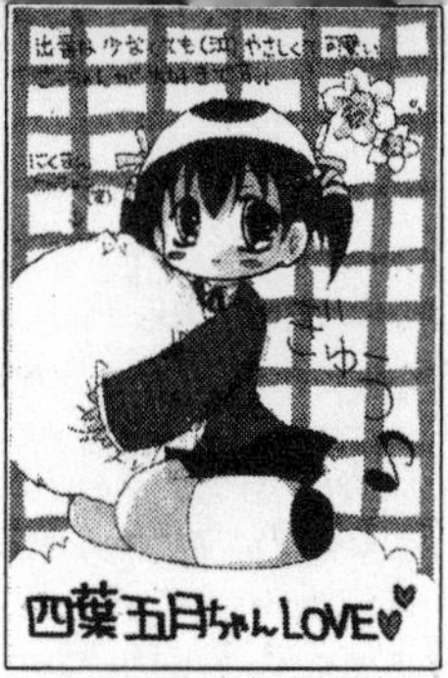
四葉五月ちゃんLOVE♡

▲ A SUPER-CUTE SAT-CHAN! (LAUGHS)

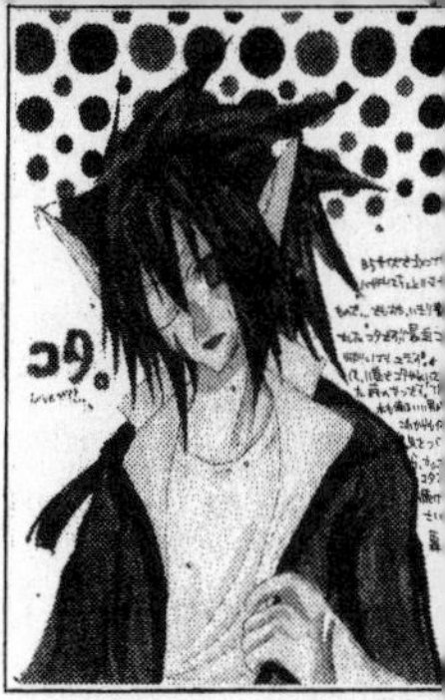
コタ。

▲ KOTARO LOOKS VERY SEXY!

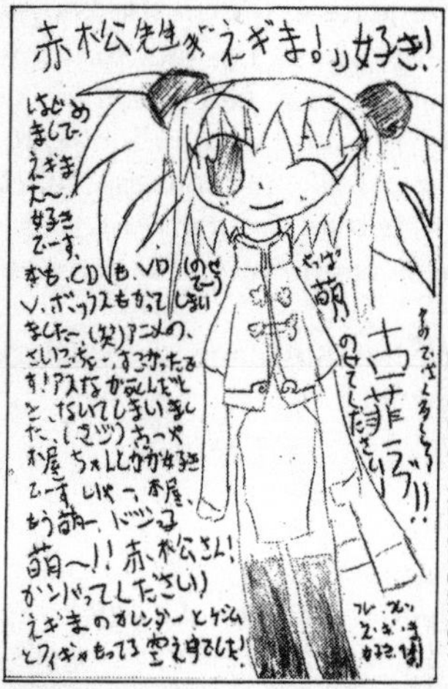
赤松先生がネギま!!好き!

◀ YOU'RE TOTALLY DIGGING KŪ FEI.♪

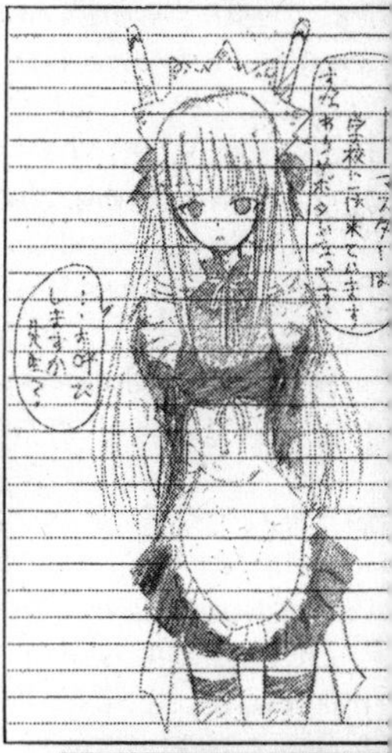

▶ CHACHAMARU LOOKING CUTE AND CASUAL.

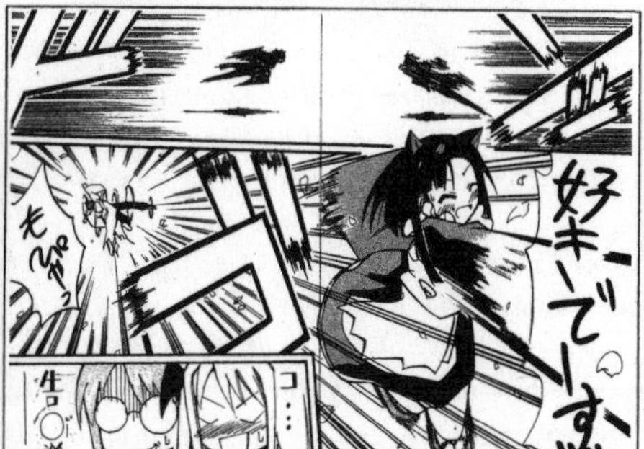
好キーでーす!!!

◀ THE PIC HAS A GREAT, NOSTALGIC FEEL. (LAUGHS)

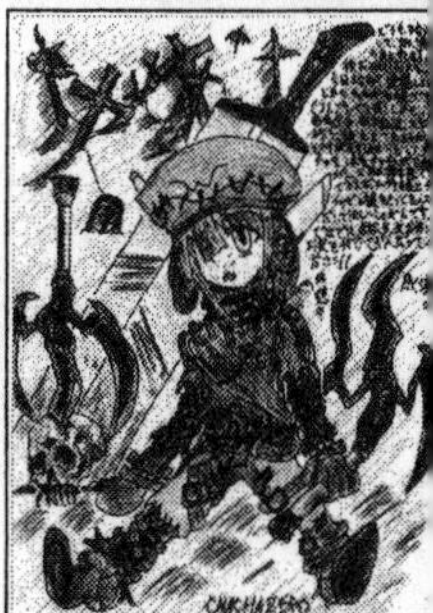
MAGISTERNEGIMAGI

▶ A VERY COOL-LOOKING CHACHAZERO.

LEXICON NEGIMARUIM
DE ARTIFACTO

■匕首 十六串呂
(Sica Sisicusiro)

Setsuna Sakurazaki is awarded this tool for her use by the power of the Pactio with Negi. *Sica* is Latin for "short sword," but *sisicusiro* is Japanese. In traditional Japanese songs and poems, *shishikushiro* is a *makura kotoba* ("pillow word," a fixed epithet in poems). It means "meat on a skewer." There are several *kake kotobas* (words which have the same sound but different meanings that are used in traditional Japanese songs and poetry) for this word. *Shishi* can mean skewered meat, but it can also stand for "beast," signifying an attack. It can also mean "four by four," which works out to the number sixteen (this is the kanji character used for this artifact). The number represents the fact that this weapon can split into sixteen separate blades that can each be controlled individually. (In the third volume of the *Manyoushu* [*Collection of Ten Thousand Leaves*], there is a an example of the Japanese characters for sixteen being read as *shishi*.) The fact that the name of this artifact is not Latin denotes the special Japanese connotation that comes from the name.

Several unadorned blades appear when the blade is activated. The one with the decorative tassel is the original.

■コチノヒオウギ／ハエノスエヒロ
KOCHI NO HIOUGI / HAE NO SUEHIRO
(Flabellum Euri / Flabellum Australe)

Through the power of the Pactio with Negi, Konoka Konoe is awarded this tool for her use. The artifact materializes along with a priest's robe with magical defense properties.

Kochi and Hae refer to an easterly wind and a southerly wind. *Hiougi* is a type of fan that can be seen starting with the Middle Ages and continuing to the Modern Era as a formal wear accessory. *Suehiro* is a type of fan that folds. The priest's robe is styled after the aristocratic robes of the Heian Period.

Flabellum means "small wind" in Latin and represents the "fan." *Euri* means "easterly wind" and comes from the ancient Greek word Ενρος. *Ausutorale* comes from the name of the southerly wind of the Mediterranean.

Konoka claims that she can cure any wounds within three minutes (126th Period), but she can't cure a crushed head (136th Period), which is the ability of the Kochi no Hiougi. The Hae no Suehiro, on the other hand, can cure conditions like putrifaction and other ailments that are considered "status anomalies" in RPG games (52nd Period) within thirty minutes. However, it would be absurd to differentiate injuries to the body and "status anomalies," as explained by French philosopher and historian Michel Foucault (1926–1984) in *La Naissance de la clinique* (*The Birth of the Clinic*). He writes, "It was given the splendid task of establishing in men's lives the positive role of health, virtue, and happiness...Medicine must no longer be confined to a body of techniques for curing ills and of the knowledge that they require; it will also embrace a knowledge of healthy man, that is, a study of non-sick man and a definition of the model man. In the ordering of human existence it assumes a normative posture" (chapter 2). According to him, a "status anomaly" is an "injury" if it causes interference with social participation. The person is not considered healthy until such conditions can be resolved or cured.

Trying to differentiate the healing capacities of Kochi no Hiougi and Hae no Suehiro to heal "injuries" and "status anomalies" is rather silly when viewed in this manner. Foucault wrote, "The clinic is both a new 'carving up' of things and principles of their verbalization in a form which we have been accustomed to recognizing as the language of a 'positive science'" (preface). Maladies such as injuries and diseases are differentiated only through language. An "anomaly" is an "anomaly," but differences arise through the use of different words. Therefore, Kochi no Hiougi and Hae no Suehiro have different healing attributes, but their words and their meaning reflect the language that the magical artifacts are based on.

[Note: English Translation of *The Birth of the Clinic* is from the 199 Vintage publication of the 1973 translation from the French by A. M. Sheridan Smith.]

■落書帝国
IMPERIUM GRAPHICES

By the power of the Pactio with Negi, Haruna Saotome is awarded this tool for her use. A magical quill, ink well, croquis tablet, and beret appear along with an artist's apron with ties embellished with a unique design element: pen tips on the ends. It is an extremely useful artifact with the special ability to summon simple golems from anything drawn on the tablet. *Imperuim* can be translated as "empire" in English; however, it can also mean "to command or control" or even "army." *Graphices* is of course, "graphics" in English, which is derived from the Latin word *grafice*, meaning "the ability to draw." So, *Imperium Graphices* can be translated as "army of drawings." By putting the *ministra* to the rear in battle, a golem can be created to defend the *ministra* as well as the mage. However, the golem is not controlled by the mage, so a certain level of skill is required of the *ministra* in order to properly control the creature.

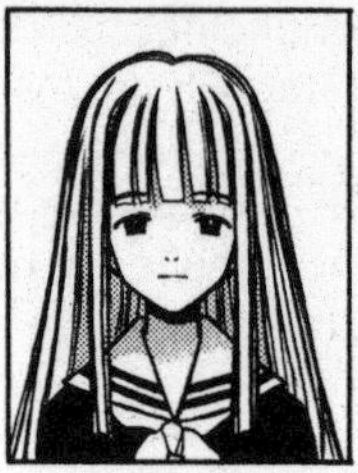

1. SAYO AISAKA

1940~
DON'T CHANGE HER SEATING

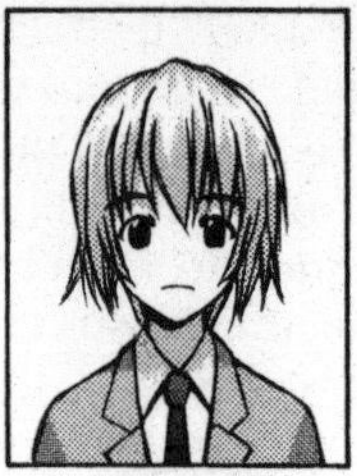

5. AKO IZUMI
NURSE'S OFFICE AIDE
SOCCER TEAM
(NON-SCHOOL ACTIVITY)

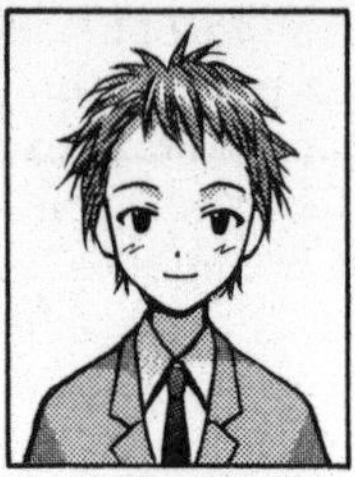

9. MISORA KASUGA
TRACK & FIELD

GRANDDAUGHTER OF SCHOOL DEAN

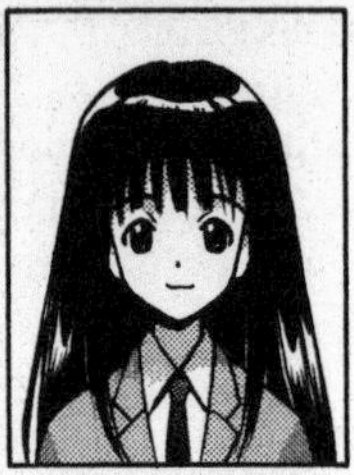

13. KONOKA KONOE
SECRETARY
FORTUNE-TELLING CLUB
LIBRARY EXPLORATION CLUB

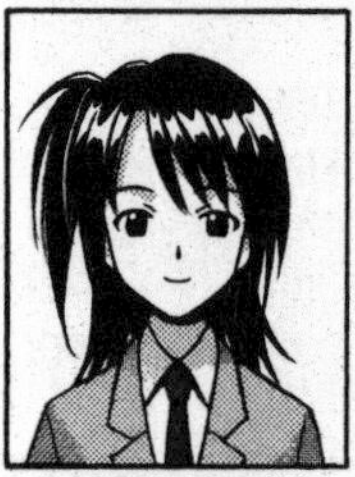

2. YUNA AKASHI
BASKETBALL TEAM

PROFESSOR AKASHI'S DAUGHTER

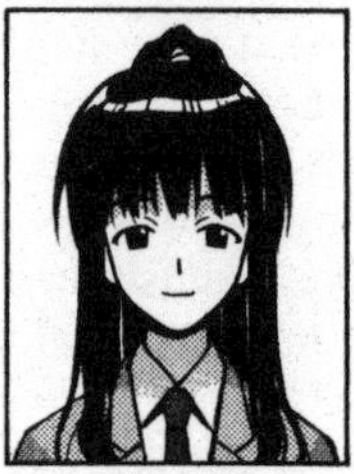

6. AKIRA OKOCHI
SWIM TEAM

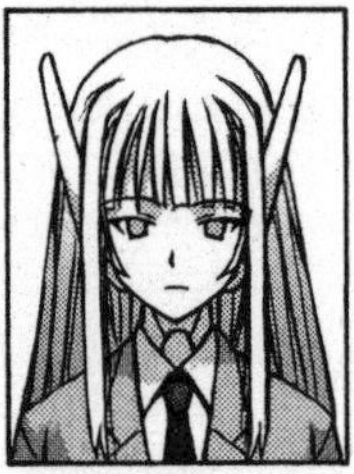

10. CHACHAMARU KARAKURI
TEA CEREMONY CLUB
GO CLUB

CALL ENGINEERING (ext. A08-7796)
IN CASE OF EMERGENCY

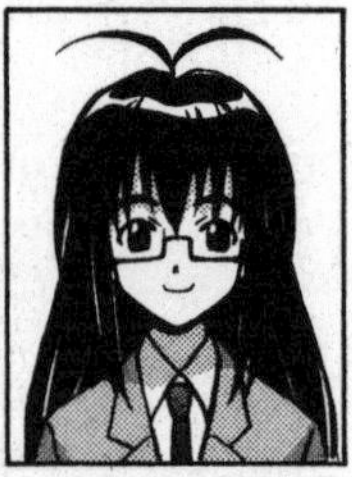

14. HARUNA SAOTOME
MANGA CLUB
LIBRARY EXPLORATION CLUB

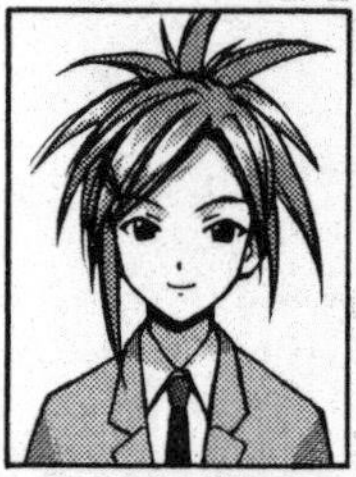

3. KAZUMI ASAKURA
SCHOOL NEWSPAPER

MAHORA NEWS (ext. 809-3780)

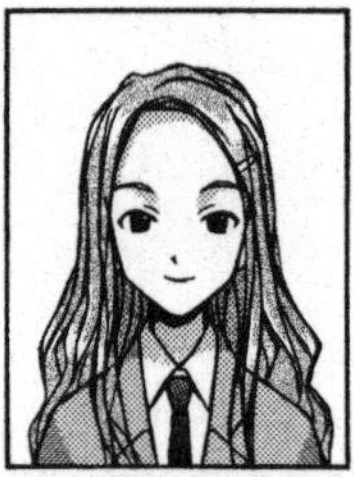

7. MISA KAKIZAKI
CHEERLEADER
CHORUS

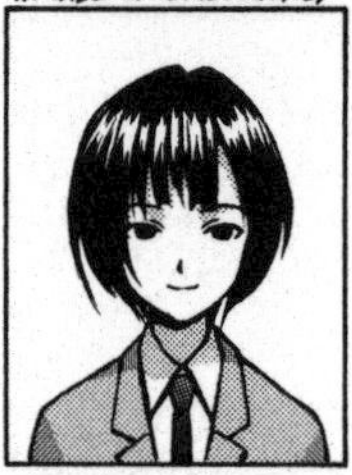

11. MADOKA KUGIMIYA
CHEERLEADER

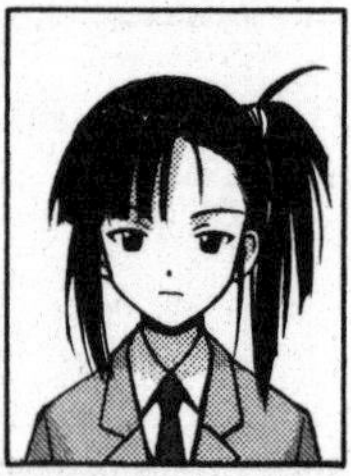

5 SETSUNA SAKURAZAKI
KENDO CLUB

KYOTO SHINMEI STYLE

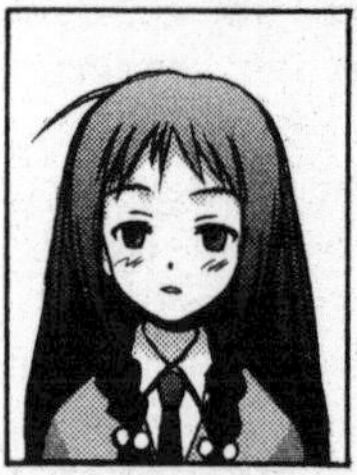

4. YUE AYASE
KIDS' LIT CLUB
PHILOSOPHY CLUB
LIBRARY EXPLORATION CLUB

A GOOD PERSON JUST AS I THOUGHT.

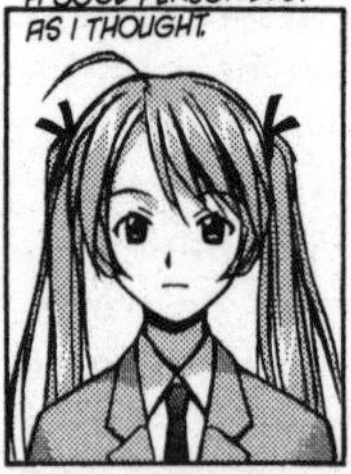

8. ASUNA KAGURAZAKA
ART CLUB
HAS A TERRIBLE KICK

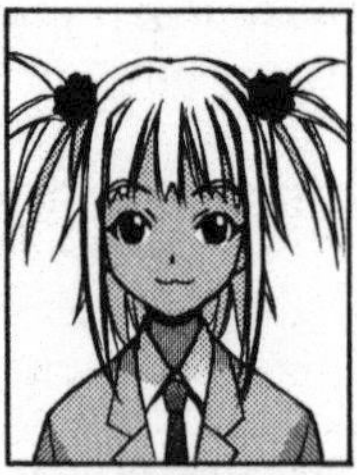

12. KŪ FEI
CHINESE MARTIAL ARTS CLUB

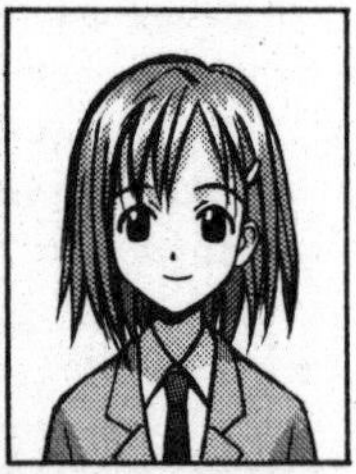

16. MAKIE SASAKI
GYMNASTICS

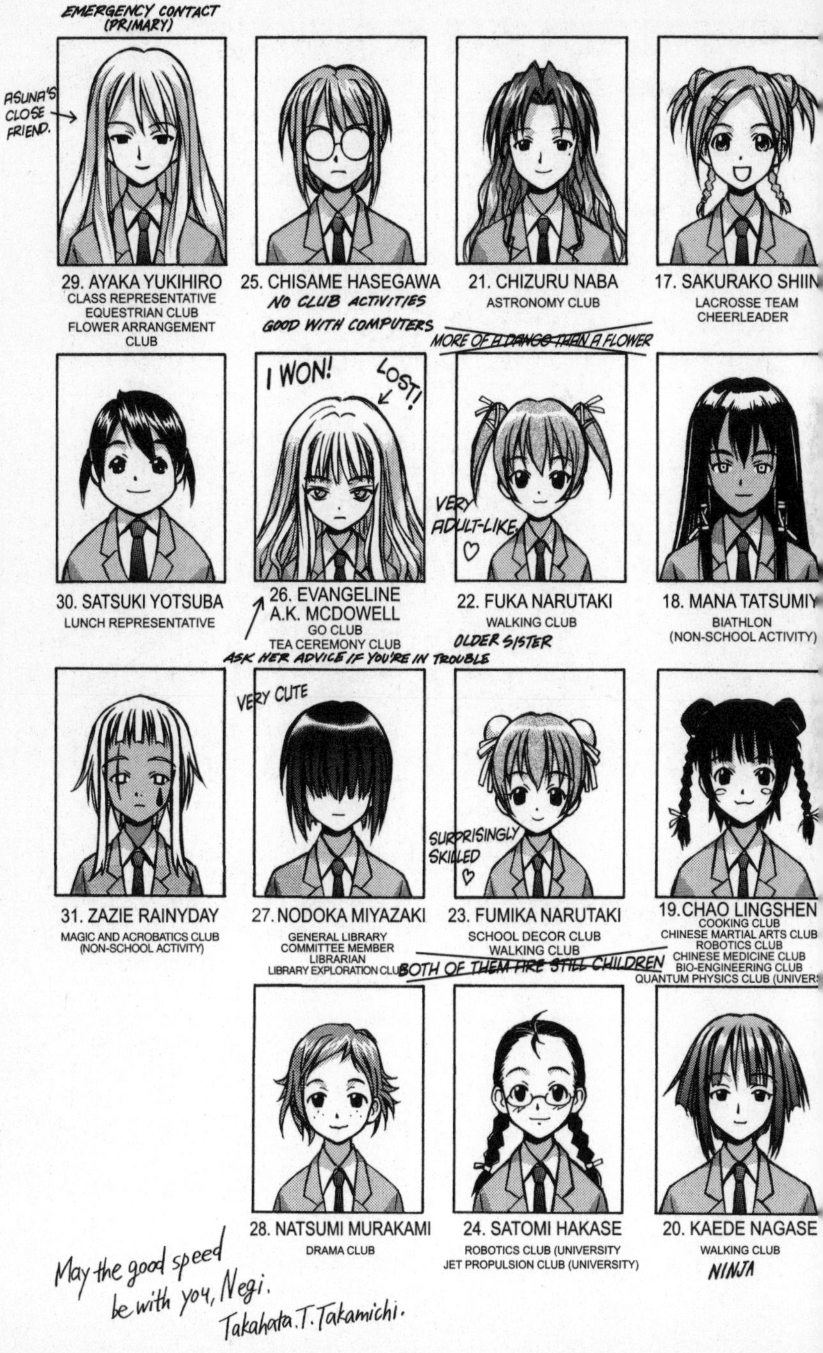
17. SAKURAKO SHIIN
LACROSSE TEAM
CHEERLEADER
18. MANA TATSUMIY
BIATHLON
(NON-SCHOOL ACTIVITY)
19.CHAO LINGSHEN
COOKING CLUB
CHINESE MARTIAL ARTS CLUB
ROBOTICS CLUB
CHINESE MEDICINE CLUB
BIO-ENGINEERING CLUB
QUANTUM PHYSICS CLUB (UNIVERS
20. KAEDE NAGASE
WALKING CLUB
NINJA
21. CHIZURU NABA
ASTRONOMY CLUB
MORE OF A DANGO THAN A FLOWER
22. FUKA NARUTAKI
VERY ADULT-LIKE ♡
WALKING CLUB
OLDER SISTER
23. FUMIKA NARUTAKI
SURPRISINGLY SKILLED ♡
SCHOOL DECOR CLUB
WALKING CLUB
BOTH OF THEM ARE STILL CHILDREN
24. SATOMI HAKASE
ROBOTICS CLUB (UNIVERSITY
JET PROPULSION CLUB (UNIVERSITY)
25. CHISAME HASEGAWA
NO CLUB ACTIVITIES
GOOD WITH COMPUTERS
I WON!
LOST!
26. EVANGELINE A.K. MCDOWELL
GO CLUB
TEA CEREMONY CLUB
ASK HER ADVICE IF YOU'RE IN TROUBLE
VERY CUTE
27. NODOKA MIYAZAKI
GENERAL LIBRARY COMMITTEE MEMBER
LIBRARIAN
LIBRARY EXPLORATION CLU
28. NATSUMI MURAKAMI
DRAMA CLUB
EMERGENCY CONTACT (PRIMARY)
ASUNA'S CLOSE FRIEND.
29. AYAKA YUKIHIRO
CLASS REPRESENTATIVE
EQUESTRIAN CLUB
FLOWER ARRANGEMENT CLUB
30. SATSUKI YOTSUBA
LUNCH REPRESENTATIVE
31. ZAZIE RAINYDAY
MAGIC AND ACROBATICS CLUB
(NON-SCHOOL ACTIVITY)
May the good speed be with you, Negi.
Takahata.T.Takamichi.

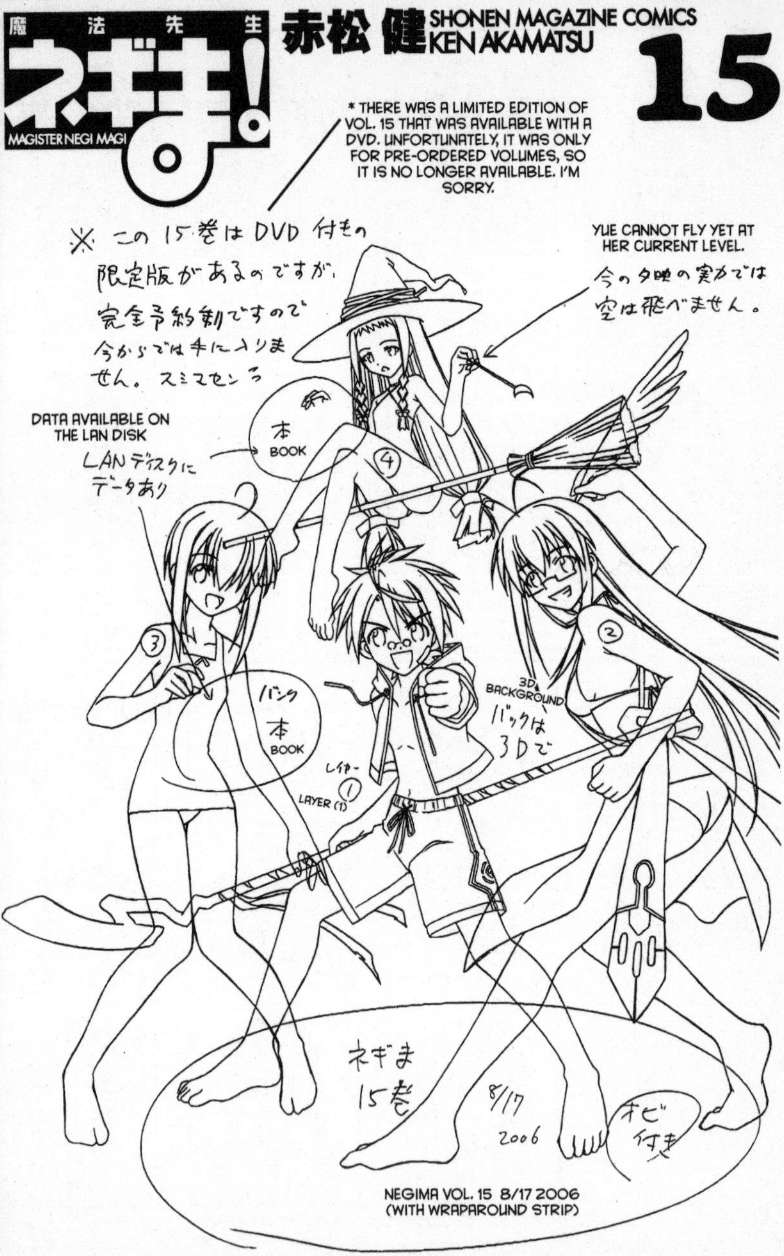
魔法先生
ネギま!
MAGISTER NEGI MAGI
赤松 健
SHONEN MAGAZINE COMICS
KEN AKAMATSU
15
* THERE WAS A LIMITED EDITION OF VOL. 15 THAT WAS AVAILABLE WITH A DVD. UNFORTUNATELY, IT WAS ONLY FOR PRE-ORDERED VOLUMES, SO IT IS NO LONGER AVAILABLE. I'M SORRY.
※この15巻はDVD付きの限定版があるのですが、完全予約制ですので今からでは手に入りません。スミマセン。
YUE CANNOT FLY YET AT HER CURRENT LEVEL.
今の夕映の実力では空は飛べません。
DATA AVAILABLE ON THE LAN DISK
LANディスクにデータあり
本
BOOK
④
③
②
バック
本
BOOK
3D BACKGROUND
バックは3Dで
レイヤー ①
LAYER (1)
ネギま 15巻
8/17 2006
オビ付き
NEGIMA VOL. 15 8/17 2006
(WITH WRAPAROUND STRIP)

キャラ解説
CHARACTER PROFILE

⑲ 超 鈴音
⑲ CHAO LINGSHEN

謎の天才クラスメート。チャオ
THIS IS THE MYSTERIOUS

リンシェンです。
CLASSMATE CHAO LINGSHEN!

まさに最強の敵！セツナや
SHE'S A TOUGH ADVERSARY! EVEN SETSUNA

カエデさえ今は勝てません！
AND KAEDE CAN'T BEAT HER!

どーすんのネギ？！
WHAT'S NEGI TO DO!?

でも普段は心優しい料理
NORMALLY, SHE'S A KIND INVENTOR

好きの発明家なんですよ。
WHO LOVES TO COOK.

3-Aの色々なイベントでも
SHE'S ALWAYS BEEN SUPPORTIVE OF THE

大活躍しているのです。
VARIOUS EVENTS HELD BY CLASSROOM #-A.

背中の
部分にヒミツが…
THERE'S A SECRET ON THE BACK
OF HER SUIT.

初代CVは大沢千秋さん。結婚おめでとう！
HER FIRST VOICE ACTRESS WAS CHIAKI OZAWA. CONGRATULATIONS ON YOUR MARRIAGE!

二代目CVとして、高本めぐみさん。期待の若手です！
THE NEW VOICE ACTOR FOR CHAO IS MEGUMI TAKAMOTO. SHE'S A ROOKIE WITH GREAT POTENTIAL!

今後ともよろしく〜♪
THANK YOU FOR YOUR CONTINUED SUPPORT♪

赤松
AKAMATSU

About the Creator

Negima! is only Ken Akamatsu's third manga, although he started working in the field in 1994 with *AI Ga Tomaranai* (released in the United States with the title *A.I. Love You*). Like all of Akamatsu's work to date, it was published in Kodansha's *Shonen Magazine. AI Ga Tomaranai* ran for five years before concluding in 1999. In 1998, however, Akamatsu began the work that would make him one of the most popular manga artists in Japan: *Love Hina. Love Hina* ran for four years, and before its conclusion in 2002, it would earn Akamatsu the prestigious Manga of the Year Award from Kodansha, as well as go on to become one of the bestselling manga in the United States.

Translation Notes

Japanese is a tricky language for most westerners, and translation is often more an art than a science. For your edification and reading pleasure, here are notes on some of the places where we could have gone in a different direction, or where a Japanese cultural reference is used.

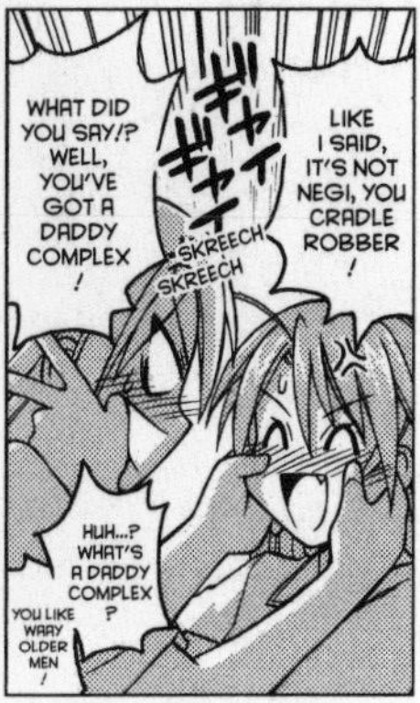
LIKE I SAID, IT'S NOT NEGI, YOU CRADLE ROBBER!
WHAT DID YOU SAY!? WELL, YOU'VE GOT A DADDY COMPLEX!
SKREECH SKREECH
HUH...? WHAT'S A DADDY COMPLEX?
YOU LIKE WAAY OLDER MEN!

Craddle robber and daddy complex, page 25

The phrases originally used were *shotacon* and *ojicon*. *Shotacon* is short for Shotaro complex, which occurs when a girl has a fondness for younger boys. It was made up as a counterpart to Lolicon, short for Lolita complex, which, as in the novel by Vladimir Nabokov, is when a male has a fondness for young girls. It's called a Shotaro complex after Shotaro, the main character in the series *Tetsujin 28-Go* (*Gigantor* in the U.S.), who usually wore a suit and tie with shorts and became the embodiment of the pretty young boy. *Ojicon* in this case is *ojin* complex. *Ojin* is slang for "an older man," hence the title of this chapter.

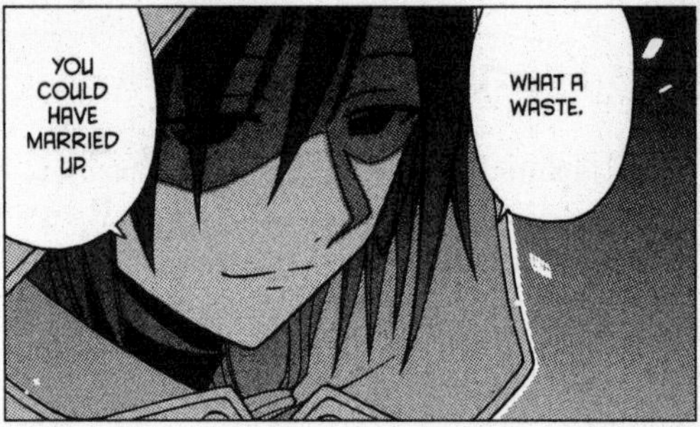
WHAT A WASTE.
YOU COULD HAVE MARRIED UP.

Married up, page 36

In panel 5, when Al says to Takahata that he could have "married up," the original Japanese used was *Gyaku Tama*. These are the characters for "reverse" and "ball," but the phrase is based on the Japanese term *Tama no Koshi*, which means "to marry into wealth." This term is usually applied to a woman looking to marry a rich or famous man. *Gyaku Tama* is used when it's a man looking to do the same. This would imply that Asuna might be someone of importance.

Cat robot and Se(xx)shi-kun, page 106

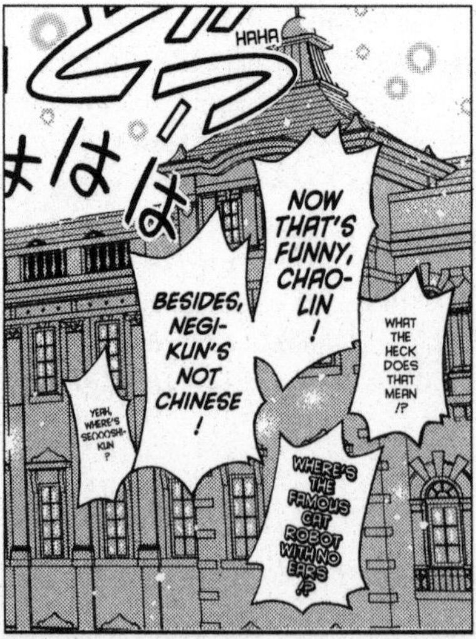
HAHA
はは
NOW THAT'S FUNNY, CHAO-LIN!
WHAT THE HECK DOES THAT MEAN!?
BESIDES, NEGI-KUN'S NOT CHINESE!
WHERE'S THE FAMOUS CAT ROBOT WITH NO EARS!?
YEAH, WHERE'S SE(XXX)SHI-KUN?

The cat robot mentioned in the second panel is, of course, Doraemon, of the famous manga, and the name with the middle letters missing is Sewashi, a descendant of Nobita, the kid who Doreamon comes to help in the present in order to make Sewashi's life better in the future. The names had to be obscured and referred to only obliquely since *Doraemon* is published by Shogakukan and *Negima!* by Kodansha.

KLINK
SIGH…
ザザァ…ン
SP-LASHH
JUST ONE MORE DAY.
もぞもぞ…
FIDGET FIDGET
うじうじ
MOPE MOPE
ズン ズン ズン
STOMP STOMP STOMP STOMP

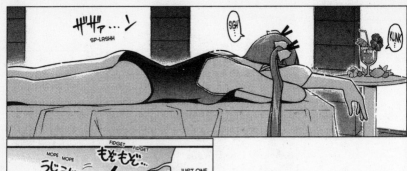

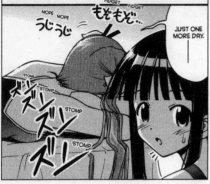

Voice actors turned manga assistants, page 109

During a visit by some of the *Negima!* anime voice actors to get material for the web radio show, the voice actor for Negi (Rina Sato) drew the sound effect of the crashing wave in panel 2. The voice actor for Setsuna (Yu Kobayashi) did the sound effects for Asuna's fidgeting in panel 7.

Red Moon Night, Blue Moon Morning, page 118

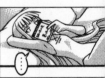

In panel 6, Eva can be seen reading a book. The title is *Akai Tsuki no Yoru, Aoi Tsuki no Asa*. This is not the title of a real book, as is often the case with books seen in *Negima!* In this case, it's a shout out by Akamatsu to the Animate TV show that the anime voice actors for Evangeline (Yuki Matsuoka) and Kazumi (Ayana Sasgawa) host.

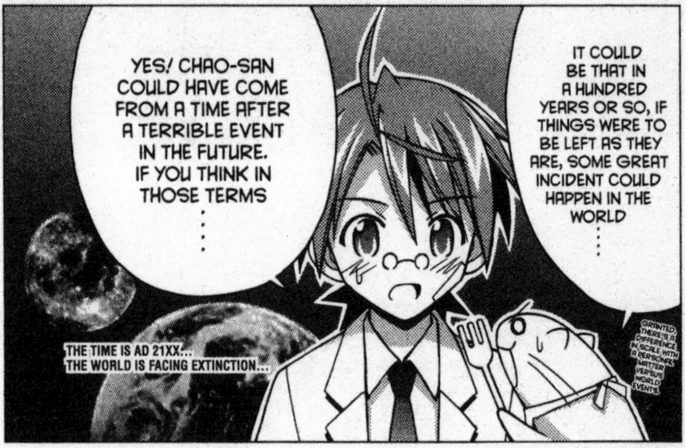
IT COULD BE THAT IN A HUNDRED YEARS OR SO, IF THINGS WERE TO BE LEFT AS THEY ARE, SOME GREAT INCIDENT COULD HAPPEN IN THE WORLD
...
YES! CHAO-SAN COULD HAVE COME FROM A TIME AFTER A TERRIBLE EVENT IN THE FUTURE. IF YOU THINK IN THOSE TERMS
...
GRANTED, THERE'S A DIFFERENCE IN SCALE WITH A PERSONAL MATTER VERSUS WORLD EVENTS.
THE TIME IS AD 21XX... THE WORLD IS FACING EXTINCTION...

The time is, page 137

Akamatsu uses this term a lot in referring to events in the future. This is most likely a homage to the TV show *Space Cruiser Yamato*. The translation really can't do this line justice, but the line is recognizable to many people. The narration that's at the start of all the movies begins with "The time is AD XXXX..." Both of the captions are actual lines from the show's narration.

DRAGON EYE

BY KAIRI FUJIYAMA

HUMANITY'S SECRET WEAPON

DRAGON EYE
1
KAIRI FUJIYAMA

Dracules—bloodthirsty, infectious monsters—have hunted human beings to the brink of extinction. Only the elite warriors of the VIUS Squad stand as humanity's last best hope.

Young Leila Mikami is one of the squad's most promising recruits, but she's not only training to battle the Dracules, she's determined to find the magical Dragon Eye, a weapon that will make her the most powerful warrior in the world.

Special extras in each volume! Read them all!

VISIT WWW.DELREYMANGA.COM TO:

- Read sample pages
- View release date calendars for upcoming volumes
- Sign up for Del Rey's free manga e-newsletter
- Find out the latest about new Del Rey Manga series

RATING T AGES 13+

DEL REY MANGA デルレイ

The Otaku's Choice™

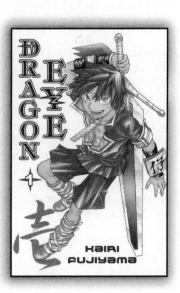

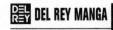

TOMARE!

[STOP!]

You're going the wrong way!

Manga is a completely different type of reading experience.

To start at the *beginning*, go to the *end*!

That's right! Authentic manga is read the traditional Japanese way—from right to left, exactly the *opposite* of how American books are read. It's easy to follow: Just go to the other end of the book, and read each page—and each panel—from right side to left side, starting at the top right. Now you're experiencing manga as it was meant to be.